Law for Business

Thirteenth Edition

John D. Ashcroft, J.D.

United States Senator, Member of the Missouri Bar

Janet E. Ashcroft, J.D.

Howard University, Member of the Missouri Bar

Prepared by
Ronald L. Taylor

Metropolitan State College of Denver

WEST **West Educational Publishing Company**
an International Thomson Publishing company I(T)P®

Cincinnati • Albany • Boston • Detroit • Johannesburg • London • Madrid • Melbourne • Mexico City
New York • Pacific Grove • San Francisco • Scottsdale • Singapore • Tokyo • Toronto

Publisher/Team Director: Jack W. Calhoun
Acquisitions Editor: Scott D. Person
Development Editor: Susanna C. Smart
Production Editor: Peggy K. Buskey
Marketing Manager: Michael Worls

Study Guide and Workbook with Quicken CD-Rom to accompany Law for Business, 13th edition
By John & Janet Ashcroft (ISBN: 0-538-88100-3)
Study Guide and Workbook to accompany Law for Business, 13th edition
By John & Janet Ashcroft (ISBN: 0-324-00659-4)

2 3 4 5 6 7 8 **PN** 5 4 3 2 1 0 9 8

Printed in the United States of America

CONTENTS

Part One   *The Legal System and The Legal Environment of Business*
Chapter 1   Introduction to Law 1
Chapter 2   Courts and Court Procedure 9
Chapter 3   Business Torts and Crimes 17
Chapter 4   Government Regulation of Business 25

Part Two   *Contracts*
Chapter 5   Nature and Classes of Contracts...31
Chapter 6   Offer and Acceptance 37
Chapter 7   Capacity to Contract...43
Chapter 8   Consideration..49
Chapter 9   Defective Agreements 55
Chapter 10   Illegal Agreements..61
Chapter 11   Written Contracts..67
Chapter 12   Third Parties and Contracts 73
Chapter 13   Termination of Contracts..79

Part Three   *Personal Property*
Chapter 14   Nature of Personal Property 87
Chapter 15   Special Bailments...95

Part Four   *Sales*
Chapter 16   Sales of Personal Property..103
Chapter 17   Formalities of a Sale...109
Chapter 18   Transfer of Title and Risk in Sales Contracts..115
Chapter 19   Warranties, Product Liability and Consumer Protection 123

Part Five   *Negotiable Instruments*
Chapter 20   Nature of Negotiable Instruments 133
Chapter 21   Essentials of Negotiability..139
Chapter 22   Promissory Notes and Drafts..145
Chapter 23   Negotiation and Discharge 153
Chapter 24   Liabilities of Parties and Holders in Due Course 159
Chapter 25   Defenses..167

Part Six   *Agency and Employment*
Chapter 26   Nature and Creation of an Agency 173
Chapter 27   Operation and Termination of an Agency 179
Chapter 28   Employer and Employee Relations 185
Chapter 29   Employees' Rights..191
Chapter 30   Labor Legislation..197

Part Seven   *Business Organization*
Chapter 31 Introduction to Business Organization 203
Chapter 32 Creation and Operation of a Partnership 209
Chapter 33 Dissolution of a Partnership 217
Chapter 34 Nature of a Corporation 223
Chapter 35 Ownership of a Corporation 229
Chapter 36 Management and Dissolution of a Corporation 237

Part Eight   *Risk-Bearing Devices*
Chapter 37 Principles of Insurance 243
Chapter 38 Types of Insurance...249
Chapter 39 Security Devices 259
Chapter 40 Bankruptcy...267

Part Nine   *Real Property*
Chapter 41 Nature of Real Property...273
Chapter 42 Transfer of Real Property 279
Chapter 43 Real Estate Mortgages...285
Chapter 44 Landlord and Tenant..291
Chapter 45 Wills, Inheritances, and Trusts 299

CHAPTER 1
INTRODUCTION TO LAW

CHAPTER OUTLINE

I. INTRODUCTION

General rules. ▸ Law: (1) Blackstone: "Law is a rule of civil conduct, commanding what is right and prohibiting what is wrong." (2) General definition: governmental rules that (a) govern conduct and (b) carry a penalty for a violation. ▸ Business law: governmental rules that regulate business transactions. ▸ Religious beliefs and social morals are not laws because (1) they are not adopted by the government and (2) they do not impose a penalty for their violation.

Examples. ▸ Law: theft is forbidden by the state; it is punished by imprisonment. ▸ Moral: society embraces belief that one should help the poor; there is no punishment for failing to do so.

Study hint. Laws may change due to society's changing perception of right and wrong.

II. OBJECTIVES OF LAW

The law establishes rules of conduct so that: (1) society can resolve disputes; (2) individuals and businesses can know the standards to which they must conform their conduct; and (3) society can effectively function because there is a stable, yet flexible, framework.

III. ROOTS OF OUR LEGAL SYSTEM

The American legal system was primarily based on the English common law and equity.

IV. THE COMMON LAW

General rule. Common law is the body of judge-made law originating from English custom.

Example. Courts have generally adopted the rule that minors can set aside most contracts.

Study hint. Common law is a source of many modern laws, such as contract and tort law.

V. EQUITY

General rules. ▸ Equity is a system of justice intended to provide (1) fairness and (2) judicial remedies other than money damages. ▸ Equity courts decide a case on the basis of what in fairness and good conscience should be done, not on the basis of fixed legal rules. Equity is carried out through certain equitable remedies including: (1) specific performance (court order requiring performance of a contract); (2) restraining orders (court orders temporarily prohibiting certain actions); and (3) injunctions (court orders permanently prohibiting certain actions).

Limitation. Equitable remedies are available only if there is no adequate remedy at law, i.e., damages (money a wrongdoer must pay) will not adequately compensate a party for a loss.

Study hint. In most states, every court can apply both legal and equitable principles.

VI. SOURCES OF LAW

Sources of law are: (1) judicial decisions; (2) constitutions; (3) statutes; and (4) administrative agency rules.

A. JUDICIAL DECISIONS

General rules. ▸ A judicial decision or interpretation of law that is adopted by the highest (appellate) courts is called a precedent. ▸ The doctrine of *stare decisis* generally requires lower courts in the same jurisdiction to follow established precedents in future, similar cases.

Study hints. ▸ The court that adopts a precedent may change the precedent in a subsequent case. ▸ The U.S. Supreme Court can reverse any federal lower court decision and a state supreme court (or equivalent) can generally reverse any decision by a lower court in that state.

B. CONSTITUTIONS

General rules. ▸ Constitution: document that defines: (1) the relationship between the branches of a government; and (2) the relations between a government and its citizens. ▸ Bill of Rights: first ten amendments to the U.S. Constitution, which establishes fundamental constitutional rights of individuals and states. ▸ The U.S. Constitution is the supreme law in the United States. No federal or state law may conflict with the U.S. Constitution.

Examples. ▸ Bill of Rights: First Amendment generally guarantees individuals the freedom of speech. ▸ State laws that discriminate against persons because of their race are invalid because they conflict with the U.S. Constitution.

Study hints. ▸ The U.S. Supreme Court has the final authority to determine whether a federal or state law violates the U.S. Constitution. ▸ A state supreme court has the final authority to determine whether a state law violates a state constitution.

C. STATUTES

General rules. ▸ Statutes: written laws created by Congress, state legislatures, and city councils.
▸ Ordinances: written laws adopted by cities. ▸ A federal statute prevails over a conflicting state statute.
▸ A state constitution prevails over a conflicting state statute.

Example. The Uniform Commercial Code (UCC) that regulates many business activities and that has been adopted in whole or in part in all states, is an important statute in business law.

Study hint. It is easier to change statutes than it is to change constitutions.

D. ADMINISTRATIVE AGENCY ORDERS

General rule. Within their area of jurisdiction, federal and state administrative agencies may adopt rules or regulations (and issue orders) that generally have the same force as other laws.

Limitation. An administrative agency can adopt laws only if it has been delegated this power by the legislature.

Study hint. Improper administrative agency orders may be challenged in court.

VII. CIVIL VERSUS CRIMINAL LAW

General rules. ▸ Civil laws relate to personal rights and duties of individuals and businesses. ▸ Criminal law prohibits offenses against society. ▸ Crime: offense against society punishable by fine, imprisonment, or death. ▸ Crimes are generally classified as: (1) felonies (serious crimes generally punishable by death or imprisonment for one year or longer); or (2) misdemeanors (minor crimes punishable by a fine or imprisonment for less than one year).

Examples. ▸ Civil laws: contract or tort laws. ▸ Felonies: murder; robbery; sexual assault.
▸ Misdemeanor: disorderly conduct.

Study hints. ▸ A criminal prosecution must be brought by a government, which is usually represented by a prosecutor or district attorney. ▸ Statutes define the acts that are crimes, and criminal laws vary from state to state.

VIII. TORT LAW

General rules. ▸ Tort: private wrong against an individual for which damages may be recovered. ▸ A tort may be: (1) intentionally committed; or (2) caused by a person's negligence (i.e., failure to exercise reasonable care toward another person).

Examples. ▸ Negligence: a worker carelessly hits a pedestrian with a board. ▸ Other torts: assault; libel; slander; trespass.

Study hints. ▸ The party injured by the tort must bring a tort action. ▸ The same act may be both a crime and a tort. However, the crime and tort are subject to separate punishments that are imposed as the result of separate legal proceedings.

IX. ETHICS

Ethics is the study of the morality of conduct, its motives, and duties. Our laws are based on society's changing concepts of right and wrong.

A. BASES FOR ETHICAL JUDGMENT

Ethical judgments, or personal opinions of what is right or wrong, are based on personal values. Values are developed from experience, cultural background, religious beliefs, and scientific knowledge.

B. ETHICAL PRINCIPLES

Ethics sometimes influences the law. Three principles that often determine the way in which ethics relates to the law are: (1) the seriousness of the consequences; (2) the consensus of the majority; and (3) changes in ethical standards.

C. SERIOUSNESS OF CONSEQUENCES

General rule. Laws are usually enacted to regulate unethical behavior that has serious consequences. Although less serious matters can involve what is right or wrong, they are not the subjects of laws.

Examples. ▸ Society believes it is wrong for one person to kill another. Laws have been enacted to try to deter and to punish those who commit murder. ▸ Society may believe it is right for a person to call a restaurant to cancel dinner reservations that won't be kept, but the consequences of not doing so are not serious enough for society to enact a law to regulate this behavior.

D. CONSENSUS OF THE MAJORITY

General rule. In a democracy, laws are designed to reflect the ethical view of the majority.

Limitation. When there are strong conflicting views on a certain subject, there may be no laws regulating the matter.

E. CHANGE IN ETHICAL STANDARDS

General rule. Society's view of what is ethical or right changes over time.

Example. As society developed the viewpoint that discrimination based on sex, color, race, national origin, or religious creed was wrong, civil rights and fair employment practices laws were enacted.

F. BUSINESS ETHICS

Businesspersons are expected to act in ways that make their firms profitable. Many businesses have also adopted codes of ethics that guide the behavior of employees. Some of these codes are legally enforceable; others are voluntary.

G. LEGALLY ENFORCEABLE

Professions, such as law, often have legally enforceable codes of ethics or codes of professional responsibility. Violators are subject to discipline and possible suspension from practice.

H. VOLUNTARY

Voluntary codes of ethics encourage certain behavior, but provide no sanctions if not followed.

CHAPTER REVIEW

REVIEW OF TERMS

Select the term that best matches a statement below. Each term is the best match for only one statement.

TERMS

a. Bill of Rights
b. Business ethics
c. Business law
d. Code of ethics
e. Crime

f. Damages
g. Equity
h. Ethics
i. Injunction

j. Law
k. *Stare decisis*
l. Tort
m. Value

STATEMENTS

Answer

_____ 1. System of justice that is premised on principles of fairness and that provides remedies other than money damages.

_____ 2. Study of the morality of conduct, motives for conduct, and duties.

_____ 3. Collection of guidelines for behavior.

_____ 4. Doctrine by which precedents must be followed by lower courts in similar cases.

_____ 5. Court order permanently prohibiting an action.

_____ 6. First ten amendments to the U.S. Constitution which guarantee individual constitutional rights.

_____ 7. Private wrong for which damages may be recovered.

_____ 8. Punishable offense against society.

_____ 9. Any governmental rule that governs conduct and imposes a penalty for its violation.

_____ 10. Governmental rules that generally regulate business transactions.

_____ 11. Money a wrongdoer must pay to an injured party.

_____ 12. Principle or ideal based on religious beliefs, experience, culture, and scientific knowledge.

_____ 13. Behavioral standards that apply to business practices.

REVIEW OF CONCEPTS

Directions: Indicate **T** for true and **F** for false in the answer column.

_____ 1. Religious beliefs and social morals are always laws.

_____ 2. Criminal law is a branch of the law that punishes wrongs against society, whereas civil law is a branch of the law that generally punishes wrongs against individuals.

_____ 3. Violation of civil law is generally punished by imposition of a fine or imprisonment, or both.

_____ 4. Primary objectives of the law include creating a stable structure for society, and establishing rules to resolve conflicts between individuals or between individuals and the government.

_____ 5. Common law is law that has been recently created by administrative agencies.

_____ 6. Courts of equity traditionally decide cases according to rigid rules of law.

_____ 7. Courts of equity may order specific performance, restraining orders, or injunctions if damages are not adequate to remedy a harm.

_____ 8. The Bill of Rights is state law that establishes certain fundamental individual rights.

_____ 9. The Uniform Commercial Code (UCC) has been adopted in whole or in part in all states.

_____ 10. An individual does not have a legal duty to obey administrative agency rules or orders.

_____ 11. A crime involves an offense against society, whereas a tort involves a wrong against an individual.

_____ 12. Laws are based on society's judgment of what is right and wrong.

_____ 13. Law regulates any unethical behavior that harms others.

_____ 14. Ethical standards stay the same, even over long periods of time.

_____ 15. Codes of ethics are not used in business since the only ethical standard applicable to businesspeople is to maximize profit for the business.

_____ 16. Codes of ethics are purely voluntary guidelines.

REVIEW OF CONCEPT APPLICATIONS

Answer

Directions: Indicate your choice in the answer column.

_____ 1. Cameron has filed a civil suit against Ann regarding a car accident. Cameron is suing Ann for money to compensate him for the destruction of his car. What remedy should Cameron request?
   a. Specific performance.
   b. Restraining order.
   c. Injunction.
   d. Damages.

_____ 2. A state supreme court has adopted a precedent holding that a promise cannot be enforced unless it is made pursuant to a contract. Kelly has filed a civil suit against Joan, suing Joan for breach of a promise that was not made pursuant to a contract. In this case:
   a. The doctrine of *stare decisis* requires the trial (lower) court to follow the precedent.
   b. The doctrine of *stare decisis* does not require the trial court to follow the precedent.
   c. If the case is appealed to the state supreme court (highest court), the doctrine of *stare decisis*.
   d. The doctrine of *stare decisis* prohibits the supreme court from changing the precedent even if it is appropriate to do so.

_____ 3. Assume that a federal law requires R&R Inc. to pay time and a half for hours worked by employees in excess of 40 hours per week. However, a state law only requires overtime pay for hours worked in excess of 50 hours per week. R&R maintains that (1) the federal statute violates the U.S. Constitution and (2) the state law prevails over the federal law. In this case:
   a. The state statute prevails over the federal statute.
   b. The federal statute prevails over the state statute.
   c. If the state supreme court holds that the federal statute is invalid because it violates the U.S. Constitution, this decision is final and cannot be reviewed by any other court.
   d. a and c.

_____ 4. Traditionally, which offense is classified as a felony?
   a. Art negligently injures Jill while he is mowing his lawn. Art is liable to Jill for damages.
   b. Michelle did not have her dog on a leash in violation of a city ordinance. This offense is punishable by a $25 fine.
   c. Lee stole a car. This offense is punishable by imprisonment for five to ten years.
   d. Rick is guilty of disturbing the peace. This offense is punishable by imprisonment in jail for one day.

_____ 5. In which of the following situations would a law be likely to be passed?
   a. The majority of people believe it is unethical to injure someone by playing with a loaded gun.
   b. Many people believe it is unethical to consume a certain product; however, many other people disagree.
   c. Most people believe it is wrong not to respond with an expression of thanks after accepting a gift.
   d. a and c.

_____ 6.   The state legislature is considering enactment of a law that would require businesses to install filtering equipment to purify wastes before they are emitted into the air. There are conflicting views among the citizens as to the need for this law, although serious lung problems have occurred in residents exposed to the unfiltered emissions. Which statement best describes the reason favoring enactment of the law?
   a.   Businesses' obligation to maximize profit.
   b.   Changes in ethical standards.
   c.   Consensus of the majority.
   d.   Seriousness of the consequences of the behavior to be regulated.

CASE PROBLEM

Diane and Steven are in a car accident. Diane was daydreaming, and she violated a duty she owed Steven to drive with reasonable care. Steven believes that he is entitled to be compensated for his losses resulting from the accident. Answer the following questions, briefly explaining your answers: (1) Are Steven's rights against Diane determined according to criminal law or tort law? (2) Will Steven or the state prosecutor bring the action to obtain compensation for Steven? (3) What remedy will Steven request?

_____

_____

_____

BUSINESS LAW PARTNER EXERCISE

Introduction

Before a person enters into a significant legal agreement or undertakes a major business transaction, it is prudent to first consult with an attorney. As a practical matter, though, a businessperson must often use forms of business documents, such as a Bill of Sale, in order to conduct day-to-day business. Occasionally, it may also be helpful if a businessperson can obtain information relating to the law without having to consult with an attorney. In order to help prepare you for these practical aspects of conducting business, each study guide chapter concludes with an exercise using the enclosed Business Law Partner CD-ROM.

The Business Law Partner Exercise requires you to use the CD-ROM in order to: (1) find and complete the appropriate form of business document; and/or (2) find requested information relating to the law. The necessary documents are included on the CD-ROM. Requested information may be obtained by using the "Online" Internet link provided by the CD-ROM.

Exercise

Using the Online feature of the Business Law Partner CD-ROM, locate the Cornell University Legal Information Institute web site. Then answer the following questions:
1. Identify the location of this web site.
2. State the five major categories of information that may be found on this web site.
3. Does this web site provide links to find information relating to both federal and state laws?

_____

_____

_____

CHAPTER 1 QUIZ

Section A

DIRECTIONS: Following each statement below, indicate your answer by placing a "T" for "True" or an "F" for "False" in the Answers column. The first statement is given as an example.

		Answers	For Scoring
0.	Law is a rule of civil conduct.	*T*	√
1.	All administrative agencies have the power to enact law.		1.
2.	Only if a sovereign state issues a rule prescribing right and wrong can it be called a law.		2.
3.	A breach of a rule of law is always a crime.		3.
4.	The standard of proof in a criminal case is proof beyond the shadow of a doubt.		4.
5.	Laws may be modified to provide rules to deal with new circumstances.		5.
6.	Common law is the source of much of our law.		6.
7.	The only remedy available in courts of equity was a judgment for money damages.		7.
8.	Administrative agencies may be given almost the same power to decide cases as the courts.		8.
9.	Only the court that makes a decision in a case may reverse that case.		9.
10.	A state supreme court is the final judge as to whether a state law violates the state's constitution.		10.
11.	Constitutions are more responsive to the changing demands of the people than are statutes.		11.
12.	A state statute prevails in a conflict with a federal statute.		12.
13.	Many governmental functions are carried on by administrative agencies.		13.
14.	A tort is a private or civil wrong or injury.		14.
15.	One benefit of the Uniform Commercial Code is that it is the same in every state.		15.

Score _____

Section B

DIRECTIONS: Complete each of the following statements by writing the missing word or words in the Answers column. The first statement is given as an example.

		Answers	For Scoring
0.	An essential part of statutory law is the constitution.		0.
1.	The sum of money a wrongdoer must pay to an injured party is a(n)		1.
2.	A temporary order forbidding a certain action is a(n)		2.
3.	A permanent order forbidding activities detrimental to others is a(n)		3.
4.	The supreme law of the land in the United States is the		4.
5.	The most important statute in the field of business law is the		5.
6.	An offense that tends to injure society as a whole is a(n)		6.
7.	The more serious crimes are		7.
8.	The less serious criminal offenses, punishable by fine or imprisonment in the county jail, or both, are called		8.
9.	Commissions that have the power to regulate particular matters or implement laws are .		9.
10.	A tort may be intentional or it may be result from a person's		10.

Score _____

Section C

DIRECTIONS: In the Answers space in Column II, place the letter of the corresponding word or words from Column I.

Column I	Column II	Answers	For Scoring
(a) administrative agency orders	1. The law dealing with the enforcement or protection of private or personal rights	_____	1._____
(b) Bill of Rights	2. Person who appoints the heads of federal administrative agencies	_____	2._____
(c) English law	3. A major root of American law	_____	3._____
(d) civil law	4. Ten amendments to the U.S. Constitution designed to protect citizens' civil rights and liberties.	_____	4._____
(e) common law	5. Custom which has come to be recognized by the courts as binding on the community	_____	5._____
(f) constitution	6. When justice demands it, deciding a case not by some rigid rule of law but by what one's conscience decides	_____	6._____
(g) criminal law	7. Document that defines the relationships of the parts of the government to each other	_____	7._____
(h) equity	8. Laws enacted by cities	_____	8._____
(i) injured person	9. Person who brings the action in criminal cases	_____	9._____
(j) President	10. Private wrong for which there may be an action for damages	_____	10._____
(k) ordinances	11. Laws enacted by legislative bodies	_____	11._____
(l) private attorney	12. Decrees that have the force of law unless courts set them aside after being challenged	_____	12._____
(m) prosecutor	13. The doctrine that makes higher court decisions binding on lower courts	_____	13._____
(n) *stare decisis*	14. That branch of the law which has to do with the punishment of wrongdoers	_____	14._____
(o) statutes	15. The person who brings a tort action	_____	15._____
(p) tort			

Score _____

CHAPTER 2
COURTS AND COURT PROCEDURE

CHAPTER OUTLINE

I. INTRODUCTION

In every state there are two separate court systems: the federal court system and a state court system.

II. FUNCTION OF THE COURTS

Courts may: (1) interpret the constitution, statutes, and other laws; (2) review the constitutionality of laws; (3) create precedents (i.e., case law); and (4) determine disputed facts and apply the law.

III. JURISDICTION OF COURTS

General rules. ▸ Jurisdiction: authority of a court to hear and determine certain types of lawsuits. ▸ To determine a case, a court must have jurisdiction over both: (1) the subject matter of the case; and (2) the persons directly involved in the case (i.e., the plaintiff and defendant).

Example. To hear a particular divorce case, a court must have jurisdiction to hear divorce cases, and it must have jurisdiction over the husband and wife involved in that case.

Study hints. ▸ Jurisdiction over the subject matter of a case is determined by what is primarily involved in case, e.g., bankruptcy. ▸ Jurisdiction over a defendant in a civil lawsuit or the accused in a criminal prosecution is obtained by serving the party with a summons (process).

IV. CLASSIFICATION OF COURTS

General rules. ▸ Classified according to the government body that created a court, a court may be: (1) a federal court; (2) a state court; or (3) a municipal court. ▸ Classified according to what a court can do, a court may be: (1) a trial court (court that hears and decides a case for the first time); or (2) an appellate court (court that reviews decisions of lower courts).

Study hints. ▸ Appellate courts typically comprise two tiers of courts: courts of appeal and supreme courts. ▸ In most states, the state supreme court is the highest state court, and it has the power to review decisions made by state trial courts and courts of appeal.

V. FEDERAL COURTS

A. SPECIAL FEDERAL COURTS

General rules. ▸ Special federal courts: trial courts with limited subject matter jurisdiction. ▸ Congress determines the jurisdiction of special federal courts.

Examples. ▸ U.S. Claims Court: hears cases against U.S. government. ▸ Tax Court: hears cases involving federal tax matters. ▸ Bankruptcy Court: hears bankruptcy cases.

B. FEDERAL DISTRICT COURTS

General rules. ▸ U.S. district court: primary trial court in federal judicial system. ▸ U.S. district courts can decide cases involving: (1) federal crimes; (2) any federal law, such as the U.S. Constitution or federal statutes or administrative rules; and (3) cases involving opposing parties who are residents of different states, if the case involves $50,000 or more.

Example. A U.S. district court can try (1) a case involving a federal antidiscrimination law, or (2) a lawsuit by an Ohio resident against an Idaho resident that involves $50,000.

C. FEDERAL COURTS OF APPEALS

General rules. ▸ U.S. courts of appeals for the twelve federal judicial circuits (twelve regions of the U.S.) hear appeals from: (1) U.S. district courts; and (2) federal agencies. ▸ Court of Appeals for the Federal Circuit hears appeals from: (1) special federal courts; (2) certain federal agencies; and (3) district courts regarding patent and claims cases.

Study hint. A court of appeals' decision is binding on lower courts in that court's circuit.

D. UNITED STATES SUPREME COURT

General rules. ▸ The U.S. Supreme Court is the highest court in the United States. ▸ The Supreme Court has original jurisdiction over cases involving ambassadors, public ministers, consuls, and cases in which a state is a party. The Supreme Court has appellate jurisdiction over: (1) cases appealed from the U.S. courts of appeals (or in limited situations, cases appealed from U.S. district courts); and (2) cases appealed from a state supreme court if the cases involve a federal constitutional question, or a federal law or treaty is invalidated by the state courts.

Limitation. In general, the Supreme Court is not required to hear an appeal. The Supreme Court can generally choose which cases it will hear. A party requesting review by the Supreme Court asks the Court to issue a writ of certiorari.

Study hint. A decision by the U.S. Supreme Court binds federal and state courts.

VI. STATE COURTS

A. INFERIOR COURTS

General rules. ▸ Inferior courts: state or local trial courts that only hear cases involving minor civil or criminal matters. ▸ Jurisdiction of inferior courts varies. Often, these courts only try cases involving misdemeanors or disputes involving amounts up to $1,000 to $25,000.

Limitation. Frequently, a party who loses in an inferior court has the right to appeal to a court of original general jurisdiction that will retry the entire case.

B. COURTS OF ORIGINAL GENERAL JURISDICTION

▸ Courts of original general jurisdiction: trial courts that are courts of record (official records of trial proceedings are kept), with the jurisdiction to try most civil and criminal cases involving state law. ▸ Common names: circuit court; district court; superior court.

C. APPELLATE COURTS

▸ Most states have two levels of appellate courts: (1) intermediate appellate courts (typically called courts of appeals); and (2) the highest appellate court (commonly called the supreme court). ▸ One generally has a right to appeal a trial court's judgment to an appellate court.

D. SPECIAL COURTS

General rule. States often have special courts that have only special (limited) jurisdiction to hear certain matters.

Examples. ▸ Probate courts: determine matters relating to wills and estates. ▸ Juvenile courts: decide cases involving delinquent, dependent, and neglected children. ▸ Domestic relations courts: hear cases involving divorces and child custody.

VII. COURT OFFICERS

▸ State inferior court officers: (1) Chief officer: judge or magistrate. (2) Executive officer: constable or bailiff.
▸ State court of record officers: (1) Chief officer: judge. (2) Executive officer: sheriff. (3) Recorder: clerk of court.
▸ Federal court officers: (1) Chief officer: judge. (2) Executive officer: marshal. (3) Recorder: clerk of court.
▸ Attorneys are officers of any court in which they appear.

VIII. PROCEDURE IN COURTS OF RECORD

Procedural law determines how a lawsuit is commenced and the procedure that is to be followed in conducting trials. Certain important rules of procedural law are discussed below.

A. FILING SUIT IN A CIVIL ACTION

- *Commencement of a lawsuit and pleadings*: In general, courts cannot determine disputes unless a party properly requests a court to do so. ▸ A plaintiff's filing a complaint (petition) with the clerk of the court begins a civil suit. The clerk then issues a summons (process), and the plaintiff has the summons served on the defendant. ▸ The defendant has a certain number of days in which to file an answer or file a motion.

- *Discovery*: ▸ Discovery: procedure by which either party can find out from the other party most information relating to the lawsuit. ▸ Types of discovery: (1) Interrogatories: written questions to be answered in writing. (2) Deposition: oral examination of a party (or witness) outside of court and under oath. (3) Admissions: requests that a party admits that certain facts are true. (4) Medical examination by a physician. (5) Access to real and personal property. Failure by a party to comply with a court order compelling discovery may be contempt of court or may entitle a judge to dismiss the case.

- *Pretrial motions*: A party may file a number of motions to obtain an early dismissal of a case or to resolve certain preliminary questions.

- *Fact finding*: ▸ A party often has the right to a jury trial. ▸ In a jury trial, the judge determines questions of law, and the jury determines all factual questions. If a case is tried without a jury, the judge determines all questions of law and fact.

B. TRIAL PROCEDURE

- *Conduct of trial*: ▸ If the trial is to be heard by a jury, the jury is selected and sworn in. Parties make opening statements. Then they present evidence in the form of testimony of witnesses and physical evidence (exhibits). The parties conclude with summations. ▸ A plaintiff has the burden to prove facts alleged in the complaint.

- *Verdict and judgment*: The judge tells the jury what law controls, and the jury determines questions of fact (including the weight to be given to evidence). ▸ The jury renders its decision, called a verdict, and the judge enters a judgment based on the verdict, unless the verdict is unsupported by the law and the evidence.

C. APPEALS

▸ Either party may appeal a judgment. However, appellate courts generally only review lower court decisions for errors of law, not errors of fact. ▸ An appellate court determines an appeal by reviewing a transcript (written record) of the trial and briefs (legal arguments) filed by the parties; the court does not hear testimony from witnesses, and it does not conduct a new trial.

IX. PROCEDURE IN SMALL CLAIMS COURTS

General rule.   The procedure for filing and trying a case in a small claims court is more informal than for a court of record. The court may furnish the necessary complaint forms and assist the plaintiff in filling them out. At trial, the judge is more active in assisting the parties in order to obtain a just decision.
Limitations.   ▸ A judge typically tries cases in small claims court; there is no jury. ▸ In some states, a party is not allowed to be represented by an attorney in small claims court.
Study hint.   Typically, either party can appeal a small claims court judgment to a court of record, in which case the court of record will try the case again in its entirety.

CHAPTER REVIEW

REVIEW OF TERMS

DIRECTIONS: Select the term that best matches a statement below. Each term may be used only once.

TERMS

a. Answer
b. Appellate court
c. Complaint (petition)
d. Court of original general jurisdiction
e. Defendant

f. Deposition
g. Discovery
h. Inferior court
i. Interrogatories
j. Jurisdiction

k. Plaintiff
l. Procedural law
m. Summons (process)
n. Trial court
o. Verdict

STATEMENTS

Answer

____ 1. Law that defines how to commence a suit and the procedure for conducting trials.

____ 2. Various procedures by which either party can find out most information relating to a lawsuit.

____ 3. Power or authority to hear and determine certain types of lawsuits.

____ 4. Court that reviews decisions of lower courts.

____ 5. Discovery consisting of an oral examination of a party or witness outside of court.

____ 6. State trial court that is a court of record with jurisdiction to try most cases that involve state law.

____ 7. Pleading stating a defendant's response to allegations made in a complaint.

____ 8. Legal notice of a lawsuit that is served on a defendant.

____ 9. State or local trial court with jurisdiction to hear cases involving only misdemeanors or minor civil disputes.

____ 10. Pleading stating a plaintiff's claim against a defendant and requesting a court to settle a claim.

____ 11. Discovery consisting of written questions that a party must answer in writing.

____ 12. Party against whom a lawsuit is filed.

____ 13. Decision of a jury.

____ 14. Court that conducts original trial of a case.

____ 15. Party who commences a civil lawsuit against another.

REVIEW OF CONCEPTS

Directions: Indicate **T** for true and **F** for false in the answer column.

____ 1. There is only one court system in the United States, and this system includes both the federal and state courts.

____ 2. Courts can only hear and decide cases; courts cannot create rules or interpret statutes.

____ 3. The United States Supreme Court has original jurisdiction to try cases involving ambassadors, public ministers, and consuls, and in cases in which a state is a party.

____ 4. A defendant must generally be served with a summons for a court to have jurisdiction over the defendant.

____ 5. In general, appellate courts can conduct trials of most cases and review lower court decisions.

____ 6. Appellate courts typically conduct a new trial when an appeal is taken from the judgment issued by a trial court.

____ 7. In general, the U.S. Supreme Court can review a state supreme court's decision if it involves an issue relating to the U.S. Constitution.

_____ 8. State courts of original general jurisdiction can only decide cases involving misdemeanors and small civil disputes.

_____ 9. In most states, the state court of appeals is the highest appellate court of the state.

_____ 10. The executive officer of an inferior state court is a marshal; the executive officer of a federal court is a constable or bailiff.

_____ 11. A court generally cannot decide a dispute unless a party files a suit requesting a court to do so.

_____ 12. Failure to comply with a court order compelling discovery may result in a dismissal of the case.

_____ 13. In a jury trial, the jury resolves questions of both fact and law.

_____ 14. When a case is tried in an inferior state court, such as a small claims court, the procedure is more informal than in a court of record, and there typically is no jury.

_____ 15. A party generally has no right to appeal a judgment rendered by an inferior court.

REVIEW OF CONCEPT APPLICATIONS

Directions: Indicate your choice in the answer column.

Answer

_____ 1. Tim, a resident of Iowa, is suing Rod, a resident of New York, for $75,000. Tim is suing for breach of contract (state law). Would a U.S. district court have jurisdiction to decide this case?
    a. Yes. Tim and Rod are residents of different states and the case involves $50,000 or more.
    b. Yes. U.S. district courts have jurisdiction to decide all civil lawsuits.
    c. No. U.S. district courts do not have jurisdiction to try cases unless federal law is involved.
    d. No. U.S. district courts do not have jurisdiction to try cases unless an issue relating to the U.S. Constitution is involved.

_____ 2. Kevin sued his employer in U.S. district court for violation of federal antidiscrimination laws. Judgment was entered in favor of the employer, and Kevin wishes to appeal the judgment. Under these facts, Kevin will appeal the judgment to which court?
    a. U.S. district court.
    b. U.S. court of appeals.
    c. U.S. Supreme Court.
    d. Tax Court.

_____ 3. In a typical state court system, which answer would be correct?
    a. Amanda is suing to obtain custody of her son from her ex-husband. A probate court would have jurisdiction of this matter.
    b. Stephanie is suing her landlord to recover her $500 security deposit. The state court of appeals would have jurisdiction to try this case for the first time.
    c. Bruce is suing Manufacturer for $60,000 for breach of contract under state law. A state court of original general jurisdiction would have jurisdiction to try this case for the first time.
    d. Kim died. A domestic relations court would have jurisdiction to administer Kim's estate.

_____ 4. Bob has filed a civil lawsuit against Acme Corp. Bob is suing Acme for physical injuries that he suffered due to Acme's negligence. All pleadings have been filed. Select the correct answer regarding Acme's right to discover information from Bob.
    a. Acme cannot discover any information from Bob.
    b. Acme can request Bob to submit to a reasonable physical examination by a doctor.
    c. Acme can take Bob's deposition regarding the accident.
    d. b and c.

_____ 5. Rosa sued T&S Co. for breach of contract. The jury returned a verdict in favor of Rosa for $5,000. Under these facts:

   a. The judge must enter judgment based on the jury's verdict even if the verdict is clearly wrong due to serious mistakes of fact and law.

   b. If the judgment is appealed, the court of appeals may reverse the judgment if the lower court committed serious errors of law.

   c. If the judgment is appealed, the court of appeals will not review the transcript of the trial proceedings.

   d. If the judgment is appealed, the court of appeals will have the witnesses testify again and it will conduct a new trial.

CASE PROBLEM

Juan hired Arco Construction Co. to build a new home for Juan. Juan alleges that Arco failed to properly build the home, and Juan wishes to sue Arco for breach of contract. Under these facts, answer the following questions, briefly explaining your answers.

1. How does Juan commence this civil lawsuit and what must be done for the court to obtain jurisdiction over Arco? What must Arco do in response to Juan's action?
2. Describe the basic procedure that will be followed at trial?
3. Who bears the burden of proof?
4. If there is a jury trial, who determines questions of fact and who determines questions of law?

_____

_____

_____

BUSINESS LAW PARTNER EXERCISE

Directions: Access your Business Law Partner CD-ROM and locate the document entitled "Defending a Business Lawsuit." Complete this document using the information provided in the following case study.

Case Study: *The Airplane that Fell From the Sky*

You are president of Airplane Resale, Inc. (ARI), a firm that buys, refurbishes, and resells used private airplanes. On January 10, ARI sold a used airplane to John Rain for $30,000 pursuant to a Contract of Sale. Mr. Rain paid $10,000 cash and signed a promissory note for the unpaid balance.

On January 14, Mr. Rain took the plane for its maiden voyage. A few minutes after take-off, the plane's engines lost power and the plane crashed. The plane was destroyed, and Mr. Rain suffered a broken arm. Gary Beck, a mechanic at the airport, witnessed the accident.

Mr. Rain alleges that he suffered $30,000 property damage, $10,000 medical costs, and $50,000 damages for pain and suffering. Mr. Rain insured the airplane with First Mutual. ARI has business insurance with Last Fidelity Insurance.

On March 1, process was served on you, as president of ARI. You have arranged a conference with ARI's attorney, and the attorney has requested that you bring a list of relevant information to your meeting.

CHAPTER 2 QUIZ

Section A

DIRECTIONS: Following each question below, indicate your answer by placing a "Y" for "Yes" or an "N" for "No" in the Answers column.

		Answers	For Scoring
1.	Are there two distinct court systems in each state?	_____	1. _____
2.	Can a court hear a case when it only has jurisdiction over the subject matter of the case?	_____	2. _____
3.	Do federal courts have exclusive jurisdiction of child custody cases?	_____	3. _____
4.	Do special federal courts have unlimited jurisdiction?	_____	4. _____
5.	Do federal district courts try all criminal cases involving a violation of federal law?	_____	5. _____
6.	Are most cases heard by the U.S. Supreme Court appealed from federal district courts?	_____	6. _____
7.	Are justice of the peace or magistrate courts types of appellate courts?	_____	7. _____
8.	Are courts of original general jurisdiction courts of record?	_____	8. _____
9.	Are some special courts, such as probate courts, the same level as trial courts?	_____	9. _____
10.	Can privileged information be obtained from a party by means of discovery?	_____	10. _____
11.	Could a party who fails to comply with a court's order compelling discovery be found in contempt of court?	_____	11. _____
12.	May a party to a case in small claims court have a trial by a jury?	_____	12. _____

Score _____

Section B

DIRECTIONS: Complete each of the following statements by writing the missing word or words in the Answers column.

		Answers	For Scoring
1.	An application by a party to the judge for an order requiring an act be done in favor of the requesting party is a(n)	_____	1. _____
2.	The power and authority of a court to hear cases is called its	_____	2. _____
3.	Courts that review cases appealed from the decisions of lower courts are	_____	3. _____
4.	The major trial courts in the federal court system are	_____	4. _____
5.	The highest tribunal in the land is the	_____	5. _____
6.	A plaintiff begins a civil lawsuit by filing with clerk of the court a pleading called a	_____	6. _____
7.	In a state court of record the chief officer is the	_____	7. _____
8.	An examination of a party that is taken outside court is called a	_____	8. _____
9.	The executive officer of a state court of record is the	_____	9. _____
10.	Laws that specify how parties are to proceed in filing civil actions and how the actions are to be tried are	_____	10. _____

Score _____

Section C

DIRECTIONS: In the appropriate blanks, fill in the names of the courts on the various levels of the federal and state court systems.

Federal Courts

Highest court .... 1. _____

Intermediate courts .... 2. _____

Trial courts .... 3. _____

Special courts .... 4. _____

State Courts

Highest court .... 5. _____

Intermediate courts .... 6. _____

Courts of Original General Jurisdiction .... 7. _____

Inferior courts .... 8. _____

Score _____

Section D

DIRECTIONS: Following each statement below, indicate your answer by placing a " T " for " True " or an " F " for " False " in the Answers column.

		Answers	For Scoring
1.	Courts must have authority over the subject matter of a case as well as over the parties involved in order to have the power to decide the case.	_____	1. _____
2.	Federal courts and state courts both hear bankruptcy cases.	_____	2. _____
3.	Appellate courts are the first courts to hear cases.	_____	3. _____
4.	A decision of a federal court of appeals is binding on all federal district courts.	_____	4. _____
5.	The normal way a case gets to the U.S. Supreme Court is by application for a writ of mandamus.	_____	5. _____
6.	Not all states provide for appeals from trial courts.	_____	6. _____
7.	One federal court of appeals cannot decide an issue one way and another court of appeals decide it the opposite way.	_____	7. _____
8.	A party in an inferior state court can normally appeal the decision to the state's highest court.	_____	8. _____
9.	A party to a lawsuit may not request the other party to have a medical examination by a physician even if the other party's physical condition is an issue in the case.	_____	9. _____
10.	The plaintiff has the burden to prove facts that are sufficient to support the allegations made in the petition.	_____	10. _____

Score _____

CHAPTER 3
BUSINESS TORTS AND CRIMES

CHAPTER OUTLINE

I. TORTS

A. INTENTIONAL TORTS

To recover, the injured party must show: (1) an act by defendant; (2) the defendant intended to cause the consequences of the act; and (3) the injury was caused by the defendant's act.

B. NEGLIGENCE TORTS

To recover, the injured party must show: (1) a duty by person committing the tort; (2) breach of that duty; (3) the breach was the actual, proximate cause of the injury; and (4) injury.

C. BUSINESS TORTS

1. Product Liability

General rule. Manufacturers may be held liable for injuries caused by their products if (1) the products were negligently designed or made, or (2) a defect in the manufacture of a product makes the product dangerous to the person using it or in the nearby vicinity.
Study hints. ▸ The injured person need not be the purchaser to recover for product liability.
▸ Product liability is a type of strict liability tort.

2. Interference with a contract or economic advantage

General rules. ▸ *Interference with contract*: party wrongfully causes another to breach a contract with a third party. Elements: (1) valid contract existed; (2) defendant knew or should have known about contract; (3) defendant intentionally interfered with contract; (4) defendant caused a breach of the contract. ▸ *Interference with economic advantage*: wrongful interference with another's reasonable expectation of future economic advantage. ▸ Elements: (1) valid business relationship exists or is likely to develop; (2) defendant knew or should have known of relationship; (3) relationship was reasonably certain to continue or occur; (4) defendant intentionally interfered; and (5) defendant acted for improper reasons, or used improper methods to interfere.
Examples. ▸ Fay was fired by her employer, Catering by Carine. To get back at Carine, Fay convinced a resort to breach a catering contract that it had with Carine. ▸ ABC Co. and XYZ Co. are negotiating a merger. Viper Co., a competitor, files unfounded lawsuits against ABC Co. in order to defeat the merger.
Limitation. More and more courts require that an interference result from an improper motive (spite or malice), occur by improper means (violation of law), or otherwise be unjustified.
Study hint. A business can use proper means (e.g., discounts) to induce a prospective customer to exercise a right to terminate a contract that the customer has with a competitor.

3. Injurious Falsehood

General rules. ▸ *Tort*: malicious, false statement that degrades another's goods or services. ▸ *Elements*: (1) false statement; (2) made maliciously; (3) statement is communicated to third party who understood it degraded goods/services; (4) statement caused damage to a party.
Example. To get back at a cafe owner, Joe stood in front of the cafe and told prospective customers the restaurant served spoiled food. As a result, many customers left.
Study hints. ▸ Malicious means spiteful or intending to harm. ▸ In some states, showing a defendant knew a statement was false, or had reckless disregard of the truth proves malice.

4. Confusion of Source

General rules. ▸ *Tort*: wrongful attempt to represent one's goods or services as those of another. ▸ This tort is based on trademark (trade name) infringement or unfair competition.

- *Trademark infringement*: ▸ Defined: unauthorized use of another's trademark. ▸ Trademark: word, name, symbol, or device that distinguishes one product from another. ▸ Federal registration, state statutes, or common law may protect trademarks. ▸ To qualify for trademark protection, a mark must (1) be arbitrary, unique, or fanciful ("7-Up"); (2) subtly suggest a product's qualities ("Duracell" battery); or (3) have acquired a secondary meaning ("Mother's Cookies"). ▸ Generic terms (e.g., motor oil) are not protected.

- *Trademark or trade name dilution*: ▸ Defined: lessening of the capacity of a famous mark to identify or distinguish a product. It may result from confusing or tarnishing a mark. ▸ Example: "Cadillac toilets."

- *Unfair competition*: ▸ Defined: product's total impression creates confusion regarding its source, i.e., whose product it is. ▸ Factors: size, packaging, names, design, colors.

Study hint.   Proving a likelihood of confusion is sufficient to establish confusion of source.

II. CRIMES

A. BUSINESS CRIMES

General rule.   Business crimes include any crimes committed against a business or in which a business is used in the commission of the crime.

Examples.   ▸ Gary shoplifted some tools from the National Auto Supplies store. ▸ Marcella, comptroller of Dentyc Corp., kept for personal use some checks that were supposed to be deposited in the corporate account. ▸ Lawry Co. was having financial problems and set fire to its business building to collect the insurance proceeds.

B. TYPES OF CRIMES

1. Theft

General rule. Theft is the taking and depriving another of property without the owner's consent and with the intent of depriving the owner of the property. Types of theft include:

- *Shoplifting*: ▸ Defined: taking goods in a store with the intent to keep them and not to pay the purchase price. ▸ Example: Pam hid a package of steaks in her coat in order to take them from the store without paying.

- *Embezzlement*: ▸ Defined: fraudulent taking of property that is lawfully in one's possession.   ▸ Example: Kurt, who was in charge of reimbursing employee expenses, embezzled his employer's funds by making out a check to a nonexistent payee and then cashing the check for himself.

- *Larceny*: ▸ Defined: Taking and carrying away property of another without his or her consent, with the intent of depriving the owner of the property. ▸ Kim committed larceny by taking diskettes and ink cartridges from the office supply room for her personal use at home.

Study hints. ▸ The elements of criminal offenses may vary somewhat from state to state.
▸ Embezzlement differs from other theft offenses because the embezzler has lawful possession of the property at the time of the offense.

2. RICO (RACKETEER INFLUENCED AND CORRUPT ORGANIZATIONS ACT)

- *Nature of law*: RICO is a federal law that was enacted to prevent organized crime from using legitimate business to further their criminal activities.
- *Elements*: (1) Conduct; (2) by an enterprise (two or more people); (3) involving a pattern (two or more incidents of wrongful conduct within ten years); (4) of racketeering activities (acts that are criminal under federal or state law, whether or not a conviction has been obtained).
- *Penalties*: ▸ RICO creates both criminal and civil penalties. ▸ A party injured by conduct that violates RICO can bring a civil action and recover treble damages (three times the actual damages) plus attorney's fees.
- *Application*: RICO is written so broadly that it has been applied to numerous cases involving professionals and businesses that have nothing to do with organized crime.
- *State RICO laws*: Many states have enacted RICO laws ("Baby RICO" laws) to regulate intrastate business, since RICO only governs interstate commerce.

3. Computer Crimes

General rules. ▸ Computer crimes are crimes that are committed through the use of a computer or that involve a computer. ▸ Conduct may be a crime as a result of federal or state law. ▸ Some computer crimes are prosecuted under existing criminal laws, e.g., theft and fraud. In other cases, new laws have been adopted.

Example. New computer law: The federal Computer Fraud and Abuse Act makes it a crime to access a computer used by or for the U.S. government and, in connection with doing so, to: (1) obtain anything of value; (2) intentionally alter or damage information; (3) prevent authorized use of the computer; or (4) deal in computer passwords thereby affecting interstate commerce.

Limitation. Some states refuse to apply traditional criminal laws to computer wrongs.

Study hint. Computer crimes include computer trespass and fraud.

a. Trespass

General rules. ▸ Computer trespass: unauthorized use of, or access to, a computer. ▸ This crime may be committed if (1) an unauthorized person uses another's computer; (2) a person exceeds the authorized limits for using a computer; or (3) an employee, agent, or third party wrongfully obtains information from, or causes damage to, a computer.

Examples. ▸ Stuart used a company's computer without permission. ▸ Employee, who is authorized to use Employer's computer, wrongfully used the computer to conduct a dating service that Employee operated as a private business. ▸ Monica planted a virus in Employer's computer to get revenge for a demotion.

Study hints. ▸ Computer trespass includes installing rogue programs (software instructions that cause malfunctions) in another's computer. Liability may result regardless of the harm that is caused by the rogue program. ▸ Laws in most states protect the confidentiality of information stored in computers, and wrongfully taking such information may be trespass.

b. Fraud

General rule. Larceny and embezzlement are types of fraud that may involve a computer. Many types of computer fraud now involve fraudulent Internet scams.

Examples. ▸ Jane used a computer to wrongfully transfer funds from Larry's bank account into her account. ▸ Jane used a computer to alter a bank's records to fraudulently increase her checking account balance from $500 to $5,000.

c. Criminal Copyright Infringement

Criminal copyright infringement requires proof that (1) there has been copyright infringement (2) that was willful (3) and was done for financial gain or business advantage.

REVIEW OF CHAPTER

REVIEW OF TERMS

Select the term that best matches a statement below. Each term is the best match for only one statement.

TERMS

a. Computer trespass
b. Confusion of source
c. Embezzlement
d. Induce breach of contract

e. Injurious falsehood
f. Interfere with prospective advantage
g. RICO
h. Rogue program

i. Secondary meaning
j. Trademark
k. Trademark infringement
l. Unfair competition

STATEMENTS

Answer

_____ 1. Intentionally causing a person to breach a contract with another.

_____ 2. Special meaning that has become associated with the name of a product.

_____ 3. False statement degrading another person's goods or services.

_____ 4. Software instructions that cause a computer to function abnormally.

_____ 5. Tort that arises if one represents his or her goods or services as being those of another. Tort includes trademark or trade name infringement, and unfair competition.

_____ 6. Wrongful interference with another's reasonable expectation of economic advantage.

_____ 7. Unauthorized access to, or use of, a computer.

_____ 8. Unauthorized use of another's trademark.

_____ 9. Fraudulent conversion of another's property by someone lawfully possessing it.

_____ 10. Federal law that creates civil and criminal penalties in connection with racketeering activities.

_____ 11. Word, name, symbol, or device used to identify and distinguish a product.

_____ 12. Tort that arises if overall impression of a product causes confusion regarding the product's origin.

REVIEW OF CONCEPTS

Directions: Indicate **T** for true and **F** for false in the answer column.

_____ 1. Business crimes include crimes committed against a business.

_____ 2. To commit a theft offense, the perpetrator must obtain the property unlawfully and must intend to deprive the owner of the property.

_____ 3. Shoplifting may consist of concealing unpaid-for goods while in a store.

_____ 4. An embezzler has lawful possession of another's property, but then converts the property with the intent to defraud the owner of the property.

_____ 5. To commit larceny, a person must take property from its owner, and the taking must be with the intent to deprive the owner of possession of the property.

_____ 6. To recover for an intentional tort, the injured person must show: (1) an act; (2) the defendant intended to cause the consequences of the act; and (3) the injury was caused by defendant's act.

_____ 7. According to some courts, intentionally causing another to breach a contract is a tort only if the conduct is done for an improper purpose or is accomplished by using improper means.

_____ 8. Beta wants to sell supplies to Acme Mfg., but Acme has a contract with Gart Co. Beta offers Acme some discounts to induce it to buy from Beta. In response, Acme exercises its right to terminate the contract with Gart. Beta has committed the tort of inducing a breach of contract.

_____ 9. The tort of interference with prospective business advantage requires that a party wrongfully cause another party to breach an existing contract.

_____ 10. Wrongfully injuring the reputation of another person is the tort of injurious falsehood.

_____ 11. The tort of confusion of source can be based on trademark infringement or unfair competition.

_____ 12. The tort of confusion of source cannot be committed unless a defendant's conduct actually confuses consumers regarding the source or origin of a good or service.

_____ 13. The name "Ira-Ban" for a bicycle is an example of an arbitrary trademark entitled to protection.

_____ 14. A mark may be entitled to trademark protection if it acquires a secondary meaning.

_____ 15. Day Co. sold a candy named "Xeri-Fun." Day Co. did not register this trademark. In this case, Day Co. will receive no protection of this mark since it was not registered.

_____ 16. Installing a rogue program in another's computer is not a crime unless it destroys the computer.

_____ 17. Using a computer to illegally obtain money from a bank is a computer crime involving fraud.

_____ 18. RICO applies to both intrastate and interstate activities.

REVIEW OF CONCEPTS APPLICATIONS

Answer

Directions: Indicate your choice in the answer column.

_____ 1. Markham's Emporium has been in business for thirty years and it has an excellent reputation. John wants his new store to be a success, so he erects a large sign over his business reading "Markham's Emporium." Under these facts, John is probably liable for the tort of:
   a. Interference with contract.
   b. Interference with prospective advantage.
   c. Injurious falsehood.
   d. Confusion of source.

_____ 2. Gourmet Co. was in the final stage of negotiating a contract with Last Airway. It appeared that a contract would be signed. To defeat Gourmet's chance for this contract, Foodway Corp. bribed union officials to conduct an illegal strike of Gourmet. As a result, Gourmet did not get the contract. What tort did Foodway Corp. commit?
   a. Inducing breach of contract.
   b. Interference with prospective advantage.
   c. Injurious falsehood.
   d. Foodway Corp. did not commit a tort.

_____ 3. Jason owns an ice cream shop that sells soft-serve ice cream. (Soft-serve ice cream is any type of ice cream that is dispensed from a machine). Jason wants to obtain a trademark for the name "soft-serve ice cream." For years, numerous stores nationwide have sold "soft-serve ice cream." Does the name "soft-serve ice cream" qualify for trademark protection under federal law?
   a. Yes. A party is entitled to trademark protection for any name of a product.
   b. Yes. This name is unique, fanciful, and arbitrary and it is entitled to trademark protection.
   c. No. The name is generic, and protection is generally not available for generic names.
   d. No. Federal law does not protect trademarks. Federal law only protects trade names.

_____ 4. In which case does Jeanne commit a computer crime?
   a. Jeanne works for a federal agency. To protest U.S. foreign policy, Jeanne sabotaged the agency's computer system, causing substantial damage to the system.
   b. Jeanne is employed by Motorworks, an exclusive car dealer in Beverly Hills. Secret customer data that cannot be obtained elsewhere is maintained on the company's computer. Jeanne secretly prints out the information and sells it to a competitor of Motorworks.
   c. Jeanne wrongfully obtains access to IBM's computerized payroll system, and she causes IBM to issue her ten checks for a total of $50,000. Jeanne cashes the checks.
   d. All of the above.

_____ 5. Blue Sky Inc. and Hawk Inc. are securities firms. These companies have recently engaged in three separate fraudulent stock offerings. Each offering violated both federal and state criminal laws, but Big Sky has not been convicted of these crimes. Jim bought stock from Big Sky in one of these offerings. Under these facts, can Jim bring a RICO action against Big Sky?

    a.   No, because Big Sky is not a criminal organization.

    b.   No, because Big Sky has not been convicted of a crime.

    c.   No, because RICO only imposes criminal penalties for violations.

    d.   Yes. Jim may bring a RICO action, and he may be able to recover treble damages.

CASE PROBLEM

Perry bought a tool to trim the weeds in the family's yard. His brother, Robert, used the trimmer to clear a ditch along the road in front of their property. Robert was injured when the trimmer threw some debris into his eye. There were no guard pieces on this particular model of weed trimmer to protect the user from flying debris picked up by the trimmer. (1) Under what tort theory might a lawsuit be brought against the manufacturer of the weed trimmer? (2) Can Robert bring suit even though he was not the purchaser of the trimmer? (3) To prove that the manufacturer was liable, what elements would Robert have to show?

_____

_____

_____

_____

BUSINESS LAW PARTNER EXERCISE

Directions: Access your Business Law Partner CD-ROM and locate the document entitled "Trademark Application Worksheet." Analyze the case study below and (1) answer whether one or more of the marks can be registered and explain your answer and (2) if one or both marks may be registered, determine what information is necessary for registration and complete the worksheet.

Case Study: *Buy Our Toys, But Don't Steal Their Names*

Fargo Corp. manufactures children's toys. Fargo Corp. has developed the following two new products: (1) a line of stuffed dolls called "Wild Rascals," and (2) a line of baseball bats called "Ball Bats." Fargo Corp. first began to market these products on January 1, 1998 in MegaVille, North Dakota, and they continue to sell these products in all regions of the United States?

_____

_____

_____

_____

CHAPTER 3 QUIZ

Section A

DIRECTIONS: Following each statement below, indicate your answer by placing a "T" for "True" or an "F" for "False" in the Answers column.

	Answers	For Scoring
1. All states view the same business activities as being torts and crimes.	_____	1. _____
2. All criminal offenses are closely related to business activity.	_____	2. _____
3. Some computer offenses are successfully prosecuted using traditional criminal laws that do not specifically relate to computers.	_____	3. _____
4. In general, the law prohibits the intentional, unauthorized access to computers regardless of the reason for the access.	_____	4. _____
5. An employee authorized to use a computer cannot be guilty of computer trespass	_____	5. _____
6. Laws do not protect the confidentiality of information stored in computers.	_____	6. _____
7. Computer fraud includes stealing as well as damaging computers.	_____	7. _____
8. RICO is a law used only against organized crime.	_____	8. _____
9. For purposes of proving a RICO violation, just two acts constitute a pattern.	_____	9. _____
10. A tort is always caused by a negligent act, which causes injury.	_____	10. _____
11. In order to recover for injury from a defective product, the injured party must have purchased the product from the manufacturer.	_____	11. _____
12. In all cases, to prove the tort of inducing breach of contract, a contract must have been breached.	_____	12. _____
13. If the defendant did not know about the contract, there can be no tort of inducing breach of contract.	_____	13. _____
14. Interference with prospective advantage is very similar to inducing breach of contract.	_____	14. _____
15. In general, a person may properly interfere with a business relationship if such interference is necessary to protect a legitimate economic interest of that person.	_____	15. _____
16. To be a tort, a false statement about another's goods must be malicious.	_____	16. _____
17. All words and symbols qualify for protection as trademarks.	_____	17. _____
18. A trademark does not have to be registered.	_____	18. _____
19. When a court is deciding whether there is a likelihood of confusion between two marks, the strength of the two marks is irrelevant.	_____	19. _____
20. The same legal principles govern trademark and service mark infringement.	_____	20. _____

Score _____

Section B

DIRECTIONS: Complete each of the following statements by writing the missing word or words in the Answers column.

	Answers	For Scoring
1. Taking another's property without consent and with the intention of depriving the owner of it is	_____	1. _____
2. Taking possession of goods in a store with the intent to use them without paying for them is	_____	2. _____

3. The fraudulent conversion of another's property by someone in lawful possession of the property is.. **3.** _____

4. As applied to business crime, the unauthorized use of a computer is .... **4.** _____

5. A set of software instructions which produces abnormal or unexpected behavior in a computer is called a(n) .... **5.** _____

6. A ??? is a person who causes an intentional or negligent injury to others..... **6.** _____

7. The doctrine that makes the manufacturer of a product liable for injury without proof of negligence is called .... **7.** _____

8. It is a tort to ??? a breach of contract. .... **8.** _____

9. The tort of interference with economic advantage requires what type of an interference?. .... **9.** _____

10. A false statement of fact that degrades the quality of another's goods is a(n) **10.** _____

11. To cause a tort, a false statement must be ??? to a third person. .... **11.** _____

12. When a person attempts to represent goods or services as being the goods or services of someone else, there occurs a tort of.. **12.** _____

13. The word "water" when used to describe H_2O cannot be registered as a trademark because it is merely .... **13.** _____

14. A word, name, symbol, device, or any combination of them adopted and used to identify and distinguish goods is a(n) .... **14.** _____

15. When the total impression a product gives to the consumer results in confusion as to the origin of the product there occurs the tort of................... **15.** _____

Score _____

Section C

DIRECTIONS: Indicate your decision in each of the following cases by filling in the Answers column.

	Answers	For Scoring

1-2. Heaton contracted with Guillen to sell him a carload of shoes. Two days later, Kruk, who knew about the contract, convinced Guillen the contract was a bad deal. Kruk told Heaton not to deliver the shoes. Heaton sued Kruk for inducing breach of contract. Will Heaton recover? .... **1.** _____

If Heaton finds another buyer who pays 10% more than Guillen had agreed to pay, does the decision change?... **2.** _____

3-5. Nunez, a computer programmer, was told he was going to be laid off from work in two weeks. He put a virus in his company's computer. Two days after his last day on the job, the virus caused the customer lists to disappear from the computer system. Moreover, before workers could fix the computer, all data in the system was erased. Is Nunez liable for this act? .... **3.** _____

What specific term describes Nunez' actions?.. **4.** _____

Did Nunez' actions constitute both a civil and criminal wrong? .... **5.** _____

Score

CHAPTER 4
GOVERNMENT REGULATION OF BUSINESS

CHAPTER OUTLINE

I. **PURPOSE OF REGULATION**

Government regulates business in order to eliminate (1) abuses by business and (2) unreasonable commercial conduct. Regulation is commonly implemented and enforced by administrative agencies.

II. **ADMINISTRATIVE AGENCIES**

General rules. ▸ An administrative agency is a government board or commission that has the authority to regulate or implement laws. ▸ Agencies are created by Congress and state legislatures to regulate complex aspects of business or society. The legislative body that creates an agency determines (1) the agency's authority and (2) the remedies that are available to question an agency's actions. ▸ An agency may have the power to: (1) adopt laws (rules and regulations); (2) investigate companies or industries; (3) commence and decide cases involving violations of government regulations; and (4) impose fines or forbid future, improper activities.
Example. Federal Trade Commission (FTC): (1) adopts rules regarding deceptive advertising; (2) investigates suspected violations; and (3) commences and decides administrative actions against suspected violators of its regulations.
Study hint. Agencies often (1) conduct research, (2) certify products that are in compliance with government regulations, and (3) establish standards for goods and services.

A. STRUCTURE OF ADMINISTRATIVE AGENCIES

Agencies are typically run by (1) an administrator (person appointed by the President with the consent of the U.S. Senate, or by a state governor), or (2) an appointed commission.

B. TYPES OF AGENCIES

- *Regulatory agencies*: ▸ Regulatory agency: agency that to some extent governs commercial activities of businesses. ▸ A regulatory agency may adopt rules, investigate violations, and enforce regulations. It can enforce regulations by (1) imposing fines and (2) issuing orders directing that certain conduct be stopped. ▸ Examples: Interstate Commerce Commission; Securities and Exchange Commission (SEC); Environmental Protection Agency (EPA).

- *Nonregulatory agencies*: ▸ Nonregulatory agency: agency created primarily to distribute government benefits or services, not to regulate business. ▸ Examples: State Department of Health; State Department of Social Services.

C. POWERS OF AGENCIES

Depending on the authority that is granted by Congress or a state legislature, an agency may have:

- *Licensing power*: ▸ Defined: authority to decide who may engage in certain professions or industries. ▸ Examples: Federal Aviation Administration; State Board of Medical Examiners.

- *Rate-making power*: ▸ Defined: authority to determine prices that may be charged for goods or services. ▸ Examples: U.S. Postal Service; State Public Utilities Commission.

- *Power over business practices*: ▸ Defined: authority to determine whether an activity is permissible or not. ▸ Example: Equal Employment Opportunity Commission.

D. RULE MAKING

General rule. A federal agency generally uses the following procedure to adopt a rule: (1) the agency investigates an activity; (2) notice of a proposed rule must be published in the *Federal Register*; and (3) the agency receives comments through formal hearings or by *notice and comment rule making* (informally receiving comments without formal hearings). After receiving comments, the agency adopts the rule as published or as modified, or it may not adopt the rule.

Limitation. An agency can only adopt rules that relate to matters within its authority.

E. STATE AGENCIES

Every state has agencies that regulate selected businesses and activities occurring within the state.

III. ANTITRUST

- *Nature of antitrust laws*: Antitrust laws are statutes that prohibit unreasonable restraints of trade, i.e., activities that unfairly limit competition.

- *Scope of antitrust laws*: ▸ Federal antitrust laws apply to commercial activities between two or more states. ▸ State antitrust laws (similar to federal laws) apply to activities within a state.

- *Standards for determining violations*: ▸ Rule of reason standard: Certain activities violate antitrust laws only if they in fact substantially lessen competition. ▸ *Per se* standard: Certain activities are illegal under the antitrust laws regardless of their effect on competition. Examples of *per se* violations: price fixing; group boycotts; horizontal territorial restraints (competitors divide territories among themselves). ▸ Limitation: Most antitrust violations require proof of an agreement between two or more persons or separate businesses.

- *Sherman Antitrust Act*: This Act prohibits (1) unreasonable restraints of trade, such as price fixing, and (2) unlawful monopolies or attempts to monopolize an industry.

- *Clayton Act*: The Clayton Act prohibits certain conduct if it substantially lessens competition. Such conduct may include: (1) price discrimination (charging different customers different prices for same goods) unless the difference is due to different costs; (2) exclusive dealing agreements (contracts to sell goods provided the buyer agrees not to use or deal in goods of a competitor); (3) acquiring an interest in a competitor's assets; and (4) interlocking directorates of competitors (directors of two competitors are the same).

- *Robinson-Patman Act*: This Act prohibits (1) price discrimination when it tends to lessen competition, and (2) selling goods at unreasonably low prices to eliminate competition.

- *Federal Trade Commission Act*: The FTC Act prohibits (1) unfair methods of competition, (2) unfair or deceptive practices in commerce, and (3) false advertising.

IV. ENVIRONMENTAL PROTECTION

To protect the environment, Congress and the states have adopted environmental laws. Congress has created the Environmental Protection Agency (EPA) to carry out the federal laws, such as:

- *Clean Air Act*: The EPA establishes minimum national standards for air quality and these standards are enforced by states under plans approved by the EPA.

- *Clean Water Act*: This Act protects the quality of U.S. waters and adjacent wetlands. This Act regulates the discharge of pollutants into naviagable waterways.

- *Resource Conservation and Recovery Act*: RCRA regulates the generation, storage, transportation, treatment, and disposal of hazardous waste.

- *CERCLA ("Superfund" law)*: CERCLA imposes cleanup liability on past and current property owners, operators of facilities, and persons who dispose of or transport hazardous wastes.

- *State laws*: Many states have enacted their own superfund environmental laws.

- *Protection from liability*: Before buying land, one should make an environmental assessment of the property.

CHAPTER REVIEW

REVIEW OF TERMS

Select the term that best matches a statement below. Each term is the best match for only one statement.

TERMS

a. Administrative agency
b. Boycott
c. Congress

d. Executive branch (President)
e. Federal Trade Commission
f. Nonregulatory agency

g. Price fixing
h. Regulatory agency

STATEMENTS

Answer

_____ 1. Branch of federal government that creates federal agencies.
_____ 2. Agreement between competitors not to do business with a third party.
_____ 3. Federal agency that enforces certain federal antitrust laws.
_____ 4. Type of agency that primarily regulates a particular type of commercial activity.
_____ 5. Type of agency that primarily distributes governmental benefits or services.
_____ 6. Branch of federal government that nominates persons to direct most federal agencies.
_____ 7. Governmental body created by Congress or a state legislature to regulate a particular activity.
_____ 8. Agreement between competitors to charge a uniform price.

REVIEW OF CONCEPTS

Directions: Indicate **T** for true and **F** for false in the answer column.

_____ 1. Government often regulates business in order to prevent unreasonable commercial conduct.
_____ 2. An agency can adopt whatever regulations it feels may be beneficial to society.
_____ 3. Most governmental regulation of business takes place through administrative agencies.
_____ 4. The legislative bodies that create the agencies appoint administrators who run them.
_____ 5. Regulatory agencies license and control activities of firms that engage in certain professions or industries.
_____ 6. Agencies cannot make laws; Congress or state legislatures can only exercise this power.
_____ 7. The general purpose of antitrust laws is to prohibit activities or agreements that unfairly or unreasonably limit competition between businesses (i.e., restrain trade).
_____ 8. Under the rule of reason, certain conduct is deemed to automatically violate federal antitrust laws, such as the Sherman Antitrust Act, even if the conduct does not substantially lessen competition.
_____ 9. Most antitrust violations require that two or more persons agree or jointly act to restrain trade.
_____ 10. Most federal agencies cannot investigate suspected violations of agency regulations; only federal law enforcement agencies can do this.
_____ 11. The Environmental Protection Agency generally administers Federal environmental laws.
_____ 12. Federal environmental laws often permit some regulation by both the EPA and states.

REVIEW OF CONCEPT APPLICATIONS

Answer

Directions: Indicate your choice in the answer column.

_____ 1. The SEC, a federal agency, has the power to license persons who sell stock in interstate commerce, and the power to regulate business conduct that is used to sell securities. However, the SEC does not have the power to establish prices for which securities may be sold. Under these facts, the SEC does *NOT* possess:
    a. Licensing power.
    b. Rate-making power.
    c. Power over business practices.
    d. a and b.

_____ 2. Which agreement by Heifer Co. does *NOT* violate the Sherman Antitrust Act?
   a. Heifer and a competitor agree to sell their respective products for the same price.
   b. Heifer and a competitor agree that Heifer will sell its products only in California, and the competitor will sell its products only in Arizona and New Mexico.
   c. Heifer gives A&A Grocery the exclusive right to sell Heifer's products in a small town. This agreement is evaluated under the rule of reason, and it does not lessen competition.
   d. All of the above.

_____ 3. Compu Co. is one of the two largest manufacturers of computers in the United States. Which action or agreement does *NOT* violate federal antitrust laws?
   a. In one market, Compu sells its X computer to some stores for $1,800, and it sells the same computer to other stores for $2,500. There is no justification for this difference in pricing, and this pricing scheme substantially lessens competition.
   b. Compu sells its Y computer in one market for $1,000, and it sells the same computer in other markets for $950. The pricing difference is due to a difference in transportation costs.
   c. Compu agrees to buy all of the assets of the other largest computer manufacturer in the United States. This agreement will substantially lessen competition.
   d. a and b.

_____ 4. Chemco manufactures and distributes chemical products. Chemco is concerned that its production, distribution, and disposal of chemical products may be subject to federal environmental laws. What federal act most directly regulates Chemco's business activities?
   a. Clean Air Act.
   b. Clean Water Act.
   c. Safe Drinking Water Act.
   d. CERCLA.

CASE PROBLEM

The EPA is a federal agency authorized to regulate national environmental matters. The EPA is considering a new rule to control pollution caused by storm water. In this case: (1) Is the EPA required to give notice of the proposed rule and, if so, how is notice given? (2) How can the EPA obtain comments on this rule? (3) After receiving comments, what are the EPA's options with regard to the proposed rule?

_____

_____

_____

BUSINESS LAW PARTNER EXERCISE

Directions: Using the Online feature of the Business Law Partner CD-ROM, answer the questions in the case below.

Case Study: *Hazardous Waste is Nothing to Fool Around With*

Toxic Corp. manufactures several products using chemicals and other hazardous substances. Toxic has tons of hazardous waste left over from its manufacturing process, and its management has asked you to determine (1) what federal environmental act directly regulates disposal of this waste, (2) what the citation is for this law, and (3) what this Act generally requires.

_____

_____

_____

Section A

DIRECTIONS: In the Answers space in Column II, place the letter of the corresponding word or words from Column I.

Column I	Column II	Answers	For Scoring
(a) Antitrust laws	1. The federal agency charged with administering laws to protect the environment	_____	1. _____
(b) Clayton Act	2. A type of administrative agency that governs to some degree the economic activity of businesses	_____	2. _____
(c) Clean Air Act	3. A type of administrative agency set up to dispense benefits for social and economic welfare	_____	3. _____
(d) CERCLA	4. An agency's power to allow a business to enter the field being regulated	_____	4. _____
(e) Environmental assessment	5. An agency's power to fix the prices a business may charge	_____	5. _____
(f) Environmental Protection Agency	6. The primary way in which administrative agencies set policy	_____	6. _____
(g) Federal Register	7. Where a notice of a proposed rule is published	_____	7. _____
(h) Federal Trade Commission Act	8. A common state regulatory agency	_____	8. _____
(i) Food Safety and Inspection Service	9. Statutes that seek to promote competition among businesses	_____	9. _____
(j) Hazardous waste	10. The most important federal antitrust law	_____	10. _____
(k) Licensing power	11. The courts' examining and ruling on anticompetitive effects on a case-by-case basis	_____	11. _____
(l) Nonregulatory agency	12. An activity that is illegal without regard to its effect	_____	12. _____
(m) Notice and comment	13. The law that prohibits price discrimination to different purchasers where price difference is not due to differences in selling or transportation cost	_____	13. _____
(n) Per se violation	14. The law that prohibits price discrimination generally, for the purpose of eliminating competition	_____	14. _____
(o) Public Service Commission	15. The law prohibiting false advertising	_____	15. _____
(p) Rate-making power	16. The law under which the EPA sets minimum national standards for air quality	_____	16. _____
(q) Regulatory agency	17. The law enacted to restore and maintain proper chemistry of wetlands	_____	17. _____
(r) Resource Conservation and Recovery Act	18. The law giving the EPA the duty of setting standards for people who operate hazardous waste disposal facilities.	_____	18. _____
(s) Robinson-Patman Act	19. The law which seeks to clean up waste from previous activities.	_____	19. _____
(t) Rule making	20. What lending institutions should require before making a loan or foreclosing on property	_____	20. _____
(u) Rule of reason			
(v) Sherman Act			
(w) Water Pollution and Control Act			

Score _____

Section B

DIRECTIONS: Following each statement below, indicate your answer by placing a "T" for "True" or an "F" for "False" in the Answers column.

		Answers	For Scoring
1.	Governmental rules and regulations affect the operation of most businesses.	_____	1. _____
2.	Government regulation is intended to make it easier for heavy industry to do business.	_____	2. _____
3.	In most cases where administrative agencies are used to regulate, it is because the area of regulation is simple.	_____	3. _____
4.	Commissions, the members of which are appointed for staggered terms, run all administrative agencies.	_____	4. _____
5.	Certain regulatory agencies dispense benefits for social and economic welfare.	_____	5. _____
6.	Regulatory power over business practices is the power to determine whether the activity of the regulated entity is acceptable.	_____	6. _____
7.	The primary way in which administrative agencies set policy is by issuing injunctions.	_____	7. _____
8.	Antitrust laws are primarily intended to regulate foreign competition.	_____	8. _____
9.	Most of the states have antitrust laws very similar to the Sherman Act.	_____	9. _____
10.	Courts determine the anticompetitive effects of price fixing and group boycotts on a case-by-case basis.	_____	10. _____
11.	Any activity that lessens competition violates federal antitrust laws.	_____	11. _____
12.	In general, the Clayton Act allows companies to engage in conduct even if their conduct substantially lessens competition or tends to create a monopoly.	_____	12. _____
13.	The Robinson-Patman Act prohibits sales at unreasonably low prices in order to eliminate competition.	_____	13. _____
14.	The states apply and enforce the national standards for air quality set by the EPA.	_____	14. _____
15.	Either the EPA or private citizens may sue under the Clean Water Act to protect wetlands.	_____	15. _____
16.	The Resource Conservation and Recovery Act requires only those who generate hazardous waste to obtain a permit from the EPA for its dispersal.	_____	16. _____
17.	The "Superfund" law may impose liability for environmental cleanup of contaminated property on a present owner even though a prior owner did the contamination.	_____	17. _____
18.	If several parties are liable for the cleanup of waste, CERCLA requires each to pay only his or her proportionate share of the cleanup costs.	_____	18. _____
19.	The only potential business costs under CERCLA are the cleanup costs.	_____	19. _____
20.	Federal agencies are the only agencies that regulate pollution and protect the environment.	_____	20. _____

Score _____

CHAPTER 5
NATURE AND CLASSES OF CONTRACTS

CHAPTER OUTLINE

I. CONTRACTS CONTRASTED WITH AGREEMENTS

General rules. ▸ A contract is a legally enforceable agreement. ▸ A contract must include an express or implied agreement between the parties. ▸ Contracts are legally enforceable. Agreements are not necessarily legally enforceable (that is, not all agreements form contracts).
Examples. ▸ Contract: Pam promises to pay $100 to Jay for his VCR and Jay promises to sell the VCR to Pam. ▸ Unenforceable agreement: Gil and a friend agree to play tennis with each other.
Study hint. The essential characteristics of a contract are: (1) by mutual agreement (2) parties create obligations that can be legally enforced.

II. CLASSIFICATION OF CONTRACTS

General rule. A contract may be classified according to: (1) its validity or enforceability; (2) how the contract arose; (3) the form of the contract; (4) the extent to which the contract has been performed; and (5) the manner by which the offer to contract can be accepted.
Study hint. The classification of a contract is important regarding: (1) how a contract is created; and (2) whether certain defenses may be used to set aside the contract.

A. VALID CONTRACTS, VOID AGREEMENTS, AND VOIDABLE CONTRACTS

General rules. ▸ Classified according to its validity, a contract or agreement may be a:

- *Valid contract*: ▸ Definition: legally binding contract made in accordance with all legal requirements. ▸ Elements: (1) mutual agreement; (2) competent parties; (3) consideration (value) is given by each party; (4) lawful purpose; (5) proper form of contract (if required, contract is written or under seal). ▸ Example: Cob agrees in writing to sell his car to Eva for $1,000.
- *Voidable contract*: ▸ Definition: contract that may be set aside by a party because of circumstances surrounding the making of the contract, or because the party lacked contractual capacity. ▸ Example: Spike (a minor) agrees to buy Vena's bike for $100.
- *Void agreement*: ▸ Definition: agreement that is of no legal effect (frequently an illegal agreement). ▸ Example: Fred agrees to buy illegal drugs from Boris.
- *Unenforceable contract*: ▸ Definition: agreement that cannot presently be enforced by judicial action. ▸ Example: Employer orally hires Chelsea for two years. The contract is not in writing as required by law and, therefore, it cannot be enforced in court.

Limitation. A voidable contract is legally enforceable, and it must be performed unless it is properly set aside by the party with the right to avoid it.
Study hints. ▸ A void agreement cannot be made valid by the parties' subsequent approval.
▸ An unenforceable contract can be made valid by certain corrective action, such as setting the terms of an oral contract down in a signed, written contract.

B. EXPRESS AND IMPLIED CONTRACTS

General rule. Classified according to how a contract arises, a contract may be either an:

- *Express contract*: contract formed by the oral or written words of the parties; or
- *Implied (in fact) contract*: contract formed by the conduct of the parties.

Study hints. ‣ Express and implied contracts are enforceable and have the same basic effect. ‣ An express contract is binding even if it does not state a term, if the omitted term will be implied by law. ‣ An implied contract arises if a person does a service for another with an expectation of payment, and the other party accepts the service knowing that payment is expected.

C. FORMAL AND SIMPLE CONTRACTS

General rule. Classified according to form, a contract is either a:

- ***Formal contract***: (1) contract under seal; (2) recognizance (agreement made before a court to do an act); or (3) negotiable instrument (check, note, draft, or certificate of deposit); or

- ***Simple (informal) contract***: any contract that is not a formal contract.

Limitation. Statutes in some states and the UCC (relating to contracts for sales of goods) do not recognize seals, i.e., an agreement is not legally binding just because it is under seal.
Study hints. ‣ In states where seals are still recognized, a seal implies that parties gave consideration sufficient to create a contract. ‣ In some states, a seal allows a party a longer time within which to sue for breach of contract. ‣ A contract is made under seal (1) by affixing a seal to a document in addition to a written signature, or (2) by signing an instrument, and writing or typing the words "seal" or "LS" after the name.

D. EXECUTORY AND EXECUTED CONTRACTS

Classified according to the degree of performance, a contract is either an:

- ***Executed contract***: contract that has been fully performed by all parties; or

- ***Executory contract***: : contract that has not been fully performed by all parties.

E. UNILATERAL AND BILATERAL CONTRACTS

General rule. Classified according to how a person can accept an offer, a contract may be a:
- ***Bilateral contract***: ‣ Definition: contract consisting of an exchange of promises; offer to contract can be accepted by promising to perform a requested act. ‣ Example: Devin promises to pay Yin $100 to paint his fence, and Yin promises to paint the fence.

- ***Unilateral contract***: ‣ Definition: contract consisting of a promise given in exchange for an act; offer to contract can be accepted only by performance of the requested act. ‣ Example: Doris offers JoJo $50 for the return of her lost dog, Rusty. JoJo finds and returns Rusty.

Limitation. An offer for a unilateral contract cannot be accepted by a promise to do a requested act; it can be accepted only by actually performing the act.
Study hint. Whether an offer is for a bilateral or unilateral contract is determined by the intent of the party making the offer. Focus on what this person is demanding.

F. QUASI CONTRACT

General rule. Quasi contract (or a contract implied in law) is an obligation to pay that may be imposed by a court in order to prevent unjust enrichment.
Example. Felix Florist mistakenly delivers a bouquet of flowers to Fran. Fran is aware of the mistake, but she does not inform Felix of the mistake and she keeps the flowers. Fran must pay the reasonable value of the flowers. Otherwise, she would be unjustly enriched.
Study hints. ‣ Quasi contract requires payment for a benefit even though there is no actual contractual agreement to pay. ‣ Under appropriate circumstances, quasi contractual relief may be awarded if: (1) a benefit is given by mistake; or (2) a benefit is given pursuant to a voidable contract that is subsequently set aside.

REVIEW OF CHAPTER

REVIEW OF TERMS

Select the term that best matches a statement below. Each term is the best match for only one statement.

TERMS

a. Bilateral contract
b. Executed contract
c. Executory contract
d. Express contract

e. Implied contract
f. Unenforceable contract
g. Unilateral contract

h. Valid contract
i. Void agreement
j. Voidable contract

STATEMENTS

Answer

_____ 1. Contract arising from a written or oral agreement.
_____ 2. Contract that may be set aside because it was not properly formed or a party lacked capacity.
_____ 3. Contract that presently cannot be enforced by judicial action.
_____ 4. Contract consisting of a promise made in consideration for an act. The offer to contract can be accepted only by the actual performance of the requested act.
_____ 5. Contract that has been fully performed by all parties.
_____ 6. Contract arising from the conduct of the parties.
_____ 7. Legally binding contract that is made in accordance with all legal requirements.
_____ 8. Contract that has not been fully performed by all parties.
_____ 9. Contract consisting of an exchange of promises. The offer to contract may be accepted by a promise to perform the requested act.
_____ 10. Agreement that is of no legal effect.

REVIEW OF CONCEPTS

Directions: Indicate **T** for true and **F** for false in the answer column.

_____ 1. Every agreement is a valid, legally binding contract.
_____ 2. An agreement is a valid contract even if it is not made in the form required by law.
_____ 3. In general, a void agreement cannot be made enforceable by the subsequent conduct of the parties.
_____ 4. A voidable contract is binding unless the party having the right to set it aside elects to do so.
_____ 5. In states that recognize seals, a seal implies that each party gave consideration.
_____ 6. A defendant's agreement to appear for trial in return for the court's releasing the defendant on bail is an example of a formal contract known as a recognizance.
_____ 7. A negotiable instrument, such as a check or certificate of deposit, is one type of simple contract.
_____ 8. A person can accept an offer for a bilateral offer by promising to perform a requested act.
_____ 9. A person can accept an offer for a unilateral contract only by performing the requested act.
_____ 10. Quasi contract requires that a person pay for any benefit that is ever received, whether the benefit constitutes unjust enrichment or not.

REVIEW OF CONCEPT APPLICATIONS

Answer

Directions: Indicate your choice in the answer column.

_____ 1. Which promise or agreement constitutes a valid contract?
a. Max promises to pay Lisa $50 if she will agree to clean his house. Lisa refuses Max's offer.
b. Char and her friend Todd agree to meet at the health club to lift weights together.
c. Stephie and her son agree that Stephie will buy him a motorcycle as a gift.
d. Tom and Helen are competent adults, and in a signed writing Tom and Helen agree that Helen will sell her car to Tom for $2,000.

_____ 2. Stan lacks the capacity to make a contract because he is a fifteen-year-old minor. Nonetheless, Stan contracts to buy a guitar from Play-It-Again-Sam Sales. Under these facts, the contract is:
   a. Void.
   b. Voidable.
   c. Valid.

_____ 3. Cindy saw Carl's Lawn Service mowing a neighbor's lawn. Cindy pointed to her lawn, gesturing that she wanted it mowed. In response, Carl mowed Cindy's lawn. Under these facts:
   a. Cindy and Carl made an implied contract, and Cindy is obligated to pay for Carl's services.
   b. Cindy and Carl made an implied contract, but Cindy is not obligated to pay for Carl's services.
   c. Cindy and Carl made an express contract, and Cindy is obligated to pay for Carl's services.

_____ 4. Jackie offered to pay Glenn $500 in consideration for Glenn's actual, complete trimming of all trees located on Jackie's property. With the intent to accept Jackie's offer, Glenn completely trimmed the trees in question. Under these facts, Jackie and Glenn's agreement is:
   a. A quasi contract.
   b. A bilateral contract.
   c. A unilateral contract.

CASE PROBLEM

Diane and Rick entered into a signed, written contract whereby Diane promised to sell a motel to Rick for $200,000 and Rick promised to pay Diane $200,000 for the motel. One week later, a dispute arose between the parties regarding the contract. At the time the dispute arose, Rick had paid the entire $200,000 sales price, but Diane had not conveyed title to the motel to Rick. Under these facts:

1. Is the contract in question a formal or simple contract?
2. Is the contract in question a bilateral or unilateral contract?
3. At the time the dispute arose, was the contract executed or executory?

_____

_____

_____

BUSINESS LAW PARTNER EXERCISE

Directions: Access your Business Law Partner CD-ROM and find the document "Defending a Business Lawsuit."

1. Help Dan complete the above-referenced document using the information provided in the following case study.
2. Is Dan obligated to pay for the engine because based on (a) an express contract or (2) quasi contract?

Case Study: *But I Never Agreed to Pay*

Dan drove his car to Ty's Garage, a sole proprietorship, and requested Ty's to fix the radio. Before leaving, Dan noticed Jake, the mechanic, getting ready to work on his car's engine. Dan overheard the Jake say that he was going to overhaul the engine. Dan did not say anything to correct this mistake. When Dan returned, Ty's had overhauled the engine. The reasonable value of this work was $500. Dan refused to pay for the engine overhaul and Ty's had the sheriff serve process on Dan.

_____

_____

_____

CHAPTER 5 QUIZ

Section A

DIRECTIONS: Complete each of the following statements by writing the missing word or words in the Answers column.

		Answers	For Scoring
1-4.	A valid contract must fulfill the following definite requirements:		
	It must be based upon a mutual...	_____	1. _____
	It must be made by parties who are..	_____	2. _____
	It must include something called ???, which is given by each party..............	_____	3. _____
	It must be for a lawful...	_____	4. _____
5.	An agreement that has no legal effect is	_____	5. _____
6.	An agreement not currently binding because it is not in the particular form required by law is a(n) ??? contract..	_____	6. _____
7.	A contract that may be set aside by one or both parties is	_____	7. _____
8.	A contract in which the duties and obligations of the parties are not expressed, but can be inferred from their conduct, is	_____	8. _____
9.	A contract that must be in a special form is	_____	9. _____
10.	An obligation entered into before a court whereby persons acknowledge they will do a specified act required by law is..	_____	10. _____
11.	A contract that has not been fully carried out by all parties is	_____	11. _____
12.	A contract that requires the offeree to perform an act in exchange for the offeror's promise is	_____	12. _____
13.	A contract consisting of a mutual exchange of promises is	_____	13. _____
14.	One person unfairly benefiting at the expense of another constitutes............	_____	14. _____

Score _____

Section B

DIRECTIONS: Following each question below, indicate your answer by placing a "Y" for "Yes" or an "N" for "No" in the Answers column.

		Answers	For Scoring
1.	To have a contract, must a written document be signed?	_____	1. _____
2.	Must a contract include a mutual agreement between the parties?	_____	2. _____
3.	Does an agreement necessarily result in a contract?	_____	3. _____
4.	Is one distinguishing feature of a voidable contract the fact that one party has the choice to either perform or not perform?	_____	4. _____
5.	Is a voidable contract ever in force or effective?	_____	5. _____
6.	Can a contract be implied solely from the parties' conduct?	_____	6. _____
7.	Is a recognizance a formal contract?	_____	7. _____
8.	Are simple contracts only those contracts that are written?......................	_____	8. _____
9.	Are the terms of oral contracts sometimes disputed by the parties?	_____	9. _____
10.	Are all oral business contracts unenforceable?	_____	10. _____
11.	Are most contracts unilateral?...	_____	11. _____
12.	Are legal obligations sometimes imposed by the law to prevent unjust enrichment?	_____	12. _____

Score _____

Section C

DIRECTIONS: Use the following information to complete the form below.

On the current date Jose Montoya, 5428 Gardner Avenue, Chicago, Illinois 60642, 961-8021, orders through you (the salesperson) one Model 49 Nocol Furnace and a 300-gallon oil tank for the combined price of $2,025. The seller also agrees for $875o to install 6 cold-air ducts and 6 warm-air ducts registers at 5428 Gardner Avenue. Terms are $875 down, $875 on delivery, and $1,150 on completion. Fill in the blanks of the form. Supply the buyer's signature.

COMMUNITY APPLIANCE COMPANY
8941 Hamilton Avenue
Chicago, Illinois 60613

(312) 271-3784   Date _____

FOR SCORING

Please deliver and install the following equipment as specified herein, and in accordance with prices, terms, and conditions made in this order.

Name of Customer_____   Phone_____   1. ____

Address_____   2. ____

_____

(NO.)   (STREET)

_____

(CITY)   (STATE)   (ZIP)

Installation Address_____   3. ____

Quantity	Model	Description of Equipment	Price	Total Price

4. ____

5. ____

Terms: With Order _____   On Delivery _____   Upon Completion _____

6. ____

It is expressly understood that there is no verbal understanding or additional written agreement existing which can change or modify the prices, conditions of sale, or terms of payment as specified herein, and acceptance of this order becomes a binding contract subject to the terms and conditions set forth herein.

Salesperson _____   Accepted by_____

(PURCHASER)

7. ____

---

8. Is the document above, when completed, a request, letter, contract, or order? _____   8. ____

9. Does it involve a business transaction or a social obligation? .... _____   9. ____

10. Is it void, voidable, or valid?... _____   10. ____

11. Is it express or implied? .... _____   11. ____

12. Is the agreement formal or simple?.. _____   12. ____

13. Is it executed or executory?... _____   13. ____

14. Is it unilateral or bilateral? .... _____   14. ____

Score _____

CHAPTER 6
OFFER AND ACCEPTANCE

CHAPTER OUTLINE

I. INTRODUCTION

General rules. ▸ One element required for a contract is a valid agreement. ▸ A valid agreement consists of (1) a valid offer made by an offeror and (2) a valid acceptance made by an offeree.
Study hint.   An offer or acceptance may be express or implied.

II. REQUIREMENTS OF A VALID OFFER

▸ Offer: An offer is an offeror's proposal to make a contract upon certain stated terms. ▸ Three requirements for a valid offer are that it be: (1) definite; (2) seriously intended; and (3) communicated to the offeree.

A. THE OFFER MUST BE DEFINITE

General rules.   ▸ An offer must be definite in order for a contract to arise. ▸ To be sufficiently definite, an offer must state the important (material) terms of the proposed contract.
Limitation.   Under the UCC, a contract for the sale of goods does not need to state all contract terms. For example, a sales contract may state that the price will be determined by the future market price or by a third party, or the contract may not even specify a price (in which case a buyer must pay the reasonable value for the goods).
Study hints.   ▸ Important terms include parties, subject matter, quantity, price, and financing. ▸ In general, an offer cannot leave important terms to be agreed upon later by the parties.

B. THE OFFER MUST BE SERIOUSLY INTENDED

General rules.   ▸ A valid offer requires that the offeror indicate an intent to be bound by the offer if it is accepted. ▸ An offeror's intent is determined by the offeror's outward expression of intent, and not by the secret intentions of the offeror.
Limitations.   ▸ A contract is not formed if an offeree should know the offer is only made in jest, fear, or anger. ▸ Social invitations typically lack the necessary intent to form a contract.

C. THE OFFER MUST BE COMMUNICATED TO THE OFFEREE

General rule.   An offer must be communicated to an offeree prior to the offeree's acceptance.
Example.   Seller contracts to sell a store. Seller later tries to add a term that excludes some assets from the sale. Since this term was not communicated to the offeree at the time the offeree accepted the offer, it is not part of the contract.

III. INVITATIONS TO MAKE OFFERS

General rule.   An invitation to the public to make offers does not constitute a valid offer because it does not indicate the required intent to contract.
Examples.   Advertisements; catalogs; price quotation sheets or lists; window displays; circulars.
Limitations.   ▸ An offer made to a particular offeree in a personal sales letter is a valid offer. ▸ On occasion an advertisement, such as a reward, may indicate an intent sufficient to be an offer.
Study hint.   A person who makes an invitation to make an offer can generally reject any offer that is made in response to the invitation.

IV.   DURATION OF THE OFFER

General rules.   ► An offer cannot be accepted if it has been terminated. ► An offer is terminated by:

- *Revocation*: ► An offeror can revoke an offer at any time before the offer is accepted. ► A revocation may result from an offeror's conduct or words that clearly indicate an intent to revoke. For example, notice to an offeree that the subject of an offer has been sold to another party revokes an offer. ► A revocation must be communicated; a mere intent to revoke does not suffice.

- *Rejection*: An offeree's statement to the offeror that an offer is unacceptable terminates the offer.

- *Lapse of time*: An offer that is not accepted automatically terminates upon: (1) expiration of the time stated in the offer; or (2) if no time is stated in the offer, within a reasonable time after the offer is made. ► What constitutes a reasonable time depends on the facts of each case.

- *Operation of law*: An offer *automatically* terminates if: (1) the offeror dies or becomes insane; or (2) the subject matter of the offer becomes illegal to perform.

Limitations.   ► An offer cannot be revoked if the offeror promises not to revoke and: (1) consideration is given for the promise not to revoke (an option); (2) the promise is made in a sealed writing (in states that recognize seals); or (3) the promise is a firm offer. ► A firm offer is a merchant's signed, written promise not to revoke an offer to buy or sell goods, which is binding for the time stated, or if no time is stated, for a reasonable time not to exceed three months. Consideration is not required to make a firm offer binding.

V.   THE ACCEPTANCE

General rules.   ► Acceptance: an offeree's clear, unconditional expression of intent to agree to an offer. ► In general, an acceptance must accept all terms of an offer without change or addition. ► To be effective, an acceptance must generally be communicated to the offeror; an uncommunicated intention to accept is insufficient to form a contract.

Limitations.   ► Under the UCC, an acceptance of an offer to buy or sell goods may state terms in addition to or different from the terms that are stated in the offer. ► An offer can be accepted only by the person to whom it is made or that person's authorized agent.

Study hint.   In general, an offeree's silence does not constitute an acceptance.

VI.   COUNTEROFFERS

General rules.   ► A counteroffer is a manifestation by an offeree that (1) an offer is not acceptable and (2) the offeree is offering to contract on terms that are different from those stated in the offer. ► A counteroffer terminates the original offer.

Study hint.   A contract is formed if the original offeror accepts a counteroffer.

VII.   INQUIRIES NOT CONSTITUTING REJECTION

General rule.   A mere inquiry does not terminate an offer; the offer may still be accepted.

Example.   Offeree inquires: "Would you be willing to consider a lower price for the property?"

VIII.   MANNER OF ACCEPTANCE

- *Manner of acceptance*: ► If an offeror states a required manner for acceptance, the offeree must accept in this manner; failure to do so renders an acceptance ineffective. ► If an offer is silent regarding the required manner of acceptance, the UCC and the modern trend allows an acceptance to be communicated in any manner, and using any method of communication, that is reasonable.

- *When acceptance is effective*: If an offeror does not specifically require actual delivery of an acceptance, an acceptance is effective when properly mailed, delivered to a telegraph company for transmittal, or faxed, even if the acceptance is never actually received by the offeror.

REVIEW OF CHAPTER

REVIEW OF TERMS

Select the term that best matches a statement below. Each term is the best match for only one statement.

TERMS

a. Acceptance
b. Counteroffer
c. Firm offer
d. Lapse of time

e. Offer
f. Offeree
g. Offeror

h. Option
i. Rejection
j. Revocation

STATEMENTS

Answer

_____ 1. Merchant's offer to buy or sell goods that is irrevocable for the time stated.

_____ 2. Party who makes an offer.

_____ 3. Binding promise to hold an offer open that is made in consideration for something of value.

_____ 4. Offeree's expression that is both a rejection of another's offer and a new offer by the offeree.

_____ 5. Party to whom an offer is made.

_____ 6. Offeror's termination of an offer.

_____ 7. Offeree's agreement to the terms of an offer.

_____ 8. Offeree's expression that an offer is not acceptable which results in a termination of the offer.

_____ 9. Termination of an offer resulting from an offeree's failure to accept an offer within a reasonable time.

_____ 10. Offeror's proposal to make a contract upon certain stated terms.

REVIEW OF CONCEPTS

Directions: Indicate **T** for true and **F** for false in the answer column.

_____ 1. An agreement necessary to form a contract consists of an offer and an acceptance.

_____ 2. Under the UCC, a sales contract may be sufficiently definite even if it does not state the purchase price.

_____ 3. An offer is not required to be communicated to the offeree.

_____ 4. An offer does not form a contract if the offeree knows that it is made in jest or extreme anger.

_____ 5. An offeror cannot accept a counteroffer; a counteroffer is merely an invitation to continue negotiations.

_____ 6. In general, a proposal that is stated in a sales letter that is sent to only one person is merely an invitation to make an offer and not an offer that can be accepted to form a contract.

_____ 7. An offeror cannot revoke an offer without allowing an offeree a reasonable opportunity to accept.

_____ 8. To be effective, an acceptance, revocation, or rejection must be communicated to the other party.

_____ 9. An acceptance is invalid if it is not made in the manner required by the offeror.

_____ 10. An offeree's silence is a valid acceptance if the offeror states in the offer that silence is an acceptance.

REVIEW OF CONCEPT APPLICATIONS

Answer

Directions: Indicate your choice in the answer column.

_____ 1. Fred signed an "offer" to buy Tony's condo. The offer describes the parties, property, and price. The price is stated to be $40,000, payable $20,000 cash with the balance to be represented by a promissory note. The offer states that in two weeks the parties will determine the interest to be paid and when the note will be due. Tony accepts the offer. Is a contract formed?

    a. Yes. An offer need not state all important terms if the parties intend to make a contract.

    b. Yes. The offer was sufficiently definite to constitute a valid offer.

    c. No. The offer was not sufficiently definite to constitute a valid offer.

_____ 2. In which situation does Bart make a valid offer?

a. Bart places an ad in a newspaper advertising his 1978 Ford for sale for $1,000.
b. Bart signs a written offer to buy land. The offer appears to be a sincere offer. Unknown to the seller, Bart does not intend to buy the land unless he can first sell some other property.
c. Bart publishes a catalog that lists hundreds of items for sale, together with their respective prices. Bart mails this catalog to thousands of homes.

_____ 3. In which case was Al legally entitled to revoke the offer in question?
a. Al offered to sell his condo to Ben. Before Ben accepted, Al gave Ben written notice that "I terminate my offer."
b. Al offered to sell a business to Will. Al promised not to revoke the offer for 24 hours in consideration for $100 paid by Will. One hour later and before Will had accepted, Al gave Will a written revocation and offered to return the $100.
c. Al (a merchant) offered to sell Lynn a car for $5,000. In a signed writing, Al promised not to revoke the offer for 24 hours. Lynn did not give any consideration for this promise not to revoke. Two hours later and before Lynn accepted, Al revoked the offer.
d. a and c.

_____ 4. Seller validly offered to sell a carpet-cleaning franchise to Joe for $25,000. Which of the following expressions by Joe would constitute a valid acceptance of the offer?
a. In writing, Joe states: "I accept the offer provided that the price is reduced to $24,000."
b. In writing, Joe states: "The offer seems good, but would you consider accepting $20,000?"
c. In writing, Joe states: "I accept the offer."
d. a and c.

CASE PROBLEM

Fawn offered to sell a coat to Missy. Fawn mailed the offer to Missy via first-class U.S. mail. (1) Can Missy accept by remaining silent or must she communicate an acceptance to Fawn? (2) How can Missy communicate an acceptance? (3) If Missy sent an acceptance via first-class U.S. mail, when would it be effective? (4) When will the offer lapse?

_____

_____

_____

BUSINESS LAW PARTNER EXERCISE

Directions: Access your Business Law Partner CD-ROM and find the document "General Contract for Services."
1. Complete the above-referenced document using the information provided in the following case study.
2. Is the contract, as completed, sufficiently definite to be a valid contract?

Case Study: *When Is Enough, Enough?*

Tom offered to hire Kim, a CPA, to perform an audit for the current calendar year of Tom's Hardware Inc. (THI). Kim must supply all necessary services, workers, and materials for which she will be paid $10,000 upon completion of her work. The audit is to be completed no later than March 1 following the end of the audit year. Kim is obligated to hold THI harmless from all liability arising from her work, and she must keep confidential all information. Nothing was stated regarding the quality of the work that Kim is to render.

_____

_____

_____

CHAPTER 6 QUIZ

Section A

DIRECTIONS: Following each question below, indicate your answer by placing a "Y" for "Yes" or an "N" for "No" in the Answers column.

		Answers	For Scoring
1.	May parties to a contract indicate their intentions by their actions?	_____	1. _____
2.	Are business contracts typically implied solely from the parties' conduct?	_____	2. _____
3.	Must the subject matter and time of performance normally be stated to have a contract?	_____	3. _____
4.	Under common law, must all offers be definite as to price?	_____	4. _____
5.	If the offeree reasonably believes an offer is seriously intended even though it is made in jest, can a binding contract be made?	_____	5. _____
6.	May an offer directed to a specific individual be accepted by anyone?	_____	6. _____
7.	Do people have the right to choose the parties with whom they deal?	_____	7. _____
8.	Are business advertisements and catalogs offers?	_____	8. _____
9.	Is an exhibition of goods in a display window at certain prices considered to be an offer?	_____	9. _____
10.	May an advertisement that offers a reward be an offer?	_____	10. _____
11.	May an offer that has been revoked be accepted?	_____	11. _____
12.	Under common law, can an offer be revoked if a term states that it will be held open for a stated time?	_____	12. _____
13.	If a firm offer does not state how long the offer will be held open, will the period during which it is held open exceed three months?	_____	13. _____
14.	Is an uncommunicated intent to withdraw an offer sufficient to revoke it?	_____	14. _____
15.	Will the lapse of a reasonable time after the offer has been made terminate the offer if no time is specified in the offer?	_____	15. _____
16.	Is an offer revoked by the death or insanity of the offeror?	_____	16. _____
17.	Does communication of a rejection of an offer to the offeror terminate the offer?	_____	17. _____
18.	Is the offer terminated if, after the offer is made, performance of the contract becomes illegal?	_____	18. _____
19.	Does silence, as a general rule, constitute acceptance?	_____	19. _____
20.	Is a counteroffer a valid acceptance of the offer?	_____	20. _____
21.	Does a counteroffer terminate the original offer?	_____	21. _____
22.	Can an offeree make a reasonable inquiry regarding quality, price, or other terms without this constituting rejection of the offer?	_____	22. _____
23.	Can the offer state the method by which acceptance must be communicated?	_____	23. _____
24.	Does an oral acceptance of an offer received by mail result in a rejection of the offer if no manner of acceptance was specified?	_____	24. _____
25.	Is it necessary to stipulate in the offer how it must be accepted?	_____	25. _____

Score _____

Section B

DIRECTIONS: Complete each of the following statements by writing the missing word or words in the Answers column.

		Answers	For Scoring
1.	A valid contract is formed when the parties reach a(n)..............................	_____	1. _____
2-3.	The two essential elements of a contract are	_____	2. _____
	....	_____	3. _____
4.	The person to whom an offer is made is	_____	4. _____
5.	The person making an offer may withdraw or ??? it anytime prior to its acceptance.	_____	5. _____
6.	A merchant's signed, written offer on goods saying it will be held open is a(n)	_____	6. _____
7.	If the offeree varies or qualifies the terms of the offer when making an intended acceptance, this becomes what is known as a(n)............................	_____	7. _____

Score _____

Section C

DIRECTIONS: Following each question below, indicate your answer by placing a " Y " for " Yes" or an " N" for " No" in the Answers column and by filling in the spaces provided.

		Answers	For Scoring
1-2.	Harmon wrote a letter offering to sell a radio to Adams. Harmon put the letter in his pocket, but forgot to mail it. Harmon told a friend about the letter. Adams was told about the offer by the friend and sent an acceptance to Harmon. Did a binding contract result?	_____	1. _____
	Reason	_____	2. _____
3-4.	Foster sent Morrison an offer to sell her house for $105,000. Changing her mind, the next day Foster sent a letter revoking the offer. When Morrison received the offer, he immediately faxed an acceptance, which Foster received that day. The following day, Morrison received the letter of revocation. Was Foster's offer accepted?	_____	3. _____
	Reason	_____	4. _____
5-6.	Kowalski had had a lot of trouble with her new car. While she was driving in the rain to an important business meeting, the car stalled and Kowalski could not get it started again. She had been stuck for half an hour when Farezzi stopped to help. The car still would not start, and Kowalski shouted, " This awful lemon! I'd sell it to you for $10." Farezzi produced a $10 bill and tried to buy the car. Is there a contract?	_____	5. _____
	Reason	_____	6. _____
7-8.	Buff offered to sell Samuels his television set for $500. Samuels replied that she would pay $450 for it--$250 when delivered, and $200 in 30 days. Did a contract result?	_____	7. _____
	What is Samuels' statement?	_____	8. _____

Score _____

CHAPTER 7
CAPACITY TO CONTRACT

CHAPTER OUTLINE

I. INTRODUCTION

General rules. ▸ The law generally presumes that everyone has the legal and mental capacity to contract. However, if a party does lack the capacity to contract, then: (1) the contract is voidable; and (2) the party who lacks contractual capacity can disaffirm (set aside) the contract.

Study hint.   Mental capacity is the ability to understand (1) that a contract is being made and (2) the essential terms of the contract.

II. MINORS

A. CONTRACTS OF MINORS

General rules. ▸ At common law, a minor is a person under the age of 21. In most states, by statute a minor is a person under the age of 18. ▸ In most cases, a contract made by minor is voidable, and the minor may disaffirm the contract.

Example.   Mona, age 17, contracted to buy tapes from a mail-order firm. The contract is voidable, and Mona can disaffirm the contract, thereby terminating her duty to buy the tapes.

Limitation.   An adult who contracts with a minor cannot disaffirm the contract.

Study hints. ▸ Capacity is determined at the time of contracting, not at the time a party seeks to avoid the contract. ▸ A minor may disaffirm a contract even if the contract is fair.

B. CONTRACTS THAT CANNOT BE AVOIDED (CONTRACTS FOR NECESSARIES)

General rules. ▸ Necessaries: food, clothing, shelter, medical care, some types of education, and other things required for the care of a minor in light of his or her circumstances. ▸ A minor is liable under quasi contract to pay the reasonable value for any benefit derived from a necessary.

Example.   Al, a minor, bought clothes on credit. Al must pay for their reasonable value.

Limitation.   A minor is not required to pay the actual contract price for a necessary.

Study hint.   In some states, a car that is needed to conduct a business may be a necessary.

C. DISAFFIRMANCE

General rules. ▸ Disaffirmance: repudiation (avoidance) of a contract. ▸ A minor can disaffirm a contract by giving notice of disaffirmance (1) prior to reaching the age of majority or (2) within a reasonable time thereafter. ▸ Upon disaffirmance: (1) a minor is only required to return those benefits the minor still has (regardless of their condition); and (2) the other party must return all money and property given by the minor.

Example.   Kip, age 16, bought a bike for $200 cash. Two weeks after he turned 18, Kip disaffirmed. Kip only needs to return the used bike and the seller must repay the $200.

Limitation.   If a minor delivers property to an adult and the adult sells the property to an innocent third party, the minor cannot recover the property from the third party. However, the minor can recover from the adult the money the adult received for the property.

Study hints. ▸ As a practical matter, in most cases a minor has at least a few months after reaching majority within which to disaffirm. ▸ In general, a minor is not required to pay for the value of benefits derived from a contract unless a necessary is involved.

D. RATIFICATION

General rules. ▸ Ratification: definite and certain expression of an intent to be bound by a contract. ▸ A minor can ratify a voidable contract only after he or she becomes an adult. ▸ A person cannot disaffirm a contract after ratifying it.

Limitations. ▸ A minor cannot ratify part of a contract and disaffirm the remainder. ▸ By itself, the making of one or two payments after majority is typically not a ratification.

Study hints. ▸ Ratification results from: (1) an express ratification made after a minor gains his or her majority; (2) waiting an unreasonable time after majority to disaffirm; or (3) taking significant new benefits after majority. ▸ Ratification of a voidable contract makes it valid.

E. MINORS' BUSINESS CONTRACTS

In many states a minor's contract that is made in a business or employment cannot be avoided.

F. OTHER ENFORCEABLE CONTRACTS

A number of states forbid minors from disaffirming a variety of contracts, commonly including education loan contracts, contracts for medical care, and banking contracts.

G. CONTRACTING SAFELY WITH MINORS

Some companies (e.g., multi-state catalog companies) run a particularly high risk of having contracts disaffirmed by minors. One way to avoid this risk is to have an adult cosign a contract with a minor. In the cosign situation, the minor can disaffirm, but the adult cannot.

H. MINORS' TORTS (MISREPRESENTATION OF AGE)

General rules. ▸ A minor commits a tort if the minor lies about (misrepresents) his or her age. ▸ In some states, a minor who misrepresents his or her age may disaffirm, but the minor must pay for damages caused by the misrepresentation. In other states, the minor cannot disaffirm.

Example. Pete, age 17, tells Seller that he is 21. As a result of Pete's misrepresentation, Seller sells a car to Pete, and Pete causes $500 damage to the car. In some states, Pete can disaffirm, but he must pay Seller $500 damages. In other states, Pete cannot disaffirm.

III.   MENTALLY INCOMPETENT PERSONS

General rules. ▸ A contract is void if it is made by a person who has been judicially declared incompetent. This rule applies even if the contract is reasonable or it is for necessaries. ▸ A contract is voidable if made by a person (1) who is incompetent but (2) has not been judicially declared incompetent.

Limitations. ▸ A person who has not been judicially declared incompetent and who is only occasionally incompetent cannot avoid a contract if he or she understood that a contract was being made. ▸ An incompetent person who disaffirms must return whatever benefits remain, and the incompetent person must pay the reasonable value for necessaries.

Study hint. An incompetent person who regains his or her sanity and is declared competent by a court also regains the capacity to contract.

IV.   INTOXICATED PERSONS

General rules. ▸ A person lacks contractual capacity if (1) the person is mentally impaired due to alcohol or drugs and (2) as a result the person does not understand the legal nature of the contract and its basic terms. This defense renders a contract voidable. ▸ A contract made by a person declared to be a habitual drunkard is invalid (although the person must pay the reasonable value for necessaries).

Limitation. The fact that a person is intoxicated when contracting or that the person would not have made a contract if sober is insufficient, by itself, to establish this defense.

V.   CONVICTS

▸ A convict is a person who has been judicially declared guilty of a major criminal offense. ▸ In some (but not all) states, the ability of convicts to contract is limited in various ways. ▸ A convict regains full contractual capacity once the convict is released from prison and is not supervised by parole officials.

REVIEW OF CHAPTER

REVIEW OF TERMS

Select the term that best matches a statement below. Each term is the best match for only one statement.

TERMS

a. Convict
b. Disaffirmance
c. Incompetent person
d. Minor

e. Misrepresentation of age
f. Necessaries
g. Ratification

STATEMENTS

Answer

____ 1. Person under the age of majority who lacks the capacity to contract.
____ 2. Food, clothing, shelter, medical care, and other things required for the proper care of a minor.
____ 3. Person who has a mental impairment due to a psychological or physical illness.
____ 4. Intentional, false statement regarding a person's age.
____ 5. Person who has been judicially found guilty of a major criminal offense.
____ 6. Express or implied agreement to be bound by a contract.
____ 7. Repudiation (avoidance) of a voidable contract.

REVIEW OF CONCEPTS

Directions: Indicate **T** for true and **F** for false in the answer column.

____ 1. In most states, a minor is a person who is under the age of 21.
____ 2. If an adult contracts with a minor, the adult has the right to disaffirm the contract.
____ 3. Businesses need not worry about contracting with minors; minors cannot disaffirm contracts made with a merchant or with a business.
____ 4. A trade school education and tools needed to carry on a trade may be necessaries.
____ 5. A minor must pay the contract price for a necessary.
____ 6. If a minor sells property to an adult and the adult in turn sells the property to an innocent third party, the minor cannot recover the property from the third party.
____ 7. A ratification of a contract may be oral or written, or it may be implied from conduct.
____ 8. A minor cannot ratify a contract until he or she becomes an adult.
____ 9. In some states, a minor cannot disaffirm a contract that is made in connection with the minor's business.
____ 10. In some states, minors cannot disaffirm banking contracts, such as a checking account agreement.
____ 11. A minor's misrepresentation of age does not affect his or her legal rights.
____ 12. A contract made by a person who has been judicially declared incompetent is void; a contract made by an incompetent person who has not been judicially declared incompetent is voidable.
____ 13. A person convicted of a crime is automatically barred from contracting for the remainder of his or her life.

REVIEW OF CONCEPT APPLICATIONS

Answer

Directions: Indicate your choice in the answer column.

____ 1. Mindy was a minor at the time she bought a stereo. (For purposes of this question, assume that 18 is the age of majority). Under these facts, select the correct answer.
    a.   Mindy can disaffirm the contract, but she must do so before she turns 18.
    b.   Mindy can disaffirm the contract, but she must pay for any depreciation to the stereo.
    c.   Mindy can disaffirm the contract, and the seller must repay all money paid by Mindy.

_____ 2. Minor lives on his own without support from his parents. Select the correct answer.
   a. Minor contracted to buy a big-screen TV for his personal pleasure. In this case, the TV is a necessary, and Minor must pay the reasonable value for the TV under quasi contract.
   b. Minor contracted to buy an ordinary jacket from a catalog seller. In this case, the jacket is a necessary, and Minor must pay the reasonable value for the jacket under quasi contract.
   c. Minor leased an apartment. In this case, the apartment is a necessary, but Minor is not obligated to pay the rentals stated in the lease or the reasonable value of the apartment.

_____ 3. Eva, age 16, contracted to buy a motor scooter from Seller. Seller sold Eva the scooter after she told him that she was twenty-one years old. After using the scooter for one year, Eva attempted to disaffirm the contract. The scooter was worth $300 less due to its use by Eva. In this case:
   a. Eva committed a tort by misrepresenting her age to Seller.
   b. In some states, Eva would not be permitted to disaffirm the contract.
   c. In some states, Eva can disaffirm but she must pay $300 damages to Seller.
   d. All of the above.

_____ 4. Which contract is *voidable*?
   a. Rene is judicially declared incompetent and a guardian is appointed to handle her personal and legal affairs. Rene then contracts to buy a condominium.
   b. Irving contracts to buy a car. Due to a mental illness, Irving cannot understand that he has made a contract and he is unable to understand the contract's basic terms.
   c. Gary contracts to buy a VCR. Gary has been drinking, and he is intoxicated. Gary understands that he is entering into a binding contract and he understands the contract terms.

CASE PROBLEM

Nancy, age 16, bought two cats on credit for $200 each. She can to love one cat ("Fluffy"), and to hate the other cat ("Fleas"). While a minor, Nancy made a number of contract payments. Nancy has just turned 18, and she is trying to decide what to do about Fluffy and Fleas. Under these facts: (1) Did Nancy ratify the contract by making payments while she was a minor? (2) Can Nancy disaffirm the part of the contract relating to Fleas, and ratify the part relating to Fluffy? (3) If Nancy keeps both cats for another year while she breeds them, can she thereafter disaffirm the contract

_____

_____

_____

BUSINESS LAW PARTNER EXERCISE

Directions: Access your Business Law Partner CD-ROM and find the document "General Contract for Products."

1. Complete this document using the information provided in the following case study.
2. Can Amy disaffirm the contract as written? What should Merchant have done differently?

Case Study: *Avoiding Minor Problems*

Amy purchased an electric organ on her seventeenth birthday. She purchased the organ from Merchant for $2,000: $1,000 down and $50 per month for the next 20 months. Merchant delivered the organ to Amy at her parent's home. Amy used the organ for a year. One month after Amy turned 18, a hurricane destroyed her parent's home and the organ. Amy immediately gave Merchant notice that she disaffirmed the contract for the organ

_____

_____

_____

CHAPTER 7 QUIZ

Section A

DIRECTIONS: Following each question below, indicate your answer by placing a "Y" for "Yes" or an "N" for "No" in the Answers column.

	Answers	For Scoring
1. Are some contracts made by a minor valid and enforceable?	_____	1. _____
2. If two minors make a contract, does each have the right to avoid it?	_____	2. _____
3. Is the purpose of the law regarding minors' capacity to contract to protect minors when dealing with adults?	_____	3. _____
4. Is a minor required to pay anything for necessaries?	_____	4. _____
5. Is a minor required to return all property received in order to disaffirm a contract?	_____	5. _____
6. In general, is an adult entitled to recover his or her losses when a minor disaffirms a contract?	_____	6. _____
7. Can a minor's continued silence after reaching the age of majority constitute a ratification of the minor's executed contracts?	_____	7. _____
8. Can a minor ratify a part and disaffirm a part of the same contract?	_____	8. _____
9. Do some states forbid disaffirmance of educational loan agreements by minors?	_____	9. _____
10. Is the law uniform among the states regarding the effect that misrepresentation of age has on a minor's right to disaffirm contracts?	_____	10. _____
11. Are contracts made by people so intoxicated they cannot understand the meaning of their acts voidable?	_____	11. _____
12. Do the contractual disabilities of convicts last for the rest of their lives?	_____	12. _____

Score _____

Section B

DIRECTIONS: Following each statement below, indicate your answer by placing a "T" for "True" or an "F" for "False" in the Answers column.

	Answers	For Scoring
1. One may lack capacity to contract because of age or physical condition.	_____	1. _____
2. Most 18-year-olds are competent to contract.	_____	2. _____
3. Minors are always incompetent to contract.	_____	3. _____
4. A minor must pay the contract price for necessaries.	_____	4. _____
5. A minor's disaffirmance completely nullifies a wholly executory contract.	_____	5. _____
6. A minor is liable for torts as fully as an adult is.	_____	6. _____
7. A person judicially declared incompetent may regain competency and be declared competent by a court.	_____	7. _____
8. An incompetent person who has not been judicially declared incompetent may make contracts during lucid intervals.	_____	8. _____
9. All contracts entered into by people who have been drinking intoxicants are voidable.	_____	9. _____
10. Many states have repealed laws restricting contractual capacity of convicts.	_____	10. _____

Score _____

Section C

DIRECTIONS: Complete each of the following statements by writing the missing word or words in the Answers column.

	Answers	For Scoring
1. For a contract to be enforceable, all parties must have legal and mental	_____	1. _____
2. A person who by law is not old enough to be competent to contract is a(n)	_____	2. _____
3. At the option of minors, most contracts they make are not void but are	_____	3. _____
4. Many business contracts made by minors are	_____	4. _____
5. Food, clothing, shelter, and medical services supplied to a minor are classified as	_____	5. _____
6. In its nature, the minor's liability for food, clothing, and shelter is	_____	6. _____
7. The election to repudiate a contract is known as	_____	7. _____
8. A restatement of willingness to be bound by a promise made during minority is known as	_____	8. _____
9. The safest way to protect oneself when contracting with a minor is to have an adult join in the contract as a(n)	_____	9. _____
10. Contracts made by people who have been formally adjudicated incompetent are	_____	10. _____
11. Contracts made by people so intoxicated they cannot understand the meaning of their acts are	_____	11. _____
12. A person convicted of a major criminal offense is a(n)	_____	12. _____

Score _____

Section D

DIRECTIONS: Following each question below, indicate your answer by placing a "Y" for "Yes" or an "N" for "No" in the Answers column.

	Answers	For Scoring
1. Several months before he turned 18, Richard purchased an automobile for $3,600. He paid $1,000 down and agreed to pay $85 a month until the automobile was completely paid for. He made his monthly payments regularly until two months after he became eighteen years of age. He then tried to avoid the contract because he made the contract when he was a minor. Is he entitled to do so?	_____	1. _____
2. Wilson was under the influence of drugs when she signed a contract to purchase a refrigerator from Sanders and she did not understand what she was signing. Two days later Sanders insisted that Wilson carry out the contract. Can he enforce the contract? .	_____	2. _____
3-4. When Green, a minor, entered college, she contracted for a room for the school year. At the end of three months she found it necessary to withdraw from college. Can Green disaffirm the executory portion of this contract?	_____	3. _____
Is Green entitled to and recover the three months' rent already paid?	_____	4. _____
5-6. Giblitz, who was incompetent at the time, contracted to purchase groceries from a wholesaler at exorbitant prices. Sometime later, after recovering his competence, he sought to avoid the contract. Can he do so?	_____	5. _____
Can he recover all his money paid under the contract?	_____	6. _____

Score _____

CHAPTER 8
CONSIDERATION

CHAPTER OUTLINE

I. **NATURE OF CONSIDERATION**

General rules. ▸ Consideration: price demanded and received in return for a promise. In general, an agreement is not a legally binding contract unless each party gives consideration. ▸ Consideration requires that a party: (1) promise to do or do an act the party is not required to do; or (2) promise to forbear from doing (i.e., not do) or in fact forbear from doing an act the party is entitled to do.

Example. *X* promised to pay $100 for *Y*'s promise not to sue *X*. *X* and *Y* gave consideration.

Limitations. ▸ A promise is consideration only if it imposes an actual legal duty to act or forbear. ▸ Everyone has numerous legal duties to do or not to do certain things. Promising to perform or performing a preexisting legal duty is not consideration. (See Section II B below.)

Study hint. A promise to do something only if you later want to do it is not consideration.

II. **ADEQUACY OF CONSIDERATION**

▸ Courts do not generally examine the adequacy of considerations exchanged. ▸ A contract is enforceable even if the considerations exchanged are not of equal value.

A. PART PAYMENT

General rule. A creditor's agreement to accept a debtor's part payment of an *undisputed debt* in return for a release of the debtor from the unpaid balance of the debt is not supported by consideration. The creditor may accept the part payment and sue for the balance of the debt.

Limitation. A debt may be extinguished without payment in full in the following situations:

- *Disputed debt*: An agreement to pay and to accept a certain amount as complete payment of a disputed debt is supported by consideration and legally binds the parties.

- *Composition of creditors*: ▸ Definition: agreement by a debtor's creditors to accept partial payment as payment in full. ▸ An agreement by creditors to accept part payment as payment in full is binding if the agreement is made pursuant to a composition of creditors.

- *Cancellation of debt*: Cancellation and return to the debtor of a promissory note or other written instrument that evidences a debt cancels the debt.

- *Gift*: If a creditor accepts partial payment and in return gives a receipt for payment in full with an intent to make a gift of the unpaid balance, the remainder of the debt is canceled.

- *Substitution of secured note*: If a note secured by collateral is given and accepted as payment for an unsecured note of a greater amount, the difference between the notes is canceled.

B. INSUFFICIENT OR INVALID CONSIDERATION

1. Performing or Promising to Perform What One is Obligated to Do (Preexisting Duty)

General rules. ▸ Promising to do or doing an act that one already has a legal duty to do is not consideration. ▸ A party may have a legal duty under: (1) criminal law; (2) civil law (e.g., tort law); or (3) an existing contract between the parties. ▸ A promise to merely complete an existing contract is not consideration sufficient to support a modification of the contract. The contract modification is effective only if both parties give consideration.

Limitations. ▸ Parties can cancel an existing contract and replace it with a new contract if the new contract contains new terms that benefit both parties. ▸ One gives consideration if he or she promises to perform an existing legal duty *and* also promises to do something else that he or she is not obligated to do. ▸ In rare cases, a reasonable price adjustment may be enforced despite a lack of consideration if unforeseen difficulties (such as unforeseen rock formations or zoning law changes) cause the parties to voluntarily adjust the price.

Study hint. Strikes, bad weather, and changes in prices are foreseeable difficulties that do not support a contract modification in the absence of consideration.

2. Refraining or Promising to Refrain from Doing What One Has No Right to Do (Preexisting Duty)

General rules. ▸ Forbearance: refraining from doing an act. ▸ Refraining from doing, or promising to refrain from doing an act that one has no legal right to do is not consideration.

Examples. ▸ Promise not to commit a tort. ▸ Promise not to breach a contract.

Limitation. A promise to refrain from doing an act that one has a legal right to do is consideration. Examples: ▸ Promise not to sue for breach of contract. ▸ Promise not to sue for injuries caused by another (insurance release). ▸ Promise not to assert a good faith claim.

3. Past Performance

General rules. ▸ Past performance: act or benefit voluntarily given in the past. ▸ A past performance cannot be consideration, and a subsequent promise to pay for this prior benefit is not legally binding.

Example. Suzanne saved Timmy from drowning, and his father later promised to pay her. Suzanne's past act cannot be consideration, so Timmy's father's promise is not binding.

III.   EXCEPTIONS TO REQUIREMENT OF CONSIDERATION

A. VOLUNTARY SUBSCRIPTIONS

▸ In general, charitable subscriptions and pledges (promises to donate money to charities) are legally binding as a matter of public policy regardless of consideration. ▸ Two theories often used to justify enforcing subscriptions are: (1) each pledge is consideration for and supports the pledges made by others; or (2) a charitable subscription is an offer for a unilateral contract which is accepted by the charity when it undertakes a liability in reliance on the subscription.

B. DEBTS OF RECORD

Debts of record (judicial agreements to pay; judgments) are enforceable due to public policy.

C. PROMISSORY ESTOPPEL

General rule. Promissory estoppel permits enforcement of a promise even though there is no binding contract if: (1) a promisor makes a promise; (2) the promisor should reasonably expect that the promise will induce the other person to act in reliance on the promise; (3) the promise induces such reliance; and (4) justice requires enforcement of the promise.

Study hints. ▸ If promissory estoppel applies, a promise is enforced even if consideration is not given for the promise. ▸ Courts often find that justice requires enforcement of a promise if a person would suffer a substantial financial or other loss if the promise is not enforced.

D. MODIFICATION OF SALES CONTRACTS

▸ Under the UCC, a good faith modification of a contract to sell goods is enforceable even if both parties do not give consideration pursuant to the modification

REVIEW OF CHAPTER

REVIEW OF TERMS

Select the term that best matches a statement below. Each term is the best match for only one statement.

TERMS

a. Adequacy of consideration rule
b. Composition of creditors
c. Consideration

d. Forbearance
e. Past performance
f. Promissory estoppel

STATEMENTS

Answer

_____ 1. Act performed prior to a promise.
_____ 2. Price that is demanded and received in exchange for a promise.
_____ 3. Principle that courts do not examine the value of considerations exchanged.
_____ 4. Doctrine that enforces a promise if a promisor should expect that a promise will induce another to rely on the promise, the promise induces reliance, and justice requires enforcing the promise.
_____ 5. Agreement by a debtor's creditors to accept a percentage of their debts as payment in full.
_____ 6. Refraining from doing (not doing) an act.

REVIEW OF CONCEPTS

Directions: Indicate **T** for true and **F** for false in the answer column.

_____ 1. An agreement is generally not a binding contract unless all of the parties give consideration.
_____ 2. Miles promised to buy Al's car for a stated sum in three days if, at that time, Miles still wants to buy the car. In this case, Miles' promise is not consideration.
_____ 3. In general, courts will not enforce contracts unless the considerations exchanged are equal.
_____ 4. Juan owed Hal $1,000. The debt was represented by a written promissory note. With an intent to cancel the debt, Hal wrote "Canceled--Paid in Full" on the note, he signed it, and he gave it to Juan. Juan did not give consideration for the cancellation. In this case, the debt is canceled.
_____ 5. Ché signed a $3,000 *unsecured* note payable to Ike. Later, Ché gave and Ike accepted a $2,000 *secured* note in place of the $3,000 note. In this case, the $3,000 note is not validly canceled.
_____ 6. Parties cannot agree to cancel a contract and replace it with another contract, even if the new contract provides additional benefits for both parties.
_____ 7. In rare cases, certain unforeseen difficulties may be consideration sufficient to support a contract.
_____ 8. A promise to complete a contract that one is already obligated to complete is consideration if performance of the contract is more difficult than anticipated due to strikes or price increases.
_____ 9. Len promises not to breach a contract with Lisa. Len's promise is not consideration.
_____ 10. A promise not to trespass on another's land (a civil wrong) is consideration.
_____ 11. A promise is legally enforceable if it is made in consideration for a past performance by another.
_____ 12. A gift does not require the donee (person receiving the gift) to give consideration.
_____ 13. Judgments and other debts of record are enforceable despite the lack of consideration.
_____ 14. Consideration is not required in order to modify a contract to sell goods.

REVIEW OF CONCEPT APPLICATIONS

Answer

Directions: Indicate your choice in the answer column.

_____ 1. Penny made these agreements. Which agreement is supported by consideration?
   a. On March 1, Penny signed a lease. Under the lease, Lessor agreed to lease a home to Penny and Penny agreed to lease the home on March 20 if on that date she still wanted the home.
   b. Penny agreed to buy Wade a ticket to a football game. Wade gave nothing in return.
   c. Penny and Ray agreed that she would pay $200 for Ray's stereo. The stereo is worth $900.

_____ 2.   In which case is the creditor entitled to sue for the unpaid balance of the debt?
   a.   Alice owed Otis $500. The debt was undisputed. Alice and Otis agreed that she would pay $200 in consideration for his promise to release Alice from the balance of the debt.
   b.   Dee hired Pete to paint her house for $1,000. There was a good faith dispute whether the work was done properly. Under a compromise agreement, Dee paid $500 as payment in full of the $1,000 debt.
   c.   Joan owed Cindy $800. Cindy and all of Joan's other creditors entered into a composition of creditors' agreement by which they agreed to accept 50 percent of their respective claims as payment in full. Pursuant to the agreement, Joan paid Cindy $400.

_____ 3.   Rod contracted to build a garage for Tim. The contract required Rod to pay for all materials. Later, Tim promised to pay Rod an extra $500. Tim's promise is binding if it is given for:
   a.   Rod's promise to perform the original contract with Tim.
   b.   Rod's promise to perform the original contract if the materials cost more than Rod expected.
   c.   Rod's promises to both perform the original contract with Tim, and construct a shed, which Rod was not obligated to build.
   d.   Rod's promise not to breach the original contract with Tim.

_____ 4.   Select the promise, agreement, or debt of record that is *not legally binding*.
   a.   Lynn pledged to pay $100 to a charity that operates a shelter for the homeless.
   b.   In a civil lawsuit, a court entered a judgment for $10,000 against Beaver.
   c.   Buyer and Seller agreed to modify a *land sale contract* by reducing the price from $15,000 to $10,000. Buyer did not give anything in return for Seller's promise to lower the price.

CASE PROBLEM

Lad lived in North Carolina. SST Co., a California firm, repeatedly called Lad and promised that SST would hire Lad if he ever lived in California. (However, Lad and SST never entered into an employment contract and Lad never gave consideration for SST's promise to hire him if he lived in California.) With SST's encouragement and in reasonable reliance on SST's promise, Lad quit his job in North Carolina, sold his home, and moved to California. When Lad arrived in California, SST refused to hire him. Is SST's promise to hire Lad enforceable under the doctrine of promissory estoppel? Briefly explain your answer.

_____

_____

_____

BUSINESS LAW PARTNER EXERCISE

Directions:

1.   Using the Online feature of the Business Law Partner CD-ROM, locate and identify the section of UCC Article 2 that governs the case below.
2.   In the case below, is the agreement to modify the contract enforceable even though Ida did not give consideration?

Case Study: *All Things Considered, Is Consideration Really Necessary?*

Tom, manager of Tom's Used Autos, contracted to sell a car to Ida for $2,500. After contracting, the parties discovered that the car's engine needed $300 worth of repairs, whereupon Ida and Tom agreed to modify the contract to reduce the price to $2,200. Later, however, Tom claimed that the contract modification was invalid and he demanded payment of the entire $2,500.

_____

_____

_____

CHAPTER 8 QUIZ

Section A

DIRECTIONS: Following each question below, indicate your answer by placing a "Y" for "Yes" or an "N" for "No" in the Answers column.

	Answers	For Scoring
1. Do courts require performance of an agreement only when it is supported by consideration?	_____	1. _____
2. In order to constitute consideration must a promise impose an obligation on the person making the promise?	_____	2. _____
3. Are all promises to do an act constitute consideration?	_____	3. _____
4. Does the adequacy of consideration determine the enforceability of a contract?	_____	4. _____
5. Can promising to give something to which the other party is already entitled constitute consideration?	_____	5. _____
6. If the amount of a debt is in dispute, would acceptance of a lesser sum in full settlement cancel the debt?	_____	6. _____
7. If each of several creditors agrees to accept a percentage of the amount due in full settlement, is the unpaid balance cancelled?	_____	7. _____
8. Would cancellation and return of a note discharge the debt evidenced by it?	_____	8. _____
9. Is a debt still owing if a lesser sum is paid and the creditor issues a receipt in full with an indication that a gift is made of the balance?	_____	9. _____
10. Is an agreement to accept a secured note in place of an unsecured note for a greater amount legally enforceable?	_____	10. _____
11. Is a promise to do something that one is already legally obligated to do sufficient consideration to support a contract?	_____	11. _____
12. Can a promise to refrain from suing another be consideration?	_____	12. _____
13. Is a past voluntary act sufficient consideration to support a present promise?	_____	13. _____
14. Is a pledge made to a charitable organization generally enforceable?	_____	14. _____
15. Is consideration necessary to support an obligation of record?	_____	15. _____
16. Does the UCC require a modification of a sales contract to be supported by consideration?	_____	16. _____

Score _____

Section B

DIRECTIONS: Complete each of the following statements by writing the missing word or words in the Answers column.

	Answers	For Scoring
1. The thing that distinguishes mere agreements from legally enforceable obligations is..	_____	1. _____
2. When several creditors agree to accept from a certain debtor a percentage of the amounts due in full settlement of their claims, the action taken by them is known as a(n) ??? of creditors.	_____	2. _____
3. Promising to refrain from doing what one has a legal right to do is known as	_____	3. _____

4. An act performed prior to the promise is called.. _____   4._____

5. Pledges to a charitable organization unsupported by anything from the organization are enforceable as .... _____   5._____

6. When a person makes a promise to a second person and that person reasonably and detrimentally relies on the promise, the promisor cannot claim that the second person did not give consideration in order to avoid the promise. This doctrine is known as..... _____   6._____

Score _____

Section C

This Agreement, made this _____(a)_____ day of _____(a)_____ A.D. 19 ____(a)____

by and between _____(b)_____ of

_____(c)_____ first part __√__

and _____(d)_____

of _____(e)_____ second part __ies__

   Witnesseth the said first part __y__ covenant __s__ and agree __s__ to and with the second parties as follows

_____

_____(f)_____

_____

And the said second part __ies__ covenant _____ and agree _____ to pay unto the said first part __y__ for

the same, the sum of _____(g)_____ Dollars, lawful money of the United

States, as follows:

_____(h)_____

_____ And for the true and faithful performance of all and every of the covenants and

agreements above mentioned, the parties to this agreement bind themselves, each unto the other, in the penal sum

of_____(i)_____ Dollars, as fixed and settled damages to be paid by the defaulting party.

   In Witness Whereof, the parties hereto have set their hands and seals the day and year first above written.

Signed, Sealed, and Delivered in the Presence of _____(k)_____ (LS.)

_____(j)_____   _____(l)_____ (LS.)

_____(m)_____   _____(n)_____ (LS.)

DIRECTIONS: Identify the parts of the contract shown above by writing the letter indicating the part named in the Answers column.

	Answers	For Scoring

1. The date of the document.. _____   1._____

2. The penal sum for nonperformance .... _____   2._____

3. The signatures of the contracting parties............................. _____   3._____

4. The consideration that supports the agreement.................... _____   4._____

5. The competent parties .... _____   5._____

6. The plan or method of payment... _____   6._____

7. The places for signatures of the witnesses .... _____   7._____

8. The lawful subject matter.. _____   8._____

Score _____

CHAPTER 9
DEFECTIVE AGREEMENTS

CHAPTER OUTLINE

I. MISTAKES

A. UNILATERAL MISTAKES

General rules.   ▸ Definition: mistake by one party to a contract. ▸ A unilateral mistake that is made at the time of contracting does not invalidate the contract.
Example.   Buyer purchases ten cases of oil, mistakenly thinking that there are 24 bottles to a case. Actually there are only 12 bottles per case. The purchase contract is still valid.

B. MUTUAL MISTAKES

General rules.   ▸ Definition: same mistake made by both parties to a contract. ▸ Mutual mistakes make contracts unenforceable.
Example.   Mechanic agrees to repair engine in Owner's car. Unknown to either party, the car has been destroyed by fire. The mutual mistake as to the existence of the subject matter of the contract makes the contract unenforceable.
Study hint.   Significant variations exist between states regarding the enforceability of contracts that involve mistakes. Some states hold a contract with a mutual mistake as to a material fact void; other states hold such a contract voidable.

C. CONTRACT TERMS GOVERN

General rule.   Parties can control what is to happen in case of a mistake by stating in their contract what result they want, even if this is a different outcome than the law provides.
Limitation.   If the contract provision is unconscionable, it is not controlling.
Study hint.   If, because of a mistake in keying or typing, a writing does not accurately reflect the oral agreement, the oral agreement controls.

D. EXCEPTIONS TO GENERAL RULE

1. Unilateral Mistakes

General rule.   There are few exceptions to the general rule that a unilateral mistake does not affect a contract.
Limitation.   Some courts will not enforce a contract with a unilateral mistake of fact, especially if the nonmistaken party caused the mistake or knew or should have known of the other party's mistake.
Study hint.   To entitle a party to relief, a mistake must be of fact, not opinion.

2. Mutual Mistakes

General rule.   Mutual mistakes usually make contracts unenforceable.
Limitation.   ▸ A contract is not affected if a mutual mistake only relates to: (a) value, quality, or price; (b) the terms of the contract; (c) the law; or (d) the parties' expectations. ▸ Barker agrees to sell an old picture frame to Fremont for $10. Barker cannot avoid the contract when they later find out that the frame is a valuable antique.

II.   FRAUD

A. FRAUD IN THE INDUCEMENT OR IN THE EXECUTION

- *Fraud in the inducement*: Fraud occurs when the defrauded party intended to make the contract, but the terms are different than they would have been if the fraud had not occurred. The contract is voidable by the defrauded party.
- *Fraud in the execution*: Fraud occurs when the defrauded party did not intend to enter into a contract. Such a contract is void.

B. ACTIVE FRAUD AND PASSIVE FRAUD

- *Active fraud by express misrepresentation*: Elements include: (1) false statement of material fact; (2) by a party who knows it is false or who has reckless disregard of its truth; (3) with the intent to induce the other party to rely on the statement; and (4) the other party relies and is induced into contracting.

- *Active fraud by concealment of material facts*: A contract is voidable if a party actively conceals material facts (e.g., seller rubs grease on a cracked engine block to hide defect). ▸ Passive fraud: A party usually has no duty to voluntarily disclose information to the other party. However, contract is voidable if: (1) parties have a relationship of trust and confidence; and (2) the party in the position of trust fails to disclose all material facts to the other party.

C. INNOCENT MISREPRESENTATION

A false statement made in the belief it was true may make the contract voidable if it was reasonable for the misled party to rely on the statement.

D. STATEMENTS OF OPINION

General rule.   In most cases fraud cannot be based on false statements of opinion.
Limitation.   Intentional misstatements of value or opinion by an expert may constitute fraud.

III.   DURESS

▸ A contract made under duress is voidable. ▸ Duress: (1) wrongful act or threat by a party (2) that deprives the other party of his or her free will (3) forcing the other party to contract. ▸ A threat may relate to: (1) physical well-being; (2) emotional pressure on a party; or (3) economic interests.

IV.   UNDUE INFLUENCE

General rules.   ▸ A contract resulting from undue influence is voidable. ▸ Undue influence: (1) domination of one contracting party by the other party (2) that deprives the weaker party of his or her free will (3) thereby compelling the weaker party to make a contract.
Limitations.   ▸ Nagging, and normal persuasion and arguments are not undue influence. ▸ Undue influence only applies if the weaker party feels helpless and feels compelled to do as told.

V.   BREACH OF CONTRACT BECAUSE OF FRAUD, DURESS, OR UNDUE INFLUENCE

General rules.   ▸ Fraud, duress, or undue influence: Contract is voidable; innocent party may (1) ratify (affirm) contract or (2) rescind (set aside) contract. ▸ Mistake: If the contract is void, it cannot be enforced by either party and no particular act is necessary to set aside the agreement. ▸ If the contract inaccurately states the parties' agreement, they may sue for reformation.
Limitation.   The party who acts improperly typically has no right to set aside a voidable contract.
Study hint.   If a party ratifies a voidable contract: (1) the contract is valid and binds the parties; but (2) the innocent party may still sue for damages sustained.

REVIEW OF CHAPTER

REVIEW OF TERMS

Select the term that best matches a statement below. Each term is the best match for only one statement.

TERMS

a. Duress
b. Fraud in the execution
c. Fraud in the inducement

d. Mutual mistake
e. Undue influence
f. Unilateral mistake

STATEMENTS

Answer

_____ 1. Domination of one contracting party by the other party that deprives the weaker party of his or her free will, thereby causing the weaker party to make a contract.

_____ 2. Situation in which defrauded party intended to make a contract but on different terms.

_____ 3. Mistake by only one contracting party regarding a fact.

_____ 4. Wrongful threat or act that deprives a party of free will and compels the party to make a contract.

_____ 5. Mistake by both contracting parties regarding a fact.

_____ 6. Situation in which defrauded party did not intend to enter into a contract.

REVIEW OF CONCEPTS

Directions: Indicate **T** for true and **F** for false in the answer column.

_____ 1. In general, a unilateral mistake by one contracting party does not affect the validity of a contract.

_____ 2. A contract may be set aside if one party makes a unilateral mistake regarding a material fact and the other party is aware of this mistake.

_____ 3. In general, contracts in which the parties made a mutual mistake are unenforceable.

_____ 4. When a contract provision specifies what is to happen in case of a mistake, the provision controls even if the law would provide otherwise.

_____ 5. A mistake regarding the value of a good being sold typically does not affect a contract's validity.

_____ 6. Buyer purchases a business from Seller. Both parties have the mistaken opinion that the business will make a profit in the future, but it does not. This mistake invalidates the contract.

_____ 7. One cannot rescind a contract merely because he or she did not read the contract.

_____ 8. Contracts based on fraud in the inducement, duress, or undue influence are void, not voidable.

_____ 9. An intentional misrepresentation regarding the value of an item by an expert seller cannot be fraud even if the statement is made to an unknowledgeable buyer who is relying on the statement.

_____ 10. If two contracting parties are in a confidential relationship, the party in the position of trust must generally disclose all material facts to the other party, and failure to do so may be fraud.

_____ 11. Wrongfully threatening to physically injure or to criminally prosecute a person may be duress.

_____ 12. A contract is voidable whenever one party persuades another party to make a contract.

REVIEW OF CONCEPT APPLICATIONS

Answer

Directions: Indicate your choice in the answer column.

_____ 1. Which contract described below is enforceable?
  a. Hal contracted to sell a cabin to Rob. The parties did not know that a flood destroyed the cabin the previous night.
  b. Marty was in a hurry and didn't read the financing contract she signed. She was later surprised to find out she was responsible for title and recording fees.
  c. Don contracts to sell a 1987 Audi to Carol. Don owns two 1987 Audis. Don thought he was selling one Audi to Carol, but Carol thought she was buying Don's other Audi.

_____ 2. Which contract is *defective* due to a mistake?
  a. Contractor submitted a bid to Owner that Owner accepted. Due to a math error the bid was $20,000, instead of $30,000 as intended. Owner was aware of Contractor's mistake.
  b. Vera bought a VCR. The VCR was not guaranteed. Vera thought the VCR was guaranteed for three years because she misread the contract. The seller was unaware of Vera's mistake.
  c. Cars-for-You contracted to sell a used car to Max for $5,000. The parties believed that the value of the car was $5,000. In fact, the car was only worth $2,500.

_____ 3. Seller contracted to sell a building to Buyer. The foundation of the building is cracked due to serious structural defects. Seller would *not commit fraud* in which situation?
  a. Seller plasters over the cracks, hiding the defective condition of the building.
  b. Seller does not hide the cracks, but Seller does not tell Buyer about the defects. Buyer does not inspect the building that would have revealed the building's structural defects.
  c. When Buyer asks about the cracks, Seller falsely tells Buyer that he has corrected the structural defects that caused the cracks. This statement induces Buyer into contracting.

_____ 4. Which contract is *voidable*?
  a. Robin and her son, Bob, have a confidential relationship; Robin does whatever Bob says. Robin sold some stock to Bob for an unfairly low price because he demanded that she do so.
  b. Jake persuaded Lou to accept a salary of $30,000 instead of $40,000 that Lou had wanted.
  c. Jan threatens to injure Carl's children and to burn Carl's home unless he lends Jan $10,000. As a result of these threats, Carl feels compelled to agree to the loan and he does so.
  d. a and c.

CASE PROBLEM

Attorney and Client are in a confidential relationship. Attorney contracted to sell land to Client without disclosing that a power plant is planned to be built near the property. The plant will significantly hurt the land's value. Client was unaware of this fact and paid Attorney the contract price. In this case: (1) Did Attorney commit fraud? (2) If Client elects to perform the contract, can Client sue Attorney for damages?

_____

_____

_____

BUSINESS LAW PARTNER EXERCISE

Directions: Access your Business Law Partner CD-ROM and locate the document entitled "Notice of Contract Default." Complete this document using the information provided in the following case study.

Case Study: *That's Your Mistake, Not Mine*

Acme submitted a bid to D&D Construction to pour the foundation of a home that Domain was building. The bid price was $20,000. Bids submitted by other subcontractors ranged from $22,000 to $30,000 for the same work. D&D accepted Acme's bid. Later, Acme realized that its estimator forgot to include any profit in the bid, and the bid should have been $25,000. Domain was unaware of this mistake when it accepted the bid. Acme demanded $25,000, but Domain refused. Acme then refused to do the work claiming that the contract was voidable due to mistake.

_____

_____

_____

CHAPTER 9 QUIZ

Section A

DIRECTIONS: Following each question below, indicate your answer by placing a "Y" for "Yes" or an "N" for "No" in the Answers column.

		Answers	For Scoring
1.	Is there a valid contract whenever an offer and an acceptance have been made?	_____	1._____
2.	Are business contracts usually completely implied from the parties' acts?....................	_____	2._____
3.	Are the states uniform in their approach regarding the effect that mistakes have on the enforceability of contracts?..	_____	3._____
4.	May the parties specify in the contract what impact a mistake will have on its enforceability?	_____	4._____
5.	Do some states allow a party who has made a unilateral mistake to raise the mistake as a defense?	_____	5._____
6.	Are knowledge and diligence the chief protections against losses due to mistakes?	_____	6._____
7.	Do unilateral mistakes as to value, quality, or price of the subject matter affect the validity of the contract?	_____	7._____
8.	Can a contract be avoided on the basis of a mistake as to the terms of the contract if a party fails to understand the meaning of the contract?	_____	8._____
9.	Are the parties expected to know what the law is when making a contract?	_____	9._____
10.	Is a contract induced by fraud void?	_____	10._____
11.	Does fraud in the execution make a contract voidable?..	_____	11._____
12.	In order to be fraud by express misrepresentation, is it necessary that the one guilty of fraud know the statement is false or make the statement with reckless disregard of truth?	_____	12._____
13.	In order to constitute fraud by express misrepresentation, must the one guilty of fraud have had an intent to induce the other to act by reason of the false statement?	_____	13._____
14.	In general, do false statements of opinion constitute fraud?	_____	14._____
15.	Is it financial duress to take advantage of the other party's urgent need to make the contract?	_____	15._____
16.	Can one be guilty of fraud because of actively concealing material facts even though no false statements are made?	_____	16._____
17.	Is it fraud for a person to remain silent when he or she has a duty to speak?	_____	17._____
18.	In order for a contract to be valid, is it necessary that the parties enter into it of their own free will?	_____	18._____
19.	Can a party who has rescinded due to a breach of contract sue for both damages and, goods or other things of value that were given to the other party?	_____	19._____
20.	In general, must contracting parties be restored to their prior positions when a contract is rescinded?	_____	20._____

Score _____

Section B

DIRECTIONS: Following each statement below, indicate your answer by placing a "T" for "True" or an "F" for "False" in the Answers column.

		Answers	For Scoring
1.	A mutual mistake as to the identity of the subject matter of a contract renders the contract void.	_____	1. _____
2.	The law is the primary way that a person can avoid losses due to mistakes.	_____	2. _____
3.	A unilateral mistake as to price, resulting from an error in typing, voids a contract.	_____	3. _____
4.	A mistake by one party as to the interpretation of the terms of a written contract affects its validity.	_____	4. _____
5.	A party's unilateral mistake of fact that is caused by the other contracting party may render a contract unenforceable.	_____	5. _____
6.	A mutual mistake of law makes a contract unenforceable.	_____	6. _____
7.	In order to constitute fraud, the false statement must be relied upon by the innocent party in making the contract.	_____	7. _____
8.	If the relationship of the contracting parties is that of trust and confidence, silence may constitute fraud.	_____	8. _____
9.	Contracts entered into through fraud, duress, or undue influence are void.	_____	9. _____
10.	An innocent party may lose the right to avoid a voidable contract by doing nothing.	_____	10. _____
11.	An innocent party cannot sue for fraud after ratifying a voidable contract.	_____	11. _____
12.	A wrongdoer can never set a contract aside and thus profit from the wrong.	_____	12. _____

Score _____

Section C

DIRECTIONS: Complete each of the following statements by writing the missing word or words in the Answers column.

		Answers	For Scoring
1.	A mistake by one party without the knowledge of the other party is described as	_____	1. _____
2.	A mistake made by both parties is described as	_____	2. _____
3.	Inducing another to enter into a contract as a result of an intentionally false statement of a material facts is	_____	3. _____
4-5.	A false statement of a material fact is a(n)	_____	4. _____
	Such a statement made in the belief it is true is a(n)	_____	5. _____
6.	Obtaining consent to a contract by threatening to do harm to a person or members of the person's family is known as	_____	6. _____
7.	A contract induced by one party in a confidential or fiduciary relationship with another, against the free will of the other, is voidable because of	_____	7. _____
8.	A victim of an act that makes a contract voidable may elect to set aside, or ???, the contract.	_____	8. _____

Score _____

CHAPTER 10
ILLEGAL AGREEMENTS

CHAPTER OUTLINE

I. INTRODUCTION

General rules.   ▸ An agreement is illegal if its purpose or performance: (1) is a crime or a private wrong, such as a tort; (2) violates certain statutes or administrative rules and regulations; or (3) violates public policy. ▸ Illegal agreements generally are void. ▸ In most cases parties to an illegal agreement are denied remedies; a court will not require performance or award damages.

Limitation.   If a contract contains legal and illegal promises and the promises can be separated, then the legal promises may be enforced but the illegal promises are void and unenforceable. (If the contract is indivisible, illegality in one part makes the entire contract invalid.)

Study hint.   Typically, a party to an illegal agreement may keep a benefit received pursuant to the agreement, and a court will not make the party pay for or return the benefit.

II. CONTRACTS PROHIBITED BY STATUTE

A. GAMBLING CONTRACTS

General rules.   ▸ In general, gambling contracts are illegal and void. ▸ Gambling debts are void and cannot be enforced. However, a person holding money being wagered by others (i.e., a stakeholder), must return the money.

Limitations.   ▸ In many states, state lotteries and betting on horse and dog races are legal. ▸ Buying stock or buying the right to goods that are to be delivered in the future at a stated price is not gambling if the seller actually intends to deliver the stock or the goods.

Study hint.   Gambling contract: (1) pay consideration; (2) for a chance; (3) to win a prize.

B. SUNDAY CONTRACTS

To varying degrees, some states forbid making certain contracts on Sunday.

C. USURIOUS CONTRACTS

General rules.   ▸ Usury laws limit the rate of interest that may be charged for certain loans. ▸ Usury is charging interest in excess of the *maximum contract rate*. ▸ The penalty for usury varies among states. In most states laws prohibit a lender from recovering the excessive interest.

Limitation.   Interest includes expressly stated interest and charges that are disguised interest.

Study hint.   If a creditor or seller is legally entitled to interest on a debt but the parties did not state the rate of interest, then the creditor or seller may collect the *legal rate* of interest.

D. CONTRACTS OF AN UNLICENSED OPERATOR

General rule.   A contract is void if performance of the contract requires a party to violate a licensing statute that is intended to protect against unqualified work.

Example.   Contracts to practice law, accounting, or medicine without a license are void.

Limitation.   A contract is valid if it violates a licensing statute intended only to raise revenue.

E. CONTRACTS FOR SALE OF PROHIBITED ARTICLES

General rule.   A contract to sell illegal goods is void.

Example.   Seller cannot sue to collect purchase price of contract to sell stolen goods.

F. CONTRACTS IN UNREASONABLE RESTRAINT OF TRADE

General rule.　A contract to unreasonably restrain (limit) trade (competition) is void.
Examples.　Contracts that may illegally restrain trade include:

- *Contract not to compete*: A contract not to compete is illegal unless: (1) it relates to a sale of a business or employment; (2) it is reasonably necessary to protect the other party; and (3) it is for a reasonable time and area.

- *Contracts to restrain trade*: Federal and state antitrust laws prohibit contracts between competitors that unreasonably limit competition, including agreements to fix prices and agreements between competitors to divide up territories.

- *Contracts to fix the resale price*: A seller and buyer cannot agree that the buyer will not resell goods below a stated price.

- *Unfair competitive practices*: The Robinson-Patman Act (federal law) prohibits a seller from charging different buyers different prices for the same goods. States also impose similar restrictions. Some states forbid selling goods at a loss or below cost if this is done with an intent to hurt competition.

Limitations.　Contract not to compete by a seller of a business: (1) area should not exceed the area in which business is conducted; and (2) duration of the promise not to compete should not exceed that necessary to allow the buyer to get established.
Study hint.　Absent a valid contract not to compete, a seller of a business can compete against the buyer of the business, and a person can compete against a former employer.

III. CONTRACTS CONTRARY TO PUBLIC POLICY

▸ An agreement or a contract term is unenforceable if it violates an important public policy. ▸ Public policy creates standards of conduct necessary to protect the government, the legal system, and fundamental social values, interests, and institutions, such as marriage.

A. CONTRACTS LIMITING THE FREEDOM OF MARRIAGE

General rule.　A contract that limits a person's right to marry violates public policy and is void.
Examples.　▸ Contract never to marry. ▸ Contract not to marry for a stated time. ▸ Contract not to marry a certain person. ▸ Contract to marry someone while married to a different person. ▸ Contract requiring a person to divorce another.
Limitations.　▸ Promise not to marry while a minor is valid. ▸ A property settlement is valid.

B. CONTRACTS OBSTRUCTING THE ADMINISTRATION OF JUSTICE

General rule.　A contract that may tend to interfere with the proper functioning of courts or the legal system violates public policy. This type of contract is void even if it does not actually interfere with the administration of justice.
Examples.　▸ Agreement to pay a witness for certain testimony or for not testifying. ▸ Agreement not to criminally prosecute a thief if stolen goods are returned. ▸ A promise to appoint a person to a legal or governmental position in return for campaign contributions.

C. CONTRACTS INJURING THE PUBLIC SERVICE

General rule.　An agreement that interferes with the performance of public duties by a public official violates public policy, and the agreement is void.
Examples.　▸ Illegal lobbying agreements. ▸ Contract to improperly use one's influence to obtain official action, such as a contract or a pardon.
Limitation.　Persons may be hired as lobbyists to support or oppose proposed laws.

REVIEW OF CHAPTER

REVIEW OF TERMS

Select the term that best matches a statement below. Each term is the best match for only one statement.

TERMS

a. Contract not to compete   c. Public policy   e. Sherman Antitrust Act
b. Gambling contract   d. Robinson-Patman Act   f. Usury

STATEMENTS

Answer

_____ 1. Principles that invalidate a contract if it endangers fundamental public interests or values.
_____ 2. Contract by which a party agrees not to compete against another party.
_____ 3. Charging a rate of interest greater than the maximum contract rate.
_____ 4. Federal law that prohibits price fixing and other unreasonable restraints of trade.
_____ 5. Federal law that may prohibit a seller from charging different buyers different prices for goods that are of the same grade, quality, and quantity.
_____ 6. Contract by which parties win or lose by chance.

REVIEW OF CONCEPTS

Directions: Indicate **T** for true and **F** for false in the answer column.

_____ 1. A contract that requires a person to commit a private wrong against another is illegal and void.
_____ 2. In nearly all states, every contract that is made on Sunday is illegal and void.
_____ 3. All forms of gambling are illegal based on state statutes.
_____ 4. Bake agrees to sell Chambers 1,000 bushels of soybeans with delivery in seven months. Although Bake does not even own any soybeans, the contract is legal if Bake intends to deliver.
_____ 5. If a creditor is legally entitled to interest on a debt but there is no agreement specifying the rate of interest, then the creditor may collect the legal rate of interest.
_____ 6. Most states regulate loans to consumers by finance companies and certain other lenders. In some states, these laws permit lenders to charge higher rates of interest for these types of loans.
_____ 7. For purposes of determining whether a lender has committed usury, interest includes only the amount that is expressly stated to be interest.
_____ 8. Contracts to divide up territories among competitors are void as unreasonable restraints of trade.
_____ 9. If a manufacturer and a retailer agree that the retailer will not resell the manufacturer's product for less than $1,000, then this contract is illegal and void.
_____ 10. If a husband and wife are preparing to divorce and they enter into a contract to divide their property, then this property settlement contract is illegal and void.
_____ 11. A contract to pay a witness a fee contingent on a favorable outcome of a suit may be illegal.
_____ 12. A contract that has a tendency to interfere with the legal system cannot violate public policy and cannot be invalid if the contract does not cause any actual harm to the public.

REVIEW OF CONCEPT APPLICATIONS

Answer

Directions: Indicate your choice in the answer column.

_____ 1. Compu Co. and Gina entered into an illegal contract whereby Gina agreed to sabotage a competitor's business. The sabotage is a crime. Gina failed to perform. Under these facts:
    a. A court will not require Gina to perform the agreement.
    b. A court will require Gina to perform the agreement.
    c. A court will make Gina pay damages for losses caused by her nonperformance.
    d. b and c.

_____ 2. Ted, a law student, made *one* contract to: (a) paint Kim's house for $500; and (b) represent Kim in a small lawsuit for $250. The painting service is legal; the legal service is illegal. In this case:
   a. The entire contract is valid.
   b. The entire contract is void.
   c. The portion of the contract relating to the painting service is valid. The portion of the contract relating to the unlicensed practice of law is void.

_____ 3. Select the correct statement.
   a. Bob bet $100 that the L.A. Lakers would win. The Lakers lost. This contract is legal and enforceable. A court will make Bob pay the bet.
   b. On a commodity exchange, Seller contracted to sell John a quantity of oil at a fixed price in one year. Seller intends to perform the contract. This contract is legal and enforceable.
   c. Cap and Sue bet one another $100 on who would win the Super Bowl. They gave the money to Leslie to hold. If requested, a court would make Leslie return the money to Cap and Sue.
   d. b and c.

_____ 4. Neal was hired as sales manager for a food distributor doing business in Pork City, U.S.A. Neal managed the important customer accounts and he was responsible for developing the company's sales strategy. When hired, Neal agreed not to compete in the food distribution business after he quit. Under these facts, Neal's agreement not to compete would be:
   a. Valid if it prohibited Neal from competing in Pork City for one year after he quit.
   b. Valid if it prohibited Neal from competing anywhere in the entire state in which Pork City is located for ten years after he quit.
   c. Void regardless of its terms. All contracts not to compete are illegal and void.

CASE PROBLEM

Todd hired Toni as general contractor to make structural repairs to a building. A person is legally required to be licensed to be a general contractor. To assure the competency of general contractors to safely repair buildings, this license requires extensive experience and successful completion of an exhaustive exam. Toni does not have this license. Under these facts: (1) Is the contract between Todd and Toni valid or void? (2) If Toni performs the contract but Todd fails to pay, can Toni enforce the contract and recover the contract price?

_____

_____

_____

BUSINESS LAW PARTNER EXERCISE

Directions:

1. Using the Online feature of the Business Law Partner CD-ROM, find and read 18 U.S.C. § 201 and identify the web site where this statute is located.
2. In the case below, is the contract between Kim and Jack Co. legal or illegal?

Case Study: *Beware of Strangers Bearing Gifts*

Kim is Director of the U.S. Department of Freeways. Kim makes the final decision for awarding federal road construction contracts. Jack Co. offered to pay $100,000 to Kim if she would "pay special attention" to its bid for a large government contract that Kim would soon award. In response to Jack's offer, Kim paid "special attention" to Jack's bid, and awarded the contract to Jack Co.

_____

_____

_____

CHAPTER 10 QUIZ

Section A

DIRECTIONS: Following each question below, indicate your answer by placing a "Y" for "Yes" or an "N" for "No" in the Answers column.

	Answers	For Scoring
1. If a contract is partly but it can be divided so that the legal part can be performed separately, is the legal portion of the contract enforceable?	_____	1. _____
2. Will courts ordinarily provide a remedy for a party to a wagering contract?	_____	2. _____
3. Does trading on the grain market represent a legitimate business transaction?	_____	3. _____
4. In general, are violators criminally prosecuted for conducting business on Sunday when it is prohibited by law?	_____	4. _____
5. Is a contract to lend money at the legal rate usurious if the borrower purchases an item at an exorbitant price?	_____	5. _____
6. May an unlicensed person who performs a service requiring a license collect the reasonable value of the services?	_____	6. _____
7. Is a contract to fix prices void?	_____	7. _____
8. Is a contract that violates an administrative agency rule illegal?	_____	8. _____
9. Is an agreement not to marry during minority valid?	_____	9. _____
10. Will the courts enforce a contract that obstructs the administration of justice?	_____	10. _____

Score _____

Section B

DIRECTIONS: Following each statement below, indicate your answer by placing a "T" for "True" or an "F" for "False" in the Answers column.

	Answers	For Scoring
1. Certain classes of gambling contracts have been legalized in some states......................	_____	1. _____
2. The stakeholder may retain the winnings in a gambling contract...................................	_____	2. _____
3. Laws and interpretations regarding Sunday contracts are uniform throughout the states.	_____	3. _____
4. The legal rate of interest is always higher than the maximum contract rate.	_____	4. _____
5. The penalty for usury varies from state to state.	_____	5. _____
6. Contracts for impose an unreasonable restraint of trade are enforceable......................	_____	6. _____
7. The courts determine whether contracts are contrary to public policy.	_____	7. _____
8. Property settlement agreements made in contemplation of divorces are void as against public policy.	_____	8. _____
9. A contract to pay a public official more than the statutory salary is valid.	_____	9. _____

Score _____

Section C

DIRECTIONS: Complete each of the following statements by writing the missing word or words in the Answers column.

	Answers	For Scoring
1. A contract that is made for an lawful purpose is...	_____	1. _____
2. Laws that limit the rate of interest that may be charged for the use of money are called..	_____	2. _____
3. The rate of interest fixed by the state as the maximum that can be charged is known as the........................	_____	3. _____
4. The amount of interest fixed by the state to be charged when the parties are silent as to the rate is known as the	_____	4. _____
5. A transaction wherein the parties stand to win or lose based on chance is a(n)	_____	5. _____
6. When the seller of a business agrees not to engage in the same business, the contract is called a contract	_____	6. _____
7-8. Two federal laws enacted to prohibit contracts which restrain interstate commerce are the..	_____	7. _____
	_____	8. _____
9. The act of Congress that attempts to eliminate certain unfair trade practices, such as discrimination in price between competing buyers, is known as the .	_____	9. _____
10-12. .... Three types of contracts contrary to public policy are contracts	_____	10. _____
	_____	11. _____
	_____	12. _____

Score _____

Section D

DIRECTIONS: Indicate your decision in each of the following cases by placing a "Y" for "Yes" or an "N" for "No" in the Answers column.

	Answers	For Scoring
1. C was a heavy loser in a game of chance played for high stakes. He threatened to sue A and B for the recovery of his losses. Is it likely that a court will hear the case and hold in favor of C?	_____	1. _____
2. X borrowed $1,000 from City Finance and was induced to sign a note for $1,060 plus interest at 10 percent. Ten percent was the maximum rate of interest that could be charged in that state. Can City Finance compel payment of the interest plus the extra $60?	_____	2. _____
3. Strobel was called as an eyewitness in a murder case. The defendant's brother agreed to pay Strobel $5,000 if Strobel would say the defendant was not the murderer. When testifying, Strobel so testified and then demanded the $5,000. Can he recover it?	_____	3. _____
4. Bennet bought out Kenyon's grocery business in order to eliminate the last competitor in that market. Kenyon signed a contract to refrain from entering the grocery business in that town for ten years from the date of contract. Do you consider this a reasonable restraint of trade?	_____	4. _____

Score _____

CHAPTER 11
WRITTEN CONTRACTS

CHAPTER OUTLINE

I.   INTRODUCTION

General rule.   Broadly speaking, oral contracts are valid and courts will enforce such contracts.
Limitation.   An oral contract is unenforceable if the Statute of Frauds requires a writing.

II.   REASONS FOR WRITTEN CONTRACTS

Important contracts should be in writing in order: (1) to prevent a party from falsely denying that a contract was made; and (2) to assist an administrator of an estate or a guardian of an incompetent person to prove the existence and terms of a contract made by a deceased or incompetent person.

III.   STATUTE OF FRAUDS

General rules.   ▸ The Statute of Frauds requires six types of contracts to be evidenced by a sufficient writing to be enforceable. ▸ If a contract is unenforceable: (1) a court will not make the parties perform the contract; but (2) if a party has given property or services for which he or she has not been paid, the party may recover the property or may recover the reasonable value for the benefits given.
Limitations.   ▸ The Statute of Frauds applies only to executory contracts. It cannot be used as a ground to rescind (set aside) a fully performed oral contract. ▸ Parties may choose to voluntarily perform an oral contract even though it does not comply with the Statute of Frauds.
Study hint.   The Statute of Frauds originated in England in 1677. Most states have adopted this law with only a few changes.

A. AN AGREEMENT TO SELL LAND OR ANY INTEREST IN OR CONCERNING LAND

General rules.   ▸ Contracts for the sale or transfer of land or any interest in land must be evidenced by a sufficient writing to be enforceable.
Examples.   ▸ Contracts for the sale of land or buildings affixed to land. ▸ Rights of way across land
(easements).   ▸ Certain contracts for the sale of minerals in the ground. ▸ Leases of real property for more than one year.
Study hint.   Some cases have held a sale of standing timber to be a sale of an interest in land.

B. AN AGREEMENT THE TERMS OF WHICH CANNOT BE PERFORMED WITHIN ONE YEAR FROM THE TIME IT IS MADE

General rules.   ▸ A contract that cannot be fully performed within one year from the date it is made must be evidenced by a writing. ▸ The one-year period begins the day after a contract is made (not when the work is to begin), and concludes the day performance will be completed.
Example.   Employer hires Becky for a fixed, three-year term.
Limitation.   A writing is not required if it is physically possible to fully perform the contract in less than one year.
Study hints.   ▸ A contract to hire a person for life is not required to be in writing; the employee may die in less than one year. ▸ An oral contract for an indefinite time is usually enforceable since it typically is *possible* to perform most contracts in less than one year.

C. AN AGREEMENT TO BE RESPONSIBLE FOR THE DEBTS OR DEFAULT OF ANOTHER

General rule. A promise to pay a debt or to perform an obligation of another party if that party fails to do so, is required to be evidenced by a sufficient writing to be enforceable.

Example. Wes promises Lender that if Lender lends money to Sal and Sal fails to repay the loan, then Wes will repay the loan. To make the promise enforceable, it must be written.

Limitations. ► A promise made to a *debtor* to pay a debt is not required to be written. ► This statute does not apply to an original promise to perform a contract, even if the other party is told to deliver a benefit to a third party. ► If the main purpose for promising to pay another's debt is to benefit the party making the promise and not the debtor, then a writing is not required.

Study hint. One type of promise that is subject to this statute is a guarantee of another's debt.

D. AN AGREEMENT OF AN EXECUTOR TO PERSONALLY PAY DEBTS OF THE ESTATE

General rule. A promise by an executor or administrator to pay a debt of an estate out of the executor's or administrator's personal funds must be evidenced by a writing to be enforceable.

Limitation. An oral promise in the name of the estate that the estate will do something does not fall within this rule, and such an oral promise may be enforced.

E. AN AGREEMENT IN WHICH A PROMISE IS MADE IN CONSIDERATION OF MARRIAGE

General rule. A promise made in consideration for a person's promise to marry (or for actually marrying) another person is required to be evidenced by a sufficient writing to be enforceable.

Limitation. This statute does not apply to promises by two persons to marry one another.

IV.   NOTE OR MEMORANDUM

General rules. ► The Statute of Frauds requires that a writing: (1) state the material contract terms (e.g., parties, subject matter, quantity, price, and financing); and (2) be signed by the party who is using the Statute of Frauds as a defense to having to perform the contract.

Limitation. Article 2 imposes different writing requirements for contracts for the sale of goods.

Study hints. ► Any writing may suffice; a written contract signed by both parties is not needed. ► A writing can be made after the time of contracting. ► A writing may be sufficient even if the party who signed it did not sign with the intention of authenticating or being bound by the contract.

V.   OTHER WRITTEN CONTRACTS

Other contracts required to be in writing include (1) contracts for the sale of goods for $500 or more, (2) contracts for the sale of stock or securities, and (3) contracts to pay a real estate broker commission.

VI.   PAROL EVIDENCE RULE

General rules. ► Parol evidence means oral statements. ► Parol evidence rule: Terms of a final, complete written contract (complete contract) cannot be added to, modified, or contradicted by evidence of oral statements or writings made before, or at the same time, a written contract was made.

Example. Seller and Buyer sign a final, complete written contract for the sale of a business. The contract clearly states that the sale does not include a computer. The parol evidence rule bars proving that Seller orally stated during negotiations that the sale might include the computer.

Limitations. ► The parol evidence rule does not exclude other writings that are referenced by and incorporated into a contract. ► If a written contract is a final statement of only part of a contract (an incomplete contract), the parol evidence rule permits proof of parol evidence and trade custom to establish terms that are not addressed by the writing. ► The parol evidence rule does not prevent the use of parol evidence to: (1) explain the meaning of an ambiguous term; (2) prove the existence of a contract defense (such as fraud, mistake, accident, or illegality); or (3) prove a contract modification that was agreed to after the making of the written contract.

REVIEW OF CHAPTER

REVIEW OF TERMS

Select the term that best matches a statement below. Each term is the best match for only one statement.

TERMS

a. Ambiguous term
b. Complete contract
c. Debt
d. Default

e. Parol evidence
f. Parol evidence rule
g. Statute of Frauds

STATEMENTS

Answer

____ 1. Law that requires certain contracts to be evidenced by a writing to be judicially enforceable.
____ 2. Oral statements.
____ 3. Obligation to pay money to another.
____ 4. Doctrine that prohibits altering a complete written contract by proving evidence of oral statements or writings that were made prior to or at the same time the written contract was made.
____ 5. Contract that is intended by the parties to be the entire, final statement of their agreement.
____ 6. Contractual term that may have more than one meaning.
____ 7. Breach of a contractual obligation that does not involve a payment of money.

REVIEW OF CONCEPTS

Directions: Indicate **T** for true and **F** for false in the answer column.

____ 1. All oral contracts are unenforceable.
____ 2. The Statute of Frauds requirements help prevent a party from falsely denying that a contract was made.
____ 3. Parties may voluntarily perform an oral contract even if it violates the Statute of Frauds.
____ 4. A fully performed oral contract can be set aside because it violates the Statute of Frauds.
____ 5. A party may recover the reasonable value of benefits that have been given pursuant to a contract that is unenforceable under the Statute of Frauds.
____ 6. In general, a promise made to a creditor to pay another person's debt must be evidenced by a writing.
____ 7. Lisa promised Violet that, if Violet borrows $1,000 to go to business school and Violet cannot repay the loan, then Lisa will repay the loan. Lisa's promise is not required to be written.
____ 8. A writing may satisfy the Statute of Frauds even if it is not a formal written contract.
____ 9. Only a few states have adopted the Statute of Frauds.
____10. Except for a sale of goods, the Statute of Frauds requires a writing to state all material terms.
____11. Contracts to pay real estate broker commissions or to sell stock are not required to be in writing.
____12. In general, the parol evidence rule forbids using evidence of prior oral statements or writings to modify or contradict a complete written contract that is subsequently made by the parties.
____13. Prior oral statements may be used to prove trade customs in order to establish missing terms in an incomplete contract.

REVIEW OF CONCEPT APPLICATIONS

Answer

Directions: Indicate your choice in the answer column.

____ 1. Which oral contract is unenforceable because it violates the Statute of Frauds?
   a. Biff orally contracts to sell his ranch to Marty.
   b. Sue orally leases her home to Larry for two years.
   c. Lin orally grants Kelly a right of way (easement) to cross over Lin's land.
   d. All of the above.

_____ 2. Which oral contract is unenforceable because it violates the Statute of Frauds?
      a.   On March 1, Lee contracts to work for Pam from June 1 until April 30 of the following year.
      b.   On June 1, Gill contracts to do a research project for R&D Inc. It is possible to complete the project in less than one year, although the parties think it will take longer.
      c.   A&A hires Al, age 40, as a consultant for the remainder of his life.
      d.   All of the above.

_____ 3. Which oral promise violates the Statute of Frauds?
      a.   Mom orders a radio from Seller, and Mom orally promises to pay the $100 contract price for the radio. However, Mom tells Seller to deliver the radio to her son.
      b.   Pete promises Lender that, if Lender loans $200 to Pete's daughter and his daughter does not repay the loan, then Pete will repay the loan.
      c.   Debtor owes Roger $1,000 but Debtor cannot repay this debt. To enable Debtor to repay the debt owing him, Roger orally promises Bank that, if Bank lends Debtor $1,000 and Debtor does not repay the loan, then Roger will repay the loan.

_____ 4. Which oral promise or contract violates the Statute of Frauds?
      a.   Claudia and Mickey promise to marry one another.
      b.   Tom orally contracts to buy a TV for $400.
      c.   Executor promises Attorney that an estate being administered by Executor will pay Attorney $100 per hour for services rendered to the estate.
      d.   Dad and Jose made an oral contract whereby Dad promised to make Jose general manager of a company in consideration for Jose's promise to marry Dad's daughter.

CASE PROBLEM

Sid bought a computer pursuant to a final, complete, written contract signed by Sid and the seller. The contract states that the price is $2,000, payable on delivery, and it guarantees the computer to be free of "serious defects," an ambiguous term. Can Sid use parol evidence to prove: (1) the meaning of the term "serious defects;" (2) that previously the parties had orally agreed that payment was to be 30 days after delivery; (3) that the seller committed fraud by intentionally misrepresenting the computer?

_____

_____

_____

BUSINESS LAW PARTNER EXERCISE

Directions: Access your Business Law Partner CD-ROM and locate the document entitled "Guaranty Agreement." Complete this document using the information provided in the following case study.

Case Study: *One Written Contract is Worth Ten Oral Contracts*

You are the manager of consumer credit at Last Bank. Stan, a customer, applied for a $10,000 personal loan. You rejected Stan's application, however, because he did not have sufficient collateral to secure repayment of the loan. Stan's parents have now agreed to repay the loan if the bank is unsuccessful in collecting payment from Stan. The bank president has requested you to complete the Guaranty Agreement that will be enforceable against Stan's parents. The president also said, "When in doubt, make sure that the provisions of the guaranty favor the bank."

_____

_____

_____

CHAPTER 11 QUIZ

Section A

DIRECTIONS: Following each statement below, indicate your answer by placing a "T" for "True" or an "F" for "False" in the Answers column.

	Answers	For Scoring
1. If there are witnesses to an oral contract there is no legal need to have it in writing......	_____	1. _____
2. The Statute of Frauds applies only to executory contracts...	_____	2. _____
3. The writing required by the Statute of Frauds when land is sold is called a deed.	_____	3. _____
4. If one has paid money under an oral contract, the executory part of which cannot be enforced, the money may not be recovered.	_____	4. _____
5. A contract that cannot be performed in one year must be in writing since the terms might easily be forgotten before the contract is completed.	_____	5. _____
6. Even if a contract may not be completed for fifty years, if it is physically possible to complete within one year, it does not have to be in writing.	_____	6. _____
7. A contract to care for another as long as the other person lives must be in writing........	_____	7. _____
8. The Statute of Frauds applies to a promise to pay the obligation of another even if the purpose of the promise is to gain some advantage for the promisor.	_____	8. _____
9. A memorandum covering an agreement must be signed by both parties........................	_____	9. _____
10. A person who signs a writing required by the Statute of Frauds must sign with the intention of being bound..	_____	10. _____
11. The five classes of contracts listed by the Statute of Frauds are the only contracts that must be written to be enforceable..	_____	11. _____
12. The terms of a complete written contract may be altered by parol evidence..................	_____	12. _____

Score _____

Section B

DIRECTIONS: Indicate your decision in each of the following cases by placing a "Y" for "Yes" or an "N" for "No" in the Answers column.

	Answers	For Scoring
1. Walker orally accepted Barnett's oral offer to sell two lots on Short Street at a quoted price. Walker asked Barnett to hold the lots for a week while he obtained funds to pay Barnett. Barnett agreed to the delay but sold the lots to a relative before the week ended. Was Barnett free to sell the lots?	_____	1. _____
2. Smitty orally agreed to rent an apartment for two years. At the end of three months he moved out because he had found an apartment at a lower rent. Was he obligated on his contract?	_____	2. _____
3. Hall sought to buy a suit on credit at Campton's Store. Stanley, a friend of Hall, said, "Let him have the suit. I will pay for it if he does not." Campton replied, "All right, I will charge it to you, Mr. Hall. But if Mr. Hall fails to pay, I will charge your account, Mr. Stanley." Is Stanley liable?	_____	3. _____
4. X, an administrator of Y's estate, gave the undertaker, Z, her oral promise that she would pay Y's funeral expenses from her own funds if Y's estate could not cover the expenses. Z sued to collect from X. Is X liable?	_____	4. _____

Score _____

Section C

DIRECTIONS: Complete each of the following statements by writing the missing word or words in the Answers column.

	Answers	For Scoring
1. The statute that requires certain classes of contracts to be in writing to be enforceable is the...	_____	1. _____
2. An obligation to pay money is a(n)...	_____	2. _____
3. The breach of contractual obligations other than the payment of money is a(n)	_____	3. _____
4. Spoken or oral testimony is..	_____	4. _____
5. The party who has been named or appointed to settle the business affairs of a deceased person is known as an executor or a(n)	_____	5. _____
6. The rule that does not allow oral testimony that varies or contradicts the terms of a written contract is the	_____	6. _____

Score _____

Section D

DIRECTIONS: Following each question below, indicate your answer by placing a " Y" for " Yes" or an " N" for " No" in the Answers column.

	Answers	For Scoring
1. Is an oral contract less enforceable than a written contract when the Statute of Frauds does not apply?	_____	1. _____
2. Is an oral contract to use a joint driveway enforceable?	_____	2. _____
3. Does the Statute of Frauds apply when a promisor promises the debtor that the promisor will pay an obligation that the debtor owes to a third person?	_____	3. _____
4. Must an agreement to transfer property in consideration of marriage be written to be enforceable?	_____	4. _____
5. Must the memorandum covering an agreement be made at the time of the contract? ...	_____	5. _____
6. Must agreements to sell goods for $500 or more be in writing to be enforceable?	_____	6. _____
7. May oral testimony clarify ambiguous terms of a written contract?	_____	7. _____
8. If an omission in an apparently complete contract is due to duress, may oral testimony be produced to prove the duress?	_____	8. _____

Score _____

CHAPTER 12
THIRD PARTIES AND CONTRACTS

CHAPTER OUTLINE

I. **WAYS TO INVOLVE A THIRD PARTY**

A. THIRD-PARTY BENEFICIARY

- ***Definitions***: ▸ *Third-party beneficiary*: party whom contracting parties intend to directly benefit by a contract. ▸ *Creditor beneficiary*: third-party beneficiary who is a creditor of a contracting party and whose obligation will be paid (in whole or in part) by performance of the contract. ▸ *Donee beneficiary*: third-party beneficiary to whom a party intends to give a benefit as a gift. ▸ *Incidental beneficiary*: party who may incidentally (indirectly) benefit from a contract even though the parties do not intend to contract for the benefit of that party.

- ***General rules***. ▸ A third party (creditor or donee) beneficiary can sue on and enforce a contract. An incidental beneficiary cannot enforce a contract. ▸ The contracting parties' intent is important in determining whether someone is a third-party beneficiary. ▸ The fact that a person receives a benefit does not, by itself, make that person a third-party beneficiary.

- ***Examples***. ▸ Creditor beneficiary: Tim owes Joe $100. Tim contracts to sell a TV to Nan, and the contract states that Nan shall pay the $100 to Joe. ▸ Donee beneficiary: Ross sold stock to Bea for $500, and the contract states that Bea shall pay the money to Ross' church. ▸ Incidental beneficiary: The New York Giants hire a quarterback for their football team. Persons holding New York Giants season tickets are incidental beneficiaries of the contract.

B. NOVATION

General rules. ▸ Novation: agreement by which a contract between two parties is terminated, and substituted in its place is a new contract between one of the original contracting parties and a new party. ▸ The contractual liability of the original party who is replaced in a novation is discharged (terminated). The substituted party is liable for performance of the new contract.

Limitations. ▸ A novation requires an agreement between all of the original contracting parties and the new party to be substituted. ▸ A novation occurs (and the original party is discharged) only if the parties intend that the second contract will replace and discharge the original contract.

C. ASSIGNMENT

General rules. ▸ Assignment: transfer of legal rights. ▸ An assignment transfers a contract right from a contracting party (assignor) to a third party (assignee). ▸ In general, an assignee can sue on and enforce an assigned right. ▸ In general, a party is free to assign most contract rights.

Limitations. ▸ Many states restrict or prohibit assignments of wages by various employees. ▸ In most cases, an employer cannot assign the right to an employee's services. ▸ In general, an assignment is invalid if the contract expressly prohibits assignments, although some courts hold such a prohibition to be invalid if only a right to money is being assigned.

D. DELEGATION

General rules. ▸ Delegation: transfer of a contractual duty. ▸ A party can delegate a duty only if the duty involves a standardized performance that can be easily evaluated according to recognized industry standards. ▸ A delegation cannot change or alter the performance required.

Limitations. ▸ A party cannot delegate a duty without the consent of the other party if: (1) the duty is personal in nature or it involves the taste, confidence, or trust of a party (e.g., painting a portrait; surgery; legal representation); or (2) the contract expressly prohibits a delegation.

Study hints.　　▸ A party who delegates a duty remains liable for performance of the duty. But the delegating party may sue the party to whom a duty is delegated if the duty is improperly performed. ▸ A duty to do many types of construction work or unskilled labor can be delegated.

II.　TECHNICALITIES OF AN ASSIGNMENT

A. NOTICE OF AN ASSIGNMENT

- *Rights between assignor and assignee*: An assignment is effective and binds the assignor and assignee when it is made, whether notice of assignment is given to others or not.

- *Multiple assignments*: In most states, if an assignor assigns the same right more than once and a debtor is notified of the assignments, the first assignee has priority.

- *Rights and duties of debtor*: ▸ Notice: If a right to receive money is assigned and the debtor is given notice of the assignment and told to pay the assignee, then payment to the assignee is required. Payment to the assignor does not discharge the debt. ▸ No notice: If a debtor is not given notice of an assignment, then payment to the assignor discharges the debt. ▸ If a right to only part of a sum of money is assigned, the debtor can either (1) continue to pay the assignor or (2) pay the amount assigned to the assignee.

B. FORM OF THE ASSIGNMENT

- *Assignment by operation of law*: On the death or bankruptcy of a party, the rights and duties of the party automatically pass to the executor of the estate or to the trustee in bankruptcy.

- *Assignment by contracting party*: ▸ Typically, an assignment can be oral or written. But, if a contract is required to be written, then an assignment must be written. ▸ Consideration is not required. ▸ An assignment must clearly indicate an intent to presently assign a right.

C. EFFECT OF AN ASSIGNMENT

- An assignee has only the same right to enforce a contract as the assignor had. A contractual defense that can be asserted against the assignor can also be asserted against the assignee.

- Unless otherwise agreed, an assignment does not excuse an assignor from any contractual duties. The assignor remains legally bound to perform all obligations.

D. WARRANTIES OF THE ASSIGNOR

General rule.　　If an assignment is made for value, the assignor automatically warrants to the assignee that: (1) the assignor owns the assigned right; (2) the assigned right is valid; and (3) the right is not subject to any defenses that have not been disclosed to the assignee.
Example.　　For value, Abe assigned to Ann the right to receive $500 from Tania. Unknown to Ann, Tania has a defense of fraud that negates her duty to pay. Abe breached a warranty.
Limitation.　　An assignee does *not* warrant that a debtor will pay or that a debtor is solvent.

III.　JOINT, SEVERAL, AND JOINT AND SEVERAL CONTRACTS

- *Joint contract*: ▸ Parties have a duty to collectively (i.e., jointly) perform the same act. ▸ Unless otherwise stated, a promise by two or more parties is presumed to be a promise to act jointly.

- *Several contract*: Each party has an obligation to individually perform the same act.

- *Joint and several contract*: Parties have an obligation to collectively perform the same act and, if requested, to individually perform the act.

REVIEW OF CHAPTER

REVIEW OF TERMS

Select the term that best matches a statement. Each term is the best match for only one statement.

TERMS

a. Assignment
b. Delegation
c. Incidental beneficiary
d. Joint and several contract

e. Joint contract
f. Novation
g. Several contract
h. Third-party beneficiary

STATEMENTS

Answer

____ 1. Third party who may indirectly benefit from a contract even though the contracting parties did not intend to make the contract for the benefit of that party.

____ 2. Contract in which two or more parties have the duty to collectively perform the same act, and each party also has a duty to individually perform that act.

____ 3. Transfer of a contract right to a third party.

____ 4. Transfer of a contractual duty to a third party.

____ 5. Third party whom contracting parties intend to directly benefit by a contract.

____ 6. Contract in which two or more parties each have an individual obligation to perform the same act.

____ 7. Contract in which two or more parties have an obligation to collectively perform the same act.

____ 8. Agreement to replace a contract with a new contract between one original party and a new party.

REVIEW OF CONCEPTS

Directions: Indicate **T** for true and **F** for false in the answer column.

____ 1. A third-party beneficiary can enforce a contract made between two other parties.

____ 2. A third-party beneficiary is anyone who may be directly or incidentally benefited by a contract.

____ 3. A person is not a third-party beneficiary unless the contracting parties intend to benefit that party.

____ 4. If a contractor contracted with a university to build a gymnasium for physical education classes, students at the university would be third-party beneficiaries of the contract.

____ 5. Tom contracted to buy a car from Hal. Tom, Hal, and Yin agreed that the contract between Tom and Hal was canceled and replaced with a contract between Hal and Yin. This is a novation.

____ 6. In a novation, the liability of the original contracting party who is replaced is not discharged.

____ 7. An assignment is a transfer of contract duties whereas a delegation is a transfer of contract rights.

____ 8. State laws frequently impose restrictions on assignments of wages.

____ 9. In general, an employer can assign the right to receive the services of an employee.

____ 10. An assignment of contract rights terminates all of the assignor's duties under the contract.

____ 11. If a debtor is not told that his or her debt has been assigned, then the debtor's payment to the assignor will discharge the debt; the assignee cannot sue the debtor to collect.

____ 12. An assignor who is paid value for an assignment warrants that he or she owns the assigned right.

REVIEW OF CONCEPT APPLICATIONS

Answer

Directions: Indicate your choice in the answer column.

____ 1. Which third party is a third-party beneficiary who can enforce the contract in question?
   a. Bank lent Alice $500 to pay bills. The loan contract states that the parties do not intend for any creditors of Alice to be third-party beneficiaries. Third party is a creditor of Alice.
   b. Ned contracted with Rock Insurance Co. whereby the insurance company agreed to pay $10,000 to Ned's sister (third party) upon Ned's death.
   c. Sara contracted to sell her car to Tom for $1,000. The contract requires Tom to pay the $1,000 directly to Last Chance Bank (third party) to whom Sara owes $1,000.
   d. b and c.

_____ 2. In most states, which right can be assigned without statutory restriction and without the consent of the party whose obligation is being assigned?

    a. Tasha wants to borrow $500. As security, Tasha wants to assign her right to her wages.

    b. Central Airlines wants to assign its right to the services of its employee, Captain Kelly.

    c. Danna contracted to pay $100 to Bret. Bret wants to assign the right to receive this money.

    d. All of the above.

_____ 3. Cody owed Don $1,000. Don orally told Cody and Sylvia: "I assign to Sylvia all of my right to be repaid the $1,000. Pay this sum to Sylvia." Sylvia did not give Don any consideration for this assignment. Under these facts:

    a. The assignment is invalid because it is oral. All assignments must be written.

    b. The assignment is invalid because Sylvia did not give Don any consideration.

    c. The assignment is valid and Cody must pay the $1,000 to Don.

    d. The assignment is valid and Cody must pay the $1,000 to Sylvia.

_____ 4. Art sold a truck to Luis for $20,000. Art misrepresented the truck. As a result, Luis has a defense and he is only obligated to pay Art $15,000. For value, Art assigned to Stella the right to receive the $20,000 from Luis. Luis was given notice of assignment. Under these facts:

    a. Luis must pay Stella $15,000.

    b. Luis must pay Stella $20,000

    c. Art did not breach any implied warranties that he made to Stella.

CASE PROBLEM

Erecto Construction Co. contracted to build a building for Owner. Without Owner's consent, Erecto delegated its duty to do excavation work to Gophers Inc. The excavation work is standardized work that does not require any special skill, and it can be easily evaluated according to recognized industry standards. Gopher did not properly do the work. Under these facts: (1) Was Erecto legally entitled to delegate its duty to Gopher without first obtaining Owner's consent? (2) Is Erecto liable to Owner for the improper work?

_____

_____

_____

BUSINESS LAW PARTNER EXERCISE

Directions: Access your Business Law Partner CD-ROM and find the document "Consulting Agreement." Complete this document using the information provided in the following case study. Supply any additional data as appropriate.

Case Study: *Want A Little Advice?*

CompCo Insurance agreed to hire Nate as a consultant to develop software for expediting payment of insured's claims. CompCo agreed to pay $25,000, payable upon installation of the software on CompCo's network. Nate agreed that the software belongs to CompCo and that he would not divulge any information to others. He also agreed that he would personally develop the software. He is to begin work on June 1, and is to be finished no later than December 1.

_____

_____

_____

CHAPTER 12 QUIZ

Section A

DIRECTIONS: Following each question below, indicate your answer by placing a "Y" for "Yes" or an "N" for "No" in the Answers column.

	Answers	For Scoring
1. Can a third person expressly benefited by the performance of the contract enforce it against the promisor if the benefit to the third party was intended by the contracting parties?	_____	1. _____
2. When an event must occur before the donee beneficiary is benefited, may the contracting parties change the beneficiary?	_____	2. _____
3. Do the terms of the contract remain the same when a novation is made?	_____	3. _____
4. Does whether rights may be assigned and duties delegated depend upon their nature and the terms of the contract?	_____	4. _____
5. Is the person to whom an assignment is made called the assignor?	_____	5. _____
6. As a general rule, can a person delegate personal duties and obligations?	_____	6. _____
7. Is it possible to delegate unskilled work or labor called for in a contract?	_____	7. _____
8. Does the delegating party escape liability by delegating to another the duties or obligations?	_____	8. _____
9. As a general rule, does the law require that notice of assignment be given?	_____	9. _____
10. If the assignor assigns a larger sum than the debtor owes, does the debtor have an obligation to pay the entire assignment?	_____	10. _____
11. Does the nonassigning party to a contract retain all rights and defenses?	_____	11. _____
12. Must the assignment be written if the law requires the original contract to be written?	_____	12. _____
13. Does the assignor warrant that the other party will perform the duties under the contract?	_____	13. _____
14. Can one party making an assignment impose new conditions upon the other without making the contract voidable?	_____	14. _____
15. Can one person be sued under the terms of a joint and several contract?	_____	15. _____

Score _____

Section B

DIRECTIONS: Complete each of the following statements by writing the missing word or words in the Answers column.

	Answers	For Scoring
1. A person who is not a party to a contract but whom the contracting parties intended to benefit is a(n)	_____	1. _____
2. A person to whom the promisee of a contract owes an obligation or duty, which will be discharged to the extent that the promisor performs the promise, is a(n)	_____	2. _____
3. A third party to whom the promisee of a contract owes no legal duty, but to whom performance of a contract is a gift, is a(n)	_____	3. _____
4. The termination of a contract and substitution of a new one with the same terms but a new party is called a(n)	_____	4. _____

5. The means whereby one party conveys rights under a contract to one who is not a party to the original undertaking is known as a(n) ....   _____   5. _____

6. The party making an assignment is known as the...   _____   6. _____

7. The one to whom contract rights are transferred by assignment is the ....   _____   7. _____

8. If one transfers duties or obligations under a contract but retains rights, the term used to describe the transfer is ....   _____   8. _____

9. A contract in which two or more persons together promise to carry out an obligation is a(n) ??? contract..   _____   9. _____

10. A contract in which two or more people individually agree to perform the same obligation even though the agreements are in the same document is a(n) ....   _____   10. _____

Score _____

Section C

DIRECTIONS: Following each question below, indicate your answer by placing a "Y" for "Yes" or an "N" for "No" in the Answers column.

Answers   For Scoring

1. Normally does one not a party to a contract have a right to the benefits to be derived from the contract?...   _____   1._____

2. May a party entitled to receive performance under a contract release the party bound to perform and permit another party to render performance?.........................   _____   2._____

3. Is everyone who benefits by the performance of a contract between others a third-party beneficiary with rights under the contract? ....   _____   3._____

4. Can one party making an assignment impose new conditions upon the other party to the contract? ....   _____   4._____

5. Can a third party acquire the rights or assume the duties of one of the original parties to a contract? ....   _____   5._____

6. Are there any laws prohibiting the assignment of certain rights? ....   _____   6._____

7. Can all contractual duties be assigned without the consent of the other contracting party? ....   _____   7._____

8. In general, does an assignment transfer all the right, title, or interest held by the assignor in whatever is being assigned? ....   _____   8._____

9. Is a special form of assignment necessary when made by operation of law? ....   _____   9._____

10. In most jurisdictions, if a party makes more than one assignment and the assignees all give notice to the obligor, is priority given according to the order in which notice was given? ....   _____   10._____

Score _____

CHAPTER 13
TERMINATION OF CONTRACTS

CHAPTER OUTLINE

I. METHODS BY WHICH CONTRACTS ARE TERMINATED

A contract may be discharged by: (1) the parties' performance of their duties; (2) operation of law; (3) agreement of the parties; (4) impossibility; or (5) acceptance of a breach of contract.

A. PERFORMANCE

▸ A contract is discharged (terminated) by the parties' performance of their contractual duties. ▸ If only one party has performed, that party is discharged, but the other party and the contract are not discharged. The party who performed can enforce the contract. ▸ Whether a performance (or offer to perform) discharges a duty depends on the concepts discussed below.

1. Time of Performance

- *Time stated*: ▸ If time for performance is stated in a contract, a party should perform within the time stated. Nonetheless, a late performance that is tendered (offered) within a reasonable time entitles a party to enforce a contract if time is not of the essence (i.e., timely performance is not vital). ▸ If time is of the essence, a party can enforce a contract only if the party performs his or her duties within the time stated in the contract.

- *Time not stated*: If time for performance is not stated in a contract, then a party is generally required to perform within a reasonable time.

2. Tender of Performance

General rules. ▸ Tender of performance: offer to perform contract duties. ▸ In general, a contracting party's refusal to accept a tender of performance by the other party (that does not involve payment of money) discharges the other party's duty to perform. The discharged party, however, retains the right to recover damages from the party refusing performance.
Example.   Olaf hires Tony to remodel Olaf's store. Tony tenders performance, but Olaf wrongfully refuses to allow Tony to do the work. Olaf's refusal discharges Tony. Tony is not obligated to remodel the store, but Tony can recover damages from Olaf.

3. Tender of Payment

General rules. ▸ Tender of payment: offer to pay money owed under a contract combined with the actual ability to pay. ▸ Refusal to accept a party's tender of payment: (1) does not terminate the duty to pay; but (2) does stop further interest and it enables the party to avoid liability for court costs that are incurred following the tender.
Example.   Loren and Greg made a contract. Loren properly offered to pay the contract price to Greg, but Greg wrongfully refused payment. Loren's duty is not discharged, but he does not have to pay interest or court costs that may accrue after he tendered payment.
Limitations.   ▸ A tender of payment requires that: (1) a party be able to pay; (2) the party offer to pay the entire debt, plus interest, costs, or attorney's fees owing; and (3) payment must be offered in legal tender (cash). ▸ Tender of a check is not a valid tender. ▸ If a creditor accepts a check, the debt is not discharged until the check is paid by the bank.

4. Satisfactory Performance

▸ If a person promises to perform to the satisfaction of a party regarding a matter of personal taste or judgment (e.g., painting a portrait), then performance is satisfactory and a duty is discharged only if the party is actually satisfied.

▸ If a mechanical or impersonal act is required to be done to the satisfaction of a party and the performance can be objectively evaluated (e.g., ordinary construction work), then a performance is acceptable and a duty is discharged if a reasonable person would be satisfied.

5. Substantial Performance

General rule.　　Modern law: A party who substantially performs contract duties can enforce a contract and can recover the contract price less damages caused by imperfect performance.

Example.　　Cassie agrees to paint Fran's house.　Cassie completes the work, except she unintentionally failed to paint one window.　Cassie can recover the price, less damages.

Limitation.　　A party cannot enforce a contract if the party intentionally fails to perform.

Study hint.　　Substantial performance typically exists if: (1) a party attempts to completely perform; (2) performance is nearly equivalent to what was required; (3) performance can be used by the other party for intended purposes; and (4) it would be unjust to deny recovery.

B. DISCHARGE BY OPERATION OF LAW

General rule.　　A contracting party's duty is discharged (cannot be enforced) if: (1) the party is discharged in bankruptcy; (2) the statute of limitations has run; (3) the other contracting party has improperly altered a material term of the contract; or (4) at the time the contract was made, it was impossible to perform the contract.

Limitations.　　▸ A debt that is barred by a running of the statute of limitations may be revived by a debtor.　Depending on the state, a debt may be revived by: (1) a written acknowledgment or promise to pay the debt; (2) part payment of principal; or (3) payment of interest.　▸ Once revived, the statute of limitations begins to run again from the date of revival.　▸ The statute of limitations is tolled (ceases to run) if a debtor leaves the state.

Study hints.　　▸ The statute of limitations begins to run only when a debt becomes due and, in the case of an open or running account, from the date of the last purchase.　▸ Discharge due to impossibility results from: (1) destruction of a specific subject matter that is essential for performing the contract; (2) a change in law that makes performance illegal; (3) death or physical incapacity of a party who is to perform a service that is of a personal nature or that involves a special skill; or (4) a wrongful act of a party.

Example.　　A doctor's contract to perform a heart transplant would be discharged by impossibility if: (1) the heart has been destroyed; (2) transplants become illegal; (3) the doctor or patient dies; or (4) the patient refuses to be operated on.

C. VOLUNTARY AGREEMENT OF THE PARTIES

A contract may be discharged as a result of (1) terms of the contract, e.g., the contract states that it ends on a certain date or (2) a mutual agreement of the parties.

D. ACCEPTANCE OF BREACH OF THE CONTRACT BY ONE OF THE PARTIES

If a party accepts a breach or anticipatory breach by the other party, the contract is discharged.

II.　　REMEDIES FOR BREACH OF CONTRACT

Under appropriate circumstances, a party may have the following remedies: (1) damages; (2) rescission; or (3) specific performance.

III. SUE FOR DAMAGES

A party can sue for damages (money) if: (1) the party can prove that the other party breached a contract; and (2) the party can reasonably prove his or her damages. Types of damages:

- *Nominal damages*: If a party can prove a breach by the other party but cannot prove any actual damages, a court may award nominal damages (e.g., $1 damages).

- *Compensatory damages*: ▸ A nonbreaching party can recover compensatory damages (damages sufficient to compensate a party for actual losses resulting from a breach). ▸ In general, a jury determines the amount of damages to be awarded.

- *Punitive (exemplary) damages*: ▸ In general: In most breach of contract cases, a party cannot recover punitive damages (damages awarded solely to punish a wrongdoer). Example: Employer fires Herman in breach of contract, but there is no tort. Herman cannot recover punitive damages. ▸ Exception: A party can get punitive damages if a breach is also a tort for which punitive damages are awarded (e.g., tenant intentionally destroys a rented home).

- *Liquidated damages*: ▸ A contract may state the amount of damages (liquidated damages) to be paid if the contract is breached. Liquidated damages are valid if: (1) actual damages are difficult to estimate; and (2) the stated amount is reasonable in light of probable damages. ▸ Example: Seller contracted to sell a business to Buyer. The contract states that if Seller breaches, Buyer can recover $10,000 liquidated damages. If damages are hard to estimate and this is a reasonable estimation of probable damages, then Buyer will recover $10,000 damages if Seller breaches. ▸ If the amount of liquidated damages is unreasonable, then the liquidated damage clause is invalid. In this event, a party can recover only his or her actual, compensatory damages.

IV. RESCIND THE CONTRACT

General rules. ▸ A party may be able to rescind a contract if the other party breaches the contract. ▸ If the rescinding party has performed, he or she may sue to recover what has been given. ▸ In a contract for the sale of goods, a party can rescind *and* sue for damages.
Example.   Eli contracted to buy a yogurt store franchise. In breach of contract, the franchise has been revoked and the business cannot use the franchise name. Eli can rescind the contract.

V. SUE FOR SPECIFIC PERFORMANCE

General rules. ▸ A party can obtain specific performance (i.e., a court order compelling performance of a contract) if damages and rescission are not adequate to remedy the harm caused by a breach. ▸ A party can obtain specific performance of a contract to buy: (1) real property or any interest in land; or (2) unique or rare goods.
Example.   A buyer can obtain specific performance of a contract to buy a house; a farm; a Picasso painting; a rare antique.
Limitation.   One cannot get specific performance of personal service or employment contracts.

VI. MALPRACTICE

▸ Malpractice is a breach of contract by an accountant, attorney, doctor, or other professional. Malpractice results from a professional's failure to use the care and skill that is typically used by other members of the profession. ▸ A professional is generally liable for damages resulting from his or her malpractice. ▸ Sometimes a third party has a right to sue a professional for malpractice.

REVIEW OF CHAPTER

REVIEW OF TERMS

Select the term that best matches a statement. Each term is the best match for only one statement.

TERMS

a. Anticipatory breach   c. Specific performance   e. Substantial performance
b. Malpractice   d. Statute of limitations   f. Time is of the essence

STATEMENTS

Answer

_____ 1. Failure to use the care and skill that is exercised by other professionals.

_____ 2. Law that limits the time within which a suit may be brought to enforce a legal right.

_____ 3. Timely performance is vital; timely performance is required to discharge a contractual duty.

_____ 4. Prior to time performance is required, a party announces that performance will not be rendered.

_____ 5. Equitable remedy requiring performance of a contract.

_____ 6. Doctrine authorizing a party to enforce a contract if the party has almost completely performed his or her contractual obligations.

REVIEW OF CONCEPTS

Directions: Indicate **T** for true and **F** for false in the answer column.

_____ 1. A contract is discharged when all parties fully perform their contractual duties.

_____ 2. If a land sale contract requires a seller to deliver title by June 1 and time is of the essence, then delivery of title on June 2 would be improper.

_____ 3. One party's refusal to accept a valid tender of performance by the other contracting party discharges (terminates) the other party's obligation to perform.

_____ 4. A valid tender of payment only requires an offer to pay the contract price; it need not include interest, costs, or attorney fees that are also due.

_____ 5. Refusal to accept a proper tender of payment by a party discharges the party's duty to pay.

_____ 6. A tender of payment must generally be made in legal tender (U.S. currency). But, if payment by check is accepted by a creditor, the debt is not discharged until the check is paid by the bank.

_____ 7. A party is not entitled to payment under a contract unless the party has perfectly performed all contractual obligations.

_____ 8. If a contracting party receives a discharge in bankruptcy, the discharge bars (prohibits) a creditor from enforcing the contract against the party who was discharged.

_____ 9. A party cannot sue to enforce a claim if the statute of limitations for the claim has run (expired).

_____ 10. The statute of limitations for a contractual debt begins to run when the contract is made, not when the debt becomes due.

_____ 11. In some states, a payment of principal or interest, or the debtor's acknowledgment of a debt may revive (renew) a debt that has been barred by the statute of limitations.

_____ 12. If a contracting party alters important terms of a contract without the consent of the other party, this act is improper, but it does not discharge the other party from the contract.

_____ 13. A contract is discharged by impossibility whenever it is harder to perform the contract than was anticipated, or when performance is delayed by foreseeable events, such as strikes.

_____ 14. In general, a party can recover punitive damages whenever another party breaches a contract.

_____ 15. Liquidated damage clauses are illegal and unenforceable.

_____ 16. A party can rescind a contract if the other party commits a major breach of contract.

_____ 17. A party can get specific performance even if damages adequately compensate for a breach.

_____ 18. Accountants and other professionals who breach a contract for professional services commit malpractice, and they may be sued for damages caused clients as a result of their malpractice.

REVIEW OF CONCEPT APPLICATIONS

Answer

Directions: Indicate your choice in the answer column.

_____ 1. Ken contracted to set up ordinary accounting books for Paul's business. The contract requires the books to be satisfactory to Paul. Ken set up the books in accordance with generally accepted accounting principles, and a reasonable person would be satisfied with the books. However, Paul refuses to pay because he is not actually satisfied with the books. Under these facts:
   a. Ken cannot enforce the contract because Paul is not actually satisfied with the books.
   b. Ken cannot enforce the contract because personal satisfaction contracts are illegal.
   c. Ken can enforce the contract because a reasonable person would be satisfied.
   d. Ken can enforce the contract because obligations to perform to another person's personal satisfaction are not enforced by courts.

_____ 2. JR contracted to renovate an historic home for June for $50,000. The renovations were completed as required, except JR unintentionally failed to refinish one oak banister. It will cost $250 to have the banister refinished. Under these facts, JR can recover:
   a. $0. JR failed to completely perform his duties. Thus, JR cannot enforce the contract.
   b. $49,750. JR substantially performed his duties. Thus, JR can enforce the contract, and June must pay for the contract price, less damages caused by JR's imperfect performance.
   c. $50,000. JR substantially performed his duties. Thus, JR can recover the full contract price.
   d. Only such amount, if any, that June may decide to pay JR.

_____ 3. Which contract is *not discharged* by impossibility?
   a. Acme Co. contracted to sell a pesticide to farmer. The contract was legal when made. Prior to performance, the FDA unforeseeably declared the pesticide illegal.
   b. XYZ contracted to sell a standard Sony stereo to Bob. Prior to performance, XYZ's stereos were destroyed by fire. XYZ can obtain the required stereo elsewhere to deliver to Bob.
   c. Larry, a rodeo star, agreed to appear in TV ads for Manufacturer's new saddle. Before the ads could be made, Larry died.
   d. Maria contracted to sew a custom-made dress for Claire. However, Claire now refuses to give her measurements to Maria.

_____ 4. Beth agreed to service a computer for AAA Tax Service. Beth unintentionally breached the contract. As a result, the computer suffered $250 damage. As could be anticipated, AAA also lost profits of $500 because it could not complete certain tax returns without the computer. Under these facts, what damages, if any, can AAA recover from Beth?
   a. AAA cannot recover any damages; Beth did not agree to pay for losses caused by a breach.
   b. AAA can only recover nominal damages of $1.
   c. AAA can only recover compensatory damages of $750.
   d. AAA can recover compensatory damages of $750, and punitive damages of $10,000.

_____ 5. Juan can obtain specific performance of which contract?
   a. Seller contracted to sell Juan a ranch. Seller wrongfully refuses to convey title.
   b. Juan bought a hybrid bull to be used for breeding. Seller wrongfully refuses to perform. The bull is unique and cannot be replaced. Damages cannot be measured.
   c. Juan hired Tex to be a ranch foreman. Tex wrongfully refuses to perform.
   d. a and b.

CASE PROBLEM

Mica Co. agreed to build a commercial storage building by September 1 for Pack Rat Storage. It was hard to predict Pack Rat's losses if the building was not completed on time. The parties estimated that Pack Rat would lose $100 in storage fees per day if the building was not completed on time. Thus, the contract required Mica to pay liquidated damages of $100 per day if the work was completed late. Mica finished 20 days late. Pack Rat actually lost $1,800 due to the breach. Under these facts:

1. Is the liquidated damage clause valid?
2. How much damages can Pack Rat recover from Mica?

_____

_____

_____

_____

BUSINESS LAW PARTNER EXERCISE

Directions: Access your Business Law Partner CD-ROM and locate the document entitled "Notice of Contract Termination."
1.   Complete this document using the information provided in the following case study.
2.   Does Acme have the legal right to terminate the contract in question?

Case Study: *Hey Buddy, You Are Terminated!*

Acme Tool Corporation hired Buddy as its district sales manager for its western district, commencing January 1, 1997. The Management Contract states that Acme may, at its option, terminate Buddy upon 60 days' prior written notice if annual gross sales of Acme's tools in Buddy's district fall below $5 million. During 1997 and 1998, sales in Buddy's district were $6 million and $5.5 million, respectively. In 1999, however, annual gross sales were only $4 million. On February 1, Acme's management instructs you to complete a Notice of Contract Termination for Buddy.

_____

_____

_____

_____

Section A

DIRECTIONS: Complete each of the following statements by writing the missing word or words in the Answers column.

	Answers	For Scoring
1. Johnson filed a petition in bankruptcy. He owed Kirk $100. Kirk received $60 in settlement of her claim. The contract was terminated by	_____	1. _____
2. Graham contracted to repair Young's house. She completed the work and received full payment. This contract was terminated by	_____	2. _____
3. Gates was injured in an automobile accident caused by Segrest. Gates wanted to be sure of the extent of his injuries and did not sue Segrest until three years after the accident. Segrest had the suit dismissed because the law prohibited the suit so long after the accident. This law is called the	_____	3. _____
4. Panovich contracted to sell 1,000 bales of cotton to O'Dell. O'Dell agreed to make a down payment of $5,000 in 7 days. O'Dell failed to make the payment, so Panovich said he was canceling the contract. Panovich has chosen to ??? the contract...	_____	4. _____
5. Ty contracted to supply Bob's Café with meat for 6 months. The price of meat went up and Ty told Bob he would not supply the meat. This is a(n) ...	_____	5. _____
6. George and Allen agreed to pool funds to purchase and restore an old car. Upon finding that he could finance the purchase without Allen's help, George asked to be released from his agreement. Allen said, "That's all right. I wasn't much interested anyhow." This contract was terminated by...	_____	6. _____
7. Eddy contracted to caulk the deck of the sloop Louise. Before he began the work, the Louise was destroyed by fire. This contract was terminated by.....	_____	7. _____
8. Jenkins bought a motor from Keene for $60 but refused to accept it or to pay for it when it was delivered. This is a	_____	8. _____
9. A suit in equity may be brought to compel a party to carry out the specific terms of the contract. This would be a suit requesting	_____	9. _____
10. A doctor negligently performed an appendectomy. The patient suffered severe complications. This constitutes	_____	10. _____

Score _____

Section B

DIRECTIONS: Following each question below, indicate your answer by placing a "Y" for "Yes" or an "N" for "No" in the Answers column.

	Answers	For Scoring
1. For a tender of payment, must the debtor offer the exact amount due to the creditor? .	_____	1. _____
2. Does proper tender of payment, even if refused, stop the running of interest?	_____	2. _____
3. If the contract requires performance to satisfy the personal taste or judgment of one of the parties, can that party reject the performance as unsatisfactory even if the performance would satisfy an ordinary, reasonable person?	_____	3. _____
4. If a construction contract is substantially performed, may the contractor demand the contract price less the damages suffered by the other party?	_____	4. _____
5. If the promisor leaves the state, does the statute of limitations continue to run?...........	_____	5. _____

6. If one party to a written contract makes an intentional material alteration of the contract without the consent of the other, is the contract terminated? .... _____ **6.** _____

7. When a contract calls for a routine performance not of a personal nature, is the contract terminated by the death or physical incapacity of the obligated party? .... _____ **7.** _____

8. Is the usual remedy for breach of contract to sue for specific performance? .... _____ **8.** _____

Score _____

Section C

DIRECTIONS: Following each statement below, indicate your answer by placing a "Y" for "Yes" or an "N" for "No" in the Answers column.

	Answers	For Scoring

1. Parties are discharged as soon as they have done all that they agreed to do. .... _____ **1.** _____

2. If the time of performance is not stated in the contract, it must be performed within a reasonable time. .... _____ **2.** _____

3. A contract is discharged due to impossibility if a party does not have sufficient money to perform the contract. .... _____ **3.** _____

4. The performing party to a contract may demand full price if the contract is substantially performed. .... _____ **4.** _____

5. Creditors do not have the right to force a person into involuntary bankruptcy............... _____ **5.** _____

6. A debt that has been barred by a statute of limitations cannot be revived. .... _____ **6.** _____

7. Any alteration to a written contract by one of the parties discharges the contract......... _____ **7.** _____

8. If the act called for in a contract is impossible to perform at the time the contract is made, there is no contract. .... _____ **8.** _____

9. Destruction of the subject matter of a contract by any cause discharges the contract because of impossibility of performance. .... _____ **9.** _____

10. The law of damages seeks to compensate the injured party for loss sustained without giving a profit for the other party's wrongdoing. .... _____ **10.** _____

Score _____

Section D

DIRECTIONS: In the Answers space in Column II, place the letter of the corresponding word or words from Column I.

Column I	Column II	Answers	For Scoring
(a) compensatory damages	**1.** An offer to perform an obligation in satisfaction of the terms of a contract	_____	**1.** _____
(b) damages			
(c) legal tender	**2.** Damages that entitle the injured party to payment of the exact amount of loss	_____	**2.** _____
(d) liquidated damages			
(e) nominal damages	**3.** Damages awarded when the plaintiff is unable to prove any loss has been suffered because of a breach of contract............	_____	**3.** _____
(f) punitive damages			
(g) satisfactory performance	**4.** An offer to pay money in satisfaction of a debt when one has the ability to pay	_____	**4.** _____
(h) substantial performance			
(i) tender of payment	**5.** A contract include a provision fixing the amount of damages to be paid in the event one party breaches the contract. Such a provision is called	_____	**5.** _____
(ii) tender of performance			
	6. Damages awarded to punish the wrongdoer, not to compensate the innocent party are called	_____	**6.** _____
	7. When the contract is performed in a manner that would satisfy an ordinary, reasonable person	_____	**7.** _____

Score _____

CHAPTER 14
NATURE OF PERSONAL PROPERTY

CHAPTER OUTLINE

I. INTRODUCTION

Property is anything that can be owned. The law protects the right to use property as well as the right to own it.

II. PERSONAL PROPERTY

General rules. ▸ Property is classified according to whether or not it can be moved. If it is movable property, it is personal property. ▸ Property that is not movable is real property. However, an interest in real property less than complete ownership, such as an easement, is usually considered personal property.
Examples. ▸ Cars. ▸ Books. ▸ Stock certificates. ▸ Furniture. ▸ Leases of land.

A. TANGIBLE PERSONAL PROPERTY

General rule. Tangible personal property is movable property that can be seen, touched, and possessed.
Examples. ▸ Clothing. ▸ Food. ▸ Silverware. ▸ Musical instruments. ▸ Desks.

B. INTANGIBLE PERSONAL PROPERTY

General rule. Intangible personal property is movable property that consists of evidences of ownership of rights or value.
Examples. ▸ Certificates of deposit. ▸ Contracts. ▸ Copyrights. ▸ Checks.

III. METHODS OF ACQUIRING PERSONAL PROPERTY

Title to property may be acquired by: (1) purchase; (2) will (property transfers on owner's death, following probate); and (3) gift (transfer without consideration). Title may also be acquired by:

- *Descent*: Property is transferred on the death of an owner who dies without a will.

- *Accession*: ▸ Property is increased by natural addition (colt is born) or by adding other property. ▸ If property owned by two parties is combined to form one product, the party who owned the largest part of the separate property owns the final product.

- *Confusion*: ▸ If goods belonging to two parties are commingled by accident or by mutual consent, each party owns a proportionate share. ▸ If one party wrongfully commingles goods with goods belonging to a second party and they cannot be separated, the second party owns the entire mass. ▸ Example: Cob pumps an unknown amount of oil into ABC's oil tank. ABC owns all of the oil.

- *Creation*: ▸ The creation of property (e.g., books, paintings, songs, inventions) gives the creator a right to obtain absolute title and exclusive use by obtaining a copyright or patent. ▸ A copyright must be registered in order for the owner to sue for copyright infringement.

IV. LOST AND ABANDONED PROPERTY

- *Abandoned property*: ▸ Defined: personal property that an owner throws away with no intent to reclaim. ▸ Example: family leaves its old lamp at the curb for the weekly trash pick-up. ▸ The person who finds and takes possession of abandoned property owns it.

- *Lost property*: ▸ Defined: personal property that an owner unintentionally loses. ▸ A person who finds lost property must return it to the true owner. Until the owner can be found, the finder has the right to possess the property. ▸ A finder of lost property may acquire title to the property if the owner cannot be found within a certain period of time. ▸ A few courts hold that lost property that is found during one's employment belongs to the employer until the owner is located.

- *Mislaid property*: ▸ Defined: property intentionally put somewhere by its owner, who then forgets about the property. ▸ The owner of the premises where mislaid property is left has the right to the property until the owner claims it. ▸ Example: Gail mislaid a watch in the Sands Hotel restroom. A person who finds the watch must turn it over to the hotel, which must hold it for Gail.

- *Uniform Disposition of Unclaimed Property Act*: This law that has been adopted in some states requires that unclaimed, abandoned property be turned over to the state.

V. BAILMENTS

General rules. ▸ A bailment is a legal relationship by which possession of personal property is delivered by one party (a bailor) to another party (a bailee), and the identical property is to be returned, delivered to a third party, sold, or accounted for in the manner agreed upon by the parties. ▸ Elements of a bailment: (1) an agreement; and (2) delivery and acceptance of personal property.
Examples. ▸ Bob holds Tom's watch for safekeeping. ▸ Al rents a car. ▸ Dan borrows a bike.
Limitation. A transfer of possession of land or real property is not a bailment.

VI. THE BAILMENT AGREEMENT

General rule. A bailment agreement may be express (oral or written), or it may be implied from the conduct of the parties.
Examples. ▸ Express: written car rental contract. ▸ Implied: Without speaking, Alice checks her shoes at the desk when she rents skates at an ice rink.

VII. DELIVERY AND ACCEPTANCE

General rules. ▸ A bailment is not made until property is delivered to a bailee and the bailee accepts the property. ▸ Delivery can be (1) actual (property is given to a bailee), or (2) constructive (property is not actually delivered, but the bailee exercises control over the property).
Examples. Actual: bailee takes rented tool. ▸ Constructive: bailee finds someone's lost tools.
Limitation. A bailment cannot occur unless a bailee accepts the property. Acceptance generally requires that the bailee know that the bailor has given the bailee possession of the property.
Study hint. A person who finds lost property holds the property as a bailee pursuant to a constructive bailment (bailment imposed by the law).

VIII. RETURN OF THE BAILED PROPERTY

General rule. A bailee must return or deliver the actual goods that the bailee received.
Limitations. ▸ Fungible goods: bailee can return different goods if goods returned are of same quality and quantity as goods originally delivered. ▸ Consignment: bailee need not return goods if they are sold. ▸ If goods are left for repair, the returned property will not be identical to the property that was left with the bailee.

IX. TYPES OF BAILMENTS

A. BAILMENTS FOR THE SOLE BENEFIT OF THE BAILOR

General rules. ▸ Nature of bailment: bailment made solely for the bailor's benefit. The bailee does not receive compensation or other benefits under the bailment. ▸ Bailee's duty: exercise slight care. ▸ Bailee's liability: liable only for gross negligence.
Example. Denise asks a friend to hold her purse while she makes a phone call.

B. BAILMENTS FOR THE SOLE BENEFIT OF THE BAILEE

General rules.   ▸ Nature of bailment: bailment made solely for the bailee's benefit. The bailor does not receive compensation or other benefits. ▸ Bailee's duty: exercise great care over the bailed property. ▸Bailor's duty: warn bailee of known dangers.

Example.   Iris borrowed Jackie's hedge clippers. Iris must take excellent care of the clippers. Jackie is required to warn Iris of known defects relating to the clippers. If Jackie knew the electric clippers had a frayed wire but didn't tell Iris, and Iris is injured because of that defect, Jackie is liable to Iris for the damages for her injury.

Limitation.   Any loss or damage to the bailed property that occurs without the bailee's fault falls upon the owner of the property.

C. MUTUAL-BENEFIT BAILMENTS

General rules.   ▸ Nature of bailment: the bailor and bailee both receive compensation or some benefit as a result of the bailment. ▸ Bailee's duty: exercise reasonable care under the circumstances. ▸ Bailee's liability: liable for ordinary negligence. ▸ Bailor's duty: furnish reasonably safe property (warning of known defects in the property is not sufficient).

Examples.   ▸ Jeanne left her car with Zeno's Garage for repairs. ▸ Kelly left a skirt with ABC Laundry for dry cleaning. ▸ Pat left furniture with R&R Storage Co. to be kept until she found a new home.

Limitation.   Unless the bailee is negligent or is using the bailed goods in an unauthorized manner, a bailee is not liable to the owner of the goods for damage caused by acts of third parties.

Study hints.   ▸ A bailee has a lien on bailed property entitling the bailee to keep the property until all storage or repair charges are paid. If the charges are not paid, a bailee may advertise and sell the property in order to obtain payment. A lien is lost if goods are voluntarily returned to a bailor. ▸ Most bailments are mutual-benefit bailments in which the bailee renders a service for which the bailee charges a fee. In some mutual-benefit bailments, the bailee may receive a benefit other than monetary payment.

D. SPECIAL MUTUAL-BENEFIT BAILMENTS

General rules.   ▸ Deposit of personal property as security for a debt or obligation creates a mutual-benefit bailment. ▸ A pawn occurs when tangible personal property is left as security for a debt or obligation. ▸ A pledge occurs when intangible personal property is left as security for a debt or obligation.

Examples.   ▸ Pawns might include automobiles, jewelry, livestock, or furniture. ▸ Pledges might include stock certificates, promissory notes, or bonds.

XI. CONVERSION OF BAILED PROPERTY BY THE BAILEE

General rules.   ▸ Conversion is the unauthorized exercise of ownership rights over someone else's property. ▸ A bailee ordinarily has no right to sell, lease, or use the bailed property as security for a debt or other obligation.

Limitations.   ▸ If the bailment is for consignment, or the purpose of the bailment is to have the bailed property sold and the proceeds given to the bailor, the bailee has the power to sell the bailed goods. Restrictions on such a bailee's right to sell are not effective unless the buyer knows of the restrictions. ▸ If the bailor has misled an innocent third person into believing that the bailee owns the bailed property, the bailee may convey good title to that third person.

Study hint.   Unless the sale fits into one of the exceptions just discussed, the sale of bailed property by a bailee does not pass good title to the purchaser.

REVIEW OF CHAPTER

REVIEW OF TERMS

Select the term that best matches a statement below. Each term is the best match for only one statement.

TERMS

a. Abandoned property
b. Accession
c. Bailee
d. Bailment for sole benefit of bailee
e. Bailment for sole benefit of bailor

f. Confusion
g. Constructive bailment
h. Bailor
i. Intangible personal property
j. Lost property

k. Mutual-benefit bailment
l. Pawn
m. Personal property
n. Pledge
o. Property
p. Tangible personal property

STATEMENTS

Answer

_____ 1. Inseparable mixing of goods of different owners.

_____ 2. Party to a bailment that delivers possession of personal property to the other party.

_____ 3. Bailment from which a bailor does not receive compensation or any benefit.

_____ 4. Party to a bailment that receives possession of personal property from the other party.

_____ 5. The acquiring of property by means of the addition of personal property of another.

_____ 6. Evidences of ownership of rights or value.

_____ 7. Property discarded by the owner with no intention to reclaim it.

_____ 8. Bailment from which a bailee does not receive compensation or any benefit.

_____ 9. Bailment imposed when someone finds and takes control of lost property.

_____ 10. Personal property that can be seen, touched, and possessed.

_____ 11. Property unintentionally left, but with no intention to discard it.

_____ 12. Tangible property (e.g., a TV) that is given as security for a debt.

_____ 13. Bailment that benefits both the bailor and the bailee.

_____ 14. Intangible property (e.g., stock) that is given as security for a debt.

_____ 15. Anything that may be owned.

_____ 16. Movable property, interests in land that are less than complete ownership, and rights to money.

REVIEW OF CONCEPTS

Directions: Indicate **T** for true and **F** for false in the answer column.

_____ 1. Stock certificates are tangible property.

_____ 2. Creation of an invention does not automatically give a creator absolute title to the invention. To get absolute title, the creator must obtain a patent.

_____ 3. A party who finds lost property is automatically the owner of the property.

_____ 4. The Uniform Disposition of Unclaimed Property Act requires finders of abandoned property to turn the property over to the state.

_____ 5. Personal property may be acquired by purchase, will, gift, descent, accession, confusion, or creation.

_____ 6. Property is considered lost if the owner discards it with no intention of reclaiming it.

_____ 7. Lessor leases a home to Lessee. This transaction is a bailment.

_____ 8. A bailment cannot be implied from the conduct of the parties. A bailment must be expressly agreed upon.

_____ 9. If a person finds lost property belonging to another, the finder holds the property as a bailee pursuant to a constructive bailment (a bailment imposed by law).

_____ 10. A bailment is created if ABC delivers a carload of barley (fungible goods) to XYZ pursuant to a contract that permits XYZ to return a carload of different barley provided it is of equal quality.

_____ 11. If a person gratuitously agrees to keep and take care of a friend's pet, this is an example of a bailment for the sole benefit of the bailor.

_____ 12. If a person takes a suit to the dry cleaners and pays to have it cleaned, a mutual-benefit bailment is created.

_____ 13. In a bailment for the sole benefit of the bailee, a bailee owes a bailor a duty of great care over the property.

_____ 14. A mutual-benefit bailee's duty to care for property is measured by a fixed test. The care required is not affected by the nature of the property of a bailee's skill or experience in caring for this type of property.

_____ 15. A bailee is liable for any damage to property even if the bailee is not negligent and damage is not due to the unauthorized use of the property by the bailee.

_____ 16. A bailee has the right to use bailment property for any purpose the bailee desires.

_____ 17. A pawn or a pledge creates a mutual-benefit bailment.

_____ 18. A person who purchases bailed property from the bailee usually gets good title.

REVIEW OF CONCEPT APPLICATIONS

Answer

Directions: Indicate your choice in the answer column.

_____ 1. George found a diamond bracelet in a wall safe that was in his hotel room. The bracelet was placed in the safe by its owner, who then forgot about the bracelet. Under these facts:
  a. The bracelet is abandoned property. George owns the bracelet.
  b. The bracelet is lost property. George may keep the bracelet until the owner reclaims it.
  c. The bracelet is mislaid property. George must turn the bracelet over to the hotel owner.

_____ 2. In the following cases involving delivery and acceptance, select the correct answer.
  a. Hill rents a boat to Neuman. The boat is located at a distant lake. Hill gives Neuman keys to the boat. Neuman drives to the lake and takes possession of the boat. In this case, Neuman is a bailee.
  b. Rose rents a locker at Airport and puts a bag in the locker. Rose keeps the locker key. In this case, Airport is a bailee of the bag.
  c. Unknown to Lonnie, Jake left a bike at Lonnie's house. In this case, Lonnie is a bailee of the bike.
  d. a and b.

_____ 3. Which of the following statements correctly describes the type of property involved?
  a. Checks, stock certificates, certificates of deposit, and contracts are types of tangible personal property.
  b. Leaseholds are normally classified as real property since they involve interests in land or buildings, which are real property.
  c. Growing crops are a type of intangible personal property.
  d. Animals, furniture, clothing, and jewelry are types of tangible personal property.

_____ 4. Quinn rents a paint spray gun from U-Rent-Um Rentals for $25 per day. This bailment is correctly described as a:
  a. Bailment for the sole benefit of the bailor.
  b. Bailment for the sole benefit of the bailee.
  c. Mutual-benefit bailment.
  d. Pawn.

_____ 5. Roxie agreed to repair Tom's TV for $100. Pursuant to their contract, Tom delivered the TV set to Roxie. Roxie properly repaired the TV. Tom now refuses to pay for the repairs. Under these facts:
   a. Roxie does not have a lien on the TV. Roxie must return the TV to Tom even if he fails to pay the repair charge.
   b. Roxie has a lien on the TV. Roxie can keep the TV until Tom pays the repair charge.
   c. Roxie has a lien on the TV even if she voluntarily returns the TV to Tom.
   d. b and c.

_____ 6. Sis rented a stereo for her apartment from Rent Co. Without authorization, Sis sold the stereo to Third Party who did not know that the stereo belonged to Rent Co. Under these facts:
   a. Sis was legally entitled to sell the stereo. Third Party received good title to the stereo.
   b. Sis should not have sold the stereo. However, since Rent Co. entrusted the stereo to Sis, Sis could transfer Rent Co.'s title and Third Party received good title to the stereo.
   c. Sis was not legally entitled to sell the stereo. Third Party did not receive title to the stereo.

CASE PROBLEM

Roger wanted to go water skiing, but he did not have any skis. Roger's friend, Manuel, lent Roger a pair of skis. Manuel did not charge Roger a rental fee. While Roger was skiing, a defective foot support tore loose, causing Roger to fall and break his leg. Manuel did not know that the foot support was defective. However, Manuel did not inspect the skis before lending them to Roger. Under these facts:

1. What type of bailment is involved in this case?
2. Describe the duty that Manuel owed to Roger.
3. Describe the duty that Roger owned to Manuel.
4. Is Manuel liable to Roger for Roger's injuries? Is Roger liable for the damage to the skis?

_____

_____

_____

BUSINESS LAW PARTNER EXERCISE

Directions: Access your Business Law Partner CD-ROM and locate the document entitled "Equipment Lease."

1. Complete the above-referenced document using the information provided in the following case study.
2. Is the lease a bailment?

Case Study: *Avoiding Minor Problems*

Ace Rentals agreed to lease a backhoe to Dillard. The lease term is three years, commencing May 1. Dillard agreed to pay an annual rent of $4,800, payable $400 on the first day of each month during the lease term. Dillard cannot remove the equipment from the county, and must have all ordinary maintenance and minor repairs done at its own expense. Ace agreed to make any major repairs that are not due to ordinary wear and tear or Dillard's negligence. Dillard must insure the backhoe for $20,000, with Ace named as an additional insured. Ace requests you, as his manager, to complete the lease, making sure that any other lease terms favor Ace.

_____

_____

_____

CHAPTER 14 QUIZ

Section A

DIRECTIONS: Following each question below indicate your answer by placing a "Y" for "Yes" or an "N" for "No" in e Answers column.

	Answers	For Scoring
1. Does registration of copyrights protect authors for their lifetime plus 50 years?	_____	1. _____
2. Do finders of lost or abandoned property both acquire title to the property?	_____	2. _____
3. In some states, does property that is found by an employee in the course of employment belong to the employer?................	_____	3. _____
4. May a bailment result from either an express or an implied agreement?	_____	4. _____
5. Must the bailee always return the identical goods to the bailor?	_____	5. _____
6. In the case of a bailment for the sole benefit of the bailor, must the bailee exercise only slight care with respect to the property?	_____	6. _____
7. In the case of a bailment for the sole benefit of the bailee, must the bailee be informed of known defects in the bailed property?	_____	7. _____
8. Is the rental of personal property an example of a bailment for the sole benefit of the bailee?	_____	8. _____
9. Can the bailee in a bailment for the sole benefit of the bailor use the property for the bailee's personal benefit?	_____	9. _____
10. Is the bailor obligated to notify the bailee of any known defects in the bailed property?	_____	10. _____
11. In the absence of an agreement to do so, must the bailee insure the property?	_____	11. _____

Score _____

Section B

DIRECTIONS: Write your answer in the Answers column.

	Answers	For Scoring
1-3. Alice borrowed Ed's pickup truck. Who is the bailor?....................................	_____	1. _____
Who is the bailee?	_____	2. _____
What degree of care must Alice exercise?	_____	3. _____
4-6. Melinda rented a car while on vacation. She was told the hatchback window was loose. While she was driving from the rental agency to her hotel, the hatchback window fell onto the street and broke. What type of bailment is this?	_____	4. _____
Who is the bailor?	_____	5. _____
The standard the bailor's property must meet is that the property must be	_____	6. _____
7-9. Sally left her watch with the Towne Jewelry Company for repair. The watch was placed in the store safe for the night along with the company's property. The safe was robbed during the night. Sally sought to recover the value of the watch from Towne. For whose benefit was this bailment?.........	_____	7. _____
What degree of care was the bailee obligated to exercise?	_____	8. _____
Was the company liable to Sally?	_____	9. _____

Score _____

Section C

DIRECTIONS: Complete each of the following statements by writing the missing word or words in the Answers column.

	Answers	For Scoring
1. Anything that may be owned, possessed, used, or disposed of is	_____	1. ____
2. All movable property is..	_____	2. ____
3. Movable property that can be seen, touched, and possessed is	_____	3. ____
4. Obtaining ownership of property by payment is acquiring ownership through	_____	4. ____
5. A transfer of property that is made without consideration is called a(n)	_____	5. ____
6. Acquiring property by the addition of movable property of another is	_____	6. ____
7. Mixing the goods of different owners so the parts belonging to each cannot be identified or separated is known as..	_____	7. ____
8. One who obtains a patent gets title to a product by..................................	_____	8. ____
9. Discarding property with no intention of reclaiming it makes the property ...	_____	9. ____
10. Property left unintentionally with no desire to discard it is called..................	_____	10. ____
11. Transfer of possession of movable property on condition it will be returned is a(n)..	_____	11. ____
12. A person who gives up possession, but not title, to personal property is a(n)	_____	12. ____
13. The person who receives possession of personal property is a(n).................	_____	13. ____
14. To create a bailment, there must be both delivery and ??? of property.	_____	14. ____
15. When control of goods is delivered and accepted without physical delivery, the delivery is said to be	_____	15. ____
16. The transfer of possession of tangible personal property as security for a debt is known as a(n)...	_____	16. ____
17. The deposit of intangible personal property as security for debt is a(n)	_____	17. ____
18. What degree of care is considered reasonable when a person takes possession of lost property?..	_____	18. ____
19. For whose benefit is the bailment when a person finds lost property?	_____	19. ____
20. In ordinary bailments, the standard of care required of the bailee is	_____	20. ____

Score _____

CHAPTER 15
SPECIAL BAILMENTS

CHAPTER OUTLINE

I.   INTRODUCTION

Mutual-benefit bailments in which the bailee was, under common law, held to a higher than normal standard of care for the bailed property are extraordinary bailments. Bailees in extraordinary bailments include common carriers and hotelkeepers.

II.   CARRIERS

A carrier is an individual or company that transports goods or persons, or both, for compensation. A carrier of goods is a bailee.

III.   CLASSIFICATION OF CARRIERS

Carriers are usually classified as private or common carriers.

A. PRIVATE CARRIERS

General rules.   ▸ Private carrier: transports goods or persons for pay, but is unwilling to do so for everyone. ▸ Characteristics: (1) services are provided under individual contracts; (2) carrier can refuse service if unprofitable; and (3) carriers can, by contract, limit their liability for loss of goods. ▸ Private carrier contracts are mutual-benefit bailments (carrier is liable only for its negligence, or the failure to exercise ordinary care).
Examples.   ▸ Moving company. ▸ Express delivery firm. ▸ Shipping line. ▸ Truck line.

B. COMMON CARRIERS

General rules.   ▸ Common carrier: transports goods or persons, for pay, for all persons who apply. ▸ A common carrier generally has a duty to provide services to all persons who request service, without discrimination. Failure to do so renders carrier liable for damages. ▸ Shipper is consignor; one to whom goods are shipped is consignee.
Examples.   ▸ Airline. ▸ Passenger train line. ▸ Bus line. ▸ Passenger ship.
Limitations.   A carrier can refuse service if: (1) the carrier does not have necessary facilities;
(2) a passenger requires unusual attention, but is not accompanied by attendant; (3) a passenger is likely to injure the carrier or other passengers; (4) a passenger is highly offensive to others (e.g., drunk); or (5) the goods to be shipped are improper.

IV.   LIABILITY OF COMMON CARRIERS OF GOODS

In general, regardless of fault, a common carrier of goods is liable for the loss of, or damage to, goods resulting from any cause. However, a common carrier is not liable for losses resulting from:

- *Acts of God*: Natural, unforeseeable occurrences, such as a hurricane, tornado, or snowstorm.
- *Acts of a public authority*: Act of a public official, such as confiscation of illegal goods by police.
- *Inherent nature of the goods*: Natural deterioration of goods, such as spoilage of vegetables.
- *Acts of the shipper*: Negligence of shipper (consignor), such as an inaccurate description of goods.
- *Acts of public enemy*: Organized warfare. This exception does not apply to riots or strikes.

V. CONTRACTUAL LIMITATIONS ON LIABILITY

- *Controlling law*: ▸ Intrastate shipment: UCC. ▸ Interstate shipment: Federal Bills of Lading Act.
- *Limitations of liability*: ▸ Carrier can limit liability to a stated amount if a shipper is given an option to ship goods for a higher fee without a limit on liability. ▸ Most states permit elimination of liability for some causes (e.g., breakage, strikes, and theft) if loss is not due to carrier's negligence.

VI. DURATION OF THE SPECIAL LIABILITY

- *During transportation*: The carrier's extraordinary liability lasts only during transportation.
- *Before and after transportation*: If a carrier holds goods prior to shipment awaiting a shipper's instructions or payment, or if the consignee does not pick up goods within a reasonable time after notification, the carrier is a mutual-benefit bailee, liable only for losses caused by its negligence.
- *Connecting carriers*: If goods are shipped using two or more carriers, the first and last carriers are liable for damages caused by a connecting carrier. In turn, they may seek reimbursement from the connecting carrier.

VII. BILLS OF LADING

▸ A bill of lading is a document of title issued by a carrier for goods to be shipped. It serves as a receipt and contract between the shipper (consignor) and the carrier. ▸ Transferring the bill of lading to a buyer may pass title to goods covered by a bill of lading. ▸ Types of bill of lading include:

A. STRAIGHT BILLS OF LADING

- *Description*: Goods sent to named party (consignee); words "bearer" or "order" are not used.
- *Delivery obligations*: Carrier may deliver goods to consignee without receiving bill of lading.
- *Third party rights*: ▸ Party to whom a consignee transfers a straight bill of lading only gets the title to goods (if any) owned by the consignee. ▸ A carrier is liable to a transferee of a bill of lading if statements in the bill regarding the contents, quantity, or weight of goods are false, unless the bill of lading states that the carrier is unaware of the shipment's contents.

B. ORDER (NEGOTIABLE) BILLS OF LADING

- *Description*: Goods are shipped "to the bearer" or "to the order" of a named person.
- *Delivery obligations*: Carrier must not deliver goods without first getting the bill of lading.
- *Third party rights*: Carrier is liable to a bona fide transferee of an order bill of lading if the carrier delivers goods to another person (e.g., consignee) without first getting a bill of lading.

VIII. COMMON CARRIERS OF PERSONS

A common carrier of persons can (1) adopt reasonable rules, (2) set the time and place for payment of fares, usually prior to boarding, (3) refuse to transport persons who do not pay the fare or whose conduct offends the other passengers, (4) stop the carrier to remove offensive persons or persons who cannot prove payment of the fare, and (5) and reserve facilities for special classes of passengers.

IX. LIABILITY OF COMMON CARRIERS OF PERSONS

▸ During transportation: As soon as a passenger boards, carrier owes a passenger the highest degree of care consistent with practical operation. However, a carrier is not absolutely liable for the safety of passengers.
▸ Prior to boarding and after disembarking: carrier owes passengers only a duty of ordinary care while in the carrier's terminal or on the waiting platform.

X. DUTIES OF COMMON CARRIERS OF PERSONS

- **Duty to provide reasonable accommodations and services**: Carrier must furnish reasonably adequate and safe service and accommodations, e.g., restroom facilities. Passenger is not necessarily entitled to a seat unless one is expressly reserved.

- **Duty to provide reasonable protection to its passengers**: ▸ Carrier must exercise highest degree of care to protect passengers, but it is not an insurer of absolute safety of passengers. ▸ Carrier is liable for an injury inflicted by an employee or fellow passenger if the injured party is not at fault.

XI. BAGGAGE

▸ Baggage: articles of personal convenience or necessity usually carried by passengers for their personal use during their trip. ▸ Test: items that a reasonable traveler would carry on a similar trip. Baggage does not include goods carried for someone other than a passenger. ▸ A passenger may be charged an extra fee for transporting goods other than baggage or for transporting baggage in excess of a reasonable amount. ▸ Baggage held by carrier: common carrier historically was absolutely liable for any damage or losses, with the five exceptions previously noted (see Section IV). ▸ Today, carriers may limit their liability for loss of baggage to a fixed maximum amount stated on the ticket.

XII. HOTELKEEPERS

General rule.   A hotelkeeper is an operator of a hotel, motel, or other facility who regularly engages in the business of offering living accommodations to transients (guests), not permanent lodgers.
Example.   Bishop Motel provides rooms for overnight guests; it is subject to hotelkeepers' law.
Study hints.   ▸ A tourist home that does not advertise as willing to accommodate all transient persons who apply is not a hotelkeeper. ▸ One who offers rooms or room and board to permanent lodgers is a boardinghouse keeper and is not subject to the laws regulating hotelkeepers.

XIII. WHO ARE GUESTS?

General rules.   ▸ Guest: transient person who stays overnight or on a temporary basis. ▸ The hotelkeeper-guest relationship begins when a person is received as a guest by the hotelkeeper. The relationship ends when the guest: (1) departs; or (2) makes arrangements to stay permanently.
Study hints.   ▸ A guest does not include: (1) a person who is merely visiting a guest at a hotel; (2) a person having dinner or attending a function at a hotel; or (3) a passerby who is only temporarily visiting an establishment. ▸ A guest need not be a traveler from a distance. ▸ An owner of a condominium or timeshare unit who rents the unit to another person is not a hotelkeeper with regard to the person who rented the unit.

A. DUTIES OF A HOTELKEEPER

- **Duty to serve all who apply**: In general, a hotelkeeper must provide accommodations to all who apply. A hotel may not discriminate based on race, color, religion, or national origin. A hotel is not obligated to provide rooms to: (1) offensive, intoxicated persons; (2) criminally violent persons; (3) persons improperly dressed in violation of reasonable hotel rules; or (4) persons seeking accommodations if the establishment is full.

- **Duty to protect a guest's person**: A hotelkeeper has a duty to exercise reasonable care to protect the safety of a guest, patron, or visitor. A hotelkeeper is only liable for injuries caused by its willful wrongdoing or its negligence. A hotelkeeper who knows of prior criminal acts on or near the premises must provide additional security.

- **Duty to care for the guest's property**: State statutes allow hotelkeepers to limit their liability.

B. HOTELKEEPER'S LIEN

A hotelkeeper has a lien on a guest's baggage for the amount of services provided. The lien is lost if the baggage is returned to a guest, even if the room charges have not yet been paid.

REVIEW OF CHAPTER

REVIEW OF TERMS

Select the term that best matches a statement below. Each term is the best match for only one statement.

TERMS

a. Baggage	f. Consignee	k. Order (negotiable) bill of lading
b. Bill of lading	g. Consignor	l. Permanent resident
c. Boardinghouse keeper	h. Guest	m. Private carrier
d. Carrier	i. Hotelkeeper	n. Straight bill of lading
e. Common carrier	j. Hotelkeeper's lien	o. Transient

STATEMENTS

Answer

_____ 1. Articles of personal convenience/necessity carried by passengers for their use during a trip.

_____ 2. Carrier that transports goods or persons for compensation, but does not hold itself out as being willing to serve all persons who request service.

_____ 3. Document of title issued by a carrier for goods to be transported.

_____ 4. Party to whom goods are shipped.

_____ 5. Bill of lading shipping goods "to the bearer" or "to the order of" a named person.

_____ 6. Carrier that transports goods or persons for compensation, for all persons who request service.

_____ 7. Party engaging in the business of shipping goods or transporting persons for compensation.

_____ 8. Party who ships goods by common carrier.

_____ 9. Bill of lading shipping goods to a named person without using the words "bearer" or "order."

_____ 10. Party who engages in the business of offering accommodations to transient persons.

_____ 11. Person who retains accommodations for a substantial, indefinite period of time.

_____ 12. Party who engages in the business of offering accommodations to permanent lodgers.

_____ 13. Transient person who is provided overnight accommodations by a hotelkeeper.

_____ 14. Legal right to retain a guest's baggage to assure payment of room charges.

_____ 15. Person who intends to stay in a location for only a short period of time.

REVIEW OF CONCEPTS

Directions: Indicate **T** for true and **F** for false in the answer column.

_____ 1. A private carrier is only required to ship goods for those parties that it may choose to serve.

_____ 2. A private carrier is liable for damage to goods that results from any cause whatsoever.

_____ 3. Subject to a few exceptions, a common carrier must provide service to anyone who requests it.

_____ 4. A common carrier is only liable for damage to goods that is caused by the carrier's negligence.

_____ 5. The Federal Bills of Lading Act governs bills of lading for goods shipped in interstate commerce.

_____ 6. Common carriers can limit their liability for loss of goods to a specified amount only if a shipper is offered the option of paying a higher fee for shipping the goods without a limitation of liability.

_____ 7. Most states allow common carriers to avoid liability for certain hazards such as fire, breakage, strikes, or theft, but only if this provision is stated on the bill of lading.

_____ 8. An initial carrier cannot be held liable for damage caused by a connecting carrier.

_____ 9. Title to goods described in a bill of lading may be passed by transferring the document to a buyer.

_____ 10. Unless otherwise notified, a carrier is entitled to deliver goods under a straight bill of lading to the consignee without first requiring that the carrier be given the bill of lading.

_____ 11. In a dispute between a bona fide transferee of a bill of lading and a carrier, statements in the bill of lading regarding contents, quantity, or weight are not binding on the carrier.

_____ 12. A person who offers accommodations to only permanent guests is classified as a hotelkeeper.

_____ 13. Leslie attended a reception held at the Freeport Hotel. In this case, Leslie is not a guest.

_____ 14. The hotelkeeper-guest relationship begins as soon as a person makes a reservation for a room.

_____ 15. In general, hotelkeepers can refuse accommodations to anyone they choose.

_____ 16. The Federal Civil Rights Act forbids certain types of discrimination, but it does not prohibit hotelkeepers from discriminating against persons on the basis of race, religion, or national origin.

_____ 17. A hotelkeeper is absolutely liable for any injury a guest may suffer.

_____ 18. A hotelkeeper has a duty to take reasonable steps to provide fire escapes and to take appropriate steps that will help contain fires that may break out at the hotel.

_____ 19. Traditionally, a hotelkeeper had a high duty to care for a guest's property. Nonetheless, a hotelkeeper was not liable for loss of property caused by an act of God or by an act of the guest.

_____ 20. In most states a hotelkeeper does not have a lien on a guest's car to secure payment of room charges.

_____ 21. Boardinghouse keepers are subject to the same laws as hotelkeepers.

REVIEW OF CONCEPT APPLICATIONS

Answer

Directions: Indicate your choice in the answer column.

_____ 1. In which case is Conn Carrier (a common carrier) liable for the damage or loss in question?
   a. During shipment, goods are confiscated by government health officials.
   b. During shipment, goods are destroyed by an unforeseeable earthquake.
   c. During shipment, goods are damaged due to improper packaging by the shipper.
   d. During shipment, goods are stolen by a thief.

_____ 2. Air Inc. (a common carrier) contracted to transport equipment for Shipper. Shipper requested Air Inc. to hold the equipment for one week prior to shipment. During this time, the equipment was damaged. Is Air Inc. liable for the damage to the equipment?
   a. Yes, if equipment was damaged due to the negligence of Air Inc.
   b. Yes, if equipment was damaged by a third party, without negligence on the part of Air Inc.
   c. No. A carrier is not liable for damage if it is merely holding goods at a shipper's request.
   d. a and b.

_____ 3. Pat shipped goods with Freight Inc. Freight Inc. issued Pat a bill of lading for the goods which directs delivery "to the bearer." Pat negotiated (transferred) the bill of lading to Steve who bought the goods and bill of lading for value and in good faith. The next day, Freight Inc. delivered the goods to Pat without first receiving the bill of lading. Under these facts:
   a. The bill of lading is a straight bill of lading.
   b. The bill of lading is an order (negotiable) bill of lading.
   c. Freight Inc. acted properly in delivering the goods to Pat, and it is not liable to Steve.
   d. a and c.

_____ 4. Ellen bought an economy ticket for a short commute on R&R Railroad, a common carrier. Ellen did not buy a reserved seat that was available. In which case would R&R be liable to Ellen?
   a. Ellen was injured when, on her way to the lounge, she fell down due to her own negligence.
   b. Ellen was injured when an R&R employee negligently dropped a suitcase on her foot.
   c. Ellen had reasonable accommodations but had to stand because there were no available seats.
   d. Ellen was asked to leave the train when she could not prove payment for her ticket.

_____ 5. In which situation is the Downtowner Hotel entitled to refuse accommodation to Paula?
   a. Paula is denied a room because she is Black.
   b. Paula is denied a room because the hotel does not have any available rooms.
   c. Paula is denied a room because she is intoxicated and she is insulting hotel guests.
   d. b and c.

_____ 6. A fire occurred at the Candlelight Motel. The fire was started by a cigarette that was negligently discarded by a visitor at the motel. Stan, a guest at the Candlelight, was injured in the fire. The Candlelight was not negligent. Under these facts, is the Candlelight liable for Stan's injuries?
   a. Yes. A hotelkeeper is absolutely liable for all injuries to guests.
   b. No. A hotelkeeper has a duty to exercise reasonable care to protect guests. Consequently, the Candlelight is not liable for Stan's injuries because it was not negligent.
   c. No. A hotelkeeper is not liable for injuries to guests.

_____ 7. Daisy checked into the Palms Motel for an overnight stay. Daisy left a coat in her room. While Daisy was having dinner, her coat was taken from her room. Under these facts:
   a. Traditionally, the Palms would have been liable for the missing coat.
   b. Traditionally, the Palms would have been liable for the missing coat only if the loss had been caused by the negligence of the Palms.
   c. In most states, statutes would prohibit the Palms from limiting its liability.

CASE PROBLEM

Larry booked passage on the Island Ferry, a common carrier. Larry was traveling to an island for a camping trip. Larry stored two bags containing clothes and camping gear with the ferry. He kept in his possession a backpack that contained personal travel items. He carried on two large crates that his employer had asked him to deliver to a store located on the island. (1) Were the bags, backpack, and crates baggage? (2) Could Larry be charged an extra fee for transportation of the crates? (3) If the checked bags were stolen without negligence on the part of the ferry, would the ferry be liable for these losses?

_____

_____

_____

_____

BUSINESS LAW PARTNER EXERCISE

Directions:

1. Access your Business Law Partner CD-ROM. Then, locate and identify the federal regulation that regulates limitations of liability by interstate common carriers.
2. For how much can Lawrence be held liable in this case?

Case Study: *All Aboard!*

Lawrence owned a business that transported passengers by bus from his hometown across the state border to a location where gambling was legal. One day, Sally bought a ticket and bordered Lawrence's bus, carrying a single suitcase. The ticket given Sally stated that Lawrence's liability was limited to $250 for lost luggage unless the passenger wanted to pay a higher tariff for greater coverage. Sally did not read this term of the ticket. When the bus arrived at the destination, everyone exited including Lawrence and Sally. Sally, however, forgot her suitcase and it disappeared from the bus. The suitcase contained $1,000 in quarters.

_____

_____

_____

CHAPTER 15 QUIZ

Section A

DIRECTIONS: Complete each of the following statements by writing the missing word or words in the Answers column.

	Answers	For Scoring
1. A party engaged in the business of transporting goods and/or persons is a(n)	_____	1. _____
2. Parties who do not hold themselves as being able or willing to offer their services to all, but who may transport specific goods/persons for a fee are...	_____	2. _____
3. A party who undertakes to transport, without discrimination, goods or persons for all who apply and whose business is so extensive as to be of public interest is a(n)	_____	3. _____
4. One who ships goods by common carrier is called the	_____	4. _____
5. The one to whom goods are shipped via a common carrier is called the	_____	5. _____
6. The document of title and evidence of contract between a shipper and a carrier for the transportation of goods is known as a(n)	_____	6. _____
7. Articles that passengers bring with them for their use are known as	_____	7. _____
8. One who supplies lodging to travelers without discrimination to all who apply is a(n)	_____	8. _____
9. A traveler who has been received and registered at a hotel is called a(n)	_____	9. _____
10. The occupant of a room in a boardinghouse is called a(n)	_____	10. _____

Score _____

Section B

DIRECTIONS: Indicate your decision in each of the following cases by filling in the Answers space.

	Answers	For Scoring
1-3. After boarding a train, Don left his bags on a seat and spent considerable time in the club car. When he returned, his bags were gone. Don sought to recover his loss. Did a bailment exist between Don and the carrier?	_____	1. _____
What degree of care for David's baggage was required of the carrier?	_____	2. _____
Would the carrier be liable if an employee on the train had stolen the baggage?	_____	_____
....................3.		
4-6. Maria rented a room with the Dillards, who rented out two rooms in their home. After living there for two years, she said she was leaving because her friend Sally was refused an empty room because she was black. Did the Dillards have an obligation to accept Sally after she applied?	_____	4. _____
Was Maria a guest or a boarder?	_____	5. _____
Must the Dillards take ordinary care of Maria's property?	_____	6. _____
7-8. Anne attended a wedding dinner at a local hotel. Her wrap disappeared while she was there. Was Anne a guest of the hotel?	_____	7. _____
Could she hold the hotelkeeper liable for the loss of her wrap?	_____	8. _____

Score _____

Section C

	Answers	For Scoring
1. Is a carrier's contract a contract for a bailment for the sole benefit of the bailee?	_____	1._____
2. Is the carrier the bailee of the goods transported?	_____	2._____
3. Is a private carrier free to refuse unprofitable service?	_____	3._____
4. Are private carriers liable for the failure to exercise extraordinary care?	_____	4._____
5. Must a common carrier provide additional equipment to accommodate customers in excess of the normal demands?	_____	5._____
6. Must a common carrier transport a person who is likely to harm other passengers?	_____	6._____
7. Are common carriers subject to regulations as to prices?	_____	7._____
8. Is a common carrier excused from losses arising from acts of God?	_____	8._____
9. Are mobs, strikers, or rioters classified as public enemies for purposes of excluding liability for acts of a public enemy?	_____	9._____
10. Can a carrier limit its liability by contract between it and the shipper?	_____	10._____
11. Do most states permit a carrier to limit liability for livestock loss due to delay over which the carrier has no control?	_____	11._____
12. If the consignee does not call for the goods within a reasonable time after being notified by the carrier that the goods have arrived, is the carrier's liability ended?	_____	12._____
13. May title to goods described in the bill of lading be passed by transferring the bill of lading to the purchaser?	_____	13._____
14. For an order bill of lading, are the goods delivered to the bearer of the bill of lading?	_____	14._____
15. Can a carrier prescribe whatever rule it chooses for the conduct of passengers?	_____	15._____
16. Does the purchase of a ticket guarantee a passenger a seat?	_____	16._____
17. If a passenger is going skiing, is ski equipment baggage?	_____	17._____
18. Does a carrier have no liability for baggage, whether retained by the passenger or placed in the carrier's possession?	_____	18._____
19. Is the test of whether a person is a hotelkeeper whether transients are lodged?	_____	19._____
20. Do the laws of hotelkeepers also apply to boardinghouse keepers?	_____	20._____
21. Are people guests of a hotel if they enter with the intention of becoming guests but change their minds before registering?	_____	21._____
22. Is a hotel permitted to segregate patrons on the basis of race as long as it does not refuse service on that basis?	_____	22._____

Score _____

CHAPTER 16
SALES OF PERSONAL PROPERTY

CHAPTER OUTLINE

I. INTRODUCTION

Contracts for the sale of goods (sales contracts) are governed by Article 2 of the UCC.

II. PROPERTY SUBJECT TO SALE (GOODS EXPLAINED)

General rules. ‣ Goods are movable personal property. ‣ Goods do not include: (1) real property (land, interests in land, and buildings and other things permanently attached to land); or (2) intangible personal property (personal property that does not physically exist, but which may be represented by a certificate or other writing).

Examples. ‣ Goods: cars, computers, equipment, airplanes, food (whether sold by producers, grocery stores, or restaurants), and clothing. ‣ Real property: land and buildings. ‣ Intangible personal property: stocks, bonds, promissory notes, copyrights, and accounts receivable.

Study hint. In general, sales contracts must satisfy the requirements for creating any contract. Article 2, however, imposes additional or special requirements that sales contracts must also meet.

III. SALES AND CONTRACTS TO SELL

General rule. Goods may be sold pursuant to (1) a sale or (2) a contract to sell.

- *Sale*: ‣ Defined: present transfer of title to goods made in consideration for a price. ‣ Example: Ken sells Buyer a specific, existing painting that Ken presently owns in consideration for $1,000. This is a sale. ‣ In a sale, title to goods passes to a buyer at time of contracting, regardless of who has possession of the goods. ‣ Once a sale is made, the buyer's creditors can immediately reach the goods.

- *Contract to sell*: ‣ Defined: contract by which title to goods will be transferred at a future time in consideration for a price. ‣ Example: Ken makes a contract to specially manufacture and sell a tool to Buyer for $1,000. This agreement is a contract to sell. ‣ Under a contract to sell, title to goods does not pass to a buyer when a contract is made; title will pass at a future date.

Study hints. ‣ Title means ownership. ‣ The difference between a sale and a contract to sell is important in determining who has title to goods, and the rights of creditors. (See Chapter 18.)

IV. SALES OF GOODS AND CONTRACTS FOR SERVICES

General rules. ‣ Article 2 governs only contracts for the sale of goods; it does not govern contracts for services or employment. ‣ If a contract requires a party to both sell goods and perform a service, the contract is classified as a sales or service contract according to the contract's predominant factor. If the sale of goods is dominant and the service is incidental, it is a contract for the sale of goods. If the service is dominant and the goods are incidental, it is a service contract.

Examples. ‣ Sales contract: Byte Co. and Nestor made a contract whereby Byte Co. sold Nestor a computer and agreed to set up the computer. The computer is the predominant factor. Thus, the contract is a sales contract. ‣ Service contract: Sue's Garage agreed to tune-up a car and to furnish spark plugs, if needed. The predominant factor is the service. Thus, this is a service contract

V.   PRICE

General rules.   ‣ The price paid for goods may be money, property, or the buyer's performance of a service. ‣ A sales contract does not need to expressly state the price to be paid. The price to be paid is (1) the price expressly stated or (2) if no price is stated, a reasonable price.

Example.   Kara makes a definite agreement to buy a bathroom sink from Plumber. The parties do not state a price. In this situation, a contract is formed and Kara must pay a reasonable price.

Study hints.   ‣ If a commodities contract (e.g., contract to buy wheat or gold) does not state a price and both parties belong to a commodity exchange, a reasonable price typically is the market price on that exchange. ‣ A contract may state that a price shall be determined by (1) a designated market price (e.g., "blue book" for a car), or (2) a formula that is stated for computing the price.

VI.   EXISTING GOODS (FUTURE GOODS AND IDENTIFIED GOODS)

General rules.   ‣ A party can make a "sale" of only existing goods. ‣ Existing goods are ones that physically exist and are owned by the seller at the time of contracting. ‣ Identified goods are ones that have been designated as being for a particular buyer.

Examples.   ‣ Existing good: Seller sells a car that Seller presently owns. ‣ Identified good: Seller sells a specific coat to Buyer and that coat is marked as being for the Buyer.

VII.   FUTURE GOODS

General rules.   ‣ A party can only make a contract to sell a future good. ‣ A future good is one that does not exist, or is not owned by the seller, at the time of contracting.

Example.   A seller contracts to sell an airplane that is to be manufactured in the future. A shipbroker contracts to sell a boat that the broker does not presently own.

Study hint.   Whether goods are existing, future, or identified goods is important in determining questions relating to title, risk of loss, and creditor's rights. (See Chapter 18.)

VIII.   BILL OF SALE

General rules.   ‣ Bill of sale: writing that evidences title to goods. ‣ Although a bill of sale is not necessary to pass title to goods, it may help a buyer prove that he or she owns certain goods.

Example.   Mary purchased some display cabinets from the North Co., which was going out of business. Mary was given a bill of sale for the cabinets. The bill of sale is not necessary to pass title, but it will help Mary prove to North's creditors that she owns the cabinets.

IX.   ILLEGAL SALES

General rules.   ‣ A contract for a sale of goods that are prohibited by law is generally illegal. ‣ If an illegal sale is executed or partially executed, a court will not require parties to return, or to pay for, any benefits received. ‣ If an illegal contract is executory, the contract will not be enforced.

Example.   A garage knowingly contracted to buy stolen car parts from J&J Inc. The garage paid part of the price to J&J. In this case, the contract is illegal and it cannot be enforced. J&J will not be required to return the money.

Limitations.   ‣ A party may recover money paid under an illegal contract if the party was defrauded into making the contract. ‣ If a sale is divisible (i.e., several items are sold with a separate price being stated for each item), a court will enforce the legal portion of the contract, but not the illegal portion. (If separate considerations are not stated, the entire contract fails.)

X.   INTERNATIONAL SALES CONTRACTS

General rule.   The United Nations Convention on Contracts for the International Sale of Goods (CISG) governs contracts for the sale of goods if the parties are from different countries that have adopted this agreement. The United States and many other countries have adopted this convention.

Limitations.   ‣ Parties may agree what law will govern a contract. ‣ Parties may agree that the CISG does not apply. ‣ The CISG does not apply if goods are bought for consumer use.

REVIEW OF CHAPTER

REVIEW OF TERMS

Select the term that best matches a statement. Each term is the best match for only one statement.

TERMS

a. Bill of sale
b. Contract to sell
c. Existing goods
d. Future goods

e. Goods
f. Identified goods
g. Intangible personal property

h. Real property
i. Sale
j. Title

STATEMENTS

Answer

_____ 1. Present transfer of title to movable personal property in consideration for a price.
_____ 2. Goods that physically exist and are owned by a seller at the time a sales contract is made.
_____ 3. Goods that do not exist, or are not owned by a seller at the time a sales contract is made.
_____ 4. Contract by which title to goods is to be transferred at a future time.
_____ 5. Land, interests in land, and things permanently attached to land.
_____ 6. Movable personal property.
_____ 7. Ownership.
_____ 8. Specific goods that have been designated as being for a particular buyer.
_____ 9. Personal property that does not physically exist, but which may be represented by a certificate or writing.
_____ 10. Writing that evidences title to goods.

REVIEW OF CONCEPTS

Directions: Indicate **T** for true and **F** for false in the answer column.

_____ 1. Contracts for the sale of goods are governed by common law, not by Article 2 of the UCC.
_____ 2. Seller sells a dresser to Buyer in consideration for Buyer's promise to repair Seller's plumbing. This contract is not a sale of goods.
_____ 3. A sale is a present transfer of title, whereas a contract to sell is an agreement to transfer title at a future time.
_____ 4. Whether a contract is a sale or a contract to sell may be important in determining who has title.
_____ 5. If a contract requires a seller to both sell goods and provide a service, the contract is a sales contract even if the predominant factor is the service and the goods are only incidental.
_____ 6. One cannot make a sale of future goods; one can only make a contract to sell future goods.
_____ 7. Seller owns an inventory of shovels, and Seller contracts to sell one of the shovels. The contract does not specify the particular shovel that is being sold. At time of contracting, the shovel being sold can be classified as an unidentified good.
_____ 8. A bill of sale is necessary to convey title to goods to a buyer.
_____ 9. In general, if an illegal sales contract has been completely or partially performed, a court will make each party return or pay for any benefits that have been received from the other party.
_____ 10. If a contract involves a divisible sale of legal and illegal goods, and the contract states separate considerations for each good, a court may enforce the legal portion of the contract.

REVIEW OF CONCEPT APPLICATIONS

Answer

Directions: Indicate your choice in the answer column.

_____ 1. Which transaction is a sale of goods that is governed by Article 2 of the UCC?
   a. Wayne sells 500 shares of UAL stock to Claire.
   b. Earl sells his farm to Mindy.
   c. Floors, Inc., a manufacturer of carpeting, sells a shipment of carpeting to Retailer.
   d. Bob sells a promissory note to Amanda.

____ 2. Which contract is a sale of goods that is governed by Article 2 of the UCC?
   a. Dr. Hanson agrees to teach for Yahoo University for one year.
   b. Zodiac Rentals rents a cement mixer to Carl.
   c. Vicky contracts to pay Ted $3,000 to paint Vicky's house. The price includes $2,500 for labor, and $500 for paint.
   d. Seller makes a contract for the sale of a movable storage shed. The contract requires Seller to assemble the shed. The contract price is $10,000, which includes $500 for Seller's labor.

____ 3. On June 1, Yuppie Inc. and Alexi entered into an agreement whereby Yuppie agreed to sell Alexi a custom-made talking watch. At time of contracting, the watch had not been made. The watch is to be delivered on July 1. Under these facts:
   a. The agreement is a sale, and title to the watch passed when the contract was made.
   b. The agreement is a contract to sell, and title did not pass when the contract was made.
   c. As of June 1, the watch would be classified as an existing good.

____ 4. Chemco and Glen entered into an agreement whereby Glen agreed to wrongfully acquire a sample of a competitor's new fertilizer product in consideration for $10,000. Performance of the agreement would be both a crime and tort. Under these facts:
   a. The agreement is an illegal contract to sell.
   b. A court would not enforce this agreement.
   c. A court would enforce this agreement if it were in writing.
   d. a and b.

CASE PROBLEM

Terri agreed to sell 500 ounces of gold to Darin. Terri and Darin are both gold traders who belong to the same commodity exchange. The parties definitely intend to contract. However, the parties' agreement intentionally does not state the price to be paid. Answer the following questions, briefly explaining your answers.

1. Is this contract subject to UCC Article 2?
2. Did the parties enter into a valid contract ? If so, what price must be paid?

_____

_____

_____

BUSINESS LAW PARTNER EXERCISE

Directions:

1. Using the Online feature of the Business Law Partner CD-ROM, locate and identify the text of the CISG.
2. Does the CISG govern the contracts between Ameri Inc. and Cannes Co., Kiev Inc., and or Felipe? Explain.
3. Is the contract between Ameri Inc. and Cannes Co. legally enforceable?

Case Study: *Buy American*

Ameri Inc., a U.S. firm, exports tennis racquets. Ameri Inc. orally contracted to sell one shipment of racquets to Cannes Co., a wholesaler located in a France, and another shipment to Kiev Inc., a Russian firm. Ameri Inc. also contracted to sell a racquet to Felipe, a Spanish citizen. The racquet is for Felipe's personal use.

_____

_____

_____

CHAPTER 16 QUIZ

Section A

DIRECTIONS: Following each statement below, indicate your answer by placing a "T" for "True" or an "F" for "False" in the Answers column.

	Answers	For Scoring
1. The largest class of contracts is contracts for the sale of goods.	_____	1. _____
2. Article 2 of the UCC governs sales of movable personal property.	_____	2. _____
3. Sales contracts must expressly state all material terms that are required to be stated in other types of contracts.	_____	3. _____
4. The rules pertaining to sales of personal property apply to all contracts.	_____	4. _____
5. A contract to sell passes title immediately.	_____	5. _____
6. In a sales contract, the buyer normally bears risk of loss.	_____	6. _____
7. If the parties to a sale specify when title or risk of loss passes, the courts will enforce this agreement.	_____	7. _____
8. The test of whether a mixed agreement is a contract for services or a sale of goods is determined by the parties' predominant purpose:	_____	8. _____
9. There can be a binding contract even though the parties state that they will agree upon the price at a later date.	_____	9. _____
10. If the price can be computed from the terms of the sales contract, the price need not be specifically stated.	_____	10. _____
11. One can make a sale of future goods.	_____	11. _____
12. It is necessary to have a bill of sale.	_____	12. _____
13. A bill of sale can be used as proof that the buyer came into possession of goods legally.	_____	13. _____
14. In general, the law will not aid either party to an illegal sales contract.	_____	14. _____
15. A major problem with an international contract for the sale of goods could be what law governs.	_____	15. _____

Score _____

Section B

DIRECTIONS: Complete each of the following statements by writing the missing word or words in the Answers column.

	Answers	For Scoring
1. A present transfer of title to goods from a seller to a buyer for a price is a(n)	_____	1. _____
2. A contract whereby a seller agrees to make a future transfer of title to goods to a buyer for a price is a(n)	_____	2. _____
3. Stock certificates and corporate bonds are <u>???</u> personal property................	_____	3. _____
4. The consideration in a sales contract that is stated in money or money's worth is called the..	_____	4. _____
5. In order to be the subject of a sale, it is necessary that the goods be	_____	5. _____
6. Specific goods that the seller and buyer have designated as being for the buyer are..	_____	6. _____
7. Goods that are not both existing and identified are called	_____	7. _____

8. Written evidence of one's title to tangible personal property is called a(n).... _____ **8.** ____

9. A sale of goods prohibited by law is called a(n) .... _____ **9.** ____

10. The United Nations Convention on Contracts for the International Sale of
Goods does not cover .... _____ **10.** ____

Score _____

Section C

DIRECTIONS: Fill out the following bill of sale as the seller with the information supplied below. Write clearly. Supply the signature of a witness to your signature.

On January 4, of the current year, you sold a one-half undivided interest in, and ownership of, the stock of merchandise, store equipment and supplies, office equipment and supplies, and other contents of the Simpson Bakery located at 7615 Keller Street, in your village or city, county, and state. The vendee, Roberta A. Bell, of 432 Mathewson Road, in your city, pays you $85,000 in full at the time of executing this instrument.

For Scoring

Bill of Sale

Purchaser .... (1)

Address .... (2)

Date _____ 199____

(3)

Property	Location or description	Price

(4) _____ (5) _____ (6) _____

For and in consideration of the sum(s) above written paid by buyer, the receipt of which is hereby acknowledged, the seller has bargained and sold, and by these presents does grant and convey, unto the said purchaser the above goods and chattels, which said above-described goods and chattels belong to and are now in the possession of seller. To Have and to Hold the same unto the said purchaser, h ___ executors, administrators, and assigns, forever.

In Witness Whereof, the seller has hereunto set h_____ hand and seal.

SELLER _____ (7)

Address _____ (8)

SIGNED _____ (9)

Signed, Sealed, and Delivered in Presence of

1._____
2._____
3._____
4._____
5._____
6._____
7._____
8._____
9._____
10._____

Score _____

CHAPTER 17
FORMALITIES OF A SALE

CHAPTER OUTLINE

I. INTRODUCTION

General rule.   The Statute of Frauds requires contracts for the sale of goods for $500 or more to be evidenced by a writing. Failure to comply with this requirement renders a contract unenforceable.
Examples.   ▸ Keri orally contracts to sell a table to Eleanor for $600. This contract is unenforceable.
▸ Ike orally contracts to sell pottery to Buyer for $200. This contract is enforceable.
Limitation.   A failure to comply with the Statute of Frauds cannot be used to set aside (rescind) a contract that both parties have fully performed.
Study hints.   ▸ Parties can voluntarily perform a contract even if it does not comply with the Statute of Frauds. ▸ If a contract is unenforceable: (1) a court will not order parties to perform the contract; and (2) a party is not liable for damages because the party does not perform.

II. MULTIPLE PURCHASES AND THE STATUTE OF FRAUDS

General rules.   ▸ If a buyer selects several items during a single shopping trip and the buyer agrees to purchase them pursuant to one contract or order, the total price for all the items is the contract price for purposes of the Statute of Frauds. ▸ If a party purchases several items and pays separately for each item, each purchase is a separate sale for purposes of the Statute of Frauds.
Example.   During a shopping trip to C&C Clothing, Betsy selected four dresses that each cost $150. One order was written for the dresses and Betsy paid $50 down. The contract price is $600.

III. WHEN PROOF OF ORAL CONTRACT IS PERMITTED

In the situations discussed below, an oral sales contract for $500 or more may be enforceable.

A. RECEIPT AND ACCEPTANCE OF GOODS

General rules.   ▸ An oral sales contract is enforceable *to the extent that* the seller delivers goods and they are received and accepted by the buyer. ▸ Receipt of goods: possession of goods. ▸ Acceptance of goods: buyer expressly or by implication agrees to be the owner of goods.
Example.   Buzz orally buys two cars for $3,000 each. Seller delivers, and Buzz receives and accepts one car. The contract is enforceable regarding the car that was accepted by Buzz.

B. PAYMENT

General rules.   ▸ An oral sales contract is enforceable *to the extent that* the contract price is paid by the buyer and accepted by the seller. ▸ In most cases, payment by a check or promissory note constitutes payment for purposes of the Statute of Frauds if the seller accepts the check or note.
Example.   Hank orally contracted to buy a motorcycle for $2,000. Hank delivered his personal check for $2,000 to Seller. Seller cashed the check. The oral contract is enforceable.
Limitation.   Payment is not made if the seller refuses a check or note.
Study hint.   If a buyer pays with a check and the seller keeps the check for an unreasonable time (e.g., 30 days), then the buyer is deemed to have paid for purposes of the Statute of Frauds.

C. JUDICIAL ADMISSION

General rule.   An oral sales contract is enforceable if (1) during judicial proceedings (2) the party who refuses to perform the contract admits that he or she made the contract.

Example.   Eva orally bought a boat for $1,000. Eva refuses to perform the contract and Seller sues her. During trial, Eva admits making the contract. The contract is enforceable.

D. NONRESELLABLE GOODS

General rule.   An oral sales contract for specially made goods is enforceable if: (1) the goods are not suitable for resale; and (2) before the buyer disavows the contract, the seller makes a substantial beginning either in making the goods or in committing to buy or obtain the goods.

Example.   Buyer orally contracted to buy a custom-made tuxedo from Tailor. Because of its special dimensions, the tux cannot be resold in the ordinary course of business. Before Buyer repudiated the contract, Tailor nearly completed the tux. The contract is enforceable.

E. AUCTION SALES

- *Auction defined*: An auction is a sale in which a seller (or a seller's agent) orally asks for bids and orally accepts the highest bid.

- *Enforceability of auctions*: An auction sale is generally enforceable even though it is oral.

- *Auction procedures*: ▸ An auctioneer can refuse an inadequate bid as a starting bid. ▸ Once bidding starts, a contract is not made until the auctioneer accepts a bid. Acceptance is commonly signified by the fall of the hammer. If a bid is made while the hammer is falling, the auctioneer may (1) reopen the bidding or (2) declare the good sold.

- *Auctioneer's memorandum*: In most states, an auctioneer is a special agent for both the seller and buyer. Therefore, a memorandum of sale signed by an auctioneer binds both parties.

- *Auctions with and without reserve*: ▸ Auction with reserve: goods may be withdrawn from an auction sale and they do not have to be sold. Unless otherwise stated, goods are presumed to be offered with reserve. ▸ Auction without reserve: goods cannot be withdrawn and they must be sold to the highest bidder once bidding commences.

IV.   NATURE OF THE WRITING REQUIRED (TO SATISFY THE STATUTE OF FRAUDS)

A. TERMS AND SIGNATURE

General rule.   To satisfy the Statute of Frauds under Article 2, a writing must: (1) indicate that the parties have made a contract; (2) state the quantity of goods sold; and (3) be signed by the party who is trying to use the Statute of Frauds as a defense (e.g., the defendant).

Example.   Lily orally contracted to buy furniture for $700. Lily signed a form. The form confirmed the making of the contract and described the furniture, but it did not state any other terms. Lily now refuses to perform the contract. The contract is enforceable against Lily.

Limitation.   The writing requirement is met for both parties if (1) the parties are merchants, (2) one party signed a sufficient written confirmation of the contract (3) that was sent to the other party, and (4) the party receiving the confirmation did not object to it in writing within ten days.

Study hints.   ▸ Both parties need not sign a writing. ▸ A signature may be initials, or it may be printed, stamped, or typewritten. Letterheads do not qualify as a signature.

B. TIME OF EXECUTION

A writing may be made at the time of contracting or at any time thereafter.

C. PARTICULAR WRITINGS

▸ A writing may satisfy the Statute of Frauds even if it is not made for that purpose, and it is not a formal written contract. ▸ Two or more writings may comprise the necessary writing. ▸ Signed bills of sale or letters may be sufficient. ▸ Purchase orders, receipts, and sales tickets are usually inadequate.

REVIEW OF CHAPTER

REVIEW OF TERMS

Select the term that best matches a statement below. Each term is the best match for only one statement.

TERMS

a. Acceptance of goods   d. Receipt of goods   f. With reserve
b. Auction   e. Statute of Frauds   g. Without reserve
c. Bidder

STATEMENTS

Answer

_____ 1. Law requiring sales contracts for $500 or more to be evidenced by a writing to be enforceable.
_____ 2. Goods put up for auction may be withdrawn after bidding begins.
_____ 3. Party whom offers to purchase goods at an auction.
_____ 4. Taking possession of goods.
_____ 5. Sale in which property is orally sold to the highest bidder.
_____ 6. Agreement by a buyer to be the owner of goods and to take them as his or her own property.
_____ 7. Goods put up for auction cannot be withdrawn after bidding begins.

REVIEW OF CONCEPTS

Directions: Indicate **T** for true and **F** for false in the answer column.

_____ 1. All contracts for the sale of goods must be evidenced by a writing to be enforceable.
_____ 2. Parties cannot voluntarily perform a contract that does not comply with the Statute of Frauds.
_____ 3. A buyer's receipt and acceptance of goods renders an oral sales contract enforceable only if the buyer has also paid the contract price to the seller.
_____ 4. Receipt of goods means that a buyer has taken physical possession of goods; acceptance of goods means that the buyer has expressly or by implication agreed to keep the goods as his or her own.
_____ 5. Seller orally contracts to sell two chairs to Buyer for $600 each. Buyer pays for one chair and Seller accepts this payment. In this situation, the entire contract is enforceable.
_____ 6. A buyer's payment with a check or promissory note that is accepted by the seller is usually sufficient payment to make an oral sales contract enforceable.
_____ 7. An oral contract for specially made goods is enforceable if the goods cannot be resold in the ordinary course of business and the seller has made a substantial beginning in making the goods.
_____ 8. An auction sale of goods is not enforceable unless the seller and buyer sign a written sales memo.
_____ 9. A sale at an auction is not made until the auctioneer accepts a party's bid.
_____ 10. In general, an auctioneer can refuse to accept an inadequate bid as an opening bid.
_____ 11. Under the UCC, a writing cannot satisfy the Statute of Frauds unless it states all contract terms.
_____ 12. Two or more related writings may be considered together in order to satisfy the Statute of Frauds.
_____ 13. A writing does not need to be a signed, formal contract in order to satisfy the Statute of Frauds.

REVIEW OF CONCEPT APPLICATIONS

Answer

Directions: Indicate your choice in the answer column.

_____ 1. Which contract(s) is required to be evidenced by a writing to be enforceable?
     a.   Tom contracts to buy a guitar for $400.
     b.   During one shopping trip to a nursery, Mercedes selected six trees from different parts of the nursery. Each tree cost $200. One purchase agreement was prepared for the six trees.
     c.   San-li made two trips to a store. On the first trip, San-li ordered a part for $300; on the second visit he ordered tools for $250. Separate orders were written for each purchase.

_____ 2. Fargo Power & Light orally contracted to buy 40 tons of coal from M&M Mining. M&M delivered 20 tons of coal to Fargo. Fargo took receipt of and accepted the 20 tons. Fargo now refuses to accept any more coal. Fargo has not paid for the coal. Under these facts:
   a. The entire contract is unenforceable.
   b. The entire contract is enforceable.
   c. The contract is enforceable to the extent that the coal was received and accepted by Fargo. The remainder of the contract is unenforceable.

_____ 3. Which contract is *unenforceable*?
   a. Peter orally contracted to sell $1,000 of nuts to Buyer. Peter did not deliver the nuts. Buyer sent Peter a check as payment, but Peter refused the check and immediately returned it.
   b. Jarvis orally contracted to sell a TV to Buyer for $600. Buyer paid Jarvis the purchase price in cash and Jarvis accepted this payment.
   c. Cy orally agreed to sell a pig for $800. No delivery or payment has occurred. Cy refuses to perform the contract because it is oral. At trial, Cy admits making the contract.

_____ 4. Which contract is *unenforceable*?
   a. A&M (a merchant) orally contracted to buy $10,000 of sugar from Refinery (a merchant). A&M sent Refinery a confirmation of the contract which stated the terms and was signed by A&M. Refinery received the confirmation, and it never objected to the confirmation.
   b. Seller sold Buyer a truck for $5,000. Both parties signed a writing that confirmed their agreement. The writing described the truck, but it did not state the contract price.
   c. Judy orally contracted to buy $800 of cosmetics. She sent the seller an unsigned purchase order for the cosmetics. The purchase order stated all of the terms of the proposed contract.

CASE PROBLEM

Maurice is an auctioneer who conducted an auction of Seller's goods. The auction was "with reserve." At the auction a couch was put up for sale. Jake's $200 bid was the highest bid for the couch. Maurice refused to sell the couch and he withdrew it from bidding. Later, Felix bid $550 for an antique table, and Maurice orally accepted the bid. On behalf of Seller and Felix, Maurice signed a memo of sale. (1) Was Jake's bid an acceptance that formed a contract? Was Maurice entitled to withdraw the couch? (2) Is the contract between Seller and Felix enforceable? Is the memo of sale binding on Seller and Felix?

_____

_____

_____

BUSINESS LAW PARTNER EXERCISE

Directions:

1. Using the Online feature of the Business Law Partner CD-ROM, locate a notice of auction that is to be conducted anywhere in the United States. Identify the web site where you found this notice.

2. Examine the announced terms of the auction regarding the seller's right to withdraw listed items. Analyze whether this auction is being conducted with or without reserve, and whether or not the seller has the right to withdraw items if the bids are unacceptable.

_____

_____

_____

CHAPTER 17 QUIZ

Section A

DIRECTIONS: Following each question below, indicate your answer by placing a "Y" for "Yes" or an "N" for "No" in the Answers column.

	Answers	For Scoring
1. Do all contracts for the sale of goods have to be written?	_____	1. _____
2. If both parties elect to abide by the terms of an oral contract that does not meet the writing requirements of the UCC, can one later avoid the contract?	_____	2. _____
3. In general, are different purchases of goods by one customer from one seller considered to be one contract if they are all made on the same day?	_____	3. _____
4. Is an oral contract for the sale of goods for $500 or more enforceable if the buyer receives and accepts the goods?	_____	4. _____
5. May an oral contract for the sale of goods for $500 or more be enforced with respect to goods for which payment has been made and accepted?	_____	5. _____
6. If the buyer offers the seller a check in payment, but the seller refuses it, has the buyer made payment for the purposes of the Statute of Frauds?	_____	6. _____
7. Is a writing required when both contracting parties admit in the course of legal proceedings that they entered into the contract?	_____	7. _____
8. Is a writing required for a sales contract involving goods made especially for the buyer and not suitable for sale in the ordinary course of business of the seller?	_____	8. _____
9. Is the record of the clerk of an auction sale sufficient to make a binding contract between the buyer and seller?	_____	9. _____
10. Must a writing be made prior to a sale to satisfy the Statute of Frauds?	_____	10. _____

Score _____

Section B

DIRECTIONS: Complete each of the following statements by writing the missing word or words in the Answers column.

	Answers	For Scoring
1. If a sales contract does not meet the writing requirements of the UCC it is ...	_____	1. _____
2. Taking possession of the goods that are the subject of the sale is called	_____	2. _____
3. The assent of the buyer to become the owner of specific goods is called	_____	3. _____
4. The law of commercial paper classifies a check as ??? payment prior to the time that the bank upon which the check is drawn actually pays it...............	_____	4. _____
5. To voluntarily acknowledge a fact in the course of legal proceedings is a(n)	_____	5. _____
6. Goods specifically made for the buyer and not suitable for sale in the ordinary course of the seller's business are	_____	6. _____
7-9. A sale in which a seller or an agent of the seller orally asks for bids on goods and orally accepts the highest bid is a(n)	_____	7. _____
The person who makes the offer at such a sale is the	_____	8. _____
If goods put up for bid may be withdrawn, they have been put up	_____	9. _____
10. When suit is brought against a person for breach of a sales contract that must be in writing, the writing must be ??? by the person being sued.	_____	10. _____

Score _____

Section C

DIRECTIONS: Following each statement below, indicate your answer by placing a "T" for "True" or an "F" for "False" in the Answers column.

	Answers	For Scoring
1. If the sales price is less than $500, the contract may be oral, written, implied, or a combination of these.	_____	1. _____
2. If separate sales slips are written for multiple purchases from one seller on the same day, each transaction is treated as a separate sale.	_____	2. _____
3. If a buyer receives and accepts any portion of the goods sold under an oral sales contract, the entire contract is enforceable.	_____	3. _____
4. An oral sales contract is enforceable if full payment on the contract has been made.	_____	4. _____
5. The delivery of a check to the seller does not make an oral contract enforceable.	_____	5. _____
6. All oral and written contracts for nonresellable goods are enforceable by a seller.	_____	6. _____
7. The signature on the writing required by the Statute of Frauds must be written by hand and in ink.	_____	7. _____
8. When a sale of goods is between merchants, there may be an exception to the writing requirement.	_____	8. _____
9. In order to satisfy the Statute of Frauds, the required writing must be a single writing.	_____	9. _____
10. A sale by auction for any amount is valid even though it is oral.	_____	10. _____

Score _____

Section D

DIRECTIONS: Following each question below, indicate your answer by placing a "Y" for "Yes" or an "N" for "No" in the Answers column.

	Answers	For Scoring
1. Roberts entered into an oral contract to sell Miller a horse on Tuesday for $1,000 to be paid at that time. Miller called for the horse and tendered payment, which Roberts refused. Roberts' defense was that if the price exceeded $500, the law would not admit oral testimony to prove the existence of a contract to sell unless there were special circumstances not present in this case. Miller demanded the horse. Would the courts find in favor of Miller?	_____	1. _____
2. Suppose that in the preceding problem Miller had paid Roberts the purchase price at the time the bargain was made and that Roberts offered to return the money, which Miller refused. Would Roberts win the suit?	_____	2. _____
3. Madson made the highest bid on a painting at an auction. The seller was not satisfied with the amount and announced he was withdrawing the painting from the auction. Madson insisted she be allowed to buy the painting at her bid price. Must the painting be sold for Madson's bid?	_____	3. _____
4-5. Gerald purchased a silo from William's Equipment Company for $1,200, which did not include the cover. When the silo was erected, Gerald was still undecided about paying $325 for an aluminum cover. William's Equipment Company asked permission to erect the cover and leave it until spring, at which time it would be removed if Gerald decided against the metal cover. Permission was granted and Williams installed a cover. Was Gerald's action an acceptance of the cover?	_____	4. _____
Would there have to be a writing for William's to enforce a sale of the cover?	_____	5. _____

Score _____

CHAPTER 18
TRANSFER OF TITLE AND RISK IN SALES CONTRACTS

CHAPTER OUTLINE

I. POTENTIAL PROBLEMS

- *Creditors' claims*: Rules relating to title often determine creditors' and purchasers' rights to goods.
- *Insurance*: Insurable interest rules determine if an insurer must pay for a loss to goods.
- *Damage to goods*: Risk rules determine whether a seller or buyer bears a loss from a casualty to goods.

II. CLASSIFICATION OF SALES TRANSACTIONS

- *Nature of the goods*: ▸ Rights relating to title, insurable interest, and risk of loss depend on whether goods are existing, future, or identified goods. (See Chapter 17 for definitions)
- *Terms of the transaction*: Delivery duties may affect parties' rights. ▸ A seller may be required to:
  (1) deliver goods at seller's business; (2) deliver goods to a carrier for shipment; (3) deliver goods at a destination; or (4) deliver a document of title (warehouse receipt or bill of lading) to a buyer.

III. TRANSFER OF TITLE, SPECIAL PROPERTY INTERESTS, AND RISK IN PARTICULAR TRANSACTTIONS

A. EXISTING GOODS IDENTIFIED AT TIME OF CONTRACTING

General rule.   If (1) goods are existing and identified at time of contracting, (2) goods are not to be transported, and (3) no documents of title are involved, then:

- *Title*: Title to goods passes to the buyer at time of contracting.
- *Insurable interest*: ▸ Seller: seller has an insurable interest if seller has title to or a security interest in goods. ▸ Buyer: buyer acquires an insurable interest at time of contracting.
- *Risk of loss*: ▸ Merchant seller: risk passes when buyer takes physical possession of goods.
  ▸ Nonmerchant seller: risk passes when delivery of goods to buyer is tendered (offered).

Limitation.   In general, if goods are to be transported, title and risk of loss pass to the buyer when the seller completes his or her shipment or delivery obligations.

Study hint.   A seller and buyer can both have an insurable interest in goods at the same time.

B. NEGOTIABLE DOCUMENTS REPRESENTING EXISTING, IDENTIFIED GOODS

If (1) goods are existing and identified at time of contracting, but (2) a seller is required to deliver a document of title to the buyer, then:

- *Title*: Title passes when seller delivers the document of title to buyer.
- *Insurable interest*: Rules are the same as stated in Section A (above) for existing goods.
- *Risk of loss*: Risk generally passes when documents of title are delivered to the buyer.

C. SELLER'S MARKING FUTURE GOODS FOR BUYER

If a contract is made for (1) future goods or (2) unidentified goods, then:

- *Title and risk of loss*: Title and risk generally do not pass to a buyer until the seller has completed his or her shipment or delivery obligations. (See Section D below)
- *Insurable interest*: ▸ Seller: seller has an insurable interest if he or she has title to or a security interest in goods. ▸ Buyer: buyer has an insurable interest when specific goods are marked, tagged, labeled, or otherwise identified as being for the buyer.

D. CONTRACT FOR SHIPMENT OF FUTURE GOODS

If a seller is required to deliver goods to a carrier for shipment to a buyer, then:

- *Title and risk of loss*: Title and risk pass to a buyer when goods are delivered to the carrier.

- *Insurable interest*: ▸ Seller: seller has an insurable interest if seller has title to or a security interest in goods. ▸ Buyer: buyer has an insurable interest as soon as goods are identified.

IV. DAMAGE TO OR DESTRUCTION OF GOODS

- *Damage to identified goods before risk of loss passes*: ▸ A contract is avoided if: (1) goods essential to the contract are identified at time of contracting; (2) risk of loss has not passed; and (3) goods are destroyed without fault of either party. ▸ If a partial loss occurs, a buyer may cancel the contract or accept the goods with an appropriate reduction in price.

- *Damage to identified goods after risk of loss passes*: If a casualty occurs and a buyer has the risk of loss, a contract is not avoided; the buyer must pay for goods and buyer bears the financial loss.

- *Damage to unidentified goods*: Casualty to unidentified goods does not affect a contract; both parties must perform and seller bears the loss. If the seller fails to deliver, the seller is in breach.

- *Reservation of title or possession (by seller)*: These actions do not affect passing of risk of loss.

V. SALES ON APPROVAL AND WITH RIGHT TO RETURN

Parties may agree that goods can be returned even if they meet contract standards. These transactions are reviewed below. If the nature of a transaction is unclear, it is a sale on approval if goods are for a consumer's personal use; it is a sale or return if goods are intended for resale by a merchant.

A. CONSEQUENCE OF SALE ON APPROVAL

- *Nature of transaction*: ▸ In a sale on approval, a sale does not occur until a buyer accepts the goods. ▸ Acceptance: failure to return goods within time agreed or within a reasonable time; use of goods for a purpose other than testing. ▸ Not acceptance: merely testing goods.

- *Return of goods*: The seller bears the risk of loss and expense for the return of goods.

- *Creditor's rights*: Buyer's creditors cannot reach goods prior to buyer's acceptance of goods.

B. CONSEQUENCE OF SALE OR RETURN

- *Nature of transaction*: ▸ A sale or return is a completed sale with an option for a buyer to return all goods or any commercial unit of goods (i.e., item or group of goods that is regarded as a separate unit). ▸ Goods must be returned when agreed or within a reasonable time if no time is stated. Goods must be returned in substantially their original condition.

- *Title and risk of loss*: General rules regarding title and risk of loss apply to a sale or return.

- *Return of goods*: A buyer bears the risk of loss and expense in returning goods.

- *Creditor's rights*: A buyer's creditors can claim goods held by a buyer under a sale or return.

C. OTHER TRANSACTIONS

Consignment: an owner (consignor) delivers goods to a seller (consignee) to sell.

VI. SALES OF FUNGIBLE GOODS

▸ Fungible goods: goods of an interchangeable nature sold by weight or measure (e.g., corn; oil). ▸ UCC: title to a portion of an identified mass of fungible goods may pass at time of contracting.

VII. SALE OF UNDIVIDED SHARES

▸ If one buys a fractional interest in a good with no intention to separate the interest, the buyer is a co-owner of the good. ▸ Example: Lex buys a one-half interest in a motorcycle belonging to Phil.

VIII. AUCTION SALES

If goods are sold at auction in separate lots, the sale of each lot is a separate transaction.

IX. FREE ON BOARD

▸ If goods are sold "f.o.b.," the seller bears the risk and expense until goods are delivered to the f.o.b. destination. ▸ Example: Seller in Miami ships goods to Buyer in Seattle. Goods are sold "f.o.b. Seattle." Seller bears the risk of loss and expense until the goods are delivered in Seattle.

X. C.O.D. SHIPMENT

C.O.D.: Seller retains right to possession until buyer pays; passing of title or risk are not affected.

XI. TRANSFER OF TITLE

General rule.   In general, a buyer receives only the title to goods (if any) held by the seller.
Example.   Thief sells a stolen TV to Innocent Buyer. Buyer does not receive title to the TV.
Limitation.   Sometimes a seller may transfer better title than a seller has. (See discussion below.)
Study hint.   If a buyer receives void (no) title or defective title, the original owner can recover the goods from the buyer and can hold the buyer liable for conversion if the goods are not returned.

A. SALE BY ENTRUSTEE

General rule.   A merchant who regularly buys and sells goods of the kind in question, and to whom a good is entrusted (voluntarily given), has the power to transfer the owner's title to a buyer in the ordinary course of business.
Example.   Joe left his bike at Ace Bike Shop for repairs. Ace buys and sells used bikes. Ace sold Joe's bike to Innocent Third Party. Third Party receives title to the bike.

B. CONSIGNMENT SALES

If (1) goods are consigned to a merchant (2) who deals in such goods, then the merchant's creditors can frequently take the consigned goods as if they belonged to the merchant.

C. ESTOPPEL

An owner's wrongful or negligent conduct may bar an owner from asserting ownership to goods.

D. DOCUMENTS OF TITLE

General rules.   ▸ Documents of title: documents that evidence ownership to goods. ▸ A good faith buyer of a document of title may acquire title to goods that are subject to the document even if the transferor of the document does not have valid title to the goods.
Example: Goods are stored and a negotiable warehouse receipt is issued (to "bearer") for the goods. Thief steals the receipt and sells it to Innocent. Innocent gets valid title to the goods.

E. RECORDING AND FILING STATUTES

A good faith buyer of goods is not subject to liens that are not properly recorded or filed.

F. VOIDABLE TITLE

General rules.   ▸ A seller has voidable title to goods if the seller: (1) paid for goods with a "bad check"; (2) bought goods in a cash sale but failed to pay the price; or (3) acquired title by fraud. ▸ A bona fide purchaser acquires valid (good) title to goods if the seller has voidable title.
Example.   Sal bought a plane, but failed to pay the cash price. Sal sold the plane to Buyer who bought it for value and in good faith. Sal had voidable title; Buyer acquires good title.

REVIEW OF CHAPTER

REVIEW OF TERMS

Select the term that best matches a statement below. Each term is the best match for only one statement.

TERMS

a. Bill of lading
b. C.O.D.
c. Commercial unit
d. Consignment
e. Document of title

f. Entrustee
g. Estoppel
h. F.O.B.
i. Fungible goods
j. Insurable interest

k. Sale on approval
l. Sale or return
m. Title
n. Voidable title
o. Warehouse receipt

STATEMENTS

Answer

_____ 1. Transaction that allows a party to return goods if the party does not accept the goods.

_____ 2. Ownership of goods.

_____ 3. Document that evidences ownership of goods (e.g., warehouse receipt or bill of lading).

_____ 4. Term that requires a shipper to not deliver goods until the buyer has paid for the goods.

_____ 5. Transaction that is a completed sale with an option for the buyer to return goods.

_____ 6. Good, or a group or quantity of goods, that is commonly regarded as a single unit.

_____ 7. Defective title acquired by a person who pays for goods with a bad check, who fails to pay a cash purchase price, or who obtains goods by fraud.

_____ 8. Transfer of goods to a party, with an authorization for the party to sell the goods.

_____ 9. Designated point to which seller bears risk and expense.

_____ 10. Document of title issued by a storage company for goods that are stored.

_____ 11. Principle that may bar an owner from asserting title to goods due to the owner's wrongful conduct.

_____ 12. Person to whom an owner of goods voluntarily transfers possession of the goods.

_____ 13. Document of title issued by a carrier for goods being shipped.

_____ 14. Goods of a homogeneous or interchangeable nature sold by weight or measure (e.g., wheat).

_____ 15. Interest in goods that is necessary to make an insurer pay for a loss to goods.

REVIEW OF CONCEPTS

Directions: Indicate **T** for true and **F** for false in the answer column.

_____ 1. Rules regarding title are important in determining whether a seller's or buyer's creditors can take goods.

_____ 2. A party has an insurable interest in goods only if the party has possession of the goods.

_____ 3. A party has an insurable interest in goods only if the party has title to the goods.

_____ 4. If a seller is required to ship future goods to a buyer, risk of loss typically does not pass to the buyer until the seller has completed its shipment or delivery obligations.

_____ 5. If a contract involves goods that are existing and identified at time of contracting but a document of title is required to be delivered to the buyer, title and risk of loss generally do not pass to the buyer until the document of title is delivered to the buyer.

_____ 6. If a contract involves future goods, a buyer does not have an insurable interest in the goods until they are marked, labeled, or otherwise identified as being for the buyer.

_____ 7. In a contract for future goods, title and risk of loss usually pass to a buyer at time of contracting.

_____ 8. If an agreement is unclear on the point, a transaction that allows a buyer to return conforming goods is a sale on approval if goods are intended for the personal use by a consumer, but it is a sale or return if goods are intended to be resold by a merchant.

_____ 9. In a sale or return contract, expense and risk of loss of returning goods are borne by the seller.

_____ 10. In a sale or return contract, a buyer may return all goods or any commercial unit of goods.

_____ 11. Creditors of a buyer under a sale on approval cannot reach goods prior to the buyer's acceptance, but creditors of a buyer under a sale or return can reach goods prior to their return by the buyer.

_____ 12. If goods are shipped C.O.D., a seller has the right to possession of goods until the buyer pays.

_____ 13. In general, a buyer receives only the title (if any) that is held by a seller. If a buyer receives voidable or void (no) title, the true owner of goods may recover them from the buyer.

_____ 14. Mr. Harris consigns equipment to N&N Equipment Sales. N&N is to sell the equipment for Mr. Harris. In this situation, N&N's creditors may be able to take the consigned equipment.

_____ 15. In an auction sale, title does not pass to a buyer until the buyer has paid for the goods.

REVIEW OF CONCEPT APPLICATIONS

Answer

Directions: Indicate your choice in the answer column.

_____ 1. On May 1, John contracted to buy an existing, identified cabinet from Seller, a merchant. Documents of title were not involved. Delivery is required at Seller's business. On June 1, Seller tendered delivery of the cabinet to John, but John failed to take it. On July 1, John took physical delivery of the cabinet. Under these facts:
   a. John had an insurable interest in the cabinet on May 1.
   b. Title to the goods passed to John on June 1.
   c. Risk of loss passed to John on July 1.
   d. a and c.

_____ 2. Seller, who is located in Atlanta, Georgia, contracted to sell a shipment of eyeglasses to SEE Co., located in Duluth, Minnesota. The eyeglasses were sold "f.o.b. Duluth." Seller duly delivered the eyeglasses to a carrier in Atlanta for shipment to SEE Co. in Duluth. The goods were damaged during shipment. Under these facts:
   a. Seller bears the loss to the glasses that occurred during shipment.
   b. SEE Co. bears the loss to the glasses that occurred during shipment.
   c. SEE Co. must pay for the cost of shipment from Atlanta to Duluth.
   d. b and c.

_____ 3. Select the correct answer. (The damage to the goods in question is not the fault of either party.)
   a. Walt contracted to buy a rare statue from Seller. The statue was both identified and existing at time of contracting. Before risk of loss passed to Walt, the statue was stolen. In this case, the contract is not avoided, and Seller is in breach of contract if Seller fails to perform.
   b. Seller contracted to sell a desk to Buyer. After risk of loss had passed to Buyer, the desk was stolen. In this case, the contract is avoided; Buyer is not required to pay for the desk.
   c. Seller contracted to sell an unidentified oven to Buyer. Before risk of loss passed, Seller's inventory of ovens was destroyed. In this case, the contract is not avoided, Seller bears the loss, and Seller is liable for breach if an appropriate oven is not delivered to Buyer.

_____ 4. Fran received a hair dryer from Seller pursuant to a sale on approval agreement. The agreement allows Fran to test the dryer for 14 days; Fran may return the dryer any time within this period if she is not satisfied. Fran received the dryer on June 1. Fran tested the dryer for seven days, and she returned it on June 9. During return shipment, the dryer was damaged. Under these facts:
   a. Title and risk of loss passed to Fran on June 1.
   b. Title and risk of loss never passed to Fran.
   c. Fran must pay for the return shipment of the dryer.
   d. a and c.

_____ 5. Nicole sold her FAX to Jasper. Jasper paid Nicole with a bad check. Jasper's bank refused to pay the check due to insufficient funds. Prior to Nicole's rescinding the sale, Jasper sold the FAX to Gary for value. Gary was unaware of the transaction between Nicole and Jasper. Under these facts:
   a. Gary received voidable title to the FAX.
   b. Gary received valid (good) title to the FAX.
   c. Nicole cannot recover the FAX from Gary.
   d. b and c.

CASE PROBLEM

Does Buyer receive Owner's title to the goods in question? Briefly explain your answer.

1. Owner delivered her diamond ring to AAA Jewelers, a merchant who regularly sells fine jewelry. AAA was supposed to clean the ring. Instead, AAA sold the ring to Buyer in the ordinary course of business.

2. Owner delivered her car to Wet N' Wild, a retail car wash. Wet N' Wild does not normally buy or sell cars. Without permission, Wet N' Wild sold Owner's car to Buyer for $8,000, a fair price. Buyer did not know that the car belonged to Owner, or that the sale was improper.

_____

_____

_____

BUSINESS LAW PARTNER EXERCISE

Directions: Access your Business Law Partner CD-ROM and find the document entitled "Consignment Agreement."

1. Complete the above-referenced document using the information provided in the following case study.
2. While the consigned goods are held by Carmen, the consignee, (a) who has title to the goods and (b) who bears the risk that the goods may be destroyed, damaged, or stolen?

Case Study: *If You Break Them, You Own Them*

Jackson has owned a tire store for many years, and he recently decided to retire. Jackson has some leftover tires and automobile wheels that he has agreed to consign to Carmen. The consignment is effective May 1, and either party may terminate it on 30 days' prior written notice. Carmen has the right to sell the goods for whatever reasonable price she determines, and she is to receive a 50 percent commission based on the gross sales price. Jackson is to be paid and provided with a written accounting within 10 days following the end of each month.

Jackson has asked you to prepare the Consignment Agreement using the foregoing information. Supply any additional information that is required to complete the document, choosing terms that reasonably favor Jackson.

_____

_____

_____

CHAPTER 18 QUIZ

Section A

DIRECTIONS: Following each question below, indicate your answer by placing a " Y" for "Yes" or an "N" for "No" in the Answers column.

	Answers	For Scoring
1. May the parties to a sales contract specify when the risk of loss passes?		1._____
2. Whenever goods are damaged without any fault of either buyer or seller, must the seller bear the loss and supply new goods to the buyer?..		2._____
3. When the terms of the contract require that the goods be shipped, are the seller's duties performed when conforming goods are delivered to the shipper?		3._____
4. If existing goods are to be transported, does title to the goods pass when the seller delivers them to the shipper?		4._____
5. Does a buyer obtain title at the time of contracting when, at this time, negotiable documents represent existing, identified goods?		5._____
6. If identified goods are damaged without the fault of either party before the risk of loss has passed, is the contract avoided if the loss is total?		6._____
7. When goods are sold "on approval" does title pass at the time of delivery?		7._____
8. Does the seller bear the risk of loss until goods are delivered at the FOB point?		8._____
9. If an owner entrusts goods to a merchant who deals in goods of that type, can the merchant transfer title to the goods to an innocent purchaser?		9._____
10. May the owner of property ever be estopped from asserting ownership?		10._____

Score _____

Section B

DIRECTIONS: Complete each of the following statements by writing the missing word or words in the Answers column.

	Answers	For Scoring
1. Evidence of ownership of property is called...		1.____
2. A document of title issued by a storage company for the goods stored is a(n)		2.____
3. The carrier's receipt showing the terms of the contract of transportation is a(n)		3.____
4. A sale that is not complete until the buyer approves the goods is called a(n).		4.____
5. A completed sale with the buyer having the right to return the goods and set aside the sale is a(n)...		5.____
6. Any article, group of articles, or quantity commercially regarded as a separate item is a(n)...		6.____
7. An agency in which goods are in the possession of a third party in order to be sold is a(n)		7.____
8. Goods of a homogeneous or like nature are called		8.____
9. The designated point to which the seller of goods bears the risk of loss and expense is called..		9.____
10. A writing that shows ownership is called a(n)		10.____

Score _____

Section C

DIRECTIONS: Following each statement below, indicate your answer by placing a "T" for "True" or an "F" for "False" in the Answers column.

	Answers	For Scoring
1. Until paid, the seller has an economic interest in a sales transaction.	_____	1._____
2. To be existing goods, the goods must be in the condition required by the sales contract.	_____	2._____
3. A merchant seller bears the risk of loss for a shorter time than a consumer seller.	_____	3._____
4. Risk of loss for damage to a motor vehicle does not pass to the buyer until a certificate of title is issued.	_____	4._____
5. Title and risk of loss pass to the buyer when the seller, for the benefit of the shipping department, marks the goods to indicate the ones to be sent.	_____	5._____
6. When a buyer orders goods to be shipped later, risk of loss passes when the goods are delivered to the carrier.	_____	6._____
7. If damage occurs to identified goods after the risk of loss has passed, it is the buyer's loss.	_____	7._____
8. During the period from the transfer of the risk of loss to the transfer of possession to the buyer, the seller has the status of a bailee.	_____	8._____
9. So long as goods are unidentified, risk of loss does not pass to the buyer.	_____	9._____
10. The fact that a seller reserves title or possession does not affect when risk of loss passes to the buyer.	_____	10._____
11. When the buyer may return goods. whether the buyer is a merchant or not determines whether the transaction is a sale on approval or a sale or return.	_____	11._____
12. Goods delivered to a buyer in a sale on approval transaction can be claimed by the buyer's creditors at any time while the buyer has possession of the goods	_____	12._____
13. A consignment is a type of agency.	_____	13._____
14. Title to fungible goods cannot pass until they are separated from the mass.	_____	14._____
15. Title to each lot sold at an auction passes independently of the other lots.	_____	15._____
16. Shipping goods COD changes the time when title and risk of loss pass.	_____	16._____
17. In general, a person who buys goods from a thief does not receive title to the goods.	_____	17._____
18. The owner of property may never be barred from asserting ownership.	_____	18._____
19. Documents of title include bills of lading and warehouse receipts.	_____	19._____
20. When a sales contract is voidable, the seller may still avoid the contract and keep possession and title to the goods even if the buyer has resold the goods to an innocent purchaser.	_____	20._____

Score _____

CHAPTER 19
WARRANTIES, PRODUCT LIABILITY AND CONSUMER PROTECTION

CHAPTER OUTLINE

I. INTRODUCTION

► A warranty is an assurance of a fact that relates to a good, or an assurance of the future performance or condition of a good. ► A warranty may be made before or after a contract is made. A warranty that is made after a sale is valid even if consideration is not given for the warranty.

II. EXPRESS WARRANTIES

- *Definition*: (1) Statement of fact or promise regarding quality or performance of a good (2) that is a basis of the bargain (i.e., the statement or promise is presumed to be part of the contract).
- *Form:* ► Express warranties can be oral or written; no special words are needed. ► Warranties may arise due to statements made in negotiations, ads, brochures, etc. An express warranty is interpreted according to its ordinary meaning, not by what the seller secretly intended.

A. SELLER'S OPINION

General rule.   Opinions and "puffing" (sales talk) do not create express warranties.
Example.   "This car is the best buy on the market" is an opinion, not an express warranty.
Limitations.   ► A seller may be liable for fraud if the seller states an opinion that the seller does not believe is true. ► A seller's opinion may create a warranty if the seller has knowledge of facts that are unknown to the buyer.

B. DEFECTS

General rule.   Express warranties do not apply to obvious defects or defects known to a buyer.
Example.   "This car has no defects" would not apply to an obviously broken windshield.

III. IMPLIED WARRANTIES

General rule. Warranties implied by law arise automatically when a sales contract is made.
Examples.   ► Warranty of merchantability. ► Warranty of fitness for a particular purpose.
Study hint.   A contract may have express and implied warranties. If warranties conflict, express warranties prevail over all implied warranties except the warranty of fitness for a particular purpose.

IV. FULL OR LIMITED WARRANTIES

► Express warranties made in sales of consumer goods are full or limited warranties. ► Among other things, a full warranty requires a seller to fix or replace a defective good within a reasonable time and without cost to a buyer. If this cannot be done, the buyer can choose to request a refund or a free replacement. ► A limited warranty is a warranty that does not qualify as a full warranty.

V. WARRANTIES OF ALL SELLERS

A. WARRANTY OF TITLE

General rule.   Every seller warrants that he or she has good title and the right to transfer title.
Limitation.   A seller does not warrant title if: (1) the contract disclaims this warranty; or (2) goods are sold by a sheriff, a creditor enforcing a lien, or an administrator of an estate.

B. WARRANTY AGAINST ENCUMBRANCES

▸ Every seller warrants that goods, *when delivered*, will not be subject to a security interest that the buyer did not actually know of at the time of contracting. ▸ Constructive notice (notice presumed because a lien is recorded) is not actual notice. It does not negate this warranty.

C. WARRANTY OF CONFORMITY TO DESCRIPTION, SAMPLE, OR MODEL

General rule.   Express warranties can be created by a description (labels), or by showing a buyer a sample (specimen of goods to be furnished) or a model (example of what goods will be like).
Limitation.   A sample or model creates a warranty only if it is a basis of the bargain.

D. WARRANTY OF FITNESS FOR A PARTICULAR PURPOSE

It is implied that a seller warrants that a good is fit for an unusual purpose if: (1) seller has reason to know a buyer intends an unusual use for a good, and that the buyer is relying on seller to select an appropriate good; and (2) buyer actually relies on seller's judgment. This warranty does not apply if: (1) goods are used only for ordinary purposes; or (2) a buyer designed the goods.

VI.   ADDITIONAL WARRANTIES OF MERCHANT

Merchant: party who deals in goods of the kind being sold or who by an occupation represents himself or herself as having special knowledge or skill regarding the goods in question.

A. WARRANTY AGAINST INFRINGEMENT

Merchant sellers generally warrant that goods do not violate others' patents or trademarks.

B. WARRANTY OF MERCHANTABILITY OR FITNESS FOR NORMAL USE

General rule.   Merchant sellers warrant that goods: (1) are fit for ordinary purposes for which such goods are used; (2) are of average quality; and (3) are adequately packaged and labeled.
Limitation.   This warranty only relates to the condition of goods at the time they are delivered.
Study hints.   ▸ Goods need not be the best or perfect. ▸ This warranty is not breached simply because goods could have been made better or safer by using a different design.

VII.   WARRANTIES IN PARTICULAR SALES

▪ *Sale of food or drink*: Warranties apply to sales of food (whether consumed on or off seller's premises). Fitness (merchantability) of food is determined by one of two tests: (1) reasonable expectation test: an unintended substance in food renders food unfit if a buyer should not expect to find the substance in the food; or (2) foreign/natural test: food is unfit if a substance is foreign (e.g., a stone in pea soup); it is fit if an unintended substance is natural (e.g., pit in a prune).

▪ *Sale of article with patent or trade name*: Selling a good on the basis of its patent or trade name does not always eliminate warranties. Warranties may still exist if this is intended by the parties.

▪ *Sale on buyer's specifications*: If goods are made according to a buyer's specifications, express or implied warranties may apply except: (1) the warranty of fitness for a particular purpose does not arise; and (2) a seller's warranty against infringement is not implied.

▪ *Sale of secondhand or used goods*: In a number of states, the warranty of merchantability applies to sales of used goods if a seller is a merchant. (It does not apply if the seller is a casual seller.)

VIII.   EXCLUSION AND SURRENDER OF WARRANTIES

General rules.   Parties can agree to disclaim any warranty, provided the disclaimer is not unconscionable.
▸ Disclaimer of warranty of merchantability: (1) may be oral or written; (2) must use word "merchantability"; and (3) must be conspicuous (noticeable to a reasonable person) if written. ▸ Disclaimer of warranty of fitness for particular purpose must be written and conspicuous.
Limitation.   Disclaimer is invalid if it is communicated to a buyer after the contract was made.

A. PARTICULAR PROVISIONS

Warranties of merchantability and fitness for a particular purpose are excluded by a general disclaimer, such as "as is," "with all faults," or other statements indicating that no implied warranties are made. To be effective, general disclaimers must be brought to a buyer's attention.

B. EXAMINATION

If a buyer examines (or refuses to examine) a good, sample, or model before contracting, no implied warranties are made regarding matters the buyer would discover by examining the good.

C. DEALINGS AND CUSTOMS

Implied warranties may be excluded by course of performance or dealing, or by usage of trade.

IX. CAVEAT EMPTOR

‣ Caveat emptor means "Let the buyer beware." At common law, caveat emptor meant that a people bought goods at their own risk, and sellers made no implied warranties. ‣ Caveat emptor has been modified by statutes, including the UCC and consumer protection statutes. ‣ Caveat emptor still applies when the buyer can examine the goods to discover any defects and the seller has not been guilty of fraud.

X. PRODUCT LIABILITY

A manufacturer may be liable for damages if the use or condition of a product causes injury.

A. BREACH OF WARRANTY (PARTIES ENTITLED TO RECOVER FOR BREACH)

- *Common law*: A person cannot sue for breach of warranty unless there is privity of contract (a direct contractual relationship) between the injured person and the defendant sued.
- *UCC*: The buyer, a member of buyer's family or household, or a guest may sue for personal injuries caused by a breach of warranty. Privity of contract is not required.
- *Trend*: ‣ The trend is to abolish the privity of contract requirement. ‣ In certain cases, some states let a party sue a manufacturer or remote seller for breach of warranty without privity of contract.

B. EFFECT OF REPROCESSING BY DISTRIBUTOR

Manufacturer may not be liable if goods are supposed to be reprocessed by a distributor.

XI. IDENTITY OF PARTIES

- *Third persons*: Some courts let employees of buyers sue for breach of warranty; others do not.
- *Manufacturer of component part*: If privity of contract is not required, a manufacturer of a component part may be sued for breach of warranty by a buyer or other plaintiff.

XII. NATURE AND CAUSE OF HARM

‣ The law is more concerned with protection of the person than protection of property. ‣ To be liable, a defendant must have caused the harm. ‣ To prove breach of warranty, a plaintiff needs to show: (1) a sale and warranty existed; (2) the goods did not conform to the warranty; and (3) an injury resulted from the nonconformity of the goods.

XIII. LEASED GOODS

General rule. Most states have adopted UCC Article 2A governing leases of goods. Article 2A provides express and implied warranties similar to those in UCC Article 2 governing sales of goods.
Limitation. The warranty of title in Article 2 is replaced by a warranty of possession without interference in Article 2A.

XIV. CONSUMER PROTECTION

A. USURY LAWS

General rules. ▸ Usury laws establish the maximum interest rate that can be charged on loans. ▸ The penalty for violating usury laws varies between states. ▸ States commonly establish several types of interest rates, including:

- **Legal rate**: This rate applies if a party is obligated to pay interest, but no rate is stated by the parties. Depending on the state, this rate may range from 5 to 15 percent.

- **Maximum contract rate**: This is the highest interest rate that can be charged. Depending on the state, this rate may range from 8 to 45 percent.

Limitations. ▸ Some states do not limit interest that can be charged. ▸ Some states allow more interest on small loans. ▸ In many states, usury laws do not apply if a debtor is a corporation.

B. PRODUCT SAFETY

The federal government imposes design standards for many goods. Penalties for violation: (1) products can be recalled; and (2) managers who authorize selling obviously dangerous goods may be fined/imprisoned.

C. DISCLOSURE AND UNIFORMITY

- *Consumer Product Safety Act*: ▸ This federal law created the Consumer Product Safety Commission (CPSC) that (1) has established safety standards for many products and (2) can ban or halt the sale of unsafe goods. ▸ Manufacturers and sellers of consumer goods must report any nonconforming or dangerous products to this Commission. ▸ This Act does not apply to motor vehicles, pesticides, airplanes, boats, food, or drugs.

- *Truth in advertising*: ▸ Federal Trade Commission (FTC) requires that statements made in advertisements must be true and be substantiated. ▸ If a statement is false or deceptive, the FTC may: (1) seek a consent order (an advertiser's voluntary agreement to discontinue an ad or to run corrective advertising); or (2) issue a cease and desist order, which prohibits a party from engaging in certain conduct. However, this order can be contested in court.

- *Truth in lending*: ▸ Federal Truth in Lending Act requires lenders (and ads) to disclose: (1) finance charges; (2) annual percentage rate (APR) (annual amount charged for a loan); and (3) number, amount, and due dates of payments, including balloon payments. ▸ If a purchase of consumer goods is secured by a mortgage on the consumer's home, the consumer has 3 days within which to rescind the agreement.

- *Product uniformity*: ▸ Unit pricing: price per ounce or other measure is stated. ▸ Some local governments require unit pricing to enable consumers to compare prices for goods. ▸ The federal government requires car dealers to publish mileage test data.

C. STATUTES PROHIBITING UNCONSCIONABLE CONTRACTS

▸ UCC Section 2-302 allows courts to void unconscionable contracts (or terms) relating to sales of goods.
▸ Unconscionable: grossly unfair; so outrageous it violates basic community standards.

XV. FAIR CREDIT REPORTING (FAIR CREDIT REPORTING ACT)

- *Important provisions of Fair Credit Reporting Act*: ▸ A creditor must notify a credit applicant when credit is denied based on a credit report. ▸ A consumer who is the subject of a credit report can find out the substance of the report. ▸ Incorrect reports must be corrected, and a consumer may add a written explanation if a report is disputed. ▸ Certain adverse information (e.g., lawsuits) cannot be reported after seven years. ▸ Credit reports can be used for legitimate business purposes only.

- *Remedies*: ▸ Persons harmed by a negligent violation of the Act may recover ordinary damages. ▸ Willful noncompliance may entitle victims to punitive damages.

- *State consumer protection agencies*: In many states, consumer protection is handled by the state attorney general or a consumer affairs office who investigate complaints, seek voluntary compliance, and exercise injunctive powers (i.e., they issue cease and desist orders forbidding improper acts).

REVIEW OF CHAPTER

REVIEW OF TERMS

Select the term that best matches a statement below. Each term is the best match for only one statement.

TERMS

a. Balloon payment
b. *Caveat emptor*
c. Conspicuous
d. Disclaimer
e. Finance charge

f. Injunctive powers
g. Privity of contract
h. Sample
i. Unconscionable
j. Usury laws

k. Warranty against encumbrances
l. Warranty against infringement
m. Warranty of fitness for a particular purpose
n. Warranty of merchantability
o. Warranty of title

STATEMENTS

Answer

_____ 1.   Authority to issue cease and desist orders.

_____ 2.   Noticeable to a reasonable person.

_____ 3.   Grossly unfair; violates conscience of community.

_____ 4.   Disavowal or elimination of a warranty.

_____ 5.   Laws that establish the maximum rate of interest that can be charged for loans.

_____ 6.   Warranty that a seller has good title and that the seller has the right to transfer title.

_____ 7.   Common law maxim "let the buyer beware"; i.e., a buyer purchases goods at his or her own risk without any implied warranties by the seller.

_____ 8.   Warranty that a good is not subject to a lien that a buyer is unaware of at time of contracting.

_____ 9.   Implied warranty that a good can perform an unusual use that is intended by the buyer.

_____ 10.   Payment that is more than twice the amount of a normal installment payment.

_____ 11.   Implied warranty that a good is fit for the ordinary purposes for which the good is sold.

_____ 12.   Warranty that a good does not violate patent or trademark rights of others.

_____ 13.   Direct contractual relationship between two parties.

_____ 14.   A portion of a whole mass that is the subject of a transaction.

_____ 15.   Total dollar amount that a borrower pays for credit. This amount includes interest and all fees that are charged in order to obtain a loan.

REVIEW OF CONCEPTS

Directions: Indicate **T** for true and **F** for false in the answer column.

_____ 1. A warranty that is made by a seller after a sales contract has been made is not binding unless consideration is given for the warranty.

_____ 2. To create an express warranty, a seller must specifically use the words "warrant" or "guarantee."

_____ 3. If express and implied warranties conflict, implied warranties always prevail.

_____ 4. Under appropriate circumstances, implied warranties, such as the warranty of merchantability, are imposed by the law in connection with sales contracts.

_____ 5. In general, an express written warranty in a sale of a consumer good is not a full warranty if a buyer must pay for repairs or if implied warranties are eliminated.

_____ 6. Only merchant sellers can make a warranty of title, a warranty against encumbrances, a warranty of conformity to a description or model, or a warranty of fitness for a particular purpose.

_____ 7. Seller showed Buyer a model of a boat that Seller offered to make for Buyer. The model was intended to be the exact replica of Buyer's boat. Seller's conduct created an express warranty.

_____ 8. All sellers warrant that goods do not infringe on the patent or trademark rights of others.

_____ 9. The warranty of merchantability obligates a seller to design and sell the safest product possible.

_____ 10. A sales contract may include warranties even if a buyer ordered a good by its trade name.

_____ 11. According to some courts, the warranty of merchantability may apply to a merchant's sale of used goods.

_____ 12. A buyer's refusal to examine goods may exclude implied warranties regarding obvious defects.

_____ 13. Under the UCC, only the buyer can sue for personal injuries caused by a breach of warranty.

_____ 14. A manufacturer or seller cannot change its warranty liability by the terms included in the sales contract.

_____ 15. In a lease of goods transaction, UCC Article 2A provides a warranty of possession without interference.

REVIEW OF CONCEPT APPLICATIONS

Answer

Directions: Indicate your choice in the answer column.

_____ 1. In which case does Seller breach an express warranty?
   a. Seller stated to Byron: "This ring is solid sterling silver." Byron then purchased the ring, but he later discovered that the ring was made of brass, with only a thin silver plating.
   b. Seller stated to Stan: "This drill is the best, most useful little drill on the market." Stan purchased the drill, but he did not find the drill to be very useful.
   c. Seller stated to Buyer: "This antique table does not have any defects." Both parties knew the tabletop was split, and they assumed that Seller was not talking about the tabletop.
   d. All of the above.

_____ 2. Select the correct statement.
   a. K&L foreclosed a lien on a debtor's goods. K&L held a sale of the goods. Prior to sale, buyers were told that only the debtor's interest, if any, was being sold. As it turns out, the debtor had defective title to the goods. In this case, K&L breached the warranty of title.
   b. Kit sold an engine to Buyer. Unknown to the parties, Kit did not have title to the engine. In this case, the warranty of title is breached.
   c. John sold a car to Sam. Unknown to Sam, the car was subject to a lien. Prior to delivery, John had the lien removed. In this case, the warranty against encumbrances is breached.
   d. All of the above.

_____ 3. In which case is the implied warranty of fitness for a particular purpose breached?
   a. Manufacturer made an unusual egg incubator and sold it to City Zoo. At time of contracting, Manufacturer knew Zoo needed an incubator for hatching ostrich eggs, an unusual purpose, and that Zoo was relying on Manufacturer to make a proper incubator. (Zoo did in fact rely on Manufacturer.) The incubator delivered did not hatch ostrich eggs; it baked them.
   b. Buyer needed paint that could withstand unusual, prolonged heat. Buyer independently developed and furnished Manufacturer with specifications for a paint. The paint was made in accordance with the specifications, but it failed to perform the unusual task.
   c. Seller sold Buyer a lawn mower. Unknown to Seller, Buyer intended to use the mower to cut three-foot tall Saltmarsh grass, an unusual purpose. The mower failed to cut this grass.
   d. a and b.

_____ 4. The implied warranty of merchantability is breached in which case?
   a. Juanita, a consumer, sold Bob a new toaster that she had received as a gift. The toaster does not toast.
   b. Seller (a merchant) sold a standard, private airplane to Buyer. The plane operates safely and it is fit for ordinary use. However, the plane is of only average quality; it is not the best plane on the market.
   c. Spokes (a merchant) sold a bike to Buyer. The bike was fit for its ordinary use when delivered. Two years later, the bike was unusable due to Buyer's constant use of the bike.
   d. None of the above.

_____ 5. M&M Cafe sold Lucy a guacamole taco. The taco had a piece of avocado pit in it (guacamole is made from avocados, which have pits). Under these facts:
   a. M&M cannot breach the warranty of merchantability; warranties do not apply to food sales.
   b. M&M cannot breach the warranty of merchantability; this warranty does not apply to merchant sellers.
   c. Under the reasonable expectation test, the taco is unfit (not merchantable) if Lucy could not reasonably expect to find the piece of pit in the taco.
   d. Under the foreign/natural test, the taco is unfit (not merchantable).

_____ 6. Chuck agreed to lend Fay some money. Under state law, Fay is obligated to pay interest on the loan if she does not repay it on time. However, the agreement between Fay and Chuck does not specify what rate of interest Fay will pay. Under these facts, Fay must pay the:
   a. Maximum contract rate.
   b. Fluctuating maximum contract rate.
   c. Prime rate.
   d. Legal rate.

_____ 7. Autos Inc. plans to advertise a car for sale on credit. The ad will state the credit price for the car. What information must this ad disclose in order to comply with the Truth-in-Lending Act?
   a. Only the fact that interest will be charged.
   b. Finance charge and APR.
   c. Finance charge; APR; and the number, amount, and due dates of payments.
   d. Nothing.

8. Susan bought a watch that cost $300. The watch was guaranteed by a written, full one-year warranty. One month later, the watch stopped running. Seller has repeatedly tried to fix the watch, but the watch still does not work. Under these facts:
   a. Susan's only remedy is to continue to ask the seller to repair the watch.
   b. Susan may request a full refund or a new, replacement watch.
   c. If Susan requests a refund or a new, replacement watch but Seller refuses, Susan cannot sue Seller for damages.
   d. b and c.

9. Brenda applied to Lender for credit to buy a car. Brenda was denied credit because of an inaccurate credit report that was negligently prepared for Lender by Reliable Credit Agency. Under these facts:
   a. Brenda can sue Reliable for ordinary damages she suffered due to the inaccurate report.
   b. Brenda can sue Reliable for punitive damages.
   c. Brenda cannot sue Reliable because Reliable did not intentionally make an inaccurate report.

CASE PROBLEM

Vision, Inc., a manufacturer of commercial microscopes, plans to sell a new microscope. Vision is concerned about its potential liability for implied warranties. Answer the following questions:

1. In general, can Vision disclaim the warranties of merchantability and fitness for a particular purpose?
2. Can Vision disclaim the warranty of merchantability by burying a term in the contract in such a manner that an ordinary person would not notice the disclaimer?
3. If Vision's sales contract conspicuously states that a microscope is sold "as is," what effect, if any, would this term have on implied warranties?

_____

_____

_____

_____

BUSINESS LAW PARTNER EXERCISE

Directions:

1. Access your Business Law Partner CD-ROM and locate the document entitled "Consumer Information Catalog." Complete this document for yourself.
2. List five types of subject matters for which consumer-related publications may be available.

_____

_____

_____

CHAPTER 19 QUIZ

Section A

DIRECTIONS: Following each question below, indicate your answer by placing a "Y" for "Yes" or an "N" for "No" in the Answers column.

		Answers	For Scoring
1.	Does a warranty made at the time of a sale become part of the contract?	_____	1. _____
2.	Does a warranty made after the sale and unsupported by a separate consideration become a part of the sales contract?	_____	2. _____
3.	Is it necessary in making a warranty that the seller use the words "warrant" or "guarantee"?	_____	3. _____
4.	Does a statement of opinion generally constitute a warranty?	_____	4. _____
5.	Does an express warranty always cover defects that are known to the buyer?	_____	5. _____
6.	Does UCC Article 2 empower courts to refuse enforcement of unconscionable contracts?	_____	6. _____
7.	Is there an implied warranty of title when property is sold by a sheriff under orders of a court?	_____	7. _____
8.	Does a warranty against encumbrances apply to goods only at the time they are delivered to the buyer?	_____	8. _____
9.	Is it a sale by sample whenever a sample is exhibited in the course of negotiations?	_____	9. _____
10.	Is there a warranty of fitness for a particular purpose when goods are ordered on particular specifications and the purpose is not disclosed?	_____	10. _____
11.	If an advertisement mentions credit terms, is it generally required that the advertisement disclose finance charges that must be paid?...	_____	11. _____
12.	Do all sellers make a warranty of merchantability?	_____	12. _____
13.	Do all merchants who sell food warrant that it is fit for its ordinary purpose--human consumption?	_____	13. _____
14.	Is there a special warranty that applies when a patented good is sold?	_____	14. _____
15.	Can warranties be excluded by agreement of the parties?	_____	15. _____
16.	Is it correct that a consumer can sue a manufacturer for breach of warranty only if the consumer purchased the good directly from the manufacturer?	_____	16. _____
17.	Does the UCC permit recovery for breach of warranty by guests of the buyer?	_____	17. _____
18-20.	Andrea's Grocery Store bought a certain brand of canned corn after testing a sample. Customer complaints and further testing showed that the corn was of inferior quality and that some of the corn was not of the same variety as the corn sampled. Was there a breach of warranty on the part of the seller?	_____	18. _____
	Does the rule of caveat emptor apply in this purchase?	_____	19. _____
	Does the fact that Andrea tested a sample affect her rights against the seller?	_____	20. _____

Score _____

Section B

DIRECTIONS: Complete each of the following statements by writing the missing word or words in the Answers column.

	Answers	For Scoring
1. The Consumer Product Safety Act regulates the safety of employees in the work place	_____	1. _____
2. A statement that "these goods are the best on the market" is called	_____	2. _____
3. When the warranty is not expressed but becomes part of the sales contract, it is called a(n)	_____	3. _____
4. A written guarantee for a consumer product that does not have an unlimited duration is a(n)	_____	4. _____
5. The FTC cannot issue cease and desist orders to prevent deceptive ads.........	_____	5. _____
6. Information or knowledge imputed by law is	_____	6. _____
7. A seller who deals in goods of the kind or who is considered, because of occupation, to have particular knowledge or skill regarding the goods involved is a(n)	_____	7. _____
8. The warranty that goods are fit for the ordinary purposes for which they are sold is the	_____	8. _____
9. The maxim that states "let the buyer beware" is	_____	9. _____
10. A contract relationship between the parties is	_____	10. _____

Score _____

Section C

DIRECTIONS: In the Answers space in Column II, place the letter of the corresponding word or words from Column I.

Column I	Column II	Answers	Scoring
(a) borrow			
(b) express	1. A portion of a whole mass that is the subject of the transaction ...	_____	1. _____
(c) full	2. Affirmations of fact or promises made by the seller to the buyer that relate to the goods and become part of the basis for the bargain are ??? warranties.	_____	2. _____
(d) implied			
(e) lease			
(f) limited	3. ??? warranties agree to remedy any defects in the consumer product in a reasonable time without charge and place no limit on the duration of implied warranties..	_____	3. _____
(g) model			
(h) sample	4. Rather than purchasing goods, many people and businesses now ??? them.	_____	4. _____
(i) seller's opinion			
(j) warranty	5. A replica of the article in question is a(n).	_____	5. _____

Score _____

CHAPTER 20
NATURE OF NEGOTIABLE INSTRUMENTS

CHAPTER OUTLINE

I. INTRODUCTION

General rules. ▸ A negotiable instrument, also called commercial paper, is a special writing that evidences an obligation to pay money, and it may be transferred from party to party. ▸ Negotiable instruments are important because one type of transferee (a holder in due course) may acquire a right to demand payment that is superior to the right possessed by the transferor.

Study hint.   A negotiable instrument is (1) a substitute for money and (2) a means to provide credit.

II. HISTORY AND DEVELOPMENT

In England, commercial paper was governed by the law merchant (rules applied by courts that were set up by merchants). In the United States, commercial paper was governed by common law rules based on the law merchant, and the Uniform Negotiable Instruments Law later governed it. Presently, commercial paper is governed by Article 3 of the UCC. Nearly all states have adopted a 1990 revision of Article 3, which uses the term "negotiable instruments" rather than "commercial paper."

III. NEGOTIATION

Negotiation transfers ownership of a negotiable instrument to another party.

IV. ORDER PAPER AND BEARER PAPER

General rule.   A negotiable instrument must be payable to the order of a named person, or to bearer.

Examples.   ▸ Order paper: draft payable "to the order of Ruth Hays" or "to Ruth Hays or order." ▸ Bearer paper: draft payable to "bearer," "order of Ruth Hays or bearer," or "cash."

Study hints.   ▸ If an instrument merely states "pay to X," it is ordinarily nonnegotiable. ▸ To be negotiable, an instrument must typically use one of these words: "order," "bearer," or "cash."

V. CLASSIFICATION OF COMMERCIAL PAPER

- *Drafts*: ▸ Defined: unconditional written order by a party directing another to pay a sum certain in money on demand or at definite time to order or bearer. ▸ Parties to draft: drawer, drawee, and payee. ▸ Types of drafts: checks and trade acceptances.

- *Promissory notes*: ▸ Defined: unconditional written promise to pay a sum certain in money on demand or at a definite time to order or bearer. ▸ Parties to promissory note: maker and payee.

VI. PARTIES TO NEGOTIABLE INSTRUMENTS

- *Payee*: ▸ Defined: party named on the face of an instrument as the party to receive payment. ▸ Example: Dave issues his check ordering his Bank to pay $100 to Paul. Paul is a payee.

- *Drawer*: ▸ Defined: party who creates and signs a draft (including a bill of exchange or check). ▸ Example: Dave signs his check ordering his bank to pay $100 to Paul. Dave is a drawer.

- *Drawee*: ▸ Defined: party ordered by a drawer to pay a draft or check. ▸ Example: Dave issues his check ordering his bank, ABC Bank, to pay $100 to Paul. ABC Bank is a drawee.

- *Acceptor*: ▸ Defined: drawee who, in writing on a draft, agrees to pay the draft. ▸ Example: Dave issues a check, ordering Bank to pay a check. Bank writes on the check that it agrees to pay.

- *Maker*: Defined: party who creates and executes a promissory note.

- *Bearer*: ▸ Defined: party who possesses an instrument that is payable to bearer. ▸ Example: Dave issues a check payable to bearer, and he delivers the check to Paul. Paul is a bearer.
- *Holder*: Defined: party to whom a negotiable instrument is originally issued and delivered, or to whom a negotiable instrument is subsequently negotiated.
- *Holder in due course*: Defined: holder who takes an instrument for value, in good faith, and without notice that it is overdue or dishonored, or that there are any defenses or claims to it.
- *Indorser*: ▸ Defined: party who signs the back of an instrument. ▸ Example: Dave issues his check payable to the order of Paul, and Paul signs the back of the check. Paul is an indorser.
- *Indorsee*: ▸ Defined: party to whom an indorsed instrument is payable. ▸ Example: Paul specially indorses a check stating "pay to Irene" on the back of the check. Irene is an indorsee.

VII.   NEGOTIATION AND ASSIGNMENT

General rules.   ▸ A negotiable instrument may be transferred by negotiation or assignment. ▸ The manner of transfer affects the rights of a transferee.   The effects of negotiation and assignment are:

- *Negotiation*: (1) transferee is a holder and may be a holder in due course; (2) transferee may have a greater right to enforce payment than the original holder; and (3) transferee may take the instrument free from certain defenses that could have been raised against the original holder.
- *Assignment*: (1) transferee cannot be a holder or a holder in due course; (2) transferee is an assignee who receives only the assignor's right to payment; and (3) any defense that could be asserted against the original holder (assignor) can be asserted against the transferee.

Examples.   ▸ Negotiation: Bob issued a negotiable note in payment for goods, but Seller failed to deliver the goods. Seller negotiated the note to Pat, a holder in due course. In this situation, Bob cannot assert his defense against Pat, and he must pay the note to Pat. ▸ Assignment: Sally signed a nonnegotiable note for goods, but Seller failed to deliver the goods. Seller assigned the note to Dick. In this situation, Dick has only the same right to demand payment as Seller. Thus, Sally can assert her breach of contract defense against Dick, and she can avoid paying the note to Dick.

Limitation.   Between the original parties to an instrument (e.g., the maker and payee under a note, or the drawer and payee under a draft), negotiable and nonnegotiable paper are equally enforceable.

VIII.   CREDIT AND COLLECTION

- *Instruments of credit*: ▸ Defined: paper issued to accomplish a credit sale of property or services. ▸ Example: Buyer buys equipment on credit, and issues a negotiable note as payment.
- *Instrument of collection*: ▸ Defined: paper used to enable a creditor to collect a debt. ▸ Example: Seth sells goods to Bob; Seth issues a draft ordering Bob to pay Bank to whom Seth owes money.

IX.   ELECTRONIC FUND TRANSFERS

In general, electronic fund transfers (EFTs) involve transfers of money that generally do not utilize commercial paper (and hence are not governed by Article 3). Common types of EFTs:

- *Check truncation*: ▸ Defined: system of processing checks that shortens the normal procedure for processing and payment of checks. ▸ Example: canceled checks are not returned to a customer.
- *Preauthorized debits*: ▸ Defined: depositor authorizes bank to automatically pay set amounts to designated creditors. ▸ Example: bank automatically pays mortgage payments.
- *Preauthorized credits*: ▸ Defined: payments are automatically credited to a depositor's account. ▸ Example: police officer authorizes employer to deposit paychecks in officer's account.
- *Automated teller machines*: Defined: electronic terminals that perform routine banking functions.
- *Point-of-sale systems*: Defined: electronic terminals that enable a merchant to deduct a purchase price from a buyer's bank account and to deposit this sum into the merchant's account.

REVIEW OF CHAPTER

REVIEW OF TERMS

Select the term that best matches a statement below. Each term is the best match for only one statement.

TERMS

a. Acceptor

b Draft

c. Drawee

d. Drawer

e. Indorsee

f. Indorser

g. Maker

h. Negotiable instrument (commercial paper)

i. Payee

j. Promissory note

STATEMENTS

Answer

_____ 1. Party who is ordered by a drawer to pay a draft or check.

_____ 2. Party who originally signs and issues a promissory note.

_____ 3. Type of negotiable instrument that is an unconditional written order signed by one person ordering another to pay on demand or at a definite time a sum certain in money to order or to bearer.

_____ 4. Drawee who agrees to pay a draft by writing such agreement on the draft.

_____ 5. Party to whom an instrument is originally made payable (party stated on face of instrument).

_____ 6. Payee or holder who signs on the back of an instrument.

_____ 7. Type of negotiable instrument that is an unconditional written, signed promise to pay on demand or at a definite time a sum certain in money to order or to bearer.

_____ 8. Party to whom *an indorsement* directs payment to be made.

_____ 9. Writing evidencing an obligation to pay money, which is governed by Article 3 of the UCC.

_____ 10. Party who originally signs and issues a draft or check.

REVIEW OF CONCEPTS

Directions: Indicate **T** for true and **F** for false in the answer column.

_____ 1. Subject to certain limits, a transferee of a negotiable instrument may acquire a right to payment that is greater than the right of the original holder.

_____ 2. In the United States, negotiable instruments are presently governed by the law merchant.

_____ 3. A writing states: "I promise to pay $1,000 to Ken Hill." This writing is not a negotiable instrument because it is not made payable to the "order" of Ken Hill, or to bearer.

_____ 4. Ralph signed an instrument that stated: "I promise to pay $500 to bearer." This instrument could not be a negotiable instrument because it does not use the word "order."

_____ 5. A bearer is a person who is given a negotiable instrument made payable to "bearer."

_____ 6. Alex issues a check payable to the order of Lou. Lou indorses the check and delivers it to Quinn. In this situation, Quinn is a holder because a negotiable instrument was negotiated to him.

_____ 7. A draft or check has two original parties: a maker and a payee.

_____ 8. The original parties cannot legally enforce nonnegotiable instruments.

_____ 9. An *assignee* of a nonnegotiable (or negotiable) instrument only acquires the same right to payment as the assignor possessed, and the assignee takes the instrument subject to all defenses.

_____ 10. Preauthorized debit and credit transactions and point-of-sale systems involve transfers of money which are accomplished by transferring commercial paper.

REVIEW OF CONCEPT APPLICATIONS

Answer

Directions: Indicate your choice in the answer column.

_____ 1. Theodore issued and signed a negotiable instrument ordering Charles to pay $100 on demand "to the order of Mike Lansing." Under these facts:

    a.   This instrument is a promissory note, and it is order paper.

    b.   This instrument is a promissory note, and it is bearer paper.

    c.   This instrument is a draft, and it is order paper.

    d.   This instrument is a draft, and it is bearer paper.

_____ 2. Johannes issued and executed a negotiable instrument promising to pay $5,000 "to bearer" on January 1, 2002. Johannes then delivered the instrument to Reggie. Under these facts:
   a. This instrument is a promissory note, and it is order paper.
   b. This instrument is a promissory note, and it is bearer paper.
   c. This instrument is a draft, and it is order paper.
   d. This instrument is a draft, and it is bearer paper.

_____ 3. Otis issued and signed his personal check ordering Last Bank to pay $500 to the order of Yuan Chan. He delivered the check to Yuan. Yuan took the check to Last Bank and an authorized bank officer wrote "accepted for payment" on the check, and signed it. Under these facts:
   a. Otis is a maker.
   b. Last Bank is a drawer.
   c. Last Bank is a drawee and an acceptor.
   d. Yuan is a drawee.

_____ 4. Sarah issued and signed a negotiable promissory note promising to pay $1,000 to the order of Martha Yeager. On the back of the note, Martha wrote "Pay to Terrence Jones, (signed) Martha Yeager," and she delivered the note to Terrence. Under these facts:
   a. Sarah is a drawer.
   b. Martha is an indorser.
   c. Martha is an indorsee.
   d. Terrence is an indorser.

CASE PROBLEM

Seller sold a tractor to Terry. Terry executed a nonnegotiable promissory note to Seller as payment. Seller also sold a commercial truck to Denny, and Denny executed a negotiable promissory note to Seller as payment. Seller assigned Terry's note to Mr. Innocent, and he negotiated Denny's note to Mr. Innocent. Mr. Innocent took the notes for value, in good faith, and without notice of any problems. As it turns out, the tractor and truck both breach certain warranties, and Terry and Denny can both claim defenses against Seller. Under these facts, discuss Mr. Innocent's right to receive payment from (1) Terry and (2) Denny.

_____

_____

_____

BUSINESS LAW PARTNER EXERCISE

Directions:

1. Using the Online feature of the Business Law Partner CD-ROM, locate and identify a company that produces and sells checks for individuals and companies.
2. What terms must each check state or leave a blank for filling in?
3. In the case below, what risks, if any, would James encounter in ordering his business checks over the Internet?

Case Study: *Penny Wise and Pound Foolish?*

James just started a new dog grooming business called "Pruned Puppies." James has little capital and he is trying to save money anywhere he can. He intends to establish a business checking account, but he is concerned with the price that banks charge for checks. He is considering buying his checks from a company that sells them via the Internet.

_____

_____

_____

CHAPTER 20 QUIZ

Section A

DIRECTIONS: Complete each of the following statements by writing the missing word or words in the Answers column.

	Answers	For Scoring
1. A writing drawn in a special form, which can be transferred as a substitute for money or as an instrument of credit, is a(n)	_____	1. _____
2. The act of transferring a negotiable instrument to another party in such a manner that the instrument is payable to that party is called	_____	2. _____
3. A person who acquires rights superior to those of the original owner of a negotiable instrument is a(n)	_____	3. _____
4. A negotiable instrument made payable to the order of a named person is	_____	4. _____
5. A negotiable instrument that can be transferred merely by handing the paper to another person is	_____	5. _____
6. An unconditional order in writing addressed by one person to another, signed by the person giving it, requiring the one to whom it is addressed to pay on demand or at a particular time a sum certain in money to order or to bearer is a(n)...	_____	6. _____
7. An unconditional promise made in writing by one person to another, signed by the maker, engaging to pay on demand or at a particular time a sum certain in money to order or to bearer is a(n)................................	_____	7. _____
8. The party to whom a negotiable instrument is made payable is the...............	_____	8. _____
9. The person who executes a draft is called the..................................	_____	9. _____
10. The person who is ordered to pay a bill of exchange is the	_____	10. _____
11. The drawee of a bill of exchange who indicates a willingness to assume responsibility for its payment is called the..	_____	11. _____
12. The person who executes a promissory note is called the...........................	_____	12. _____
13. If the payee of a negotiable instrument is indicated as "Myself," "Cash," "Payroll," or some similar name, the term is equivalent to...........................	_____	13. _____
14. The person in possession of a negotiable instrument and to whom it was delivered and made payable is called the......................................	_____	14. _____
15. The payee who signs the back of negotiable instrument before delivering it to another party is called a(n)..	_____	15. _____
16. A person who becomes the holder of a negotiable instrument by an indorsement naming him or her as the person to whom the instrument is negotiated is called the..	_____	16. _____
17. A transfer of funds initiated electronically, telephonically, or by computer...	_____	17. _____
18. Shortening a check's trip from the payee to the drawer is called...................	_____	18. _____
19. The authorized, automatic deduction of a bill payment from a person's checking account each month is a(n)	_____	19. _____
20. An ATM terminal capable of performing routine banking services is a(n)	_____	20. _____

Score _____

Section B

DIRECTIONS: Following each question below, indicate your answer by placing a "Y" for "Yes" or an "N" for "No" in the Answers column.

	Answers	**For Scoring**
1. Are negotiable instruments different from commercial paper?	_____	1. _____
2. May a creditor refuse to accept a negotiable instrument in payment of a debt?	_____	2. _____
3. May the one to whom a negotiable instrument is transferred acquire rights superior to those of the original owner?	_____	3. _____
4. Does a negotiable instrument payable to the bearer require indorsement in order to be transferred?	_____	4. _____
5. May order paper be paid to any person in possession of the paper?	_____	5. _____
6. Are checks a type of draft?	_____	6. _____
7. Can a draft, which is not immediately payable, be accepted by an acceptor signing the draft a and writing "Accepted" on the face of it?	_____	7. _____
8. Is the obligation of the maker of a promissory note similar to that of the acceptor of a draft?	_____	8. _____
9. Are both a nonnegotiable instrument and a negotiable instrument equally enforceable between the original parties?	_____	9. _____
10. Are the rights given to subsequent parties the same whether an instrument is transferred by negotiation or assignment?	_____	10. _____
11. Does the assignee of a nonnegotiable instrument receive rights superior to those of the assignor?	_____	11. _____
12. If a defense of one of the original parties to a nonnegotiable contract is valid against the assignor, is it also valid against the assignee?	_____	12. _____
13. Can a transfer of funds that starts with a check be an EFT?	_____	13. _____
14. Are EFTs more expensive than the transfer of paper instruments?	_____	14. _____
15. Are banks required to disclose a customer's potential liability for unauthorized EFTs no later than the time the customer is charged for them?	_____	15. _____
16. Do many banks keep the actual cancelled checks and give customers a list of them?	_____	16. _____
17. May checking account customers authorize that recurring bills be automatically deducted from their checking accounts each month?	_____	17. _____
18. Do preauthorized credits benefit only the payor of a check?	_____	18. _____
19. Do all automatic teller machines have the same capabilities?	_____	19. _____
20. Does a point-of-sale entry reduce the customer's bank account?	_____	20. _____

Score _____

CHAPTER 21
ESSENTIALS OF NEGOTIABILITY

CHAPTER OUTLINE

I. INTRODUCTION

General rules. ▸ If an instrument is a negotiable instrument (i.e., it satisfies the requirements of negotiability discussed below), a transferee of the instrument may be a holder in due course, enabling the party to take it free of many defenses that could have been raised against the original holder. ▸ If an instrument is nonnegotiable (i.e., it does not satisfy the requirements of negotiability), a transferee has only the rights of an assignee and takes the instrument subject to all defenses.
Study hint.   Negotiability of an instrument is determined when it is first issued or completed.

II. REQUIREMENTS (OF NEGOTIABILITY)

To be negotiable, an instrument must: (1) be written and signed by a maker or drawer, (2) contain a promise or order (3) of an unconditional nature (4) to pay a fixed amount of money (5) on demand or at a definite time (6) to the order of a payee or bearer and (7) a payee and drawee must be named.

A. A SIGNED WRITING

General rules.   ▸ The required writing can generally be in any form. ▸ Any name, mark, or other signature is sufficient if placed on an instrument with the intent to bind the party signing.
Example.   Leslie Mays wrote out a promissory note partly in pen, and partly in pencil. Leslie signed using her nickname, Les Mays. The writing and signature requirements are met.
Limitation.   A signature cannot be made on a separate paper that is attached to an instrument.
Study hints.   ▸ A signature may be written, printed, typed, or stamped. ▸ An agent can sign an instrument. ▸ A maker's or drawer's signature is usually made in the lower right-hand corner of an instrument. However, a signature is valid even if placed elsewhere on an instrument.

B. AN ORDER OR A PROMISE TO PAY

General rule.   Promissory note must contain promise to pay; draft must contain an order to pay.
Limitation.   A mere acknowledgment of a debt (e.g., IOU) is not a negotiable instrument.
Study hint.   The word "promise" need not be used if language shows a definite intent to pay.

C. UNCONDITIONAL

General rule.   A promise or order to pay must be unconditional. A promise or order cannot be dependent on any condition or on any event that is not certain to occur.
Example.   Conditional promise: Promise to pay only if a party performs a contract.
Limitations.   ▸ Negotiability is not affected if a government agency promises to pay from a certain fund. ▸ Stating the consideration paid for an instrument does not affect negotiability. ▸ Under revised Article 3, an order to pay from a specific fund is not conditional.

D. A FIXED AMOUNT OF MONEY

General rules.   ▸ A negotiable instrument can be payable only in money (currency acceptable where payment is to be made). Payment in stock, property, or services is not permitted. ▸ An instrument must state principal and amount (or rate) of interest to be paid. ▸ The amount cannot depend on future events or impose a duty to pay a sum that cannot be determined until the future.
Examples.   ▸ Negotiable: "I promise to pay $100 plus 15 percent interest...." ▸ Nonnegotiable: "I promise to pay 20 percent of all profits earned by ABC Corp. in 2002." "I promise to pay $10,000, plus all future insurance and tax costs regarding subject property."

Limitation.   An instrument is negotiable even if it requires payment of a variable rate of interest.

Study hints.   ▸ Permitted terms: installment payments; debtor agrees to pay collection costs and attorney's fees. ▸ If terms conflict: amount stated in words wins over amount stated as a number; handwritten amount wins over typed amount; typed amount wins over printed amount.

E. PAYABLE ON DEMAND OR AT A DEFINITE TIME

General rules.   ▸ Instrument must be payable on demand or at a definite time. ▸ Payable on demand: payable "on demand" (demand note); payable "at sight" (sight draft); no time for payment is stated. ▸ Payable at definite time: pay on or before stated date (e.g., May 1, 2003).

Limitation.   Paper is nonnegotiable if payment is contingent on event that (1) may not occur ("pay after I earn $50,000"), or (2) is uncertain when it may occur ("pay 30 days after I die").

Study hint.   Permitted terms: acceleration clause (clause entitling a holder to demand payment in full if the debtor defaults in making one or more payments); prepayment clause (clause entitling a debtor to make early payments of principal and/or interest).

F. PAYABLE TO ORDER OR BEARER

General rules.   ▸ To be negotiable, an instrument must be payable to order or bearer. ▸ Under revised Article 3, a check (not other drafts or notes) stating "Pay to John Doe" is negotiable.

Examples.   ▸ Payable to order: "pay to the order of Randy Clark"; "pay to Randy Clark or order"; "pay to Randy Clark or assigns." ▸ Payable to bearer: "pay to bearer"; "pay to Randy Clark or bearer"; "pay to cash"; "pay to the order of cash."

Limitation.   A negotiable instrument may be payable to order without using the word "order" if the instrument is clearly payable to a named person *or* a transferee. However, this is rarely done.

G. PAYEE AND DRAWEE DESIGNATED WITH REASONABLE CERTAINTY

A payee of order paper and a drawee of a draft must be reasonably named or identified.

III.   ISSUE AND DELIVERY (REQUIREMENTS FOR ISSUANCE/NEGOTIATION OF PAPER)

▪ *Issuance*: An instrument has no legal effect until it is issued, i.e., drawer or maker (1) relinquishes control of instrument and (2) delivers it to a payee.

▪ *Negotiation of order paper*: Requirements: (1) proper indorsement by person to whom it is then payable (i.e., payee or subsequent indorsee); and (2) physical delivery of instrument to transferee.

▪ *Negotiation of bearer paper*: Requires only physical delivery of instrument to transferee.

▪ *Conditional delivery*: ▸ If paper is issued or transferred but delivery is conditioned on an event or act, issuance or negotiation does not occur until the condition is met. ▸ Exception: defense that delivery was conditional and condition is not satisfied cannot be used against holder in due course who later obtains the paper and demands payment.

IV.   DELIVERY OF AN INCOMPLETE INSTRUMENT

If a drawer or maker signs an incomplete instrument and delivers it to a payee with directions for completion, the drawer or maker: (1) is liable to a payee (or a holder) for the amount authorized; but (2) is liable to a holder in due course for the amount actually filled in, even if more than authorized.

V.   DATE AND PLACE

▪ *Date*: A negotiable instrument can be undated, antedated (dated earlier than date issued), or postdated (dated later than date issued). ▸ A holder can fill in correct date if the date is left blank.

▪ *Place*: A negotiable instrument does not need to state where it was issued or where it is payable.

REVIEW OF CHAPTER

REVIEW OF TERMS

Select the term that best matches a statement below. Each term is the best match for only one statement.

TERMS

a. Acceleration clause
b. Demand instrument
c. Issue

d. Negotiable instrument
e. Nonnegotiable instrument
f. Payable to bearer

g. Payable to order
h. Prepayment clause
i. Unconditional

STATEMENTS

Answer

_____ 1. Instrument that satisfies the seven requirements for negotiability.
_____ 2. Term that allows a holder to demand payment of entire debt if debtor fails to make a payment.
_____ 3. Payable to a named payee or any subsequent party to whom the instrument is negotiated.
_____ 4. Instrument that does not satisfy all seven requirements for negotiability.
_____ 5. Instrument that is payable immediately upon request by a holder.
_____ 6. Term that allows a debtor to make pay principal or interest earlier than required.
_____ 7. To relinquish control, and deliver an instrument to a payee.
_____ 8. Without qualification, limitations, conditions, or contingencies.
_____ 9. Payable to anyone in possession of the instrument when payment is due.

REVIEW OF CONCEPTS

Directions: Indicate **T** for true and **F** for false in the answer column.

_____ 1. A payee cannot enforce a nonnegotiable instrument.
_____ 2. A maker cannot authorize an agent to sign an instrument on behalf of the maker.
_____ 3. A note is nonnegotiable if it states: "I promise to pay $1,000 on demand to the order of Henry Feder out of the proceeds, if any, from the sale of my business."
_____ 4. A note is nonnegotiable if it states: "I promise to pay eight carloads of coal to bearer on demand."
_____ 5. A note is nonnegotiable if payments are to be paid in installments.
_____ 6. A note is nonnegotiable if a term in a note authorizes a holder to accelerate the due date if the maker defaults.
_____ 7. A payee cannot enforce a negotiable instrument until the maker or drawer issues it.
_____ 8. If delivery of a negotiable note by a maker to a payee is conditioned on the payee's doing an act, then, between the maker and the payee, issuance does not occur until the condition is met.
_____ 9. If a payee is given a partially completed instrument with instructions to fill in the amount, the payee can enforce the instrument for only the amount that he or she was authorized to fill in.
_____ 10. Carrie executed a promissory note that would ordinarily be negotiable. However, the note does not state when Carrie must pay. In this situation, the note cannot be negotiable.
_____ 11. If a draft or check is postdated, it cannot be a negotiable instrument.

REVIEW OF CONCEPT APPLICATIONS

Answer

Directions: Indicate your choice in the answer column.

_____ 1. Thomas Blue wrote out a promissory note in longhand. He signed the note "T. Blue." His signature was written in the left-hand corner of the instrument. Under these facts:
  a.   The note is nonnegotiable because it is handwritten.
  b.   The note is nonnegotiable because Mr. Blue did not sign his full name.
  c.   The note is nonnegotiable because Mr. Blue signed in the left-hand corner of the instrument.
  d.   The note satisfies the writing and signature requirements, and it may be negotiable.

_____ 2. Which writing may be a negotiable instrument?
   a. Kyle signed a note promising to pay $1,000 on demand to bearer. The note states that the note and the duty to pay are both subject to the terms of a separate loan agreement.
   b. Kyle signed a writing acknowledging that he owed Esther $300. The writing does not contain a promise or order to pay this sum.
   c. Kyle signed a note promising to pay $900 on demand to bearer. The note states that the note is given in consideration for a stereo that Kyle purchased from ABC Inc.

_____ 3. Which note may be negotiable?
   a. Pete signed a note promising to pay $1,000 and 100 bushels of wheat on demand to bearer.
   b. Pete signed a note promising to pay $1,000 on demand to the order of Liz Kelly. In the note, Pete also promised to pay reasonable collection costs and attorney fees if he defaults.
   c. Pete signed a note promising to pay $1,000 to bearer. Pete promised to pay 60 days after he is promoted to general manager. It is not certain whether Pete will be promoted.

_____ 4. Select the correct answer.
   a. Tom signed a negotiable note payable to the order of Sid. Tom still has the note; he did not deliver the note to Sid. In this case, Sid can enforce the note since it has been issued.
   b. Jake signed and delivered a negotiable draft payable to the order of Carl. To negotiate this draft, Carl must indorse the note and deliver it to a transferee.
   c. Patty signed a negotiable note payable to bearer, and she delivered it to Rose. To negotiate this note, Rose must indorse the note and deliver it to a transferee.

CASE PROBLEM

Roger is considering four forms of promissory note. Roger requests you to tell him: (1) whether the forms can create a negotiable instrument or not; and (2) if negotiable, whether the note created would be payable to order (order paper) or payable to bearer (bearer paper). Relevant portions of the forms read:

1. Form 1: "I promise to pay $1,000 to Sam West on demand...."
2. Form 2: "I promise to pay $1,000 to the order of Sam West on demand...."
3. Form 3: "I promise to pay $1,000 to the order of Sam West or bearer on demand...."
4. Form 4: "I promise to pay $1,000 to cash on demand...."

_____

_____

_____

BUSINESS LAW PARTNER EXERCISE

Directions: Access your Business Law Partner CD-ROM and find the document entitled "Promissory Note."

1. Complete the Promissory Note using the information provided in the following case study.
2. Is the Promissory Note, as completed, bearer paper or order paper?

Case Study: *Promises, Promises*

On December 1, 1998, Rita purchased a $5,000 motorcycle from Jim, paying $1,000 cash and signing a promissory note for the balance. Rita promised to pay the principal in 40 equal monthly payments together with accrued interest at the rate of 10 percent. The note may be accelerated if she is more than 30 days late in making any payment, and the interest would be 20 percent following any such default. The motorcycle secures payment of the note. Jim has asked you to help him complete the note, making sure that any other terms reasonably favor his interests.

_____

_____

_____

CHAPTER 21 QUIZ

Section A

DIRECTIONS: Following each question below, indicate your answer by placing a "Y" for "Yes" or an "N" or "No" in the Answers column.

Russellville, Tenn. Jan. 2, 19___

I owe John Hart of Morristown Two Thousand Dollars for office equipment purchased under terms of a separate written agreement, which sum I contract to pay to him or his assigns with 6% interest on May 1 of this year, or sooner if I get my income tax refund early.

JoAnn Graham

by A. B. Vance

	Answers	**For Scoring**
1. If the above instrument were executed partly in typing and partly in printing, could it still be negotiable?	_____	1._____
2. So long as the intention of the maker or drawer is clear, is the location of the signature of significance?	_____	2._____
3. Would the instrument be negotiable if the signature were placed on a separate piece of paper that was attached to the instrument?	_____	3._____
4. Is Graham liable on this instrument?	_____	4._____
5. Does the note contain a promise or an order to pay?	_____	5._____
6. Does the reference to a separate agreement make this instrument nonnegotiable?	_____	6._____
7. Does this instrument provide for the payment of a sum certain in money?	_____	7._____
8. If there is a John L. Hart, John S. Hart, and John W. Hart in Morristown, is the payee designated with reasonable certainty?	_____	8._____
9. Assuming the note is negotiable and was delivered on condition the office equipment be received, if the office equipment was never received, would a holder in due course be able to collect on the instrument?	_____	9._____
10. As stated, is this a negotiable instrument?	_____	10._____

Score _____

Section B

DIRECTIONS: Following each statement below, indicate your answer by placing a "T" for "True" or an "F" for "False" in the Answers column.

	Answers	**For Scoring**
1. An instrument must meet seven requirements to be negotiable.	_____	1._____
2. A nonnegotiable instrument cannot be enforced between the original parties................	_____	2._____
3. A negotiable instrument cannot be written in pencil..	_____	3._____

4. To be negotiable, an instrument cannot be signed with a trade name. .... _____   4. _____

5. A draft or a check must contain a definite command (order) to pay. .... _____   5 _____

6. It is not necessary to use the word "order" to make a draft negotiable. .... _____   6. _____

7. The mere acknowledgment of a debt is not a negotiable instrument. .... _____   7. _____

8. A draft that orders payment upon the retirement of the payee is negotiable. .... _____   8. _____

9. A reference to the consideration in a note destroys its negotiability. .... _____   9. _____

10. If the payee of a note may choose payment in pesos or gold, the note is nonnegotiable. _____   10. _____

11. A term in an instrument that requires payment of costs of collection if the maker or drawer defaults does not affect the negotiability of a note or draft. .... _____   11. _____

12. If the rate of interest called for in a note is variable, the note is nonnegotiable. .... _____   12. _____

13. If there is a conflict between the words and the figures stating the amount to be paid, the words prevail. .... _____   13. _____

14. A term in an installment note that requires immediate payment of all principal and interest upon any default renders the note nonnegotiable. .... _____   14. _____

15. To be negotiable, an instrument must indicate where it is to be paid. .... _____   15. _____

Score _____

Section C

DIRECTIONS: Complete each of the following statements by writing the missing word or words in the Answers column.

	Answers	For Scoring

1. In a negotiable instrument, the order or the promise to pay must be .... _____   1. _____

2-3. Commercial paper must be payable to ??? or ???. .... _____   2. _____
.... _____   3. _____

4. If the drawer or maker has the option to pay in money or goods, then the instrument is .... _____   4. _____

5. The amount must be ??? from the wording of the instrument itself in order for the instrument to be negotiable. .... _____   5. _____

6. A provision making the whole note immediately due and payable if one installment is in default is a(n) .... _____   6. _____

7. A provision allowing the maker to pay the note early to save interest is a(n). _____   7. _____

8. An instrument does not have any effect until ??? by the drawer or maker. .... _____   8. _____

9. If a negotiable instrument is signed, but only partly filled out, at the time of delivery to the payee, then the maker or drawer is ??? if the blanks are completed in accordance with the maker's or drawer's instructions. .... _____   9. _____

10. An undated instrument ??? be a negotiable instrument. .... _____   10. _____

Score _____

CHAPTER 22
PROMISSORY NOTES AND DRAFTS

CHAPTER OUTLINE

I.   NOTES

▸ Negotiable promissory notes are negotiable instruments that are governed by UCC Article 3.
▸ The parties to a note are the maker (party who issues and promises to pay note) and the payee.

A. LIABILITY OF THE MAKER

- *Liability to pay amount of note*: A maker agrees to pay a note issued by the maker.
- *Admissions*: A maker admits the existence of the payee and the payee's competency to transfer the note.

B. TYPES OF NOTES

- *Bonds*: A bond is a written obligation to pay a debt. A corporation or a governmental body generally issues a bond. Types of bonds include:

  ▸ *Coupon bond*: Interest for this bond is represented by coupons (in bearer form) that are presented for payment. Anyone in possession of a coupon can obtain payment of interest.

  ▸ *Registered bond*: Bond that is issued to a named person. The issuer of the bond keeps a record of owners, and transfer of a bond requires registration under the new owner's name.

- *Collateral notes*: ▸ Defined: notes that are secured by intangible personal property (e.g., stock or bonds) or tangible personal property (goods). ▸ If a collateral note is not properly paid, the creditor can sell the collateral to obtain payment. Excess proceeds belong to the debtor.

- *Real estate mortgage notes*: Defined: notes that are secured by an interest in real estate.

- *Debentures*: Defined: unsecured bonds (or notes) that are issued by a business.

- *Certificates of deposit* ▸ UCC definition: "An acknowledgment by a bank of a receipt of money with an engagement to repay it." ▸ UCC Article 3 treats certificates of deposit as notes. ▸ Transactions involving negotiable certificates of deposit are governed by Article 3.

II.   DRAFTS

General rules.   ▸ A draft is an instrument by which a drawer orders a drawee to pay a sum of money to a payee. ▸ A drawee has no liability to pay the draft until the drawee accepts the draft.
Study hint.   Two types of drafts are: (1) inland (domestic) draft: draft issued and payable in the United States; and (2) foreign draft: draft issued or payable outside the United States.

A. FORMS OF DRAFTS

- *Sight drafts*: ▸ Defined: draft that is payable at sight or upon presentation for payment by a payee or holder. ▸ Examples: checks and money orders.

- *Time drafts*: ▸ Defined: draft that is payable: (1) on a specific, future date; or (2) a stated period of time after sight (i.e., the date a payee or holder presents a draft for acceptance). ▸ If a time draft is payable after sight, the instrument must be presented for acceptance because the due date is calculated from the date of presentment, not from the date of issuance.

B. TRADE ACCEPTANCE

General rules.   ▸ Trade acceptance: draft issued by a seller (drawer) ordering a buyer of goods (drawee) to pay money to payee. ▸ A trade acceptance is a type of draft governed by Article 3.
Example.   ABC Piano Inc. sold a piano to Roger for $4,000 on 60 days credit. ABC issued a time draft ordering Roger to pay $4,000 to ABC's bank in 60 days.

C. PRESENTMENT FOR ACCEPTANCE

General rules.   ▸ A drawee is not obligated to pay a trade acceptance until the drawee accepts the draft. On acceptance, a drawee becomes an acceptor with primary liability to pay. ▸ Place for presentment: drawee's business or, if none, drawee's home. ▸ Party to whom presentment is made: drawee or drawee's authorized agent.
Limitation.   A conditional or qualified acceptance of a draft destroys negotiability.
Study hint.   Only trade acceptances and drafts that are payable a stated time after sight *must be presented for acceptance*. For other instruments, *presentment for acceptance* is optional.

D. FORM OF ACCEPTANCE

- ▪ ***Form of acceptance***: ▸ Typically, an acceptance is written on the face of an instrument and the drawee or an authorized agent signs it. ▸ The word "acceptance" need not be used; any words indicating an intent to accept will suffice. ▸ An oral acceptance is not valid.

- ▪ ***Acceptance refused***: If a drawee refuses to accept a draft, the drawee is not liable to pay.

E. ADMISSIONS OF THE ACCEPTOR

General rule.   By accepting an instrument, an acceptor: (1) agrees to pay the instrument when due; and (2) admits that the drawer's signature is genuine, the drawer has the capacity and authority to issue the draft, and the payee has capacity to indorse the instrument.
Limitation.   In accepting a draft, a drawee does not admit the genuineness of a payee's indorsement.
Study hint.   Due to the foregoing admissions, after acceptance an acceptor cannot refuse to pay an instrument because the drawer's signature was forged, or because the drawer or an indorser is a minor.

F. ACCEPTANCE BY THE BUYER'S FINANCING AGENCY

Sometimes a borrower may issue a trade acceptance for the amount of a prearranged loan. The lender, as drawee, then accepts the trade acceptance in order to complete the loan transaction.

G. MONEY ORDERS

A money order is an instrument issued by a bank, post office, or business indicating that a payee is to receive the amount stated. UCC Article 3 governs negotiable money orders.

III.   CHECKS

General rules.   ▸ A check is a special type of (sight) draft. ▸ Unique features: (1) drawee of a check is always a bank; and (2) a check is demand paper.
Study hint.   Federal regulations require checks that are processed by federal clearinghouses to be imprinted at the bottom with numbers in magnetic ink. However, checks without this printing are valid negotiable instruments, and drawee banks generally accept them.

A. SPECIAL KINDS OF CHECKS

- ▪ ***Certified check***: ▸ Defined: a check that is accepted by an officer of drawee bank. ▸ Certification: "certified" or a comparable word is written on the face of a check and a bank officer signs it. ▸ Effect: the drawee must pay it, and the drawee makes warranties of an acceptor. ▸ Certification is obtained by: (1) a drawer; or (2) a holder, which discharges the drawer's and indorses' liability to pay. ▸ The drawer of a draft that is accepted by the bank is discharged regardless of who obtains certification.

- *Cashier's checks*: Defined: a check drawn by a bank on itself; check is accepted for payment when issued.
- *Bank drafts*: Defined: a check that is drawn by one bank on another bank.
- *Voucher checks*: ▸ Defined: a check with an attached voucher that states the purpose for its issuance. ▸ A payee who indorses a voucher check may be bound by the statements on a voucher.
- *Traveler's checks*: Defined: a check that is similar to cashier's check except that a party purchasing the check is required to sign the check at the time of purchase and to re-sign it when it is negotiated.

B. POSTDATED CHECKS

▸ Defined: a check that is dated later than the date on which it is issued. ▸ A postdated check is not payable until the date stated on the check. ▸ In general, postdated checks are permitted, although a payee can refuse a postdated check if current payment is required. This is because payment with a postdated check is not present payment; it is only a promise to pay in the future. ▸ A bank is not liable for paying a postdated the check before its date unless the drawer gave the bank prior notice that a postdated check was issued.

C. BAD CHECKS

▸ Issuing a check with insufficient funds to pay the check and with an intent to defraud renders a drawer civilly liable for damages and criminally liable under bad check laws. ▸ An intent to defraud is often presumed if a check is not paid within a certain time after notice of dishonor.

D. DUTIES OF THE BANK

- *Confidentiality*: A bank must generally keep customer information confidential.
- *Forged signature of drawer*: If a drawee bank pays a check and the drawer's signature is forged, the bank is liable for the loss. The check cannot be charged to the drawer's account.
- *Refusal of bank to pay*: ▸ A bank owes its customer (the drawer) a duty to pay checks to the extent the customer has sufficient funds. Failure to do so renders the drawee bank liable *to the drawer*. ▸ A drawee bank does *not* owe any duty to a payee or holder to pay a check, even if there are sufficient funds to do so.
- *Stale check*: ▸ Defined: check presented more than six months after the date issued. ▸ A bank may pay a stale check, but it is not required to do so unless the check is certified.
- *Stopping payment*:
  - ▸ *Stop payment order*: A drawer notifies a drawee bank not to pay a check.
  - ▸ *Manner*: Orders may be oral or written. ▸ Oral orders are effective for only 14 days unless confirmed in writing during that time. ▸ Written orders are effective for six months.
  - ▸ *Effect*: Stopping payment does not alter any rights. A drawer remains liable to a holder in due course if the reason for stopping payment cannot be asserted against that party.
  - ▸ *Liability for violation*: A drawee bank is liable to its customer for failure to obey a proper order, but the customer has the burden to prove that the drawer actually suffered a loss.
  - ▸ *Limitation*: A drawer cannot stop payment of a certified or cashier's check.
- *Payment after depositor's death*: A drawee bank can pay or certify a check for ten days after receiving notice of a depositor's death unless the bank is told not to do so by a party in interest.

IV.   BANK CUSTOMER'S RESPONSIBILITY

▸ A bank customer owes a bank many duties including examining bank statements and notifying the bank "with reasonable promptness" of any forged signatures. ▸ A customer who fails to report an unauthorized signature or alteration within one year cannot assert the loss against the bank.

REVIEW OF CHAPTER

REVIEW OF TERMS

Select the term that best matches a statement below. Each term is the best match for only one statement.

TERMS

a. Bond
b. Cashier's check
c. Certificate of deposit
d. Certified check
e. Check

f. Coupon bond
g. Debenture
h. Money order
i. Registered bond
j. Sight draft

k. Stale check
l. Time draft
m. Trade acceptance
n. Traveler's check
o. Voucher check

STATEMENTS

Answer

_____ 1. Form of draft that is payable upon presentation for payment by a payee or holder.

_____ 2. Bond issued to a named person; ownership is registered with the issuer of the bond.

_____ 3. Check that is drawn by a bank on itself; check is accepted for payment when issued.

_____ 4. Special type of draft ordering a drawee bank to pay the draft on demand.

_____ 5. Form of draft that is payable on or after a future date, or after a stated time following presentment.

_____ 6. Check accepted by a drawee bank by writing "certified" or comparable words on the check.

_____ 7. Check that has an attached voucher.

_____ 8. Written payment obligation issued by a corporation or a governmental body.

_____ 9. Bond with detachable coupons that represent the right to receive interest payments.

_____ 10. Instrument issued by a bank acknowledging receipt of funds, with a promise to repay the funds.

_____ 11. Instrument issued by a bank or business indicating that a payee can receive the money stated.

_____ 12. Unsecured bond issued by a business.

_____ 13. Draft that is drawn by a seller of goods (as drawer) on the purchaser of the goods (as drawee).

_____ 14. Check presented more than six months after the date it was issued.

_____ 15. Check that requires the signature and re-signature of the party purchasing the check in order to negotiate the check.

REVIEW OF CONCEPTS

Directions: Indicate **T** for true and **F** for false in the answer column.

_____ 1. Molly issued a negotiable promissory note to John. In this case, Molly is a maker and she is liable to pay the note.

_____ 2. Bosco Inc. issued coupon bonds, and Aretha bought one of the bonds. Aretha lost the bond and Eddie found it. In this case, Eddie can collect the interest represented by the bond's coupons.

_____ 3. UCC Article 3 classifies a certificate of deposit as one type of promissory note.

_____ 4. Ajax Inc. issued a sight draft to Ann, as payee, and the drawee accepted the draft. In this case, this draft is payable on demand whenever Ann presents it to the drawee for payment.

_____ 5. On April 1, 1999, Jean issued a draft that was payable May 1, 2000. This draft is a time draft.

_____ 6. A negotiable trade acceptance is not a draft governed by UCC, Article 3.

_____ 7. Carrie issued a draft. The draft ordered Ben Isaac, as drawee, to pay money to a payee. This draft cannot be a check since the drawee is not a bank.

_____ 8. A check is not a valid instrument if it does not have numbers imprinted on it in magnetic ink as required by federal banking regulations.

_____ 9. It is a crime to issue a postdated check.

_____ 10. Under Article 3, a bank is liable for paying a postdated check before the stated date even if the drawer never gave the bank notice that the drawer was issuing this check.

_____ 11. A drawer may be criminally prosecuted under bad check laws if the drawer issued a check with insufficient funds in his or her account to pay the check, with the intent to defraud a payee.

_____ 12. Thief stole Dan's checkbook and forged Dan's signature on a check. Dan's bank cashed the check. In this case, Dan's bank must bear the loss; it cannot charge the check to Dan's account.

_____ 13. A drawee bank is liable to a drawer (depositor) for paying a check in violation of a stop payment order only to the extent that the drawer can prove that he or she suffered an actual loss.

_____ 14. A written stop payment order is effective for one year.

_____ 15. A drawer cannot stop payment of a certified or cashier's check.

REVIEW OF CONCEPT APPLICATIONS

Answer

Directions: Indicate your choice in the answer column.

_____ 1. RBK Inc. borrowed $500,000 from Lender and RBK issued a promissory note for this amount to Lender. Payment of the note is secured by stock, bonds, and equipment owned by RBK. Subsequently, RBK defaulted in payment of the note. Under these facts:
   a. The note is properly described as a real estate mortgage note.
   b. The note is properly described as a debenture.
   c. Lender can sell the stock, bonds, and equipment to obtain payment of the note, but any excess proceeds belong to RBK.
   d. Lender can sell the stock, bonds, and equipment to obtain payment of the note. Lender can keep all proceeds from the sale even if it is more than the unpaid balance of the note.

_____ 2. Dave issued a check to Payee. Payee indorsed the check and delivered it to Harold. At Harold's request, the First Bank of Fruita (drawee bank) certified the check. Under these facts:
   a. Certification discharged Dave from his liability to pay the check.
   b. Certification binds First Bank of Fruita to the admissions made by an acceptor.
   c. Certification caused First Bank of Fruita to become liable to pay the check.
   d. All the above are correct.

_____ 3. Select the correct answer.
   a. Ken does all his banking with City Bank. Ken's creditor asks City Bank for private information regarding Ken's assets and debts. In this case, City Bank owes Ken a duty to protect the confidentiality of this information; it should not disclose this information.
   b. On March 1, Anna issued a check to Lee. On October 1, Lee presented the check and Anna's bank cashed it. In this case, the bank acted improperly in cashing this "stale check."
   c. On May 1, Jim died. Jim's bank was notified of his death on May 4. On May 9, a check issued by Jim was presented. In this case, Jim's bank is prohibited from paying the check.
   d. a and b.

____ 4. Oscar issued a check payable to Juanita. Juanita negotiated the check to Laura (a holder in due course). On October 1, Oscar gave his bank an oral stop payment order. On October 10, Laura presented the check for payment and Oscar's bank paid the check. Under these facts:
   a. The stop payment order was invalid. Oral stop payment orders are invalid.
   b. The stop payment order was invalid. Oral stop payment orders are valid for only seven days.
   c. The stop payment order was valid, and it terminated Oscar's liability to pay the check.
   d. The stop payment order was valid, but it does not automatically terminate Oscar's liability to pay the check.

____ 5. Cody has a checking account with State Bank. Cody has $1,000 in his checking account. Cody issued a check payable to Payee for $500 in payment of a debt. Payee properly presented the check for payment to State Bank, but State Bank dishonored the check. As a result, Cody incurred $50 damages and Payee incurred $25 damages. Under these facts:
   a. State Bank is not liable to Cody or Payee.
   b. State Bank is liable to Cody for $50 damages; State Bank is not liable to Payee.
   c. State Bank is liable to Payee for $25 damages; State Bank is not liable to Cody.
   d. State Bank is liable to Cody for $50 damages, and it is liable to Payee for $25 damages.

CASE PROBLEM

Gary Phillips sold a $10,000 painting to A&A Art Gallery on 30 days credit. Gary (as drawer) signed a negotiable instrument ordering A&A (as drawee) to pay $10,000 to Fawn Tremont, one of Gary's creditors. Gary then delivered the instrument to Fawn. Fawn is uncertain what this instrument is and what her rights are to collect this instrument. Please advise Fawn regarding the following: (1) What type of draft is this instrument? (2) Where and to whom must Fawn present this instrument for acceptance? (3) How can this instrument be accepted? (4) Prior to acceptance, is A&A obligated to Fawn to pay this instrument? (5) After acceptance, is A&A obligated to Fawn to pay this instrument?

BUSINESS LAW PARTNER EXERCISE

Directions:

1. Using the Online feature of the Business Law Partner CD-ROM, find an advertisement for a financial institution that issues certificates of deposit in foreign currencies. Identify the web site where this advertisement is located.
2. What benefits and risks may you experience in buying a CD issued in a foreign currency?
3. Would a CD issued in a foreign currency qualify as a negotiable instrument?

CHAPTER 22 QUIZ

Section A

DIRECTIONS: Fill in the blanks in the following note dated October 22, 19--. It is to be payable in sixty days at your local bank. Make the note payable to the Campbell-Charles Co. Bank for $972.50, with 10 percent interest. Sign it. Then answer the questions in the spaces provided at the right.

```
 $ _____              19 _____

 _____ after date _____ I promise to pay to

 the order of _____

 _____ Dollars

 Payable at_____

 Value received with interest at _____ percent per annum

 Due _____
                                          _____
```

		Answers	For Scoring
1.	Would this still be a note if, instead of the word "promise," the words "guarantee to pay" were used?	_____	1. _____
2.	Is this a collateral note?	_____	2. _____
3.	Does the maker admit the existence of the payee and warrant the payee's competency to transfer the note?	_____	3. _____
4.	Is this note negotiable?	_____	4. _____
5.	May this note be transferred by delivery alone?	_____	5. _____

Score _____

Section B

DIRECTIONS: Complete each of the following statements by writing the missing word or words in the Answers column.

		Answers	For Scoring
1.	A bond payable to a specific person whose name is recorded by the issuer is a(n)	_____	1. _____
2.	An unsecured bond is called a(n)	_____	2. _____
3.	An acknowledgment by a bank of a receipt of money with an engagement to repay it is a(n)	_____	3. _____
4.	A draft payable upon presentation by the holder is a(n)	_____	4. _____
5.	A draft ordering the drawee to pay money a certain number of days after date or after sight is a(n) ??? draft.	_____	5. _____
6.	An instrument issued by a bank post office or express company indicating that the payee may request and receive the amount indicated on the instrument is a(n)	_____	6. _____
7.	A draft payable on demand and drawn on a bank is a(n)	_____	7. _____
8.	A check that is accepted by an official of the drawee bank is a(n)	_____	8. _____
9.	A check drawn by a bank on its own funds and signed by an officer of the bank, usually the cashier, is known as a(n)	_____	9. _____
10.	An instrument much like a cashier's check of the issuer except that it requires signature and countersignature by its purchaser is a(n)	_____	10. _____

Score _____

Section C

DIRECTIONS: Following each statement below, indicate your answer by placing a "T" for "True" or an "F" for "False" in the Answers column.

	Answers	For Scoring
1. The maker of a promissory note expressly agrees to pay it according to its terms.		1. _____
2. A bond issued by a corporation is always secured by a deed of trust on the property of the corporation..		2. _____
3. The holder of a coupon bond automatically receives interest payments by mail as long as the bond is owned..		3. _____
4. A creditor in possession of collateral securing a note is liable to the debtor for losses resulting from the creditor's failure to reasonably care for the collateral......................		4. _____
5. The maker of a real estate mortgage note generally retains possession of the real estate.		5. _____
6. The signature of a person not clearly the drawer on a draft is construed to be the signature of an indorser.		6. _____
7. The date a time draft payable after sight is accepted determines the date of maturity....		7. _____
8. A draft with more than one drawee may normally be presented to just one drawee.......		8. _____
9. The drawee of a time draft is liable to pay it even before the drawee accepts it............		9. _____
10. A draft may be accepted orally.		10. _____
11. A drawer cannot assert a forged signature if the drawer fails to notify the bank within one year after the drawer receives a bank statement that indicates the forged item		11. _____
12. The material on which a check is written does not affect the validity of a check.		12. _____
13. Certification of a check by the bank has the same effect as an acceptance......................		13. _____
14. It is both a civil wrong and a crime in most states to draw a check on a bank with intent to defraud the payee..		14. _____
15. A stop-payment order may be written or oral.		15. _____

Score _____

Section D

DIRECTIONS: Answer the following questions in the Answers column.

```
        Middletown, Ky.  __January 8__  20____    No. _____
        Middletown Deposit Bank

PAY TO THE
ORDER OF_____Harris Clothing Store_____    _____
 Forty Nine and 50/100_____DOLLARS
                                    Ann Lu Smith
                      _____
```

	Answers	For Scoring
1. What kind of instrument is shown above?		1. _____
2. Who is the payee?		2. _____
3. What is the name of the drawee?		3. _____
4. By signing the instrument, Smith becomes the ???.		4. _____
5. When should the instrument be presented for payment?		5. _____
6. Who is the acceptor of this instrument?		6. _____
7. When must the instrument be presented for acceptance?..............................		7. _____
8. Must the magnetic ink coding appear on the instrument for it to be valid?		8. _____
9. If it is not yet January 8, is it illegal to have written out the instrument?		9. _____
10. Can this instrument require immediate payment on demand?		10. _____

Score _____

CHAPTER 23
NEGOTIATION AND DISCHARGE

CHAPTER OUTLINE

I. INTRODUCTION (NEGOTIATION IN GENERAL)

General rules. ▸ Negotiation: transfer of a negotiable instrument in the manner required for a transferee to be a holder (or holder in due course). ▸ Manner of negotiation: (1) Order paper: proper indorsement by payee or indorsee and delivery to transferee. (2) Bearer paper: delivery of instrument.

Study hints. ▸ Negotiation passes ownership of paper to a transferee. ▸ The required manner of negotiation is determined by whether an instrument is order or bearer paper. ▸ Whether an instrument is order or bearer paper is determined each time that it is transferred. ▸ An instrument may change back and forth between being order and bearer paper.

II. PLACE OF INDORSEMENT

- ***Manner of indorsement***: An indorsement (indorser's signature) must be made on an instrument or on a paper securely attached to it (an allonge). ▸ Banks generally require check indorsements to be on the back and within 1 and ½ inches of the trailing edge. ▸ If a party signs an instrument and it is unclear in what capacity the party signed, the party is presumed to be an indorser.

- ***Misspelled name***: A payee or indorsee whose name is misspelled can: (1) indorse the misspelled name; (2) indorse the name spelled properly; or (3) indorse by writing both the misspelled and properly spelled names. ▸ A misspelling of a name does not affect negotiability of an instrument.

III. KINDS OF INDORSEMENT

A. BLANK INDORSEMENTS

- ***Description***: Indorser signs indorser's name without indicating to whom the instrument is to be paid.

- ***Example***: Beth Thomas (payee) indorsed a check "Beth Thomas."

- ***Effect of blank indorsement***: ▸ Creates bearer paper. ▸ Imposes secondary liability on indorser if instrument is not paid. ▸ Gives rise to implied warranties by the indorser.

- ***Converting blank indorsement***: ▸ A holder receiving paper following a blank indorsement may write above the blank indorsement the name of a person to whom the paper is to be paid. Doing so converts the paper into order paper. ▸ Example: Beth Thomas indorsed a check "Beth Thomas" and delivered it to Chris Brown. Chris may write above Beth's indorsement "Pay to Chris Brown." Doing so creates order paper. To negotiate the paper, it is now necessary for Chris Brown to indorse the check and deliver it to a transferee.

B. SPECIAL INDORSEMENTS

- ***Description***: Signature of indorser coupled with words specifying the person to whom the instrument is to be paid.

- ***Example***: Beth Thomas (payee) indorsed a check "Pay to Ina Kay, (signed) Beth Thomas."

- ***Effect of special indorsement***: ▸ Creates order paper. ▸ Imposes secondary liability on indorser if instrument is dishonored. ▸ Creates implied warranties by indorser. ▸ To negotiate paper, indorsee (person named) must indorse paper and deliver it to a transferee.

C. QUALIFIED INDORSEMENTS

- *Description*: Indorsement limiting indorser's liability by words "without recourse" or "without recourse or warranties."

- *Effect of qualified indorsement*: ‣ Does *not* impose liability on indorser to pay amount of instrument. ‣ Qualified indorser may make certain warranties.

D. RESTRICTIVE INDORSEMENTS

- *Description*: Indorsement that: (1) imposes condition on holder's right to payment; or (2) restricts to whom proceeds of instrument can be paid or how proceeds can be used.

- *Examples*: ‣ Beth indorsed a note "Pay to Chris Brown when he delivers car title (signed) Beth Thomas." ‣ Beth Thomas indorsed a check "For deposit only, Beth Thomas."

- *Effect of restrictive indorsement*: Limits holder's right to payment, or limits use of proceeds. Under Article 3, conditional indorsements are effective only between the indorser and indorsee. Revised Article 3 does not use the term "restrictive indorsements."

IV. LIABILITY OF INDORSER

A. LIABILITIES FOR PAYMENT OF INSTRUMENT

- *Unqualified indorser*: Subject to presentment, dishonor, and notice of dishonor, unqualified indorsers have secondary liability to pay an instrument.

- *Qualified indorser*: No liability to pay amount of paper even if primary party fails to pay.

B. WARRANTIES OF THE INDORSER

- *Unqualified indorser*: Warrants certain matters to all holders.

- *Qualified indorser*: Under revised Article 3, an indorser "without recourse" makes the same warranties that an unqualified indorser makes.

- *Nature of warranty liability*: Warranty liability of indorsers and other parties who negotiate a negotiable instrument is not conditioned on proper presentment, dishonor, or notice of dishonor.

V. OBLIGATION OF NEGOTIATOR OF BEARER PAPER

General rule.   If a party negotiates bearer paper without indorsing it, the party: (1) does not have any liability to pay the face amount of the paper; but (2) it is implied that the party warrants *to the immediate transferee* all matters warranted by an unqualified indorser.
Example.   Ty forged a drawer's signature and delivered the check to Toni. Toni negotiated the check to Cob without indorsing the check. Toni has warranty liability to Cob due to the forgery.
Study hint.   An indorsement is not needed to negotiate bearer paper. However, if a party indorses bearer paper, the party has the same liabilities as any other indorser.

VI. DISCHARGE OF THE OBLIGATION

- *Payment*: Payment of an instrument by a party with primary liability discharges an instrument.

- *Cancellation*: A party entitled to payment can discharge an instrument by an act, such as intentionally mutilating a note that manifests an intent to invalidate the instrument.

- *Renunciation*: ‣ A party may unilaterally give up (renounce) a right to be paid. ‣ Examples: Payee returns a note to Maker with intent to discharge note. Payee signs a separate writing giving up his or her right to be paid. ‣ Consideration is not required to make a renunciation binding.

- *Other causes of discharge*: ‣ Discharge in bankruptcy. ‣ Running of statute of limitations.

- *Lost instrument*: Loss or accidental destruction of instrument does not discharge the instrument.

REVIEW OF CHAPTER

REVIEW OF TERMS

Select the term that best matches a statement below. Each term is the best match for only one statement.

TERMS

a. Allonge
b. Blank indorsement
c. Cancellation

d. Converting a blank indorsement
e. Negotiation
f. Qualified indorsement

g. Renunciation
h. Restrictive indorsement
i. Special indorsement

STATEMENTS

Answer

_____ 1. Indorsement signed "without recourse" which eliminates an indorser's secondary liability.

_____ 2. Indorsement that conditions right to receive payment or restricts use of proceeds of instrument.

_____ 3. Paper that is firmly attached to and becomes a part of an instrument.

_____ 4. Holder writing above a blank indorsement a statement designating a special indorsee to be paid.

_____ 5. Indorsement that states the person to whom the instrument is to be paid.

_____ 6. Mutilation or destruction of paper or other act that indicates an intent to discharge an instrument.

_____ 7. Indorsement that consists of only the signature of the indorser.

_____ 8. Unilateral act giving up rights in an instrument or against a party, e.g., returning a note to a maker, or signing a writing renouncing rights against a party who is liable to pay an instrument.

_____ 9. Transfer of a negotiable instrument in the manner required for a transferee to be a holder.

REVIEW OF CONCEPTS

Directions: Indicate **T** for true and **F** for false in the answer column.

_____ 1. If a payee's name is misspelled, a payee must indorse the misspelled name to negotiate the paper.

_____ 2. Title to an instrument cannot be passed to another unless the transferor indorses the instrument.

_____ 3. A special indorsement converts bearer paper into order paper.

_____ 4. Payee indorsed a note "Pay to X if X graduates from college by June 1, 1999, Payee." This indorsement is a restrictive indorsement; X is not entitled to payment unless the condition is met.

_____ 5. Pat indorsed a check "For deposit only to Pat Jones' account, (signed) Pat Jones." Pat's agent took the check to Pat's bank. In this case, the bank must credit the check to Pat's account.

_____ 6. A transferor has no *warranty liability* unless an instrument is properly presented for payment, it is dishonored, and proper notice of dishonor is given.

_____ 7. A person negotiating a note by delivery only (no indorsement) does not make any warranties.

_____ 8. A holder's renunciation is not valid unless consideration is given for the renunciation.

_____ 9. Maker issued a note and delivered it to Stan. Later, in a signed writing, Stan renounced all rights against Maker on the note and Stan gave the writing to Maker. In this case, Maker is discharged.

_____ 10. Drawer issued a check on June 1. On July 1 drawer filed for bankruptcy and received a discharge in bankruptcy. In this case, drawer's liability on the check is discharged.

_____ 11. If a payee accidentally loses a note, the note is discharged and the payee has no right to be paid.

REVIEW OF CONCEPT APPLICATIONS

Answer

Directions: Indicate your choice in the answer column.

_____ 1. Drawer issued a check payable to the order of Penny Thompson. Penny indorsed the check "Penny Thompson" and delivered it to Terry. Under these facts:

    a. Penny's indorsement is a special indorsement.

    b. The check is order paper after Penny's indorsement.

    c. Penny may have secondary liability to pay the check if it is dishonored.

    d. Penny did not make any warranties to subsequent holders.

_____ 2. Drawer issued a check payable to the order of cash, and delivered it to Peter Bryan. Peter indorsed the check "Pay to Tip Wilson, (signed) Peter Bryan." Under these facts:
   a. Peter's indorsement is a special indorsement. To further negotiate this check, Tip must indorse the check and deliver it to a transferee.
   b. The check is bearer paper after Peter's indorsement.
   c. Peter would not have secondary liability to pay the check if it is dishonored.
   d. Peter did not make any warranties to subsequent holders.

_____ 3. Maker issued her negotiable promissory note to Barry Mills. Barry transferred the note to Hans for value. Barry indorsed the note "Without recourse, Barry Mills." Under these facts:
   a. Barry's indorsement is a qualified indorsement.
   b. Barry does not have secondary liability to pay the note if Maker fails to pay.
   c. Barry did not make any warranties to subsequent holders.
   d. a and b.

_____ 4. Maker issued a negotiable note and delivered it to Rose. The note is payable to bearer. Rose negotiated the note to Wilbur without indorsing it. Under these facts:
   a. Rose may have secondary liability to pay the note if Maker fails to pay.
   b. Rose does not have secondary liability to pay the note if Maker fails to pay.
   c. Rose did not make any warranties to Wilbur regarding the note.
   d. b and c.

CASE PROBLEM

Drawer issued a check payable to the order of Carol Fay. Carol indorsed the check "Carol Fay" and delivered it to Belin. Belin transferred the check to Holmes without indorsing the check. When Holmes presented the check, payment was refused due to insufficient funds. All requirements for presentment, dishonor, and notice of dishonor have been met. In this case: (1) What type of indorsement is Carol's indorsement? Does Carol have any liability to pay the check to Holmes? (2) Did Belin negotiate the check to Holmes? Did Belin's delivery of the check transfer title to Holmes? Is Belin liable to pay the check?

_____

_____

_____

BUSINESS LAW PARTNER EXERCISE

Directions:

1. Access your Business Law Partner CD-ROM and find the document entitled "Bad Check Notice." Complete this document using the information provided in the case below. This Notice is to be sent to *PAM, THE INDORSER*.
2. Does Pam have liability to pay the bad check? Explain.

Case Study: *Watch the Bouncing Check*

Dee issued a $100 check payable to the order of cash and delivered it to Pam Wright as payment of a debt. Pam indorsed the check "Pam Wright" and cashed it at Jack's Groceries, a neighborhood market. When Jack's presented the check to Dee's bank, it refused payment because Dee's account had been closed. Jack's tried to contact Dee, but she had moved and left no forwarding address. Jack's now plans to send Pam notice of the bad check.

_____

_____

_____

CHAPTER 23 QUIZ

Section A

DIRECTIONS: Following each question below, indicate your answer by placing a "Y" for "Yes" or an "N" for "No" in the Answers column.

	Answers	For Scoring
1. May an instrument payable to "order" be negotiated by delivery?	_____	1. _____
2. If a signature is not placed on the back of the instrument and it is not clear in what capacity it was made, will it be considered an indorsement?	_____	2. _____
3. Can a party to a negotiable instrument avoid liability as an indorser by assigning the instrument?	_____	3. _____
4. Is it always necessary to correct an irregularity in the name of a party to an instrument?	_____	4. _____
5. If a check is made payable to and is intended for Ray K. Brown, but it comes into the possession of Ray D. Brown, can the latter person legally indorse it and receive payment?	_____	5. _____
6. If a check is indorsed in blank and then stolen or lost, can the thief or finder of the check obtain payment for it?	_____	6. _____
7. If an indorsee converts a blank indorsement to a special indorsement, is the contract between the indorser and indorsee altered?	_____	7. _____
8. Does a qualified indorser warrant payment of the instrument?	_____	8. _____
9. Does a person who indorses a negotiable instrument "without recourse" warrant that the instrument has not been altered?	_____	9. _____
10. May a bank that receives a check for deposit with a restrictive indorsement ignore the restriction?	_____	10. _____
11. Does one who negotiates a bearer instrument by delivery alone guarantee payment? ..	_____	11. _____
12. Does the accidental destruction of a negotiable instrument discharge the obligation? ..	_____	12. _____

Score _____

Section B

DIRECTIONS: Complete each of the following statements by writing the missing word or words in the Answers column.

	Answers	For Scoring
1-2. A negotiable instrument payable to the order of the payee or holder can be negotiated only by ???	_____	1. _____
and ???.	_____	2. _____
3. The left side of a check when looking at it from the front is called the	_____	3. _____
4. A paper so firmly attached to an instrument as to become a part of it is	_____	4. _____
5. An indorsement that attempts to prevent the use of the instrument for anything except the stated use is a(n) ??? indorsement.	_____	5. _____
6. The unilateral act of the holder of an instrument giving up rights on the instrument is called	_____	6. _____

Score _____

1-4. Use the following Roman numerals, which identify types of indorsements, to indicate in the Answers column the type of indorsement illustrated.

I. Blank

II. Qualified

III. Restrictive

IV. Special

1.	Without recourse, /s/ *Alice Walker*
2.	Pay to the order of Tom Young /s/ *Clara Roberts*
3.	/s/ *Tom Young*
4.	Pay to Jersey Savings & Loan, for collection only /s/ *Bob Hartwell*

1. _____   1. _____

2. _____   2. _____

3. _____   3. _____

4. _____   4. _____

5. Illustrate the manner in which the holder, Jeannie Fuller, would change a blank indorsement to a special indorsement

ENDORSE HERE

_____

/s/ *Ellen Tracy*

_____

5. _____

6. Illustrate at the right the manner in which Donald Kean should indorse in blank a negotiable instrument that is made payable to him as "Ronald Kean."

ENDORSE HERE

_____

_____

_____

6. _____

7. Illustrate at the right the manner in which Delia Pagan should indorse a negotiable instrument in order to avoid having to pay the instrument whether because of insolvency, refusal to pay, or any defense.

ENDORSE HERE

_____

_____

_____

7. _____

Score _____

CHAPTER 24
LIABILITIES OF PARTIES AND HOLDERS IN DUE COURSE

CHAPTER OUTLINE

I. INTRODUCTION

General rule.　　There are two types of liability that one may have in connection with a negotiable instrument. One may have (1) liability to pay the face amount of paper or (2) warranty liability.

Study hint.　　With one exception, indorsers may have both types of liability. Other parties typically have liability to pay the face amount of an instrument, *or* warranty liability.

II. LIABILITY FOR THE FACE OF THE PAPER (LIABILITY CAUSED BY SIGNING)

General rule.　　With one exception, any party who signs a negotiable instrument has either primary or secondary liability to pay the face amount of the instrument.

Limitation.　　Parties that do not have liability for the face amount of an instrument: (1) qualified indorser (indorses "without recourse"); (2) transferor who does not indorse paper; and (3) drawee prior to acceptance.

Study hint.　　Liability for face amount of instrument does not arise unless one signs the instrument.

A. PRIMARY LIABILITY

- *Parties with primary liability*: (1) Maker of a promissory note; (2) drawee bank after acceptance of a check; and (3) drawee after acceptance of a draft.

- *Nature of liability*: A party with primary liability must pay an instrument when it is due. The party's duty to pay is *not* dependent on presentment, dishonor, or notice of dishonor.

B. SECONDARY LIABILITY

- *Parties with secondary liability*: (1) Drawer of a draft or check and (2) unqualified indorser.

- *Nature of liability*: A party does not have any liability unless: (1) an instrument is presented on time for payment or acceptance; (2) it is dishonored; and (3) timely notice of dishonor is given to the party.

- *Presentment*:

  ▸ *Presentment defined*: (1) Demand on a drawee for acceptance of a draft or check; or (2) demand on a maker, drawee, acceptor, or other payor for payment of an instrument.

  ▸ *Manner of presentment*: ▸ Presentment must be made in a timely manner and it should be made to the party who may have primary liability to pay (e.g., maker; acceptor; drawee).

  ▸ *Time of presentment*: ▸ Paper that is payable on a stated date: presentment is required on that date. ▸ Paper does not state a payment date: presentment within a reasonable time. ▸ A reasonable time for presentment of checks is presumed to be: (1) drawers - within 30 days after the date of the check or the issue date, whichever is later; and (2) indorsers - within 7 days after indorsement.

  ▸ *When presentment is not required*: (1) Presentment is waived. (2) Presentment cannot be made despite reasonable attempts. (3) Maker, acceptor, or drawee has died or become insolvent. (4) Secondary party has no reason to expect that instrument will be paid.

  ▸ *Effect of improper presentment*: ▸ Primary party: improper presentment does not avoid liability. ▸ Secondary party: failure to present when due may discharge a secondary party.

- *Dishonor*: Instrument is dishonored if presented for acceptance or payment to a party who may have primary liability, but acceptance or payment is refused or cannot be obtained.

- *Notice of dishonor*:

  ▸ *Notice of dishonor defined*: Party who may be liable to pay an instrument is notified that the instrument has been dishonored. Notice must be given only to (1) drawers whose drafts are accepted by someone other than a bank and (2 indorsers.

- *Requirements for notice*: Notice may be mailed. Otherwise, there are no special rules for giving notice except that notice regarding instruments issued or payable outside of the U.S. must be certified by an appropriate official (i.e., "protest" must be given).
- *Time for notice*: ▸ A bank must give notice before midnight of next business day after the bank's receipt of a check or notice of dishonor. ▸ Persons other than banks must give notice before midnight of third full business day after dishonor or receiving notice of dishonor.
- *When notice is not required*: (1) Notice waived. (2) Delay or failure to give notice is unavoidable. (3) Party entitled to notice had no reason to expect payment would be made.
- *Effect of improper notice*: ▸ Primary party: improper notice does not affect liability. ▸ Secondary party: failure to give notice may discharge secondary party from liability.

C. LIABILITY OF AGENTS

- *Agent authorized to sign*: If an agent is authorized to sign an instrument for a principal, then whether a principal or agent is liable on an instrument may depend on how the agent signed.
    - *Signature identifies principal and indicates agent is signing as agent*: ▸ Liabilities: principal is liable; agent is not liable. ▸ Example: "Acme Co., by Eli Downs, President."
    - *Signature does not identify principal nor indicate agent is signing as agent*: ▸ Liabilities: principal is not liable; agent is liable. ▸ Example: Eli intends to sign an instrument for Acme Co., but he signs the instrument "Eli Downs."
    - *Signature identifies principal, but does not indicate agency capacity*: ▸ Liabilities: principal and agent are both liable. ▸ Example: Eli signs "Acme Co. and Eli Downs."
    - *Signature does not identify principal, but agency capacity indicated*: ▸ Liabilities: principal is not liable; agent is liable. ▸ Example: Eli signs "Eli Downs, President."
    - *Article 3 Exceptions*: ▸ In the last three examples, a holder in due course (HDC) without knowledge that the agent is not supposed to be liable can enforce liability against the agent. In these examples, if a HDC is not involved, then the agent is liable on the instrument unless the agent can prove that the original parties did not intend for the agent to be liable. ▸ An agent is not liable on a check even if the agent does not disclose his or her representative capacity if the agent signs a check that is drawn on an identified principal's checking account.
- *Agent is not authorized to sign*: The principal is not liable on the instrument, but the agent is liable.

D. GUARANTORS

- *Payment guaranteed*: Indorsing an instrument "payment guaranteed" creates primary liability.
- *Collection guaranteed*: Indorsing an instrument "collection guaranteed" creates only secondary liability, which can be enforced only if a judgment against the party with primary party cannot be collected.

III. LIABILITY FOR WARRANTIES

General rule.   In general, a party who transfers an instrument for consideration warrants that: (1) the party has good title or is authorized to obtain acceptance or payment; (2) all signatures are genuine and authorized; (3) there are no material alterations; (4) no defense of any party is good against the party; and (5) the party has no knowledge of an insolvency proceeding against the maker, acceptor, or drawee of an unaccepted draft.

Limitations.   ▸ A transferor may specifically exclude warranties. ▸ The warranty obligations of a qualified indorser and a party transferring bearer paper without indorsing are more limited than for unqualified indorsers.

IV. HOLDERS IN DUE COURSE (INNOCENT PURCHASERS)

- *Importance of holder in due course*: ▸ A HDC (innocent purchaser) may have a greater right to demand payment than his or her transferor. ▸ Certain defenses (limited defenses) that may be used against a transferor cannot be used against a HDC.
- *Holder in due course defined*: A HDC is a holder who takes a negotiable instrument by negotiation: (1) for value and in good faith; (2) without notice that the instrument is overdue or has been dishonored; and (3) without notice of any defense or adverse claim.

A. FOR VALUE AND IN GOOD FAITH

- **Value.** ▸ *Defined*: something of value actually given in consideration for an instrument. ▸ *Example of value*: A note is negotiated to a CPA as payment for services actually performed. ▸ *Example of no value*: An instrument is negotiated in exchange for property that has not been delivered. ▸ *Partial payment*: If a holder pays only part of the price and then receives notice of a defense, then the holder is an innocent purchaser only to the extent that value was given before receiving notice.

- **Good Faith.** ▸ *Defined*: A holder takes an instrument in good faith if the holder does not know: (1) that the instrument is not genuine; (2) that its transfer is improper; or (3) that someone has a defense or claim to the instrument. ▸ *Example*: Abe issued a note to Lu, who negotiated the note to Bob. Abe claims a defense. Bob acted in good faith if he did not know of the defense when he took the note.
  ▸ *Bad faith*: A holder acts in bad faith if, at the time of negotiation, the holder knows that: (1) an instrument was issued for services that were improperly done; (2) someone else claims to own the instrument; or (3) a party who may be liable to pay claims a defense that would avoid the duty to pay.

B. NO KNOWLEDGE THAT INSTRUMENT IS PAST DUE OR DISHONORED

General rules. ▸ A holder is not an innocent purchaser if *at the time of negotiation* the holder has notice that an instrument is past due or has been dishonored. ▸ Past due: (1) time instrument: day after payment is due; (2) demand instrument: reasonable time after issuance; (3) check: presumed to be 30 days after the check is issued. ▸ Dishonor defined: maker, acceptor, or drawee refuses to pay instrument.

Examples. ▸ Past due: Note due May 1, 2000 is negotiated to Holder on June 1, 2000. Check dated April 1, 2001 is negotiated to Holder on July 1, 2001. ▸ Dishonored: The maker refuses to pay a promissory note, or a drawee bank refuses to accept or pay a customer's check.

Limitation. The fact that an instrument has been dishonored does not prevent a party from being a HDC if the party was unaware of the dishonor at the time of negotiation.

Study hints. ▸ A party taking paper on its due date may be an innocent purchaser. ▸ A party is not an innocent purchaser if the party takes an instrument with notice that payment has been accelerated, or that there is an uncured default in payment of an instrument in the same series.

C. NO KNOWLEDGE OF ANY DEFENSE OR ADVERSE CLAIM TO THE INSTRUMENT

- *Notice of defense*: ▸ A holder cannot be an innocent purchaser if the holder takes an instrument with notice that a party who may be liable to pay has any defense to paying the instrument. ▸ Examples of defenses: (1) a party claims fraud, illegality, mistake, or other contractual defenses; (2) a fiduciary negotiated an instrument as payment for a personal debt; (3) any party was a minor; or (4) there is an obvious forgery or alteration of the instrument.

- *Notice of adverse claim*: ▸ A holder is not an innocent purchaser if the holder knows another person claims to own the instrument. ▸ Example: party claims a check was stolen from him.

II. HOLDER THROUGH A HOLDER IN DUE COURSE

▸ *Holder through a holder in due course defined*: Any holder who possesses a negotiable instrument after it has been held at any time by a HDC. ▸ *Example*: Drawer issued a check to Payee. Payee negotiated the check to Gary, a HDC. Gary negotiated the check to Alice, who did not pay value and who had notice that the check was overdue. Alice is a holder through a HDC. ▸ *Rights*: same rights as a HDC.

III. HOLDERS OF CONSUMER PAPER

- *Definitions*: ▸ Consumer goods or services: goods or services for personal, family, or household use. ▸ Consumer credit transaction: credit sale of consumer goods or services. ▸ Setoff: claim by a party being sued against the party suing.

- *Modification of UCC*: As a result of FTC rules and state laws, a holder of an instrument that arose out of a sale of consumer goods or services generally takes the instrument subject to all defenses or setoffs that can be raised by the consumer, whether the holder qualifies as a HDC or not.

- *FTC rule*: The FTC requires a contract in a consumer credit transaction to contain a notice that a buyer can use all defenses against any person enforcing a negotiable promissory note given in such transaction.

- *Limitation*: The foregoing limits on the rights of a HDC only apply if a loan is arranged, or directly made, by the seller or lessor.

REVIEW OF CHAPTER

REVIEW OF TERMS

Select the term that best matches a statement below. Each term is the best match for only one statement.

TERMS

a. Acceptance
b. Collection guaranteed
c. Dishonor

d. Notice of dishonor
e. Payment guaranteed
f. Presentment

g. Primary liability
h. Protest
i. Secondary liability

STATEMENTS

Answer

_____ 1. Notification that acceptance or payment of an instrument has been refused or cannot be obtained.

_____ 2. Guarantee made by a party signing an instrument that creates primary liability to pay.

_____ 3. Liability to pay amount of instrument regardless of presentment, dishonor, or notice of dishonor.

_____ 4. Guarantee made by a party signing an instrument that creates secondary liability to pay.

_____ 5. Demand for acceptance or payment that is made upon a maker or drawee.

_____ 6. Liability to pay instrument that is conditioned on presentment, dishonor, and notice of dishonor.

_____ 7. Certification of a notice of dishonor by an authorized official.

_____ 8. Agreement by drawee to accept or pay instrument, which agreement is written on the instrument.

_____ 9. Refusal by a maker, acceptor, or drawee to accept or pay an instrument.

REVIEW OF CONCEPTS

Directions: Indicate **T** for true and **F** for false in the answer column.

_____ 1. A drawee cannot be held liable to pay a draft unless the drawee has accepted the draft.

_____ 2. An acceptor of an instrument has only secondary liability to pay the instrument.

_____ 3. Sara issued a negotiable note due June 1. Katrina, the payee, did not present the note to Sara until August 1. In this case, the delayed presentment terminates Sara's primary liability to pay.

_____ 4. Presentment is excused if a maker dies, becomes insolvent, or cannot be found.

_____ 5. A secondary party is not obligated to pay an instrument unless it has been dishonored.

_____ 6. Rosa issued a check. Rod is payee and Last Bank is drawee. Rod indorsed the check and delivered it to Last Bank on Monday, March 15. Last Bank dishonored the check. In this case, notice of dishonor by Last Bank should by given to Rosa and Rod by midnight on March 16.

_____ 7. Todd (agent) signed a note on behalf of Chris (principal). Todd had no authority to sign the note for Chris. In this case, neither Todd nor Chris is liable on the note.

_____ 8. Al indorsed an instrument "payment guaranteed." Al has primary liability to pay the instrument.

_____ 9. Hal indorsed a check and negotiated it to Nancy. Unknown to Hal, the amount of the check had been improperly altered by a prior party. In this case, Hal breached a warranty to Nancy.

_____ 10. Yen negotiated a check to Earl without indorsing the check. Unknown to Yen, the drawer's signature was forged. In this case, Yen did not breach a warranty; she did not indorse the check.

_____ 11. Indorsers may have secondary liability to pay the amount of an instrument *and* warranty liability.

_____ 12. A holder may lack good faith if circumstances surrounding the negotiation of an instrument to the holder would indicate to a reasonable person that the negotiation is improper.

_____ 13. A holder may lack good faith if the holder knows that a fiduciary is negotiating an instrument to the holder in payment of the fiduciary's personal debt.

_____ 14. A holder lacks good faith whenever the holder pays a discount for an instrument.

_____ 15. Maker issued a $1,000 note to Payee. Payee negotiated the note to Lynn. Lynn agreed to pay Payee $1,000 for the note. After paying $400 to Payee, Lynn learned that Maker claimed a defense. In this case, Lynn may be a holder in due course to the extent of $400.

_____ 16. Drawer issued a check dated June 1. Payee negotiated the check to Holder for value on July 15. Holder may be a holder in due course; a check is not overdue until 60 days after issuance.

_____ 17. A party may be a holder in due course even if an instrument is taken with knowledge that there has been a default in payment of *interest* on the instrument.

_____ 18. Dick deposited a check in his bank account and he withdrew the entire sum from the account. In this case, Dick's bank has given value for the check.

_____ 19. A party cannot be a holder through a holder in due course if the party has notice of a defense.

_____ 20. A holder through a holder in due course has the same rights as a holder in due course.

_____ 21. In a consumer credit transaction, FTC rules require that a contract include a notice allowing a consumer to use all defenses against a holder of a note, even if a holder is a holder in due course.

REVIEW OF CONCEPT APPLICATIONS

Answer

Directions: Indicate your choice in the answer column.

_____ 1. Select the correct answer.
   a. Mark issued a negotiable note. In this case, Mark has secondary liability to pay the note.
   b. Wally issued a check that was drawn on Peoria Bank, as drawee. Peoria Bank accepted the check for payment. In this case, Peoria Bank has primary liability to pay the check.
   c. Dorothy issued a check that was drawn on ABC Bank, as drawee. ABC Bank has not accepted the check. In this case, ABC Bank has primary liability to pay the check.

_____ 2. In which situation may Nick Ames have *secondary* liability to pay the face amount of the check?
   a. Nick indorsed a check "Nick Ames," and negotiated it to a holder.
   b. Nick received a check payable to cash. Nick transferred the check without indorsing it.
   c. Nick signed and issued a check payable to cash.
   d. a and c.

_____ 3. Martha issued a negotiable note to Paula. The note was due May 1. Paula indorsed the note and negotiated it to Harry. On May 1, Harry presented the note to Martha and Martha refused to pay. On May 3, Harry gave written notice to Paula that Martha had refused to pay. In this case:
   a. Paula does not have secondary liability to pay the note because it has not been dishonored.
   b. Paula does not have secondary liability to pay the note because Harry was required to give Paula notice of dishonor by midnight of May 2.
   c. Paula is obligated to pay the note based on her secondary liability.

_____ 4. B&K, Inc. authorized its president, Tim Blue, to borrow $50,000 from Bank. Tim negotiated a loan and he signed a note in the manner indicated below. In this case, select the correct answer.

   B&K, Inc. By: _____Tim Blue_____
   Tim Blue, President of B&K, Inc.
   a. B&K, Inc. is liable to pay the promissory note.
   b. B&K, Inc. is not liable to pay the promissory note.
   c. Tim Blue is personally liable to pay the promissory note.
   d. a and c.

_____ 5. In which case does Holder give value?
   a. Drawer issued a check to Paul. Paul negotiated the check to Holder as a gift.
   b. Maker issued a check to Rod. Rod negotiated the check to Holder in payment for services that Holder promised to perform for Rod. Holder did not perform the services.
   c. Maker issued a note to Priscilla. Priscilla negotiated the note to Holder in payment for equipment that Holder delivered to Priscilla.
   d. b and c.

6. Maker signed a note for $10,000 which is payable May 1, 2000. Maker delivered the note to Paul. On June 1, 1999, Paul negotiated the note to Antonio. Antonio would *NOT* be acting in good faith in which situation?
   a. Antonio bought the note from Paul for $9,000 (a reasonable discount).
   b. Antonio bought the note from Paul for $1,000 (an unreasonably large discount). Under the circumstances, a reasonable person would have known that something was improper.
   c. Antonio bought the note from Paul for $10,000. Unknown to Antonio, Maker claimed that he had a breach of warranty defense that he could assert against Paul.

7. In which case did Holder have notice that the note was overdue or had been dishonored?
   a. Maker issued a note that was due June 1. Payee negotiated the note to Holder on June 2.
   b. Maker issued a note due May 1, 2001. The note was negotiated to Holder on April 1, 1998. At time of negotiation, Holder knew that time for payment of the note had been accelerated.
   c. At the time a note was negotiated to Holder, Holder knew that the maker had failed to pay some interest on the note.
   d. a and b.

8. In which case did Holder take the check with notice of a defense or adverse claim?
   a. Drawer issued a check as payment for a car. The car was misrepresented to Drawer. One hour after the seller negotiated the check to Holder, Holder learned of the misrepresentation.
   b. Drawer issued a check for Payee's services. At the time Payee negotiated the check to Holder, Holder knew that Drawer claimed that Payee had improperly performed the services.
   c. At the time a check is negotiated to Holder, Holder knows that the check was postdated.

CASE PROBLEM

Luis issued a negotiable promissory note that is due and payable January 1, 2000. Luis delivered the note to the payee, Ward Bates. Ward indorsed the note "Ward Bates" and delivered it to Noel. In this case: (1) What type of liability do Luis and Ward have to pay the face amount of the note? (2) What conditions must be met in order to hold Ward liable to pay the note? (3) Could Noel hold Ward liable to pay the face amount of the note if she did not present it to Luis for payment until March 1, 2000? Would it matter that Noel did not present it sooner because Luis was hiding and could not be found?

BUSINESS LAW PARTNER EXERCISE

Directions:

1. Using the Online feature of the Business Law Partner CD-ROM, find and identify the FTC rule that regulates the rights of a HDC in connection with consumer credit transactions.
2. Does this FTC rule apply in the case below? Must Mindy pay the amount of the note to Harry?

Case Study: *Sometimes Being a HDC Is Not Enough*

Mindy issued a negotiable note to P&P Co. to pay for a stove for her home. The note contains all notices required by FTC rules. The stove breached various warranties. P&P negotiated the note to Harry, who took it for value, in good faith, and with no notice of the breach. Mindy now claims that she does not have to pay the note because the stove is defective.

CHAPTER 24 QUIZ

Section A

DIRECTIONS: Following each statement below, indicate your answer by placing a "T" for "True" or an "F" for "False" in the Answers column.

	Answers	For Scoring
1. The law of commercial paper imposes liability upon the parties to a negotiable instrument based solely upon the nature of the paper..............................	_____	1. _____
2. Parties whose signatures do not appear on the paper are not liable for its payment.	_____	2. _____
3. A person may incur liability on a negotiable instrument by signing an assumed name..	_____	3. _____
4. When a negotiable instrument is due, no conditions need be met by the holder of the paper prior to the demand being made upon one who is primarily liable......................	_____	4. _____
5. The parties who ordinarily have the potential of primary liability are makers and drawees.	_____	5. _____
6. The drawee is made liable for a negotiable instrument by the mere order of the drawer.	_____	6. _____
7. A drawee has no liability on the instrument until it is accepted..................................	_____	7. _____
8. The demand for acceptance or payment made upon the maker, acceptor, drawee, or other payor of a negotiable instrument is called notice.	_____	8. _____
9. The nature of the instrument is the sole determinant as to what length of time is reasonable for presentment for payment...	_____	9. _____
10. With respect to the liability of a drawer to pay his or her check, presentment within 30 days is presumed to be reasonable.	_____	10. _____
11. Proper presentment is not a condition of secondary liability on a note when the maker has died or has been declared insolvent..	_____	11. _____
12. If, after a diligent effort, a holder cannot find the maker of a note, the holder is excused from the requirement of presentment..	_____	12. _____
13. Dishonor may consist of refusal to accept a draft as well as a refusal to pay.	_____	13. _____
14. The return of a check because of a missing proper indorsement constitutes dishonor. ..	_____	14. _____
15. Notice of dishonor may not be given by mail.	_____	15. _____
16. Notice of dishonor may not be waived by the terms of a negotiable instrument.	_____	16. _____
17. In general, an agent who signs a negotiable instrument "Ralph Gordon by Sam Smith" may have liability to pay the instrument..	_____	17. _____
18. Jane Doe, an agent, would not be bound on an instrument she signs "John Smith and Jane Doe".	_____	18. _____
19. An agent signing for a corporation should sign above or below the corporation's name and indicate after the signature what office is held.	_____	19. _____
20. One's signature must appear on the instrument in order to be liable as a warrantor.......	_____	20. _____

Score _____

Section B

DIRECTIONS: Complete each of the following statements by writing the missing word or words in the Answers column.

	Answers	For Scoring
1. Makers of notes and drawees of drafts are the two parties who ordinarily may have ??? liability on a negotiable instrument...	_____	1. _____
2. Indorsers and drawers are the parties whose liability on a negotiable instrument is ordinarily ???.	_____	2. _____
3. The demand for acceptance or payment made upon the maker, acceptor, drawee, or other payor is	_____	3. _____

4. The maker's refusal to pay when demanded by a holder is .... 4. _____

5. A holder desiring to hold indorsers liable must give them........................ 5. _____

6. The requirement that a notice of dishonor of an instrument drawn or payable outside the United States be certified is called................................. 6. _____

7. An agent who signs an instrument that identifies the principal and indicates a(n) ??? capacity is not be liable on it... 7. _____

8. The ordinary indorser incurs primary liability to pay an instrument. . ... 8. _____

9. A party who incurs primary liability by signing and agreeing to pay an instrument is called ???... 9. _____

10. Warranties are made by every ??? of a negotiable instrument....................... 10. _____

Score _____

Section C

DIRECTIONS: Indicate your decision in each of the following cases by filling in the Answers column.

	Answers	For Scoring

1-2. Green executed and delivered a check payable to Dwight. The bank refused to pay the check because of insufficient funds. Dwight notified Green and said Green was liable. Green thought he remembered from his business law course that drawers were not primarily liable and therefore he should not have to pay. Is Green correct that he is not primarily liable? .... 1. _____

Is Green liable on the check? .... 2. _____

3-4. Smithson was an agent for Jackson. In the course of her agency, Smithson signed a note " Smithson, Agent." The third party did not know Smithson was an agent for Jackson. Who is liable on the instrument? .... 3. _____

If the third party had known Smithson was Jackson's agent, who would be bound? .... 4. _____

5. Could Smithson introduce parole evidence to prove the agency?.................. 5. _____

Score _____

Section D

DIRECTIONS: Place an X in the Answers column to indicate that the condition specified below would prevent you, a prospective purchaser of the instrument, from becoming a holder in due course. Place a O in the Answers column if the condition specified would have no effect.

	Answers	For Scoring

1. You pay a 5 percent discount for the instrument. .... 1._____

2. The instrument is a gift. .... 2._____

3. All interest payments due on the instrument have been made, but one principal payment is overdue. .... 3._____

4. The instrument is a check that is dated 60 days previous. .... 4._____

5. The instrument falls due on the day it is offered. .... 5._____

6. The instrument is stamped " paid." .... 6._____

7. The instrument is offered to pay for consumer goods and the seller arranged for the loan. .... 7._____

8. The holder is aware the instrument is postdated. .... 8._____

9. There has been a default in the payment of interest....................................... 9._____

10. A consumer gave a note for goods that were never delivered............................ 10._____

Score _____

CHAPTER 25
DEFENSES
CHAPTER OUTLINE

I. INTRODUCTION

General rules. ▸ A maker, drawer, or indorser who ordinarily has liability to pay an instrument may have a defense that avoids this liability. Defenses may be classified as (1) limited (personal) defenses or (2) universal (also called real) defenses. ▸ Limited defenses can be used against an ordinary holder, but they cannot be used against a holder in due course (HDC) or a holder through a holder in due course. ▸ Universal defenses can be used against anyone.

Examples. ▸ *Limited defense*: June issued a $50,000 note to Seller as payment for property. Seller negotiated the note to a HDC. Seller did not convey title to June (failure of consideration, a limited defense). June cannot use this defense against the HDC; June must pay the note. June must sue Seller for breach of contract for $50,000.
▸ *Universal defense*: Rosa, age 17, issued a check as payment for a debt. The payee indorsed the check and negotiated it to an innocent purchaser. Rosa can use the defense of minority (a real defense) against the innocent purchaser, avoiding her liability to pay the check. The innocent purchaser must sue the payee based on his or her liability as an indorser or on warranty liability.

Study hint. Certain defenses, classified as hybrid defenses, may be limited or universal defenses.

II. CLASSIFICATION OF DEFENSES

A. LIMITED DEFENSES

- *Ordinary contract defenses*: Most contract defenses, such as breach of warranty and failure of consideration (party fails to perform a contractual promise), are limited defenses.

- *Fraud that induced the execution of the instrument*: ▸ Defense: A party knowingly executes a negotiable instrument, but the party has been fraudulently induced into signing the instrument. ▸ Example: Buyer issued a check in payment for a car that was misrepresented.

- *Conditional delivery*: ▸ The fact that an instrument is subject to secret, unmet conditions is a limited defense. ▸ Example: Max issued a note to Pete, subject to an oral condition that it was not payable until Pete delivered goods to Max. Pete negotiated the note to Irene, an innocent purchaser. The conditional delivery from Max to Pete cannot be asserted against Irene. Max must pay Irene even if Pete does not satisfy the condition.

- *Improper completion*: ▸ Unauthorized completion of an instrument is a limited defense. ▸ Example: Liz issued a check leaving the amount blank. Liz gave the check to her son, telling him not to complete it for more than $20. The son filled in $200 and negotiated it to a holder in due course. The son's unauthorized completion cannot be asserted against the holder in due course. Liz must pay $200 to the holder in due course.

- *Payment or part payment*: ▸ The fact that a party has already paid an instrument is a limited defense.
  ▸ Example: Mandy issued a note to Chris payable June 1. On March 1, Mandy prepaid the note, but she did not get the note back. On April 1, Chris negotiated the note to a holder in due course. Mandy's prior payment is a limited defense, and it cannot be asserted against the holder in due course. ▸ Partial payment: If someone makes a partial payment of an instrument and *this fact is noted on the instrument*, a person taking the instrument is charged with notice of payment and the right to be paid is reduced accordingly.

- *Nondelivery*: ▸ The fact that an instrument was delivered without a party's authorization is a limited defense. ▸ Example: Larry issued a check payable to Kim, and he placed it in his coat. Without permission, Kim took the check and negotiated it to an innocent purchaser. The unauthorized delivery to Kim cannot be used as a defense against the innocent purchaser.

- **Theft**: ‣ The fact that an instrument was stolen is a limited defense. ‣ Example: Rex issued a check payable to cash and gave it to Nancy. Thief stole the check and negotiated it to an innocent purchaser. The innocent purchaser can enforce the check despite the theft.

B. UNIVERSAL DEFENSES

- **Minority**: Lack of contractual capacity due to minority is a universal defense.

- **Forgery**: Unless their negligence made the forgery possible, makers, drawers, or indorsers can assert against anyone the defense that their signatures were forged.

- **Fraud as to the nature of the instrument and its essential terms**: ‣ If a maker or drawer is defrauded regarding the legal nature or important terms of an instrument, this creates a universal defense that can be asserted against anyone. ‣ Example: An elderly man, thinking that he is only signing a request for credit, is defrauded into signing a promissory note. ‣ This defense is unavailable if a maker's or drawer's negligence enabled the fraud to occur.

- **Discharge in bankruptcy proceedings**: ‣ A discharge in bankruptcy that negates a duty to pay an instrument can be asserted against anyone. ‣ Example: In 1995, Wayne signed a note payable June 1, 2003. In 1998, Wayne filed for bankruptcy and he received a discharge in bankruptcy. Wayne can use the discharge in bankruptcy as a defense against anyone.

C. HYBRID DEFENSES (DEFENSES MAY BE LIMITED OR UNIVERSAL DEFENSES)

Certain defenses may be limited or universal defenses depending on the facts and state law that apply to a given case. These defenses are:

- **Duress**: ‣ Duress is a limited defense if it renders a contract voidable under state law. ‣ Duress that renders a contract void under state law is a universal defense.

- **Incapacity other than minority**: ‣ Lack of capacity (excluding minority) is a limited defense if, under state law, it renders a contract voidable. ‣ Incapacity that renders a contract void is a universal defense.

- **Illegality**: Illegality is a universal defense if an instrument arises out of a transaction that violates a law that states that instruments are void or unenforceable.

- **Alteration**: ‣ Alteration defined: material, fraudulent changing of the terms of an instrument that is done by a party to the instrument (e.g., a holder). ‣ An alteration is a partial defense against a holder in due course, i.e., the instrument can be enforced by a holder in due course according to its original, unaltered terms. ‣ Example: Dick issued a check for $100, and Payee changed the amount to $1,000. Payee negotiated the check to Kelly, a holder in due course. Kelly can enforce the check for $100. Kelly must sue Payee for the other $900.

III. MISCELLANEOUS MATTERS

A plaintiff seeking to enforce an instrument may confront the following additional defenses:

‣ Statute of limitations has run and bars collection of the instrument.

‣ Defendant has a limited defense that can be used against plaintiff because paper is not negotiable, or the instrument was not negotiated to plaintiff (i.e., plaintiff is not a holder in due course).

‣ Defendant only has secondary liability, and requirements of presentment, dishonor, or notice of dishonor were not satisfied, thereby discharging the defendant's liability.

‣ Defendant claims that he or she did not sign the instrument and therefore is not liable to pay.

REVIEW OF CHAPTER

REVIEW OF TERMS

Select the term that best matches a statement below. Each term is the best match for only one statement.

TERMS

a. Alteration
b. Failure of consideration
c. Fraud as to the nature of an instrument
d. Fraud which induced execution of an instrument

e. Hybrid defense
f. Limited defense
g. Universal defense

STATEMENTS

Answer

_____ 1. Misrepresentation that misleads a maker or drawer regarding the legal character of an instrument.

_____ 2. Defense to payment that can be asserted against any party, including a holder in due course.

_____ 3. Material change made to the terms of an instrument by a party to the instrument.

_____ 4. Misrepresentation that induces a party to sign a negotiable instrument, although the party knows that he or she is signing a negotiable instrument.

_____ 5. Defense that may be limited or universal, depending on the facts and law in a given case.

_____ 6. Contractual defense that a party did not receive consideration from the other party.

_____ 7. Defense to payment that can be asserted against an ordinary holder, but not against a holder in due course.

REVIEW OF CONCEPTS

Directions: Indicate **T** for true and **F** for false in the answer column.

_____ 1. Limited defenses can be used against an ordinary holder, but not against a holder in due course.

_____ 2. Limited defenses cannot be asserted against a holder through a holder in due course.

_____ 3. Universal defenses can be used against an ordinary holder, but not against a holder in due course.

_____ 4. Hybrid defenses are defenses that can never be asserted against a holder in due course.

_____ 5. Most ordinary contract defenses are limited defenses.

_____ 6. Maker issued a note due May 1. Maker paid the note on March 1, but Maker did not take back the note. The note was negotiated by the payee to a holder in due course on April 1. In this case, Maker must pay the note to the holder in due course.

_____ 7. Maker issued a $5,000 note due May 1. Maker paid $2,000 to the payee on March 1 and this payment was stated on the face of the note. The payee negotiated the note to a holder in due course. In this case, the holder in due course can enforce the note for only $3,000.

_____ 8. The defense that an instrument was stolen from the rightful owner is a limited defense.

_____ 9. The defense of unauthorized completion is a universal defense.

_____ 10. Every type of fraud is a universal defense.

_____ 11. Duress is a universal defense if, under state law, duress would render a contract voidable.

_____ 12. The defense that a maker has been discharged in bankruptcy is a universal defense.

_____ 13. A holder in due course of a check cannot collect anything if the check was previously altered.

REVIEW OF CONCEPT APPLICATIONS

Answer

Directions: Indicate your choice in the answer column.

_____ 1. Denise issued three checks to various payees. In which case does Denise have a limited defense?
   a. Denise issued a check to Contractor in payment for certain remodeling work. Contractor performed the work improperly, a breach of contract.
   b. Denise issued a check that was not paid by her bank due to insufficient funds. After issuing the check, Denise filed for bankruptcy and she received a discharge in bankruptcy.
   c. Denise issued a check in payment for illegal drugs. Under state statutes, negotiable instruments issued for illegal drugs are void and unenforceable.

____ 2. Maker issued three negotiable notes. In which case does Maker have a universal defense?
   a.   Maker issued a note to Hill. Maker prepaid the note, but Maker failed to get the note back.
   b.   Maker issued a note to Stockbroker. Delivery of the note was conditioned on Stockbroker's delivering certain shares of stock to Maker. Stockbroker failed to deliver the stock to Maker.
   c.   Maker issued a note to Lender. Maker issued the note due to the wrongful threats of Lender. Under state law, the duress exerted by Lender would render a contract void.

____ 3. Mr. Conrad issued a negotiable promissory note payable to Seller in payment for a new crane. Seller negotiated the note to Mr. Innocent, a holder in due course. Which defense can Mr. Conrad use against Mr. Innocent?
   a.   Mr. Conrad has a defense of breach of warranty because the crane is defective.
   b.   Mr. Conrad has a defense of fraud because he was induced into purchasing the crane as a result of Seller's fraudulent misrepresentations.
   c.   Mr. Conrad has a defense of insanity because he had been previously declared incompetent by a court. Under state law, this defense renders a contract void.

____ 4. Vanessa issued a check for $500 in payment for some goods. The seller negotiated the check to an innocent purchaser. Which defense can Vanessa assert against the innocent purchaser?
   a.   Vanessa has a defense of failure of consideration. The seller never delivered the goods.
   b.   Vanessa has a defense of minority. Vanessa is 17 years old.
   c.   Vanessa has a defense of intoxication. Vanessa was intoxicated at the time of contracting. Under state law, this defense renders a contract voidable.

CASE PROBLEM

Joan has been sued by a holder in due course for payment of three checks. Joan has these defenses: ▸ Check 1: Joan issued an incomplete check which she gave to Employee with directions to complete it for $100. Employee completed the check for $200. ▸ Check 2: Thief stole Joan's checkbook and issued a check for $250 by forging her signature as drawer. ▸ Check 3: Joan issued a check for $50. Payee raised the amount of the check to $500. For each check: (1) What is the name of the defense in question? Is the defense a limited, universal, or hybrid defense? (2) How much must Joan pay to the holder in due course?

_____

_____

_____

BUSINESS LAW PARTNER EXERCISE

Directions:

1. Use the Online feature of the Business Law Partner CD-ROM to help Jill find the desired company in the case below.
2. Describe two risks that this type of company faces in cashing checks of strangers, such as Jill.
3. Suggest a strategy that this type of company can use to minimize or avoid the risks described above.

Case Study: *New Kid on the Block*

Jill moved to town a few days ago and she has not had time to open a bank account. However, she has a check from her parents for $500 that she needs to cash in order to put a deposit on an apartment. Jill has asked you to help her find a service advertised on the Internet that may help her.

_____

_____

_____

CHAPTER 25 QUIZ

Section A

DIRECTIONS: Complete each of the following statements by writing the missing word or words in the Answers column.

		Answers	**For Scoring**
1.	Those defenses that cannot be raised against a holder in due course are ??? defenses.	_____	1. ____
2.	Theft of an instrument is a(n) ??? defense.	_____	2. ____
3.	Universal defenses can be asserted against	_____	3. ____
4.	Limited defenses are also called ??? defenses.	_____	4. ____
5.	When a negotiable instrument is a gift, the limited defense of ??? may be available.	_____	5. ____
6.	A person who knows a negotiable instrument is being executed, but who is persuaded to execute it because of false statements, has what kind of defense?	_____	6. ____
7.	An instrument is delivered subject to a condition. This is a(n) ??? defense.	_____	7. ____
8.	If a blank term in a a negotiable instrument is filled in without authority, this is	_____	8. ____
9.	Ruth paid $400 on a $600 note held by Martin. Martin failed to make the payment on the note. What defense will Ruth raise if sued for $600 by Martin?	_____	9. ____
10.	When a note is taken from the maker without permission, the defense of ??? might be raised.	_____	10. ____
11.	If a nonnegligent person is induced by fraud to sign an instrument believed to be an instrument of another character, the mistake renders the contract void, and the defense that may be offered against any holder is fraud as to the	_____	11. ____
12.	The defense of a discharge in bankruptcy is a(n) ??? defense.	_____	12. ____
13-15.	Some defenses may be either universal or limited. Three are	_____	13. ____
		_____	14. ____
		_____	15. ____
16.	Hybrid defenses are normally universal when they ??? the underlying contract.	_____	16. ____
17.	If an instrument is paid in a transaction prohibited by law, the defense of ??? may be raised.	_____	17. ____
18.	If a party to an instrument fraudulently makes a material change in it, this is a(n)	_____	18. ____
19.	Forgery may not be raised against any holder when the forgery was made possible by the ??? of the defendant.	_____	19. ____

Score _____

Section B

DIRECTIONS: Following each question below, indicate your answer by placing a "Y" for "Yes" or an "N" for "No" in the Answers column.

	Answers	**For Scoring**
1. In the case of *Richardson v. Carpenter,* the instrument in question read in part as follows: "Please pay Lee Barnett or order $500 for value received out of proceeds of claim against Franklin estate now in your hands for collection when same shall have been collected by you." Is this a negotiable instrument?	_____	1. _____
2. Tubb drew a check and delivered it to Yate in settlement of a debt. Yate negotiated it by indorsement and delivery to Zimmerman to cover his loss in a poker game. Tubb stopped payment on the check at Yate's request. Zimmerman threatened suit to collect from Tubb. Tubb's defense was that it was given to cover an illegal transaction. Does Tubb, the drawer, have a good defense?	_____	2. _____
3-4. Simkus had a criminal record for forgery. Onay hired her without checking her record. Simkus frequently signed papers for Onay when he did not want to be bothered. She forged Onay's signature to a $1,000 note and then sold it for $1,000 to Jessup, who did not know about the forgery. On the due date, Jessup demanded $1,000 from Onay, who replied that his signature was forged and he had a universal defense. Does Onay have a good defense against Jessup?	_____	3. _____
Is Simkus liable on the note?	_____	4. _____

Score _____

Section C

DIRECTIONS: Following each question below, indicate your answer by placing a "Y" for "Yes" or an "N" for "No" in the Answers column.

	Answers	**For Scoring**
1. Are all defenses a party to a negotiable instrument has against the party dealt with good against any subsequent party to the paper?	_____	1. _____
2. Will limited defenses bar recovery by one not a holder in due course?	_____	2. _____
3. Are universal defenses good against a holder in due course?	_____	3. _____
4. If a negotiable instrument is held by a holder in due course, is the maker's defense of failure of consideration effective?	_____	4. _____
5. Is the defense of failure of consideration effective against a holder in due course?	_____	5. _____
6. Is the defense of fraud relating to the reason for executing an instrument good against a holder in due course?	_____	6. _____
7. As against a holder in due course, can an individual who would be liable on the instrument refuse to pay by showing the instrument, absolute on its face, was delivered subject to an unperformed condition?	_____	7. _____
8. Is the defense of fraud relating to the reason for executing an instrument good against a holder in due course?	_____	8. _____
9. Can a holder in due course require payment of an instrument which has been improperly completed?	_____	9. _____
10. Since a thief cannot pass good title, is a holder in due course who receives an instrument from a thief unable to require payment of it?	_____	10. _____
11. Since minors can avoid their contracts, can they successfully raise their minority as a defense against holders in due course?	_____	11. _____
12. Is the defense that the plaintiff is not a holder usable against one who claims to be a holder in due course?	_____	12. _____

Score _____

CHAPTER 26
NATURE AND CREATION OF AN AGENCY
CHAPTER OUTLINE

I.   INTRODUCTION

- A contract of agency is created when one party (a principal) appoints another party (an agent) to make a contract on behalf of the principal with a third party.
- Principals, agents, and third parties may be individuals, partnerships, or corporations.

II.   IMPORTANCE OF AGENCY

Agency relationships are important because it is frequently necessary for businesses to delegate commercial transactions and contractual dealings to agents.

III.   WHAT POWERS MAY BE DELEGATED TO AN AGENT?

General rule.   A principal can delegate to an agent the power to do any act the principal can do.
Limitation.   A principal cannot delegate the power to do acts that must be done personally or that are illegal. Thus, a principal cannot appoint an agent to vote, serve in the military, or execute a will.

IV.   WHO MAY APPOINT AN AGENT?

General rule.   Any legally competent person can appoint, and act through, an agent.
Limitation.   In most states, if a principal is a minor, the minor's contract appointing an agent is voidable. In some states, a minor's contract appointing an agent is void.

V.   WHO MAY ACT AS AN AGENT?

General rule.   In general, there are no qualifications for being an agent; anyone may be an agent.
Limitation.   Some agents, such as real estate agents, must be licensed to perform certain duties.

VI.   CLASSIFICATION OF AGENTS

- *General agents*: ▸ Definition: agents authorized to carry out a particular business for a principal (e.g., mortgage loan officer) or all business of a principal that is conducted at a specific location (e.g., general manager of a store). ▸ General agents may have broad authority, and they can sometimes act without being expressly authorized to do so by a principal.

- *Special agents*: ▸ Definition: agents authorized to do only a specific act or acts. ▸ Powers of special agents are limited to powers expressly given by a principal. ▸ Example: real estate agent.

VII.   ADDITIONAL TYPES OF AGENTS

- *Factors (commission merchants)*: ▸ Defined: parties who receive another's property to sell for a commission (factorage). ▸ Factors can bind a principal to terms that are (1) expressly authorized by the principal or (2) that are customary for the type of business in question.

- *Factors del credere*: ▸ Defined: factors who (1) sell property for a principal on credit and (2) guarantee that the price will be paid by the buyer or the factor. ▸ This agency contract is a form of guarantee, but a writing is not needed to create this agency.

- **Brokers**: ▸ Defined: special agents who bring two contracting parties together. ▸ In some situations, a broker does not have the power to bind a principal to any contract. ▸ In real estate and insurance transactions, a broker generally represents the buyer.

- **Attorney in facts**: ▸ Defined: general agents appointed by a written instrument called a power of attorney (warrant). ▸ The power of attorney establishes the existence of the agency relationship and the extent of the agent's authority.

VIII. EXTENT OF AUTHORITY

General rule.   A general agent can bind a principal to a contract with a third party if the agent acts with: (1) express authority; (2) implied authority; (3) customary authority; or (4) apparent authority.

- **Express authority**: authority specifically given to an agent in the agency agreement.

- **Implied authority**: authority to do acts reasonably necessary to carry out express authority.

- **Customary authority**: authority to do acts that are customarily done by this type of agent.

- **Apparent authority**: authority arising because a principal misleads a third party into believing that an agent has authority to do an act.

Study hints.   ▸ A third party is not bound by limits that a principal places on an agent's authority if the third party is unaware of such limits. But, a party is bound by limitations that are known to the party. ▸ The party who will benefit from proof that authority existed must prove such authority.

IX. CREATION OF AN AGENCY

- **Appointment**: ▸ In general: Contracts appointing an agent may be oral or written; formal or informal.
  ▸ Exception: An agency contract must be written if it: (1) grants an agent the authority to act for more than one year from the date the contract is made; or (2) authorizes an agent to convey title to real estate.

- **Ratification**: ▸ Defined: approval of an unauthorized act. ▸ A principal is bound by an agent's unauthorized act if the principal subsequently ratifies the act. ▸ Requirements for ratification are: (1) agent contracted on behalf of a disclosed principal; (2) principal had the capacity to authorize the contract at the time it was made; (3) principal has the capacity to authorize the contract at the time it is ratified; (4) principal knows all material facts; (5) principal must ratify the entire contract; (6) contract is legal; and (7) ratification occurs before the third party withdraws. ▸ Effect of ratification: a ratified contract is treated as if it were expressly authorized.

- **Estoppel**: ▸ An agency by estoppel may be created when a person's words or acts mislead another person into believing that a third party is that person's agent, and it is necessary to recognize an agency in order to avoid injustice. ▸ Example: Bob allowed John to falsely act as if he were Bob's agent.

- **Necessity**: ▸ If a parent fails to provide necessaries for a child, the child may purchase the necessaries and charge them to the parent. ▸ An agent may contract on behalf of a principal if doing so is made necessary due to an emergency.

X. OTHER EMPLOYMENT RELATIONSHIPS

- **Independent contractor**: ▸ Defined: party who contracts to perform a job for a stated price and who retains control over the manner of performing the job, subject only to the duties stated in the contract. ▸ Example: contractor agrees to replace a roof for a homeowner. ▸ In general, a party hiring an independent contractor is not liable for torts of the independent contractor, and does not have to pay employment taxes that must be paid for employees (e.g., social security taxes). ▸ Note: Independent contractors are employers of the persons they employ.

- **Employer - employee**: ▸ Defined: person hired to perform a job subject to the control of an employer regarding the result and manner of doing the job. ▸ An employer is liable for employees' torts committed within the scope of employment, and an employer must pay certain employment taxes.

REVIEW OF CHAPTER

REVIEW OF TERMS

Select the term that best matches a statement below. Each term is the best match for only one statement.

TERMS

a. Agent
b. Apparent authority
c. Customary authority
d. Express authority

e. Factor
f. General agent
g. Implied authority

h. Independent contractor
i. Principal
j. Special agent

STATEMENTS

Answer

_____ 1. Party on whose behalf an agent is authorized to make a contract.

_____ 2. Authority that arises because a principal misleads a third party into believing that an agent has authority to do an act.

_____ 3. Party who is authorized to make a contract on behalf of a principal.

_____ 4. Agent who is authorized to do only a specific act on behalf of a principal.

_____ 5. Authority specifically granted to an agent by an agency agreement.

_____ 6. Agent who is authorized to carry out a particular business for a principal, or all business that is conducted at a particular location.

_____ 7. Authority to do acts that are customarily done by this type of agent.

_____ 8. Authority to do acts that are reasonably necessary to carry out an agent's express authority.

_____ 9. Party who receives goods belonging to another to sell for a commission.

_____ 10. Party who is hired to do a task and who retains control over the method for completing the task.

REVIEW OF CONCEPTS

Directions: Indicate **T** for true and **F** for false in the answer column.

_____ 1. An agent who is authorized to make all purchases for a principal is a special agent.

_____ 2. A factor del credere sells goods for a principal on credit, and the factor guarantees to the principal that the purchase price will be paid by the buyer or the factor.

_____ 3. A third party is bound by all limitations that a principal places on an agent's authority whether or not the third party is aware of such limitations.

_____ 4. A general agent can represent a principal only to the extent the agent has express authority.

_____ 5. An agent's unauthorized action is treated as if it were expressly authorized if the principal ratifies the action.

_____ 6. A principal cannot ratify only part of an unauthorized contract.

_____ 7. A minor child may have authority by necessity to buy necessaries and to charge them to a parent.

_____ 8. A principal always has the burden to prove that a person was or was not the principal's agent.

_____ 9. A party must pay employment-related taxes if the party hires either an employee or an independent contractor.

_____ 10. A person who hires an independent contractor generally controls the method used by the independent contractor to perform a required task.

REVIEW OF CONCEPT APPLICATIONS

Answer

Directions: Indicate your choice in the answer column.

_____ 1. Perry (a minor) signed a contract authorizing Allied Inc. (a licensed real estate corporation) to sell and convey title to land that belonged to Perry. In many states, this contract of agency is:

a. Invalid. An agent cannot be authorized to sell or convey land on behalf of a principal.

b. Invalid. A corporation cannot be an agent.

c. Voidable. Perry is a minor and he can disaffirm the contract of agency.

d. Valid. Allied was properly authorized to sell and convey the land, and Perry cannot disaffirm this contract of agency.

_____ 2. Owner hired Jack as manager of a florist shop. Managers of such stores can customarily hire employees. But, Owner told Jack not to hire employees without Owner's consent. Dan applied for a job. Owner referred Dan to Jack, misleadingly stating "Jack handles all employment matters." Jack hired Dan without Owner's consent. Dan did not know that Jack's authority had been limited. Jack had what type of authority to hire Dan?
   a.   Implied authority.
   b.   Customary authority.
   c.   Apparent authority.

_____ 3. Without any authority to do so, Avery contracted to buy a printer on behalf of his principal, P&P Printing. After making the contract, Avery told P&P about the contract and explained the terms. P&P told Avery that the contract was acceptable, and P&P kept and used the printer. At all relevant times, P&P was capable of contracting, and the contract was legal. Under these facts:
   a.   The contract is binding on P&P. A principal is bound by any contract made by its agents.
   b.   The contract is binding on P&P. P&P ratified the contract.
   c.   The contract is not binding on P&P. Avery did not have express authority to contract.

_____ 4. Tosco Mfg. hired Roadway, Inc. to build a road at Tosco's plant. Roadway was to build the road in accordance with basic plans stated in the contract. Roadway was to use its own tools, employees, and methods; Tosco did not have the right to control the manner by which Roadway built the road. During construction, Roadway negligently injured a third party. In this case:
   a.   Roadway is an independent contractor.
   b.   Roadway is an employee.
   c.   Tosco is liable for the third party's injuries that were caused by Roadway's negligence.
   d.   b and c.

CASE PROBLEM

George is manager of a Hardi Hardware store. In his contract George was authorized by Hardi to buy inventory and to manage the store's business. Nothing was said regarding hiring a bookkeeping service or placing advertisements. It was necessary to hire a bookkeeping service to conduct the store's business, and it is customary for agents, such as George, to place ads. On behalf of Hardi, George: (1) bought ten saws for inventory, (2) employed a bookkeeping service, and (3) placed an ad in a local newspaper. What type of authority, if any, did George have to make these contracts?

_____

_____

BUSINESS LAW PARTNER EXERCISE

Directions:

1. Access your Business Law Partner CD-ROM and find the documents "Power of Attorney – General" and "Power of Attorney – Special."
2. In the following case, help Carla choose the most appropriate power of attorney form to use and then complete the form using the information provided.

Case Study: *I Want To Empower You, Carla*

George and Sally Bonner live at 455 Orange Street in Draco, State of *X*. The Bonners recently retired and listed their house for sale for $80,000. The Bonners, however, have already purchased a retirement home in Arizona and want to move there immediately. They asked Carla, their daughter who lives in Draco, if she would handle the sale of their residence, and Carla agreed. They told Carla that she could sell their home for $75,000 or more, payable in full at the closing. They told her that she could decide the other terms of the sale in her own discretion.

CHAPTER 26 QUIZ

Section A

DIRECTIONS: Complete each of the following statements by writing the missing word or words in the Answers column.

	Answers	For Scoring
1. The person who appoints another party to enter into contracts with third parties in the name of the first person is a(n)......................................	_____	1. _____
2. The party appointed by another to enter into contracts with third parties is a(n)...	_____	2. _____
3. One authorized to carry out all of the principal's business at a particular place or all of the principal's business of a particular kind is a(n) <u>???</u> agent.	_____	3. _____
4. One who is authorized by the principal to transact a specific act or a specific series of acts is a(n)	_____	4. _____
5. Commonly called a commission merchant, one who receives possession of another's property for sale on commission is a special type of agent known as a(n)	_____	5. _____
6. A commission merchant that sells on credit and guarantees the price will be paid is called a(n)..	_____	6. _____
7. A special agent whose task is to bring two contracting parties together is a(n)...	_____	7. _____
8. A general agent appointed by a written authorization is called a(n)	_____	8. _____
9. The authority an agent possesses, which is clearly within the scope of the authority stated in the agency agreement, is called	_____	9. _____
10. The authority an agent has to do things in order to carry out express authority is	_____	10. _____
11. A general agent has authority that one in his or her position usually possesses. This authority is known as...	_____	11. _____
12. When the principal behaves in a way or makes statements that mislead a third party into mistakenly believing that the agent has authority, this authority is called	_____	12. _____
13. A written instrument appointing an agent is a(n)	_____	13. _____
14. The approval by a person of an unauthorized act done in the person's name is known as	_____	14. _____
15. When a person by words or conduct misleads another person to believe that a third person is an agent, the relationship of agency is created by...............	_____	15. _____
16. When agency is created by an unforeseen emergency through the pledging of another's credit, agency is created by	_____	16. _____
17. A person hired to perform tasks for a fee but independent of the control of the other contracting party in performance of the contract is a(n).................	_____	17. _____
18. A person who performs work for another and is under the other's control both as to the work to be done and as to the manner in which it is to be done is called a(n)..	_____	18. _____
	Score	_____

Section B

DIRECTIONS: Following each statement below, indicate your answer by placing a "T" for "True" or an "F" for "False" in the Answers column.

	Answers	For Scoring
1. Every contract an agent negotiates involves at least three parties.	_____	1. _____
2. The general principles of contract law govern agency agreements.	_____	2. _____
3. All things that one has a right to do personally may be done through an agent.	_____	3. _____
4. The contract by which a minor appoints an agent to act is normally voidable.	_____	4. _____
5. A corporation cannot appoint agents to act on its behalf.	_____	5. _____
6. Unlike other agents, factors normally sell in their own name, not that of their principal.	_____	6. _____
7. The only authority a general agent has is that which is specifically stated in the contract with the principal.	_____	7. _____
8. Since the agreement between a factor del credere and the principal is a form of contract of guaranty, it must be in writing.	_____	8. _____
9. Limitations upon an agent's authority are binding upon third parties even if they are not aware of such limitations.	_____	9. _____
10. People legally competent to act for themselves may act through agents.	_____	10. _____
11. A corporation may be an agent.	_____	11. _____
12. All written agency contracts must be notarized.	_____	12. _____
13. A principal is bound by acts of agents even if the agents exceed both their actual and apparent authority.	_____	13. _____
14. In order to ratify an act, the one attempting to ratify must have been capable of authorizing the act at the time the act was done.	_____	14. _____
15. Parents' credit may be pledged without their consent for necessaries with which minor children are not reasonably supplied.	_____	15. _____
16. An independent contractor may be a person's agent.	_____	16. _____
17. The person who contracts with an independent contractor is liable for injuries negligently caused to third parties by the independent contractor.	_____	17. _____
18. An agent is always the employee of the principal.	_____	18. _____

Score _____

CHAPTER 27
OPERATION AND TERMINATION OF AN AGENCY

CHAPTER OUTLINE

I. INTRODUCTION

The law establishes numerous duties that a principal and agent owe to each other, and to third parties.

II. AGENT'S DUTIES TO PRINCIPAL

- *Loyalty and good faith*: Principals and agents have a fiduciary relationship that requires loyalty and good faith on the agent's part. An agent acts in bad faith or is disloyal if the agent:
  - secretly owns an interest in a business that competes with the principal;
  - discloses a principal's confidential information to others;
  - sells to or buys from a principal without disclosing the agent's interest; or
  - represents both the principal and a competitor (or other contracting party) at the same time.
  Liability for breach of duty: no right to compensation or reimbursement; principal can fire agent; principal can recover wrongful profits made by the agent; principal can sue agent for damages.

- *Obedience*: ▸ An agent must precisely follow routine instructions (orders regarding matters not involving an agent's judgment) unless they are illegal or fraudulent. ▸ An agent must carry out discretionary instructions (matters requiring one's judgment) by using the agent's best judgment.

- *Reasonable skill and diligence*: ▸ It is implied that an agent warrants that the agent has the skill required to perform and that the agent will diligently carry out the agency. An agent is liable for damages if these warranties are breached. ▸ An agent cannot appoint a subagent to do the agent's work unless (1) this is permitted by the agency contract, (2) the work is clerical, or (3) it is customarily delegated. Appointing subagents does not relieve an agent of liability if work is done improperly.

- *Accounting*: An agent: (1) must account to a principal for all money and property in the agent's possession; and (2) must not commingle the agent's money or property with that of the principal.

- *Information*: An agent must inform a principal of facts that are relevant to protecting a principal's interests. An agent is not entitled to be paid for information that is required to be disclosed.

III. PRINCIPAL'S DUTIES TO AGENT

- *Compensation*: ▸ A principal must pay an agent (1) the compensation stated in the contract, or (2) if compensation is not stated, a reasonable or customary compensation. ▸ Contingent compensation: If compensation is subject to a contingency (e.g., completing a sale), compensation is due only if the condition is met. Example: a sales commission is due only if goods are sold.

- *Reimbursement*: ▸ Duty: Principal must reimburse an agent for personal funds spent by the agent in carrying out agency. ▸ Limit: no reimbursement for expenditures arising from unlawful acts.

- *Indemnification*: ▸ Duty: Principal must compensate an agent for losses or damages incurred by the agent as a result of carrying out the agency. ▸ Example: Carl (agent) is in an accident while performing an agency. Carl is liable to a third party who was injured in the accident. Carl's principal must pay Carl for the amount that Carl owes to the third party.

- *Abidance by the terms of the contract*: A principal must comply with all terms of the agency contract, and a principal must cooperate fully with an agent so that the agent can fulfill agency duties.

IV. AGENT'S LIABILITIES TO THIRD PARTIES

General rule.   An agent is not liable to a third party if (1) the agent makes a contract for a principal, (2) the agent had any type of authority, and (3) the name and existence of the principal was disclosed.

Limitation.   An agent is liable to a third party if the agent: (1) contracts in the agent's own name without disclosing the principal's name and existence; (2) agrees to be personally bound by a contract; (3) contracts for a principal with no authority to do so (and the contract is not ratified by the principal); or (4) commits fraud or other wrongful acts.

V. PRINCIPAL'S DUTIES AND LIABILITIES TO THIRD PARTIES

General rules.   ▸ A principal is liable on a contract made for the principal by an agent if: (1) agent had any type of authority to make the contract; or (2) the principal ratified the contract. ▸ Principal (and agent) is liable for damages caused by an agent while acting within the scope of employment.

Examples.   ▸ Agent with apparent authority makes a contract for Principal. Principal is bound. ▸ Agent defrauds Buyer while acting within scope of agency. Principal is liable for Agent's fraud.

Limitations.   ▸ Principal is not liable for a contract if an agent had no authority to make the contract.
▸ Principal is not liable for injuries caused by an agent who was acting on his or her own.

VI. TERMINATION OF AN AGENCY BY ACTS OF THE PARTIES

- *Original agreement*: Agency contract terminates on the date stated or when its purpose is fulfilled.

- *Subsequent agreement*: A principal and agent can agree to terminate an agency at any time.

- *Revocation*:

    ▸ *Legal right*: Principal has the right to terminate an agency if an agent commits a material breach of contract. Examples: agent fails to perform agency duties; agent embezzles money.

    ▸ *Power*: Principal has the power to terminate an agency at any time, but the principal is liable to agent for damages if termination is wrongful. Example: Acme hires Jan as agent for two years. Acme can terminate Jan at anytime, but Acme is liable for damages if termination was unjustified.

    ▸ *Agency coupled with an interest*: Principal has no power to terminate an agency coupled with an interest (agent has an interest in either the authority or the subject matter of the agency). Example: Principal owes money to Agent. Principal authorizes Agent to collect funds, and to keep the funds as payment of the debt owed by Principal. Principal cannot terminate this agency.

- *Renunciation*: An agent has the power to terminate an agency relationship at any time, but the agent is liable to the principal for damages if the termination violates the agency contract.

VII. TERMINATION BY OPERATION OF LAW

By operation of law, certain occurrences automatically terminate an agency. These events are:

- *Subsequent illegality (of subject matter)*: Subject matter of agency becomes illegal.

- *Death or incapacity*: The death or incapacity of the principal or agent terminates an agency. An exception is a durable power of attorney, which survives the incapacity of the principal.

- *Destruction (of subject matter)*: Example: Agency to sell a home ends if the home burns down.

- *Bankruptcy*: Bankruptcy of a principal (but not of an agent) terminates an agency.

- *Dissolution*: If either party is a corporation, dissolution of the corporation terminates the agency.

- *War*: Agency ends if parties are citizens of different countries that go to war against one another.

VIII. NOTICE OF TERMINATION

▸ A principal who terminates an agent must give notice of this fact to third parties that have dealt with the agent. Otherwise, the agent may bind the principal to contracts with third parties that are unaware of the termination.
▸ Notice is not required if an agency is terminated by operation of law.

REVIEW OF CHAPTER

REVIEW OF TERMS

Select the term that best matches a statement below. Each term is the best match for only one statement.

TERMS

a. Accounting
b. Agency coupled with an interest
c. Discretionary instruction

d. Fiduciary relationship
e. Indemnification
f. Routine instruction

STATEMENTS

Answer

____ 1. Relationship that exists between a principal and agent.
____ 2. Principal's order regarding a matter that does not involve an agent's judgment.
____ 3. Principal's duty to pay an agent for losses suffered by the agent in carrying out the agency.
____ 4. Principal's order regarding a matter that requires an agent to exercise the agent's best judgment.
____ 5. Agency in which the agent has a personal, financial interest because the agent has paid consideration to the principal.
____ 6. Agent's duty to keep a record of the money and property of a principal.

REVIEW OF CONCEPTS

Directions: Indicate **T** for true and **F** for false in the answer column.

____ 1. In general, an agent cannot compete against a principal during the term of the agency relationship.
____ 2. Lucy is an agent of Lapco Inc. Lapco is negotiating to sell property to ABC Co., a company that is owned by Lucy. In this case, Lucy must disclose to Lapco that she owns ABC Co.
____ 3. If an agent acts in bad faith, the only remedy of the principal is to discharge the agent; the principal cannot sue the agent for damages.
____ 4. An agent is entitled to use the agent's best judgment to determine whether the agent should follow a principal's routine instructions.
____ 5. It is implied that an agent warrants to a principal that the agent has the skill reasonably necessary to carry out the duties of the agency.
____ 6. An agent can generally delegate to subagents duties that merely involve clerical work.
____ 7. An agent has a duty to keep a principal's property separate from the agent's property.
____ 8. An agent does not have a duty to disclose any information to a principal unless the principal expressly requests disclosure of information by the agent.
____ 9. An agent may be liable to a third party if the agent makes a contract in the agent's name and the agent does not disclose the name or existence of the principal.
____ 10. An agent may be personally liable for a wrong that the agent commits while acting for a principal.
____ 11. An agent may agree to be personally bound by a contract that the agent makes for a principal.
____ 12. Death of a principal or agent automatically terminates an agency.
____ 13. Bankruptcy of a principal does not terminate an agency.
____ 14. A principal cannot be liable on a contract that is made by an agent who has been terminated.

REVIEW OF CONCEPT APPLICATIONS

Answer

Directions: Indicate your choice in the answer column.

____ 1. Duke is an agent for Rork Co. Unknown to Rork Co., Duke also represents a competitor and Duke disclosed Rork Co.'s confidential marketing strategy to the competitor. Under these facts:
a. Duke violated his duty of loyalty and good faith to Rork Co.
b. Duke did not violate his duty of loyalty and good faith to Rork Co.
c. Rork Co. can sue Duke for damages that it may suffer as a result of Duke's conduct.
d. a and c.

_____ 2. Lisa was a sales agent for DRG. By contract, DRG agreed to pay Lisa a $1,500 monthly salary plus a commission of 10 percent of the price of goods sold by her. Prior to her discharge: (1) Lisa was owed one month's salary; (2) Lisa sold goods for $10,000; and (3) Lisa incurred $50 phone charges in making sales. Prior to her discharge, Lisa had also been negotiating a $20,000 sale of goods, but the sale was never completed. How much does DRG owe Lisa?
   a. $1,500.
   b. $2,500.
   c. $2,550.
   d. $4,550.

_____ 3. Juan Martinez is a purchasing agent for Viper Inc. On behalf of Viper, Juan contracted to buy a truck from Cory Truck Sales. Juan had express authority to make the contract. Juan signed the contract "Viper Inc., by Juan Martinez, purchasing agent." Under these facts:
   a. Juan is personally obligated to perform the contract.
   b. Viper Inc. is obligated to perform the contract.
   c. Juan and Viper Inc. are both obligated to perform the contract.

_____ 4. Katherine Frick is a general manager for C&C Clothing Co., which owns a clothing store. On behalf of C&C, Katherine agreed to buy from Seller all of the assets of another clothing store that was quitting business. Katherine had no authority to make this contract. Under these facts:
   a. Katherine is liable to Seller for damages.
   b. C&C Clothing Co. is obligated to perform the contract with Seller.
   c. C&C Clothing Co. is not obligated to perform the contract with Seller.
   d. a and c.

CASE PROBLEM

On January 1, 2001, George was hired as district sales manager by Carbo Inc. for an annual salary of $60,000. The agency contract stated that George was hired for a fixed, three-year term. Later, Carbo's business declined and it decided to terminate George even though he had properly performed his duties. On July 1, 2002, Carbo discharged George. Under these facts: (1) Did Carbo have the legal right to discharge George? (2) Did Carbo have the power to discharge George? (3) What remedies are available to George?

_____

_____

_____

BUSINESS LAW PARTNER EXERCISE

Directions:

1. Access your Business Law Partner CD-ROM and find the document "Employment Agreement (Short Form)."
2. Complete the document using the information provided in the foregoing Case Problem dealing with George and Carbo Inc.
3. What term should Carbo Inc. have added to the Employment Agreement to have better protected itself?

_____

_____

_____

CHAPTER 27 QUIZ

Section A

DIRECTIONS: Following each question below, indicate your answer by placing a "Y" for "Yes" or an "N" for "No" in the Answers column.

	Answers	For Scoring
1. Does the law impose upon the agent duties not set out in the contract?	_____	1. _____
2. Does the relationship created by agency impose upon the principal and the agent certain duties and obligations to third parties?	_____	2. _____
3. Does the relationship of an agent and principal created by an agency contract call for the same degree of faith and trust as do most other contractual relationships?	_____	3. _____
4. Does an agent violate any duties if the agent secretly owns an interest in a firm that does business with the principal?	_____	4. _____
5. May the principal's instructions to the agent be discretionary as well as routine?	_____	5. _____
6. Is an agent ever justified in disobeying routine, legal instructions?	_____	6. _____
7. Is an agent who does not have the skill required to perform the duties required by the agency liable for damages for loss from failure to have such skill?	_____	7. _____
8. In general, may agents appoint subagents?	_____	8. _____
9. May an agent deposit the principal's money in the agent's bank account?	_____	9. _____
10. When the agent's compensation is to be a percentage of the selling price, can the agent collect part of the compensation before the sale?	_____	10. _____
11. If the cooperation of the principal is required in order to enable an agent to perform his or her duties, does the principal have a legal duty to cooperate?	_____	11. _____
12. Are agents personally liable on a contract when they contract in their own names without disclosing the names of the principals?	_____	12. _____
13. Can agents escape liability by signing their own names to contracts and simply adding the word "Agent" after their names?	_____	13. _____
14. May an agent be liable to the principal if the agent materially departs from the authority granted by the principal?	_____	14. _____
15. Is a principal liable for all wrongful acts committed by an agent?	_____	15. _____
16. If no date is set for the termination of the agency in the original agreement, can it be terminated at any time by subsequent agreement?	_____	16. _____
17. Can a principal terminate an agency at any time by revoking the agent's authority?	_____	17. _____
18. In general, does an agent have the legal right to renounce an agency if the agent has not yet completed the agency contract?	_____	18. _____
19. May an agency be terminated by operation of law?	_____	19. _____
20. Does death or incapacity of the principal normally terminate the agency?	_____	20. _____
21. Does bankruptcy of the agent ordinarily terminate the agency?	_____	21. _____
22. Must notice to the agent or to third parties be given in all instances when an agency is terminated by operation of law?	_____	22. _____

Score _____

Section B

DIRECTIONS: Complete each of the following statements by writing the missing word or words in the Answers column.

	Answers	For Scoring
1. An agent who discloses confidential information commits a breach of..........	_____	1. _____
2. The duty of the agent to carry out the instructions from the principal is called	_____	2. _____
3-4. The two types of instructions an agent may receive from the principal are....	_____	3. _____
....	_____	4. _____
5. The duty of the agent to keep a record of all money transactions pertaining to the agency and to report to the principal is the requirement of making a(n)..	_____	5. _____
6. The agent's duty to advise the principal of all facts pertinent to the agency is called...	_____	6. _____
7. The principal's duty to pay the agent for any disbursements that the agent makes from his or her personal funds in carrying out the agency is called....	_____	7. _____
8. The right of the agent to be reimbursed by the principal for a loss incurred by the agent while carrying out his or her agency duties is the right to	_____	8. _____
9. When a principal terminates the agency because of a material breach of contract by the agent, the agency is terminated by........................	_____	9. _____
10. A written appointment of agency that survives the incapacity of the principal is a(n)..	_____	10. _____

Score _____

Section C

DIRECTIONS: Answer each of the following questions in the Answers column.

	Answers	For Scoring
1-2. Prentiss owns a gift shop that is operated by, and in the name of, her agent, Roberts. Contrary to instructions of his principal, Roberts sold merchandise on credit to Scott. If Scott fails to pay for the goods, is Roberts liable to Prentiss?...	_____	1. _____
If the goods are defective can Prentiss escape liability if her identity as a principal is discovered on the grounds that Roberts exceeded his authority?	_____	2. _____
3-4. Sestak was an agent of Zia to manage Zia's apartment complex. Without Zia's knowledge Sestak placed the property insurance for the complex through an insurance agency she owned. Since the insurance cost less than the insurance previously carried on the complex, was Sestak living up to her duty as an agent?	_____	3. _____
Are Sestak's profits on the insurance hers to keep?........................	_____	4. _____
5-6. Hall, the treasurer of the Northern Recreation Center, opened a bank account in her own name and deposited funds for the Center in it. The bank failed and the Northern Recreation Center sought to hold Hall for loss of the funds. Is Hall liable for the loss?	_____	5. _____
Who would be liable for the loss if Hall had deposited the funds in the name of the Northern Recreation Center?..	_____	6. _____
7-8. Willis was a salesman for Underwood. While driving to see a customer, he ran into Adams' car. .... Is Underwood liable for the damage Willis caused?	_____	7. _____
If Willis was speeding when the accident occurred and is fined $100, can he require Underwood to reimburse him for the fine?	_____	8. _____

Score _____

CHAPTER 28
EMPLOYER AND EMPLOYEE RELATIONS

CHAPTER OUTLINE

I.   CREATION OF EMPLOYER AND EMPLOYEE RELATIONSHIP

An employer-employee relationship can be created only by an express or implied contract. A contract may be implied if the parties' conduct shows their intent to be employer and employee.

A.   LENGTH OF CONTRACT

General rules.   ▸ *Contract period*: Employment contracts may be made for one of three periods: (1) period expressly stated in contract; (2) period that is implied from the manner of compensation (e.g., a contract is for a period of a week if wages are paid weekly); or (3) an indefinite period, i.e., employment at will. ▸ *Right to compensation*: (1) If an employer discharges an employee without cause during an express or implied period of employment, the employer is liable for wages through the end of the period. (2) In an employment at will, either party can terminate the employment at any time and for any reason without liability.

Examples.   ▸ Express period: Hilda is hired for one year. Without reason, Hilda is fired after six months. Hilda must be paid for the full year. ▸ Employment at will: Wanda is hired for an indefinite time. Employer can fire Wanda at any time and for any reason without liability.

Limitations.   ▸ Some courts do not imply a contract period from a manner of payment; an employee is an employee at will if a contract does not state an express term of employment. ▸ Some union contracts and statutes prohibit discharging employees at will without good cause.

B.   DETERMINATION OF CONTRACT TERMS

General rule.   Contractual terms of employment may be set by law, custom, or union contracts. In some cases, terms may be implied from statements made in an employer's policy manual.

Example.   Employee Handbook states that vacation time is earned at the rate of two weeks per year. In some cases, this term may legally entitle employees to two weeks of vacation.

C.   UNION CONTRACTS

A union may negotiate a union contract (collective bargaining agreement) between an employer and all employees regarding certain terms, such as wages and hours. In this case, an employer individually contracts with employees, but contracts must be consistent with the union contract.

II.   DUTIES AND LIABILITIES OF THE EMPLOYER

At common law, an employer owes the following duties to employees: (1) duty to use reasonable care; (2) duty to provide a reasonably safe workplace; (3) duty to provide safe tools; (4) duty to provide sufficient, competent employees for a task; and (5) duty to train employees in order to avoid foreseeable hazards. ▸ At common law, an employer is liable to an employee for breaching any of these duties.

III.   COMMON-LAW DEFENSES OF THE EMPLOYER

General rule.   At common law an employer is not liable for an employee's injury if:

- *Contributory negligence rule*: the employee's negligence caused or contributed to the injury;
- *The fellow-servant rule*: another employee caused the injury; or
- *Assumption-of-risk rule*: the injury is a normal risk of the job and the employee assumed this risk.

Examples.   ▸ Contributory negligence: Employee cut his finger with a saw when he carelessly gazed out a window. ▸ Fellow-servant: Employee is hit on the head by an object that was negligently dropped by another employee. ▸ Assumption-of-risk: Lumberjack is crushed by a falling tree.

IV.   STATUTORY MODIFICATION OF COMMON LAW

A.   MODIFICATION OF COMMON-LAW DEFENSES

Federal and state laws have changed common law defenses in relation to employment in various industries.

IV. STATUTORY MODIFICATION OF COMMON LAW

A. MODIFICATION OF COMMON-LAW DEFENSES

Federal and state laws have changed common law defenses in relation to employment in various industries.

B. WORKERS' COMPENSATION

General rules. ▸ Every state has workers' compensation laws. These laws compensate covered employees (or surviving family members) for injuries or death that occur within the employee's scope of employment. ▸ An employee is entitled to benefits even if the employer is not negligent and the employee is negligent.
Limitations. ▸ Statutes often forbid recovery if: (1) an injury occurs while an employee is intoxicated; or (2) an injury is self-inflicted. ▸ Although some states allow recovery for any work-related disease, others compensate for only a few listed diseases (e.g., brown-lung disease).
Study hint. An injured employee may be able to sue a fellow employee who caused an injury.

C. OCCUPATIONAL SAFETY AND HEALTH ACT

Occupational Safety and Health Act applies to all employers in interstate commerce, except governments. OSHA sets workplace safety standards and inspects to assure compliance. Employers must keep records of job-related injuries. Violations of the Act may result in fines.

V. LIABILITIES OF THE EMPLOYER TO THIRD PARTIES

An employer is liable to a third party for injuries caused by an employee if: (1) the third party was injured while the employee was acting in the course of employment; (2) the employer directed an employee to do an act; (3) the employer knew of and agreed to the act; or (4) the injuries resulted from the employer's own negligence.

VI. EMPLOYEE'S DUTIES TO THE EMPLOYER

General rules. ▸ An employee must perform duties honestly and with ordinary skill, and must not disclose confidential business or trade secrets. ▸ Inventions: Unless otherwise agreed, an employee's invention belongs to the employee. ▸ Shop right: If an invention is developed during working hours and using employer resources, an employer has a "shop right" to use the invention without charge in the employer's business
Limitation. If a person is hired to develop an invention, the invention belongs to the employer.

VIII. FEDERAL SOCIAL SECURITY ACT

A. OLD-AGE AND SURVIVORS' INSURANCE

- *Who is covered?*: ▸ Most workers are covered by the part of the Act relating to retirement and survivor's benefits except for certain persons who work for close relatives. ▸ State and local government employees may be covered by means of agreements between state and federal governments.
- *Eligibility for retirement benefits*: Retirement benefits are paid to a covered worker who: (1) lives to be 62; (2) is "fully insured" (i.e., worked equivalent of ten years); and (3) applied for benefits.
- *Eligibility for survivor's benefits*: If a covered worker dies before retirement, his or her dependents may receive survivors' benefits if, at the time of death, the worker met certain requirements.

B. ASSISTANCE TO PERSONS IN FINANCIAL NEED

Monthly supplemental social security income payments may be made to a person who is in financial need if the person is: (1) 65 or older; (2) blind; or (3) disabled.

C. UNEMPLOYMENT COMPENSATION

▸ Unemployment compensation pays benefits to unemployed workers. ▸ Most workers are covered, except for domestic and agricultural workers, government workers, and employees of non-profit firms. ▸ Eligibility test: (1) ready, available, and able to work; (2) do not refuse appropriate work; and (3) meet other requirements. ▸ Ineligible persons: self-employed persons; persons on strike; persons who voluntarily quit without cause.

D. DISABILITY AND MEDICARE BENEFITS

A disabled person is (1) unable to be employed (2) due to a physical/mental impairment (3) that is expected to end in death or to last for 12 months. Medicare covers certain medical/hospital costs for persons 65 and older.

E. TAXATION TO FINANCE THE PLAN

Old-age and survivor's benefits are paid for by employer and employee contributions (FICA).

REVIEW OF CHAPTER

REVIEW OF TERMS

Select the term that best matches a statement below. Each term is the best match for only one statement.

TERMS

a. Assumption-of-risk rule
b. Collective bargaining agreement
c. Contributory negligence rule
d. Disability benefits
e. Employment at will
f. Fellow-servant rule
g. Old-age benefits
h. OSHA
i. Shop right

STATEMENTS

Answer

_____ 1. Monthly payments to a person who is unable to work because of a physical or mental impairment.

_____ 2. Contract negotiated on behalf of employees by a union representative.

_____ 3. Common law defense prohibiting an employee from recovering damages from an employer for an injury if the employee's negligence caused the injury.

_____ 4. Employment for an indefinite term that may be terminated by either party at any time.

_____ 5. Federal-paid retirement benefits.

_____ 6. Employer's right to use an invention that was developed by an employee during work hours.

_____ 7. Common law defense prohibiting an employee from recovering damages from an employer for an injury that was caused by another employee.

_____ 8. Federal agency that enforces federal health and safety laws.

_____ 9. Common law defense prohibiting an employee from recovering damages from an employer for an injury that was a normal risk of a job that the employee voluntarily agreed to do.

REVIEW OF CONCEPTS

Directions: Indicate **T** for true and **F** for false in the answer column.

_____ 1. An employment relationship can only be created by an express contract.

_____ 2. If an employment contract does not state a fixed period of employment, some jurisdictions will not imply a period of employment from compensation terms.

_____ 3 In general, an employer can discharge an employee at will without incurring any liability even if the employee did nothing to justify being fired.

_____ 4. Clara is hired for six months. After four months, Employer fired Clara without having good cause for doing so. In this case Employer must pay Clara her wages for the six-month period.

_____ 5. In some cases, statements in an employer's policy manual may be part of an employment contract.

_____ 6. At common law, an employer could be sued by an employee who suffered an injury because the employer failed to provide enough employees to safely perform a job.

_____ 7. At common law, an employer does not have a duty to train new employees to avoid risks of harm. At common law, an employee is solely responsible for obtaining needed training.

_____ 8. The Federal Employers' Liability Act bars an employee from suing the federal government.

_____ 9. The Occupational Safety and Health Act applies to all private and governmental employers.

_____ 10. An employer may be fined for violating OSHA safety regulations.

REVIEW OF CONCEPT APPLICATIONS

Answer

Directions: Indicate your choice in the answer column.

_____ 1. Joe is employed by Nordic Sporting Goods Store. Joe's employment contract does not state a fixed term of employment. Joe is paid on a weekly basis. Joe works in a state that does not imply a period of employment from terms of compensation. Under these facts:

a. Joe is *not* an employee at will.

b. Nordic can discharge Joe at any time. Nordic does not need good cause to discharge Joe.

c. Nordic can discharge Joe at any time. However, if Nordic discharges Joe during a work week, Nordic must pay Joe's wages for the entire week.

d. Nordic has the right to discharge Joe only if Nordic has good cause for doing so.

_____ 2.   Marsha is employed as a welder by Acme Inc. Marsha is covered by worker's compensation. One day, Marsha is injured in an accident that occurred while she was performing a welding job for Acme. In which situation would Marsha be denied worker's compensation?
   a.   Marsha was negligent and her negligence caused the accident.
   b.   Marsha was intoxicated and her intoxication caused the accident.
   c.   A third party caused the accident. Acme was not negligent or responsible for causing the accident.
   d.   Marsha cannot recover worker's compensation in any situation. Worker's compensation laws no longer exist in any state.

_____ 3.   Bob was hired by Ramco Inc. as a tool and die maker. Bob's employment contract did not mention inventions. Bob was neither hired nor instructed to work on new products. However, during working hours and using Ramco's equipment, Bob invented a new piece of equipment that was applicable to Ramco's business. What rights does Ramco have to Bob's invention?
   a.   Ramco owns the invention.
   b.   Ramco has a shop right that entitles it to make and sell products that embody the invention.
   c.   Ramco has a shop right to use the invention in conducting its business.

_____ 4.   Select the answer that is correct under the federal Social Security Act.
   a.   Orville is 65 years old. Orville worked a total of five years of covered employment. In this case, Orville is entitled to receive old-age retirement benefits.
   b.   Mary is 67 and blind. Mary is in severe need of financial aid, but she has never worked. In this case, Mary is _not_ entitled to receive supplemental social security income payments.
   c.   John is 45 years old. John cannot work due to a permanent illness. John's illness is expected to last for the rest of his life. In this case, John is entitled to disability benefits.

CASE PROBLEM

The four individuals discussed below applied for unemployment benefits. Determine whether each applicant would be entitled to unemployment compensation in most states. If an applicant is not eligible for unemployment compensation, briefly explain why benefits are not available.

(1) Mary quit her job because it was boring. (2) Jim was laid off from his job as a construction worker due to a recession in the building industry. (3) Frank cannot find work because he is incapable of working due to a serious back injury. (4) Elizabeth is unemployed because she is presently on strike.

_____

_____

_____

BUSINESS LAW PARTNER EXERCISE

Directions:

1.   Access your Business Law Partner CD-ROM and find the document "Work for Hire Agreement."
2.   Help Acme complete the above-referenced document using the information provided in the following case study.

Case Study: _Mine, Mine, Mine_

Angela was hired by Rodents Inc. to help develop a new rat poison. Rodents agreed to pay Angela $50,000 as a lump sum compensation for working on this project. The parties agreed that all of Angela's work product would belong exclusively to Rodents. Also, Angela agreed to keep confidential all information that she learned while working on this project. Angela was not required to sign a covenant not to compete. Angela agreed to work 40 hours per work from January 1 until June 30. She is to be paid upon completion of her work.

CHAPTER 28 QUIZ

Section A

DIRECTIONS: Following each question below, indicate your answer by placing a "Y" for "Yes" or an "N" for "No" in the Answers column.

	Answers	For Scoring
1. Are employment relationships completely governed by common law rules?	_____	1. _____
2. Is the law regarding employers and employees uniform throughout the United States?	_____	2. _____
3. Can the relationship of employer and employee be imposed without consent?	_____	3. _____
4. Ordinarily, are all terms of an employment contract expressly stated?	_____	4. _____
5. If an employee is fired without cause, may the employer pay wages due only to the time of the firing?	_____	5. _____
6. In an employment-at-will relationship, is the employer the only party who may terminate the relationship at any time and for any nondiscriminatory reason?	_____	6. _____
7. Does a union contract obligate an employer to include certain basic terms in every covered employee's contract?	_____	7. _____
8. Under the Federal Safety Appliance Act, must the employee still prove negligence on the part of the employer in order to recover damages?	_____	8. _____
9. Is recovery under workers' compensation limited and set at a prescribed amount?	_____	9. _____
10. Is the Occupational Safety and Health Act intended to ensure safe and healthful working conditions?	_____	10. _____
11. Must most employers keep detailed records of work-related injuries?	_____	11. _____
12. Does the Occupational Safety and Health Act apply to government employees?	_____	12. _____
13. Are employers liable for all torts committed by their employees?	_____	13. _____
14. Can an employee be discharged for not performing duties faithfully and honestly?	_____	14. _____
15. Can an employer use an employee's invention without paying royalties if it was made during working hours and with the employer's material and equipment?	_____	15. _____
16. Does a shop right allow an employer to make and sell machines that embody an employee's invention?	_____	16. _____
17. Are survivors' benefits paid only to retired workers?	_____	17. _____
18. Is everyone covered by old-age and survivors' insurance?	_____	18. _____
19. Are unemployment compensation benefits paid by the federal government?	_____	19. _____
20. Are the life insurance and annuity insurance benefits of the Social Security Act financed solely by taxes on employees?	_____	20. _____

Score _____

Section B

DIRECTIONS: Following each statement below, indicate your answer by placing a "T" for "True" or an "F" for "False" in the Answers column.

	Answers	**For Scoring**
1. State labor legislation covers all employees...	_____	1. _____
2. The length of the contract period is always mentioned when the employer-employee relationship is created.	_____	2. _____
3. In some cases, wrongfully discharged employees may sue to be restored to their jobs..	_____	3. _____
4. What the common law considered to be a safe place to work depended upon the nature of the work...	_____	4. _____
5. Statutes have made it easier for employees to win lawsuits against employers.............	_____	5. _____
6. An employee has a duty of confidentiality regarding certain business matters.	_____	6. _____
7. In the absence of an agreement otherwise, inventions belong to the employee who devised them...	_____	7. _____
8. An employee can recover worker's compensation benefits for a work-related injury even if the employee was negligent and responsible for his or her injury....................	_____	8. _____
9. You must be at least 65 to be eligible for social security retirement benefits................	_____	9. _____
10. Medicare covers all hospital and medical services...	_____	10. _____

Score _____

Section C

DIRECTIONS: Following each question below, indicate your answer by placing a "Y" for "Yes" or an "N" for "No" in the Answers column.

	Answers	**For Scoring**
1. While painting a theater sign, Chase accidentally dropped a pail of paint, injuring a pedestrian. Is her employer liable?	_____	1. _____
2. If Chase left the job site to have lunch with a friend and spilt paint on a third party while enjoying her lunch, would Chase's employer be liable to the third party?	_____	2. _____
3-4. Erdmann retired at age 63. Will she automatically receive old-age benefits?	_____	3. _____
Assuming she will receive old-age benefits, will they be the maximum amount?	_____	4. _____
5-6. Fredericks owns an interstate construction company. Is his company subject to OSHA safety regulations?	_____	5. _____
Fredericks is a heavy smoker. Could his state's law ban him totally from smoking?	_____	6. _____
7-8. Earle suffered an injury on a construction job due to the negligence of a co-worker. Can Earle recover workers' compensation benefits?	_____	7. _____
If Earle's employer disputes the applicability of workers' compensation, may Earle's case be heard without going into court?	_____	8. _____

Score _____

CHAPTER 29
EMPLOYEES' RIGHTS

CHAPTER OUTLINE

I. DISCRIMINATION

There are a number of federal laws that prohibit various types of discrimination in employment. Each law forbids discrimination against one or more specific classes of individuals.

A. CIVIL RIGHTS ACT OF 1964

- *Scope*: Title VII of the Civil Rights Act of 1964 prohibits discrimination applies to employers in interstate commerce with 15 or more employees, and labor unions with 15 or more members. It does not apply to the U.S. government (except Congress) or private clubs.

- *Protection*: ▶ Title VII prohibits discrimination against job applicants and employees on the basis of race, color, national origin, religion, and sex (protected classes). ▶ The prohibition against sex discrimination bars the taking of any action against a person based on pregnancy, childbirth, or related medical conditions. ▶ Title VII forbids discrimination in connection with any aspect of the employment relationship including hiring, discharge, promotions, training, and pay.

- *Enforcement*: The Equal Employment Opportunity Commission (EEOC) enforces Title VII and other federal discrimination laws relating to employment. A charging party (job applicant or employee) must first file a claim. Then the EEOC may attempt to resolve the dispute through conciliation. If this is unsuccessful, the EEOC may file suit or it may give the charging party a "right-to-sue letter," entitling the party to file suit in federal court.

- *Remedies*: Remedies include injunction, attorney's fees, compensation for economic losses, such as back pay, and reinstatement. Punitive damages may be awarded for intentional discrimination.

- *Types of discrimination theories*: A discrimination claim under Title VII is typically based on either a disparate treatment violation, disparate impact violation, or a sexual harassment violation.
    1. *Disparate treatment*: A disparate treatment claim exists when an employer intentionally treats a job applicant or employee less favorably because of his or her race, color, national origin, religion, or sex. A person may establish this type of violation by showing actual, intentional discrimination based on one of the protected characteristics. Alternatively, a person can prove a prima facie violation by showing (a) the person belongs to a protected class, (b) was qualified for the position, (c) was rejected for the job or was not hired, and (d) a person who was not a member of the protected class was accepted or hired.
    2. *Disparate impact*: Disparate impact exists when a neutral employment practice has a significantly different, negative impact on a protected group.
    3. *Sexual harassment*: ▶ This type of Title VII violation occurs if the workplace becomes a hostile work environment because it is poisoned with unwelcomed sexual conduct, such as unwelcome sexual propositions, insults, suggestive pictures, and/or physical contacts. ▶ Whether a work environment is "hostile" is determined by the facts of each case. However, to recover an employee must generally show that (a) there was unwelcomed sexual conduct (b) that a reasonable person would find abusive, and (c) that the employee personally found such conduct to be abusive.

B. EQUAL PAY

GENERAL RULE. The Equal Pay Act requires that employers must pay male and female employees the same wage for jobs that are substantially equal.

LIMITATION. Differences in pay for male and female employees are permissible if they are the result of (1) a seniority system, (2) a merit system, (3) a pay scale based on quality or quantity of production, or (4) any factor other than the sex of the employees.

C. AGE DISCRIMINATION

GENERAL RULE.   The Age Discrimination in Employment Act (ADEA) prohibits employers, unions, and employment agencies from arbitrarily discriminating against persons who are forty years of age or older on the basis of their age.

LIMITATIONS.   ▸ An employer may consider age in certain types of employment that involve significant safety considerations, such as commercial airline pilots and law enforcement officers. ▸ As with most types of discrimination laws, bona fide seniority systems are exempt from the ADEA.

D. DISCRIMINATION AGAINST PERSONS WITH DISABILITIES

GENERAL RULES.   ▸ The Americans with Disabilities Act (ADA) prohibits discrimination against persons with (1) a physical or mental impairment that (2) substantially limits one or more major life activities. A person cannot be discriminated against on account of such a disability if he or she is qualified for the job, either with or without a reasonable accommodation by the employer. ▸Employers must make reasonable accommodations for employees with disabilities including: (1) making existing facilities accessible to and usable by persons with disabilities; and (2) restructuring jobs, (3) modifying schedules, and (4) acquiring or modifying equipment or devices.

LIMITATIONS.   ▸ Employers are not required to make accommodations that would cause them an "undue hardship." ▸ The ADA does not forbid discrimination because of temporary impairments, such as a broken arm, or certain chronic conditions, such as current, illegal use of drugs, compulsive gambling, kleptomania, or pyromania.

II.   TESTING

- *Polygraph testing*: ▸ The Employee Polygraph Protection Act forbids private employers from giving polygraph tests (lie detector tests) to employees unless: (1) the employer believes an employee has committed a theft or stolen company secrets; (2) the employer provides security services; or (3) the employer is a drug company. ▸ This federal law does not apply to or restrict the use of polygraph tests by federal, state, or local governments.

- *AIDS testing*: ▸ There is no uniform law addressing the issue of AIDS in employment. ▸ Federal law forbids discrimination against certain employees because they are infected with the AIDS virus. Some state and local laws may also provide protection from discrimination on this basis.

- *Drug testing*: Government agencies may require drug testing for certain employees and prospective employees. Random drug testing is permitted if necessary to (1) maintain the integrity of employees in their essential mission, (2) promote public safety, or (3) protect sensitive information.

III.   PROTECTIONS

- *Family and Medical Leave*: Federal law allows an employee to take an unpaid leave of up to 12 work weeks in a 12-month period for the following reasons: (1) birth, adoption, or foster care of the employee's child; (2) care for employee's spouse, child, or parent with a serious health condition; or (3) serious health condition that makes the employee unable to perform the job.

- *Plant closing notification*: the federal Worker Adjustment and Retraining Notification Act requires a business that employs 100 or more employees to give 60 days' written notice of a plant closing or mass layoff.

- *Smoking*: Many states and municipalities protect employees by requiring employers to adopt smoking policies, or to designate smoking and non-smoking areas.

REVIEW OF CHAPTER

REVIEW OF TERMS

Select the term that best matches a statement below. Each term is the best match for only one statement.

TERMS

a. Age Discrimination in Employment Act (ADEA)
b. Americans with Disabilities Act (ADA)
c. Discrimination
d. Disparate impact
e. Disparate treatment

f. EEOC
g. Employee Polygraph Protection Act
h. Equal Pay Act
i. Hostile work environment
j. Reasonable accommodation

STATEMENTS

Answer

_____ 1. Discrimination resulting from neutral employment practice that has different effect on a protected class.
_____ 2. General category of conduct against a person based on the person's race, color, religion, sex, national origin, or other personal characteristic.
_____ 3. Law that forbids paying male and female employees different wages for substantially equal work.
_____ 4. Law that forbids requiring employees to take a lie detector test except in certain limited situations.
_____ 5. Law that prohibits discrimination against persons over forty years of age.
_____ 6. Type of Title VII violation that results from unwelcome sexual conduct that poisons the workplace.
_____ 7. Law that prohibits discrimination against qualified persons with disabilities.
_____ 8. Discrimination that exists when an employer intentionally discriminates against a person on the basis of the person's race, color, religion, sex, or national origin.
_____ 9. Federal agency that administers Title VII and other federal discrimination laws.
_____10. Employer action required by the ADA to make a workplace accessible to employees with disabilities.

REVIEW OF CONCEPTS

Answer

Directions: Indicate **T** for true and **F** for false in the answer column.

_____ 1. Disparate treatment exists when a neutral employment practice has a disproportionate, negative impact on a protected class.

_____ 2. Title VII prohibits discrimination against males and whites.

_____ 3. The ADA requires an employer to reasonably accommodate an employee who has a disability if the employee can perform the essential job functions with such accommodation.

_____ 4. The ADEA forbids discrimination based on a person's age, regardless of what age the person may be.

_____ 5. A combination of severe and widespread sexual intimidation, propositions, and the displaying of nude pictures in the workplace may constitute sexual harassment.

_____ 6. Under the ADEA, employers may treat employees differently on account of their age if their jobs involve significant safety concerns.

_____ 7. Federal law allows any employee to take a paid leave for up to 12 weeks in the event of a family emergency.

_____ 8. The ADA requires employers to provide reasonable accommodation for employees who use illegal drugs.

_____ 9. It is not a violation of the Equal Pay Act to pay different wages to male and female employees if the difference is due to a bona fide seniority system.

_____10. In general, it is a violation of the Equal Pay Act for an employer to pay a male employee more than a female employee for performing the same job.

REVIEW OF CONCEPT APPLICATIONS

Answer

        Directions: Indicate your choice in the answer column.

_____ 1. In which situation is there a violation of the Civil Rights Act of 1964?
    a. Acorn Inc. conducts solely intrastate business and it has two employees. Acorn refused to hire Kent because he is a male and Catholic.
    b. Best Inc. engages in interstate commerce and employs 50 workers. Best refused to hire Stella as an electrician because she is a woman. Stella was qualified for the job.
    c. Core Inc. engages in interstate commerce and employs 40 workers. Core fired Harry, an Afro-American. The termination was due to a recession and was unrelated to Harry's race.

_____ 2. Select the correct answer.
    a. Employer is a government agency that makes nuclear weapons. In this case, Employer may require employees who make the weapons to take reasonable drug tests.
    b. Employer is a private firm that owns a stereo store. Employer wants to avoid thefts by dishonest employees. In this case, Employer can make all employees take polygraph tests.
    c. Employer is a private laboratory that prepares donor organs for human transplants. In this case, federal law prohibits Employer from requesting that employees be tested for AIDS.
    d. All of the above are correct.

CASE PROBLEM

Kim Pak was born in Korea and she recently became a U.S. citizen. Kim speaks fluent English, but she has a mild Korean accent. Her accent does not interfere with her ability to communicate with others. Kim applied for the job of manager at the Jasper Hotel in a large Midwest city. However, Kim was not hired for this position.

    Explain whether the following reasons are proper reasons for not hiring Kim: (1) Kim speaks with a slight Korean accent; (2) Kim is fifty years old, and she may not work for as many years as someone younger; (3) Kim has a hearing disorder and the hotel would have to spend $250 to purchase a special telephone for her.

_____

_____

_____

BUSINESS LAW PARTNER EXERCISE

Directions: Using the Online feature of the Business Law Partner CD-ROM, identify the location of the EEOC home page and briefly summarize what Sarah must do to file a sexual harassment claim.

Case Study: *Boys will be Boys*

Sarah was an employee at Cook Corp. for two years. During that time, she was subject to repeated, unwelcomed sexual advances and lewd behavior on the part of her male employees and her supervisor. Also, several male workers tried to kiss her and touch her inappropriately. She complained several times to the company's managers, but they merely said: "Boys will be boys. Just learn to live with it." Finally, it became so intolerable that she quit. She has asked you to help her determine what she must do to file a sexual harassment claim against Cook Corp.

CHAPTER 29 QUIZ

Section A

DIRECTIONS: Following each question below, indicate your answer by placing a "Y" for "Yes" or an "N" for "No" in the Answers column.

	Answers	For Scoring
1. Is the entire federal government subject to Title VII?.....................................	_____	1. _____
2. Can an employer be held liable for sexual harassment caused by the employer's workers?...	_____	2. _____
3. Does Title VII forbid discrimination based on an employee's religion?	_____	3. _____
4. Do all federal, state, and local discrimination laws apply to all employers?	_____	4. _____
5. Employer refused to hire Carl because he is Hispanic. Is this an example of disparate treatment?	_____	5. _____
6. Employer refused to hire Jane because she is 8-months pregnant even though Jane was qualified for the job in question. Is this a violation of Title VII?..........................	_____	6. _____
7. Can an employer be found liable for violating Title VII even if the employer never intended to discriminate against any particular person or protected class?	_____	7. _____
8. Is it necessary to show economic harm in order to establish a sexual harassment violation of Title VII?	_____	8. _____
9. Can an employee establish a sexual harassment violation of Title VII even though a reasonable person would not have found the work environment to be hostile?	_____	9. _____
10. Can state and local governments adopt ordinances that forbid smoking in public workplaces?	_____	10. _____
11. Can governmental and private employers conduct whatever employee drug tests that they want?	_____	11. _____
12. Is an employer required to pay male and female workers the same pay even if a seniority system requires otherwise?	_____	12. _____
13. Are employers liable for all torts committed by their employees?	_____	13. _____
14. Can an employee be discharged for not performing duties faithfully and honestly?	_____	14. _____
15. Can an employer use an employee's invention without paying royalties if it was made during working hours and with the employer's material and equipment?	_____	15. _____

Score _____

Section B

DIRECTIONS: Following each statement below, indicate your answer by placing a " T" for " True" or an " F" for " False" in the Answers column.

	Answers	**For Scoring**
1. Title VII applies to all employers that engage in interstate commerce..	_____	1._____
2. The Equal Employment Opportunity Commission enforces Title VII as well as most other federal discrimination laws..	_____	2._____
3. Title VII does not forbid discrimination based on a person's sexual preference, i.e., heterosexual etc...	_____	3._____
4. Federal law forbids companies to close any plant that employs 100 or more workers...	_____	4._____
5. Federal law has completely outlawed the use of polygraph tests in employment..........	_____	5._____
6. The Equal Pay Act only requires an employer to pay the same wage to men and women who perform the same work or substantially the same work..	_____	6._____
7. Sue found her work place to be hostile because male workers occasionally made sexual jokes. This is enough to prove a sexual harassment violation of Title VII.	_____	7._____
8. Employer refused to hire Carl because he is 65 years old and employer is afraid that Carl may retire in a few years. Employer has not violated the ADEA...........................	_____	8._____
9. Employer refused to hire June because she presently abuses illegal drugs. Employer has not violated the ADA	_____	9._____
10. An employee who has an ADEA claim must file a complaint with the EEOC within 180 days.	_____	10._____
11. Employer fired John as a carpenter because John broke his hand and cannot work for three weeks. Employer has violated the ADA	_____	11._____
12. The ADA requires an employer to make a reasonable accommodation for an employee's covered disability.	_____	12._____
13. Governments are not forbidden from giving polygraph tests to their employees.	_____	13._____
14. An employee who adopts a child may be entitled to 12 weeks unpaid leave.	_____	14._____
15. A "mass layoff" that triggers the federal Worker Adjustment and Retraining Notification means an employment loss during a 30-day period of 33 percent of the full-time employees or at least 500 full-time employees.	_____	15._____

Score _____

CHAPTER 30
LABOR LEGISLATION

CHAPTER OUTLINE

I. THE FAIR LABOR STANDARDS ACT

▸ Fair Labor Standards Act creates a minimum wage ($5.15 an hour) and requires employers to pay time and a half for work over 40 hours per week. ▸ Purposes of Act: (1) set a floor for wages for employees in interstate commerce; (2) discourage long work weeks, thereby spreading employment.

A. EXCLUSIONS FROM THE (FAIR LABOR STANDARDS) ACT

This law does not apply to: (1) workers in intrastate (within a state) commerce; (2) agricultural workers; (3) executives, administrators, and outside salespeople. ▸ Workweek provisions (overtime pay) do not apply to: (1) transportation workers governed by the Interstate Commerce Commission; (2) workers in fish canneries; (3) outside buyers of poultry, eggs, cream, or milk.

B. CHILD LABOR PROVISIONS

General rules.   ▸ With certain exceptions, children under the age of 16 cannot be employed. ▸ Children between the ages of 16 and 18 cannot work in hazardous industries.
Example.   In the 1800s children worked in mines; today such work is prohibited.
Limitation.   Children under 16 may be employed as actors or agricultural workers. They may also be employed by parents or guardians, or in jobs specifically exempted by regulation.

C. CONTINGENT WAGES

General rule.   Employees paid by commission or piece-rate must be paid the minimum wage.
Example.   Guy is paid commissions on sales. Guy earned commissions equal to $3.50 per hour. Employer must pay Guy an amount that will increase his pay to at least minimum wage.

II. NATIONAL LABOR RELATIONS ACT AND LABOR MANAGEMENT RELATIONS ACT

The Labor Management Relations Act (the "Act") seeks to equalize the bargaining power of employees and employers. The Act applies to all workers in interstate commerce except: (1) railroad workers; (2) agricultural laborers; (3) domestic servants; (4) supervisory employees (management); and (5) government employees. Key provisions of the Act are discussed below.

A. THE NATIONAL LABOR RELATIONS BOARD (NLRB)

▸ The Act authorizes the NLRB, which is a five-member board appointed by the President. ▸ The NLRB: (1) investigates complaints of unfair labor practices by employers or unions; (2) obtains injunctions to halt unfair practices; (3) supervises elections to select bargaining representatives; and (4) in disputed cases, determines the size and nature of each bargaining unit (e.g., group of employees that is represented by a union). ▸ In certain cases, the President may seek an injunction to postpone a strike for 80 days.

197

B. DECLARATION AS TO THE RIGHTS OF EMPLOYEES

General rule.   Employees are authorized to: (1) organize; (2) bargain collectively; (3) strike; and (4) decide whether to join a union or not (unless a majority of employees votes for union shop).
Study hint.   Union shop: business in which all employees are required to be union members.

C. DECLARATION AS TO THE RIGHTS OF EMPLOYERS

General rule.   Employers can: (1) request an investigation of a union's claim that it represents workers; (2) refuse to bargain collectively with supervisory employees; (3) file charges of unfair labor practices; (4) sue for breach of union contracts; and (5) ask workers not to join a union.
Limitation.   Employers cannot promise benefits or threaten reprisals, such as threatening to eliminate overtime work, in order to persuade employees to vote against union representation.

D. PROHIBITION OF EMPLOYERS' UNFAIR LABOR PRACTICES

General rules.   ▸ Employers cannot: (1) interfere with employees' rights; (2) refuse to bargain collectively with employees; (3) interfere with or contribute money to a labor organization; (4) discriminate against or in favor of employees based on union membership; or (5) discriminate against an employee who files charges under the Act. ▸ Improper conduct may be prohibited by a cease and desist order, or by an injunction.
Limitation.   In union shops an employer can fire a nonunion worker for not being in a union.

E. PROHIBITION OF UNFAIR UNION PRACTICES

Unions (and their leaders) cannot: (1) coerce workers or limit their rights; (2) picket an employer to force bargaining with an uncertified union; (3) refuse to bargain collectively with an employer; (4) charge excessive fees; (5) bar a worker from a union except for not paying dues; (6) engage in secondary boycotts (with exceptions); or (7) charge employers for services not rendered.

III.   THE LABOR-MANAGEMENT REPORTING AND DISCLOSURE ACT

This law seeks to protect union members from wrongful acts of union officials. Key provisions:

- *Bill of rights*: Guarantees union members the right to: (1) meet with other union members; (2) express opinions at union meetings; and (3) express views on candidates for union office.

- *Additional unfair labor practices:* This law: (1) prohibits certain types of unauthorized picketing by employees; (2) expands the kinds of secondary boycotts that are prohibited; (3) prohibits "hot cargo agreements" (agreements between a union and an employer not to use nonunion materials) except in the construction and garment industries.

- *Reporting requirements:* ▸ Unions must file certain information. ▸ Union officials must disclose interests in, or benefits received from, employers. ▸ Persuader activities must be disclosed.

REVIEW OF CHAPTER

REVIEW OF TERMS

Select the term that best matches a statement below. Each term is the best match for only one statement.

TERMS

a. Collective bargaining agreement
b. Hot cargo agreement
c. Secondary boycott
d. Strike
e. Uncertified union
f. Union shop

STATEMENTS

Answer

_____ 1. Union that has not been legally recognized to represent employees.

_____ 2. Refusal to work for economic reasons or to protest unfair labor practices by management

_____ 3. Union contract

_____ 4. Attempt by a union to prevent suppliers or other third parties from dealing with an employer.

_____ 5. Agreement between a union and an employer that the employer will not use nonunion materials.

_____ 6. Workplace in which union membership is required as a condition of employment.

REVIEW OF CONCEPTS

Directions: Indicate **T** for true and **F** for false in the answer column.

_____ 1. Employers who engage in only intrastate commerce are subject to the Fair Labor Standards Act.

_____ 2. Under federal law, children under the age of 16 can never be employed.

_____ 3. Fair Labor Standards Act requires an employer to pay an employee who is paid by commissions an additional sum if necessary to assure that the employee receives at least the minimum wage.

_____ 4. Employers are legally required to pay the minimum wage to most workers in interstate commerce.

_____ 5. Employers can legally refuse to bargain collectively with supervisory employees.

_____ 6. Employees cannot picket in order to force an employer to bargain with an uncertified union.

_____ 7. The Labor Management Relations Act generally authorizes unions to engage in secondary boycotts of employers so long as the boycotts do not involve violence.

_____ 8. Joe is an officer of Local 404 which represents Ajax Co. employees. Joe received a paid vacation from Ajax Co. as a bonus. In this case, Joe must make an appropriate report of this bonus.

_____ 9. Local 202 represents 500 laborers. The union only allows white men to join. In this case, the union's action does not violate the Civil Rights Act of 1964 because the union is not an employer.

_____ 10. Children who are at least 16 years old may work in hazardous positions, but children under the age of 16 cannot.

REVIEW OF CONCEPT APPLICATIONS

Answer

Directions: Indicate your choice in the answer column.

_____ 1. Sunshine Bakers sells bakery products throughout the United States. Sunshine wants to hire additional workers, and it wants to extend the hours for some existing employees. Sunshine does not want to violate the Fair Labor Standards Act. Under these facts, select the correct answer.

a. Sunshine is not subject to this Act since it engages in only interstate commerce.

b. Sunshine cannot employ anyone under 18 to do janitorial work at its plant.

c. Sunshine must pay its bakers time and a half for hours exceeding 40 hours per week only if Sunshine's collective bargaining agreement requires such overtime pay.

d. Sunshine must pay its bakers at least minimum wage.

_____ 2. Wholesome Foods engages in interstate commerce in connection with several farms and grocery store chains that it operates. The company has been informed that it must comply with the National Labor Relations Act. Which employees are covered by the Act?
   a. Agricultural laborers who harvest produce on the company's farms.
   b. Retail clerks in the company's stores.
   c. Company managers who supervise the company's business operations.

_____ 3. A union wishes to represent the employees of Karsten Co. Karsten believes that its employees would be better off without union representation. What action can Karsten take to discourage employee approval of the union without violating the Labor Management Relations Act?
   a. Promise to increase employee medical benefits if union representation is voted down.
   b. Threaten to lay off employees if union representation is approved.
   c. Meet with employees to discuss the disadvantages of union representation.
   d. Limit the work hours of employees who support union representation.

_____ 4. Ben's employment contract with Employer states that Ben can be terminated only for "good cause." Under these facts, Ben *cannot* be fired for which of the following reasons?
   a. Ben used illegal drugs during working hours.
   b. Ben participated in lawful union activities.
   c. Ben disclosed his employer's confidential customer list to a competitor.
   d. Ben falsely stated on his employment application that he had a required college degree.

CASE PROBLEM

Roger works for Halifax Inc., which manufactures and sells goods in interstate commerce. Roger wants to organize a union of Halifax assembly line workers. Roger has a several questions regarding his rights under the Labor Management Relations Act. Please advise Roger regarding the following: (1) Does Roger have a right to organize a union of the Halifax employees? (2) Do the Halifax workers have a right to bargain collectively with Halifax? Can Halifax refuse to bargain with an employee union? (3) If the Halifax employees approve a union shop, do Halifax employees have to join the union?

_____

_____

_____

BUSINESS LAW PARTNER EXERCISE

Directions:

1. Using the Online feature of the Business Law Partner CD-ROM, locate and identify the federal statutes and administrative regulations, if any, that apply to the case below.
2. Which teenager(s), if any, can Tracy hire for the positions in question?

Case Study: *Hey Kid, Want a Job?*

Tracy owns a cafe and she is having a difficult time finding workers for certain positions. She has the following openings: (1) dishwasher who can work on weekends for three hours each day during lunch hour; and (2) short-order cook who can use an electric grill, meat cutter, deep fryer, and vegetable chopper. Three teenagers have applied for these jobs; their ages are 14, 16, and 18. Tracy has asked you if there are any federal laws that prohibit her from hiring any of these teenagers for the jobs in question.

_____

_____

_____

CHAPTER 30 QUIZ

Section A

DIRECTIONS: Complete each of the following statements by writing the missing word or words in the Answers column.

	Answers	For Scoring
1. A process by which the employer and the union agree on the terms of employment is a(n)	_____	1. _____
2. A work setting in which all employees must be union members is a(n)	_____	2. _____
3. When the NLRB finds that an unfair practice exists, it has the power to enjoin the practice by seeking a(n)	_____	3. _____
4. An attempt to cause a third party to a labor dispute to stop dealing with the employer is a(n)	_____	4. _____
5. An agreement between a union and an employer that the employer will not use nonunion materials is a(n)	_____	5. _____
		Score _____

Section B

DIRECTIONS: Following each statement below, indicate your answer by placing a "T" for "True" or an "F" for "False" in the Answers column.

	Answers	For Scoring
1. The Fair Labor Standards Act covers all employees in interstate commerce..................	_____	1. _____
2. The Fair Labor Standards Act sets the minimum wage.	_____	2. _____
3. Sixteen- to eighteen-year-olds are not allowed to work in industries particularly hazardous to health.	_____	3. _____
4. The Fair Labor Standards Act allows the use of commission and piece-rate payments to evade the minimum-wage provisions of the Act.	_____	4. _____
5. The National Labor Relations Act of 1935 applies to all employers engaged in interstate commerce.	_____	5. _____
6. Members of the NLRB are elected by union members.	_____	6. _____
7. If a strike threatens the national health or safety, the president may ask for an 80-day postponement of it.	_____	7. _____
8. The NLRB may determine the size and nature of the bargaining unit.	_____	8. _____
9. Employers may refuse to bargain collectively with supervisory employees..................	_____	9. _____
10. It is an unfair labor practice for employers to plead with workers to refrain from joining a union even when no threats of reprisal or promises of benefit are made.	_____	10. _____
11. Union leaders may picket an employer to force this employer to bargain collectively with their union even though another union is the legally recognized bargaining agent.	_____	11. _____
12. The union reports required by the Labor-Management Reporting and Disclosure Act must be made available to the union members.	_____	12. _____
		Score _____

Section C

DIRECTIONS: In the Answers space in Column II, place the letter of the corresponding word or words from Column I.

Column I	Column II	Answers	For Scoring

Column I

(a) Fair Labor Standards Act

(b) Immigration Reform and Control Act of 1986

(c) Labor-Management Relations Act

(d) Labor-Management Reporting and Disclosure Act

(e) National Labor Relations Act

(f) National Labor Relations Board

Column II

1. Supervises elections among employees seeking union representation .... _____ 1. _____

2. Requires unions and their officers and employees to file detailed public reports .... _____ 2. _____

3. Requires employers to recognize and bargain with unions... _____ 3. _____

4. The law that makes it illegal for an employer to knowingly hire an undocumented alien .... _____ 4. _____

5. Requires employers to pay time and a half for all hours over 40 .... _____ 5. _____

6. The act that outlaws "hot cargo agreements" .... _____ 6. _____

7. An agency that hears complaints of unfair union practices .... _____ 7. _____

8. The act that permits a suit against a union for breach of the union contract .... _____ 8. _____

9. Allows employers to refuse to bargain collectively with supervisory employees................................... _____ 9. _____

10. Requires employers to pay time and a half for all hours over 40 worked in a week .... _____ 10. _____

Score _____

CHAPTER 31
INTRODUCTION TO BUSINESS ORGANIZATION

CHAPTER OUTLINE

I.   INTRODUCTION

Common forms of business organizations are sole proprietorships, partnerships, and corporations.

II.   SOLE PROPRIETORSHIP

A. NATURE

General rules.   ▸ Defined: business that is owned and carried on by one person (a proprietor). ▸ Formation and termination: No formalities are required to either form or terminate a sole proprietorship. A proprietor only needs to commence doing business, or to cease doing business.

Limitations.   ▸ Fictitious name statutes: The name of a sole proprietorship must be registered with a designated state office if the business name is different from the owner's name. ▸ A sole proprietorship may be required to obtain a license to engage in certain trades or businesses.

Study hint.   A sole proprietorship normally terminates upon the death of the proprietor. However, the business of a sole proprietorship may be passed to another by will.

B. ADVANTAGES

- ***Flexible management***: ▸ A proprietor controls all decisions. ▸ A sole proprietorship may hire employees or agents, but doing so does not reduce the owner's control.
- ***Ease of organization***: Nothing is required to create a sole proprietorship.

C. DISADVANTAGES

- ***Unlimited liability***: Owner has unlimited personal liability for business debts and obligations.
- ***Limited management expertise***: Management skills are mainly limited to those of the owner.
- ***Capital***: Capital for the business is generally limited to the owner's assets.

III.   PARTNERSHIP

General rule. A partnership is a (1) voluntary association of two or more persons (partners) (2) who combine their money, property, or services to carry on as co-owners (3) a business for profit.

Limitation.   A partnership cannot be formed to carry on an illegal business or a nonprofit activity.

A. CLASSIFICATION

- ***Ordinary, or general, partnerships***: ▸ Defined: partnerships formed to carry on a business for profit without limitation on partners' rights or duties. ▸ Law: Uniform Partnership Act.

- ***Limited partnerships***: ▸ Defined: partnerships composed of at least one general and one limited partner. ▸ Control: general partners control business. ▸ Liability: general partners have unlimited liability; limited partners' liability is limited to capital contributions. ▸ A limited partnership may be treated as a general partnership if not properly formed. ▸ Law: Uniform Limited Partnership Act or Revised Uniform Limited Partnership Act.

- ***Trading and nontrading partnerships***: ▸ Trading partnership: partnership engages in buying and selling goods. Example: partnership owns a clothing store. ▸ Nontrading partnership: partnership that primarily engages in providing services. Example: law firm. ▸ A partner in a nontrading partnership cannot customarily borrow money on behalf of the partnership.

B. WHO MAY BE PARTNERS?

- *In general*: Any person who is competent to make a contract can be a partner.

- *Minors*: ▸ A minor can be a partner, but can disaffirm the partnership contract and withdraw. ▸ Prior to withdrawal, a minor is liable for his or her share of partnership debts.

C. KINDS OF PARTNERS

- *General partner*: ▸ Defined: partner publicly known as a partner who participates in the business. ▸ General partners have unlimited personal liability for partnership obligations.

- *Silent partner*: ▸ Defined: partner who is perhaps publicly known as a partner, and who does not participate in the business. ▸ If known to the public as a partner, a silent partner may be called a limited partner. ▸ Liability of limited partners is limited to their investment.

- *Secret partner*: partner not publicly known as a partner, who participates in the business.

- *Dormant partner*: partner not publicly known as a partner, who is not active in the business.

- *Nominal partner*: person who is falsely held out as being a partner.

D. ADVANTAGES OF THE PARTNERSHIP

▸ Increased capital. ▸ Increased management skills. ▸ Increased cost efficiency and profitability.

E. DISADVANTAGES OF THE PARTNERSHIP

- *Liability*: All partners (except limited partners) have unlimited liability for partnership debts.

- *Duration*: Partnerships are unstable; death or withdrawal of a partner causes a dissolution.

- *Reduced control*: Each partner has a right to participate in the management of a partnership.

F. ORGANIZATIONS SIMILAR TO PARTNERSHIPS

- *Joint-stock companies*: ▸ Defined: business entity that issues stock and whose owners have unlimited liability for business debts. ▸ Shareholders cannot act on behalf of the company.

- *Joint ventures*: ▸ Defined: association of two or more persons to engage in a single business transaction with profits and losses being shared equally unless otherwise agreed. ▸ Example: Harvey and Peter agree to jointly operate a Christmas tree lot. ▸ Compare: (1) joint venture: accomplish single enterprise; with (2) partnership: conduct an ongoing business.

- *Limited liability companies*: ▸ Defined: business organization similar to a partnership, but with the advantage of limited liability. ▸ Owners, called members, sign an operating agreement that must be filed with the appropriate state office.

IV. CORPORATIONS

A corporation is an artificial legal entity created in accordance with the law. A corporation has an existence separate from that of its owners, and it enjoys most rights enjoyed by natural persons.

A. IMPORTANCE OF CORPORATIONS (ADVANTAGES OF CORPORATIONS)

- *Pooling of capital*: Corporations can obtain investments from many individuals.

- *Limited liability*: Investors have limited liability (liability is limited to investment). In special cases, courts may ignore the corporate entity and hold a corporate investor personally liable.

- *Piercing the corporate veil*: In exceptional situations, a court may "pierce the corporate veil," meaning that it will ignore the corporate shell and hold the shareholders personally responsible for the corporation's obligations. This may occur when there are few shareholders and they fail to act as a corporation.

B. DISADVANTAGE OF CORPORATIONS

Majority shareholders may exercise sole control over the business of the corporation.

REVIEW OF CHAPTER

REVIEW OF TERMS

Select the term that best matches a statement below. Each term is the best match for only one statement.

TERMS

a. Corporation
b. General partner
c. General (ordinary) partnership
d. Joint venture

e. Limited partner
f. Limited partnership
g. Nominal partner

h. Secret partner
i. Silent partner
j. Sole proprietorship

STATEMENTS

Answer

_____ 1. Partner who participates in management of business and is known to the public as a partner.
_____ 2. Artificial legal entity that is created in accordance with legal requirements.
_____ 3. Partner who participates in management of business but is not publicly known as a partner.
_____ 4. Partner who is known to the public as a partner, who does not participate in management of the business, and whose liability is limited to capital contributions.
_____ 5. Partnership formed to carry on a business for profit without limits on partners' rights or duties.
_____ 6. Business relationship similar to a partnership that is formed to carry out a specific transaction.
_____ 7. Person who is falsely held out as being a partner.
_____ 8. Partnership composed of at least one general partner and one limited partner.
_____ 9. Business that is owned and operated by one owner.
_____ 10. Partner who does not participate in management of business but is perhaps known as a partner.

REVIEW OF CONCEPTS

Directions: Indicate **T** for true and **F** for false in the answer column.

_____ 1. Many states require a fictitious name for a sole proprietorship to be registered with a state official.
_____ 2. A sole proprietorship may be owned by only one person.
_____ 3. A partnership engaging in the practice of accounting is an example of a trading partnership.
_____ 4. Usually, a partner in a nontrading partnership does not have the authority to borrow money for the partnership.
_____ 5. Minors cannot be partners.
_____ 6. Ernie is a partner in XYZ Partnership. Ernie does not participate in the management of the business, and he is not publicly known as a partner. In this case, Ernie is a dormant partner.
_____ 7. Shareholders in a joint-stock company may be held personally liable for debts of the company.
_____ 8. A joint venture is similar to a partnership. The major difference is that a joint venture is formed to carry out a specific transaction, but a partnership is intended to conduct an ongoing business.
_____ 9. Horace and Ivan wish to form a business to own and operate a nonprofit shelter for the homeless. In this case, the parties can properly use a general partnership to conduct this business.
_____ 10. A corporation is a legal entity that is separate from its owners.

REVIEW OF CONCEPT APPLICATIONS

Answer

Directions: Indicate your choice in the answer column.

_____ 1. Alex is starting a home repair business. Alex wants to control the entire business, and he does not want to have to do anything to create the business organization. These are Alex's only concerns. Under these facts, which form of business organization is most appropriate for Alex?
   a.   Sole proprietorship.
   b.   General partnership.
   c.   Corporation.
   d.   Joint venture.

_____ 2. Frances owns and operates Fran's Donut Shop as a sole proprietorship. The business has failed to pay the rent. Frances is considering terminating the business. Under these facts:
   a. To terminate the business, Frances must comply with numerous legal formalities.
   b. Frances' liability for the unpaid rent is limited to the amount she invested in the business.
   c. Frances has unlimited personal liability for the unpaid rent.

_____ 3. Betty and Dan agreed to pool their resources, and they formed a particular type of business organization to own and operate a catering business. Betty and Dan jointly own and manage the business, and they each have unlimited personal liability for the obligations of the business. Under these facts, what type of business organization did Betty and Dan create?
   a. Sole proprietorship.
   b. General partnership.
   c. Limited partnership.
   d. Corporation.

_____ 4. Jesse and John plan to form a limited partnership to engage in real estate development. John will be a general partner, and Jesse will be a limited partner. Under these facts:
   a. The parties cannot form a limited partnership. Limited partnerships are illegal.
   b. The parties do not need to comply with any statutes in order to create the limited partnership.
   c. Jesse will have unlimited personal liability for obligations of the partnership.
   d. Jesse's liability for partnership obligations will be limited to his investment in the partnership.

CASE PROBLEM

Kelly and Rene want to form a business to own a manufacturing firm. It is important that the business owners not have personal liability for business obligations. It is also important that the business be able to pool capital contributions from hundreds of investors. In this case, which form of organization would be most appropriate for this business?

_____

_____

BUSINESS LAW PARTNER EXERCISE

Directions:

1. Access your Business Law Partner CD-ROM and locate the document "Business Entity Planning Worksheet."
2. Using the information provided in the case below, complete the worksheet. Furnish additional information as needed to fill out the document.
3. Based on the information provided, what forms of business organizations may be appropriate?

Case Study: *What Should We Be When We Go Into Business?*

Jason plans to open a sporting equipment store. He has $40,000 that he recently inherited and other personal belongings. He is planning to lease the necessary store space and buy used trade fixtures. Jason's uncle, Cal, is willing to invest $25,000 in Jason's company, but he does not want to be personally liable for any business debts. Jason and Cal are uncertain whether they want the company or themselves to be taxed on business profits and losses.

_____

_____

_____

CHAPTER 31 QUIZ

Section A

DIRECTIONS: Complete each of the following statements by writing the missing word or words in the Answers column.

	Answers	For Scoring

1. The simplest and most common form of business is a(n) .... _____   1. _____

2. The person who owns the above form of business is a(n).............................. _____   2. _____

3. A law that requires the operator of a business under an assumed name to register with the state is known as .... _____   3. _____

4. When business debts are payable from personal, as well as business, assets there is said to be .... _____   4. _____

5. The individuals who form a partnership and constitute its members are called _____   5. _____

6. A partnership must be formed to carry on a(n)...................................... _____   6. _____

7. When two or more persons voluntarily contract to pool their capital and skill to conduct some business for profit, with no limitations upon their rights and duties, they have created a(n) ??? partnership. .... _____   7. _____

8. A partnership in which the liability of one or more of the partners for the firm's debts cannot exceed the amount of their investment is a(n) ??? partnership. .... _____   8. _____

9. A partnership engaged in the buying and selling of merchandise is a(n) ??? partnership. .... _____   9. _____

10. A partnership devoted to providing professional services is a(n) ??? partnership. .... _____   10. _____

11. A business organization similar to a partnership but without unlimited liability is a(n)... _____   11. _____

12. A partner who takes no active part in the management of the business is a(n) ??? partner. .... _____   12. _____

13. An active partner who attempts to conceal his or her partner status from the public is a(n) ??? partner. .... _____   13. _____

14. A partner who is unknown to the public as being a partner and who takes no part in the management of the partnership is a(n) ??? partner........................ _____   14. _____

15. People who hold themselves out as partners when in fact they are not partners are called ???.. _____   15. _____

16. An entity that issues shares of stock and whose investors have unlimited liability is a(n)... _____   16. _____

17. A business relationship similar to a partnership that is entered into for a single transaction is a(n)... _____   17. _____

18. It is called ??? when a court ignores the corporate entity. .... _____   18. _____

19. An association of people in an entity created by law is a(n).......................... _____   19. _____

20. An investor whose maximum business loss is the amount of his or her investment has .... _____   20. _____

Score _____

Section B

DIRECTIONS: Following each statement below, indicate your answer by placing a "T" for "True" or an "F" for "False" in the Answers column.

	Answers	For Scoring
1. A proprietor owns every asset of a sole proprietorship.	_____	1. _____
2. A proprietor need only begin doing business to start a sole proprietorship.	_____	2. _____
3. A sole proprietorship normally ends upon the death of the proprietor.	_____	3. _____
4. The sole proprietor's financial risk can be limited to what is invested in the business.	_____	4. _____
5. One of the advantages of a sole proprietorship is extensive management ability and capital.	_____	5. _____
6. A sole proprietor is liable for the activities of the business.	_____	6. _____
7. Partners cannot act as agents for the partnership.	_____	7. _____
8. The attempt to form a partnership to operate an unlawful business does not result in a partnership.	_____	8. _____
9. In all partnerships, capital and skill are increased, labor is made more efficient, the ratio of expenses per dollar of business is reduced, and management is improved.	_____	9. _____
10. A limited partnership that does not comply strictly with the law can be held to be a general partnership.	_____	10. _____
11. It is implied that a partner in a nontrading partnership can borrow money in the name of the firm and obligate the firm for the debt.	_____	11. _____
12. A partner who is a minor cannot bind the partnership on contracts.	_____	12. _____
13. A silent partner normally has limited liability.	_____	13. _____
14. A dormant partner whose status becomes known by the public is liable for the debts of the firm to the same extent as a general partner.	_____	14. _____
15. A partnership may be dissolved by the death of one of the partners.	_____	15. _____
16. Shareholders in a joint-stock company have authority to act for the firm.	_____	16. _____
17. A joint venture must be completed within one year.	_____	17. _____
18. A limited liability company may be formed for any legal business.	_____	18. _____
19. Courts never disregard the entity concept of the corporation.	_____	19. _____
20. In a corporation, the people who own or control a majority of the voting stock have the controlling voice in management.	_____	20. _____

Score _____

CHAPTER 32
CREATION AND OPERATION OF A PARTNERSHIP

CHAPTER OUTLINE

I. PARTNERSHIP AGREEMENTS

A partnership is created by an express or implied contract. Express contracts can be oral or written.

A. WRITTEN AGREEMENT

A written partnership agreement is commonly known as articles of partnership. Articles usually include terms regarding contributions, profits and losses, duties, and rights on dissolution.

B. IMPLIED AGREEMENT

General rules. ▸ A partnership agreement may be implied from parties' conduct. A partnership is implied if conduct evidences an agreement that meets the requirements for a partnership (i.e., business for profit carried on and managed by the parties as co-owners). ▸ Uniform Partnership Act (UPA) holds that an agreement to share profits is *prima facie* evidence of a partnership.
Example. Implied partnership agreement: Rick and Sue each contribute $25,000 to purchase a grocery store. Rick and Sue jointly control the business, and they share the net profits.
Limitation. Sharing profits does not imply a partnership if profits are paid as wages or rent, or they are paid to satisfy a debt.

C. PARTNERSHIP BY ESTOPPEL

General rule. A party may be held liable to a creditor if: (1) the party misled, or allowed another to mislead, the creditor into reasonably believing that the party was a partner; and (2) the creditor extended credit to the other party in reliance on the misrepresentation.
Example. Kim misrepresented to Vick that she was Hal's partner. Vick lent $1,000 to Hal. Kim cannot deny that she is Hal's partner, and she is liable for the loan if Hal fails to repay it.

II. PARTNERSHIP FIRM NAME

General rule. A partnership can adopt a firm name, although it is not required to do so.
Limitation. A name must not violate others' rights (e.g., cannot be same as another firm's name) and, in some states, a name must not use words "and Company" unless there are additional partners.
Study hint. A partnership can sue or be sued, and can own property, in its own name or in the name of its partners. Partnership property may be conveyed to partners "d/b/a" the partnership.

III. PARTNER'S INTEREST IN PARTNERSHIP PROPERTY

- *Partner's interest*: ▸ Partners own partnership property by tenancy in partnership. This means: (1) partners may use property for partnership business; but (2) a partner cannot sell his or her interest in any item of partnership property; (3) on a partner's death, surviving partners do not own the deceased partner's interest; and (4) a partner's creditors cannot force a sale of partnership property. ▸ Partners do *not* own partnership property in joint tenancy or tenancy in common.

- *Creditors*: A partner's creditor can get a court order allowing the creditor: (1) to receive the partner's share of profits and (2) to force a sale of the partner's interest in the partnership.

- *Sale of interest*: If a partner sells his or her partnership interest, the buyer cannot demand to be made a partner. The buyer only has a right to receive the partner's share of profits.

IV. DUTIES OF PARTNERS

A. EXERCISE LOYALTY AND GOOD FAITH

General rule.　　A partner is a fiduciary of the partnership. Thus, a partner cannot: (1) take advantage of co-partners; (2) make secret profits in connection with partnership business; or (3) act in a manner that advances a partner's personal interests to the detriment of a partnership.

Example.　　　On behalf of a partnership, Brenda (a partner) sold partnership property. Brenda secretly earned a $1,000 commission on the sale. This commission belongs to the partnership.

B. WORK FOR THE PARTNERSHIP

General rules.　▸ A partner must use reasonable care and skill in transacting partnership business. ▸ If a partner negligently injures a third party, both the partner and the partnership are liable to the third party, but the partnership may recover its loss from the partner.

Example.　　　While delivering goods for her partnership, Karen negligently injured Tex. Both the partnership and Karen are liable to Tex. The partnership may recover its loss from Karen.

Limitation.　　A partner is not liable to a partnership for losses resulting from honest mistakes or mere errors of judgment (e.g., a partner is not liable for a loss from an unprofitable contract).

C. ABIDE BY MAJORITY VOTE

Unless the partnership agreement provides otherwise, the majority of partners bind the partnership on ordinary matters within the scope of its business. For extraordinary matters, such as confessing a judgment, unanimous consent of the partners is needed.

D. KEEP RECORDS

A partner must maintain appropriate records of all partnership transactions.

E. INFORM

A partner must inform the partnership of all matters relating to partnership affairs and any matters that may affect the partnership.

V. RIGHTS OF PARTNERS

A. PARTICIPATE IN MANAGEMENT

- *Individual partner's right*: Unless otherwise agreed, each partner has an equal right to participate in the management of a partnership.

- *Required vote of partners*: ▸ The decision of a majority of partners controls regarding most matters arising in the usual course of partnership business no matter how important a matter may be. ▸ Unanimous consent of all partners is required if: (1) a matter relates to a basic change of the partnership (e.g., amending a partnership agreement or a sale of all assets); or (2) the partnership agreement requires unanimous approval.

B. INSPECT THE BOOKS

Each partner has the right to inspect the books and records of a partnership.

C. CONTRIBUTION

- *Contribution*: If a partner pays a partnership debt with his or her personal funds, the partner is entitled to recover from the other partners their proportionate share of the debt.

- *Indemnity*: ▸ A partnership must indemnify (pay) for expenses or liabilities that are incurred by a partner in carrying out partnership business. ▸ Indemnification is not required if a partner acted in bad faith or negligently, or agreed to bear an expense.

D. WITHDRAW ADVANCES

- *Contributions*: ▸ A partner cannot withdraw contributions (investments) without the consent of the other partners. ▸ A partner is not entitled to interest on his or her contributions.

- *Loans*: A partner is entitled to be repaid a loan (with interest) once it comes due.

E. WITHDRAW PROFITS

A partner has the right to withdraw his or her share of profits from a partnership: (1) at the times stated in the partnership agreement; or (2) at the times authorized by a majority of the partners.

VI. LIABILITIES OF PARTNERS

- *Contracts*: ▸ In general: Every partner (except a limited partner) is personally liable for contract obligations of a partnership. ▸ Unauthorized contract: A partnership is not liable on a contract if it was made by a partner with no authority to do so. In this event, the other partners are also not liable. However, the partner making the contract is personally liable to the third party.

- *Torts*: A partnership is liable for torts committed by partners who are doing partnership business.

- *Crimes*: The partnership and a partner who committed a crime in the ordinary course of business have liability for the crime. Innocent partners cannot be punished.

VII. NATURE OF PARTNERSHIP LIABILITIES

- *In general*: Partners are jointly liable on partnership contracts (partners must be sued together). Partners are jointly and severally liable for tort liabilities of the partnership.

- *Extent of partner's liability*: A partner must pay the full amount of any debt if the partnership and other partners fail to pay. The partner who pays has a right of contribution from other partners.

- *Withdrawing partner*: A partner is liable for all partnership debts incurred prior to withdrawal.

- *Incoming partner*: An incoming partner's liability for *existing debts* is limited to the partner's contribution. Incoming partners have unlimited liability for debts arising after becoming partners.

VIII. AUTHORITY OF A PARTNER

General rule.   A partner has the following authority to act for a partnership: (1) express authority given by a partnership agreement or by the required number of partners; and (2) customary authority.
Study hint.   A partnership can limit a partner's authority, but the limit may not be binding on an innocent third party. A partner is liable to a partnership for violating a limit on his or her authority.

A. CUSTOMARY OR IMPLIED AUTHORITY

A partner in a *trading partnership* has the customary or implied authority to: (1) compromise and release claims; (2) receive payments and give receipts; (3) employ or discharge ordinary agents and employees; (4) issue and receive checks and notes; (5) acquire and cancel insurance; and (6) buy goods on credit and sell goods in the ordinary course of business.

B. AUTHORITY NOT IMPLIED

A partner has no implied authority to: (1) assign assets to creditors; (2) agree to arbitration; (3) pay personal debts with partnership assets; or (4) do any act that makes it impossible for a partnership to do business. A partnership is not bound by such acts unless expressly authorized.

IX. SHARING OF PROFITS AND LOSSES

▸ An allocation of profits and losses in a partnership agreement is binding and cannot be changed by a majority of the partners. If not stated, however, profits and losses are shared equally, regardless of contributions. ▸ A majority of partners can authorize a distribution of profits at any time.

REVIEW OF CHAPTER

REVIEW OF TERMS

Select the term that best matches a statement below. Each term is the best match for only one statement.

TERMS

a. Articles of partnership   d. Partnership by estoppel   g. Tenancy in partnership
b. d/b/a   e. *Prima facie*   h. Uniform Partnership Act
c. Joint tenancy   f. *Prima facie* evidence

STATEMENTS

Answer

_____ 1.   Written partnership agreement.

_____ 2.   Evidence that, on its face, indicates that a fact is true, e.g., that a business is a partnership.

_____ 3.   Ownership rights of a partner in items of partnership property.

_____ 4.   Term indicating that parties are doing business under another name.

_____ 5.   Ownership of property whereby surviving co-owner receives interest of deceased co-owner.

_____ 6.   Law that governs ordinary, general partnerships in many states.

_____ 7.   Doctrine that may hold a person liable for another's obligation if the person who holds himself out, or permits others to hold him out, as a partner when this is not true.

_____ 8.   On the face of something.

REVIEW OF CONCEPTS

Directions: Indicate **T** for true and **F** for false in the answer column.

_____ 1.   In general, partnership agreements must be written to be enforceable.

_____ 2.   Articles of partnership do not generally state how partners will share profits and losses.

_____ 3.   A partnership cannot be created unless parties expressly call their relationship a partnership.

_____ 4.   The fact that parties share profits that are earned by a business is *prima facie* evidence that the parties' business relationship is a partnership.

_____ 5.   Josie was present when Isaac misrepresented to Seller that Josie was Isaac's partner. On the basis of this misrepresentation, Seller sold Isaac goods on credit. If Isaac fails to pay Seller, Josie may be held liable to Seller for the price of the goods under the doctrine of partnership by estoppel.

_____ 6.   The UPA does not permit a partnership to sue, or own property, in its own name.

_____ 7.   Pam, Wes, and Jonas are partners in a general partnership. Jonas dies. In this case, Jonas' interest in the partnership and partnership property belongs to Pam and Wes.

_____ 8.   A partner is not entitled to make secret personal profits in partnership dealings.

_____ 9.   A partner must disclose any information to the partnership that relates to partnership affairs.

_____ 10. A partnership involves a fiduciary relationship between the parties.

_____ 11. In general, a decision by a majority of partners controls regarding ordinary partnership contracts.

_____ 12. Unless otherwise agreed, partners generally have an equal vote on partnership matters.

_____ 13. Rory and Merl are equal partners in R&M Partnership. R&M owes Doc $500 that it can't pay. If Rory pays Doc the $500, Rory has a right of contribution to recover $250 from Merl.

_____ 14. A partnership is required to indemnify a partner for expenses the partner pays for the partnership.

_____ 15. A partner can withdraw his or her contributions to the partnership at any time the partner chooses.

_____ 16. A partner can withdraw profits from a partnership only when permitted by the partnership agreement, or when duly authorized to do so by a majority of the partners.

_____ 17. A partnership cannot be held liable for torts committed by a partner.

_____ 18. Partners are jointly and severally liable for tort liabilities of a partnership.

_____ 19. A partnership is bound by a contract that is made on its behalf by a partner with apparent authority.

_____ 20. A partnership is bound by a contract that is made on its behalf by a partner even if the partner did not have any authority to make the contract.

_____ 21. Rosalyn and Melissa are the only partners in a general partnership. Rosalyn contributed $10,000 to the partnership and Melissa contributed $5,000. Nothing is stated regarding division of profits and losses. In this case, profits and losses are allocated 50-50 among the partners.

_____ 22. An incoming partner has unlimited personal liability for existing partnership obligations.

REVIEW OF CONCEPT APPLICATIONS

Answer

Directions: Indicate your choice in the answer column.

_____ 1. In which situation does a partnership exist between Felix and Art?
   a. Felix owns a shop and he pays Art, his landlord, 10 percent of the shop's profits as rent.
   b. Felix owns an insurance agency. As compensation, Felix pays Art 5 percent of the premiums paid on insurance policies that are sold by Art.
   c. Felix and Art co-own a furniture store. Felix and Art jointly control the business and they share the net profits and losses derived from the store.
   d. None of the above. A partnership can be created only by an express partnership agreement.

_____ 2. Cal, Oscar, and Len are partners in a general partnership. Cal's creditor has obtained a court order against his partnership interest. Oscar wants to sell his interest in a truck that is owned by the partnership. Len sold his interest in the partnership to Third Party. Under these facts:
   a. Cal's creditor can force a sale of Cal's interest in the partnership.
   b. Cal's creditor can force a sale of specific items of partnership property.
   c. Oscar can sell his interest in the partnership truck.
   d. Third party has a right to demand to be made a partner and to manage the partnership.

_____ 3. Kit was a partner in a general partnership that sold hospital supplies. Which action by Kit would breach a duty that she owed to the partnership?
   a. With actual authority to do so, Kit bought supplies for the partnership. Kit acted reasonably, and she exercised care and skill, but the partnership lost money on the purchase.
   b. Kit set up a company that sold goods to the partnership. Kit did not disclose that she owned the company. Kit personally profited from sales made to the partnership.
   c. The partnership agreement required that each partner work at least 40 hours per week. Over an extended period of time, Kit worked only 20 hours per week on partnership business.
   d. b and c.

_____ 4. Cooper, Tex, and Chien are the partners in CTC, a general partnership. Cooper contributed $50,000 to the partnership, and Tex and Chien each contributed $25,000. The partnership agreement is silent regarding the partners' right to manage the partnership. Under these facts:
    a.   Cooper has the exclusive right to manage the partnership.
    b.   Cooper, Tex, and Chien are each entitled to an equal vote regarding partnership matters.
    c.   Unanimous consent of all partners is required to authorize any partnership transaction.
    d.   Cooper and Tex can properly authorize the partnership to sell all of its assets or to dissolve.

_____ 5. Don and Rene are partners in a general partnership that owns a retail liquor store. Under these facts, Don would *NOT* have customary or implied authority to make which of the following contracts on behalf of the partnership?
    a.   Contract to purchase a case of wine on credit.
    b.   Contract to hire a sales clerk who is needed to run the store.
    c.   Contract to sell the entire store.
    d.   Contract to purchase fire insurance for the store.

CASE PROBLEM

Harry and Al were general partners in a partnership that owned a drug store. On behalf of the partnership, Harry bought inventory from Seller on credit for $5,000. Harry had customary authority to make this contract. The partnership cannot pay the contract price. The partnership agreement states that Harry and Al shall each bear 50 percent of partnership losses. Under these facts: (1) Is the partnership bound by the contract made by Harry? (2) If the partnership fails to pay the contract price, does Al have personal liability for this debt? (3) If Harry refuses to pay any portion of the contract price, is Al liable to Seller for the full amount of the debt?

_____

_____

_____

BUSINESS LAW PARTNER EXERCISE

Directions:

1.   Access your Business Law Partner CD-ROM and locate the document entitled "Partnership Worksheet."
2.   Using the information provided in the case below, complete the worksheet. Furnish additional information as needed to fill out the document.
3.   Based on the information provided, should the parties form a general or limited partnership?

Case Study: *Wow, There Is A Lot To Consider Before Forming A Partnership!*

Rhonda, Liz, and Wanda have decided to form a business that will operate a health clinic for women. They have agreed that each person shall have an equal voice in managing the business, and they will each contribute $5,000 to the business. The business will commence May 1. They are not certain how well the clinic will do, so there is no fixed duration for the business. Also, any person can withdraw at any time without penalty. Profits and losses are to be shared equally.

_____

_____

_____

CHAPTER 32 QUIZ

Section A

DIRECTIONS: Following each question below, indicate your answer by placing a "Y" for "Yes" or an "N" for "No" in the Answers column.

	Answers	**For Scoring**
1. Is a partnership the result of a contract?..	_____	1._____
2. Must there be a written agreement in order to form a partnership?	_____	2._____
3. In the case of a false impression of a partnership, will the law ever hold that the apparent partners are estopped from denying that a partnership exists?.........................	_____	3._____
4. Is it legally required that a partnership have a firm name?	_____	4._____
5. Does the law impose upon each partner fiduciary duties in all partnership dealings with the other partners?	_____	5._____
6. Can personal creditors of one partner force the sale of specific items of partnership property in order to obtain payment of the partner's personal debts?	_____	6._____
7. May a fine be levied on partnership assets for the criminal acts of just one partner?.....	_____	7._____
8. Unless otherwise agreed, does each partner have a right to participate equally in the management of the partnership?...	_____	8._____
9. Is a partner entitled to withdraw any part of his or her original partnership investment without the consent of the other partners?...	_____	9._____
10. If the authority of a partner is restricted by agreement, should notice of this restriction be given to third parties?...	_____	10._____

Score _____

Section B

DIRECTIONS: Following each statement below, indicate your answer by placing a "T" for "True" or an "F" for "False" in the Answers column.

	Answers	**For Scoring**
1. The written contract providing for the formation of a partnership must be in a particular form.	_____	1._____
2. If persons do not call themselves partners, a partnership cannot exist............................	_____	2._____
3. In some states it is not permissible to identify the partnership by using the name of a person who is not a member of the firm.	_____	3._____
4. A fictitious or trade name used for a partnership normally must be registered...............	_____	4._____
5. A person who buys a partner's interest in the partnership business cannot become a partner unless all of the other partners so agree..	_____	5._____
6. A partner is not liable for a crime committed by another partner unless the first partner agreed to or participated in the crime.	_____	6._____
7. Partners have no duty to work on behalf of the partnership..	_____	7._____
8. Any loss resulting to the firm because of a partner's failure to use reasonable skill and care in transacting business must be borne by that partner..	_____	8._____
9. The majority view of the partners is decisive in all decisions that come before the firm.	_____	9._____
10. A partner is entitled to be paid interest on his or her partnership investment.	_____	10._____

Score _____

Section C

DIRECTIONS: Assuming that the powers of the partners in a trading partnership are not restricted by agreement, indicate by use of the identifying letter whether a partner would have or would not have the implied power to do the acts in question.

A.   Partner has the implied power

B.   Partner does not have the implied power

	Answers	For Scoring
1. Insuring partnership property		1. ____
2. Assigning the firm's assets for the benefit of creditors		2. ____
3. Submitting a partnership controversy to arbitration		3. ____
4. Employing agents for services needed in the business		4. ____
5. Buying inventory on the firm's credit		5. ____
6. Purchasing additional inventory on credit		6. ____
7. Indorsing a negotiable instrument for accommodation		7. ____
8. Accepting drafts in the firm name		8. ____
9. Selling all of the merchandise in stock in the regular course of business		9. ____
10. Disposing of the goodwill of the business		10. ____
11. Doing an act that makes it impossible to continue the partnership's business		11. ____
12. Giving proof of a fire loss		12. ____
13. Canceling a fire insurance policy		13. ____
14. Discharging a personal debt by setting it off against one due the firm		14. ____
15. Compromising and releasing claims against third parties		15. ____

Score _____

Section D

DIRECTIONS: Indicate your decision in each of the following cases by filling in the space at the right.

	Answers	For Scoring
1-2. Bayer, a partner in the firm of Bayer and Black, used firm money in a speculative venture in her own name and realized a profit. Could Black claim that the profit belongs to the firm?		1. ____
Who would bear the loss if the venture failed?		2. ____
3-4. The partnership ABC Company was made up of partners A, B, and C. Through negligence, while engaged in partnership activity, C committed a tort damaging the property of X. X sued A, B, and C jointly. A and B contend that they are not liable. Is X barred from bringing suit against all of the partners?		3. ____
If C had intentionally caused the damage, would your answer change?		4. ____
5. Sue and Montoya were partners in a real estate company for the purpose of owning and managing two apartment buildings. While Montoya was on vacation for two months, Sue, who considered herself knowledgeable about the commodities market, decided to make more money for the partnership by investing some of the profits in commodities transactions. When Montoya returned, he was furious to learn of this, since he considered it a very risky investment. He said he would get the partnership dissolved. Can he?		5. ____

Score _____

CHAPTER 33
DISSOLUTION OF A PARTNERSHIP

CHAPTER OUTLINE

I. INTRODUCTION

▸ Dissolution is a change in the purpose of a partnership from that of pursuing an ongoing business to concluding its business. A dissolution can result from an act of the parties, court decree, or by operation of law. ▸ After dissolution, a partnership continues to exist while it winds up (completes outstanding business and distributes assets). After affairs are wound up, a partnership terminates.

II. DISSOLUTION BY ACTS OF THE PARTIES

A. AGREEMENT

- *Definite term*: ▸ A partnership dissolves at the time stated in the partnership agreement. ▸ Limitation: By *unanimous* consent, partners can change the time for dissolution.

- *Indefinite term*: If a partnership agreement does not state a definite term but a purpose for the partnership is stated, the partnership dissolves when the purpose is accomplished. If no purpose is stated, the partners can mutually agree to dissolve the partnership at any time.

B. WITHDRAWAL OR ALIENATION

1. Permitted Withdrawal

If a partnership is formed for an indefinite term, a partner can withdraw any time and for any reason without liability, and the withdrawal dissolves the partnership. After creditors are paid, the withdrawing partner is entitled to: (1) return of contributions; (2) payment of undistributed profits; and (3) repayment of loans made to the partnership.

2. Wrongful Withdrawal

General rules. ▸ A partner has the power (but not the legal right) to withdraw from a partnership at any time even though the withdrawal breaches the partnership agreement. ▸ A partner who wrongfully withdraws is liable for damages caused by the withdrawal. These damages are deducted from the amounts otherwise payable to the partner.
Example: The partnership agreement for ABC Partnership states that the partnership will continue until January 1, 2010. Bev (a partner) wrongfully withdraws June 1, 2000. Bev has effectively withdrawn, but she is liable for damages caused by her withdrawal.
Study hint. Although a wrongful withdrawal may dissolve a partnership, in certain cases the remaining partners may have the right to continue the partnership business.

3. Sale of a Partner's Interest

The sale or assignment of a partner's interest does not cause a dissolution. The purchaser is only entitled to receive the selling partner's share of capital and profits when distributed.

C. EXPULSION

A partnership agreement may allow partners to expel another partner for certain reasons. An expulsion of a partner causes a dissolution. However, the partnership agreement may permit the remaining partners to continue the partnership business without winding up the partnership.

III. DISSOLUTION BY COURT DECREE

A partner may obtain a judicial dissolution of a partnership for the following reasons:

- *Insanity of a partner*: Another partner is judicially declared insane.
- *Incapacity of a partner*: Another partner suffers a permanent disability rendering the partner incapable of performing his or her duties. Temporary disability is not a sufficient justification.
- *Misconduct*: ▸ Another partner engages in serious misconduct that endangers the partnership. ▸ Examples: habitual drunkenness; wrongful competition against partnership; repeated violations of duties; serious disagreements among partners that make it impractical to continue business.
- *Futility*: ▸ It becomes reasonably impossible to accomplish objectives of a partnership and the business can be operated only at a loss. ▸ Temporary unprofitability does not justify a dissolution.

IV. DISSOLUTION BY OPERATION OF LAW

- *Death*: ▸ In general, the death of any partner dissolves a partnership. ▸ A partnership agreement can provide that surviving partners may liquidate a partnership over a period of time or that the surviving partners may continue the business. ▸ The personal representative of a deceased partner is entitled to receive payment for the partner's interest in the partnership, but the personal representative is not entitled to act as a partner or to be made a partner.
- *Bankruptcy*: Bankruptcy of a partnership or of any partner dissolves the partnership.
- *Illegality*: If the business of a partnership becomes illegal, this automatically causes a dissolution.

V. EFFECTS OF DISSOLUTION

General rules. ▸ Unless otherwise agreed, upon dissolution partners must wind up the partnership's affairs and, after doing so, terminate the partnership. ▸ During winding up, the following actions are permitted: (1) existing contracts may be completed; (2) minor contracts necessary to complete partnership business can be made; and (3) contracts necessary to wind up the partnership are allowed.
Study hints. ▸ Partners' duties to each other continue until the partnership is *terminated*. ▸ In some cases, a third party may be able to hold a partnership liable on new contracts that a partner improperly makes while winding up the partnership.

VI. NOTICE OF DISSOLUTION

- *Liability to third parties*: A partnership and every partner is liable for an improper contract made by another partner following dissolution if (1) the contract relates to the partnership business, and (2) the third party was not given proper notice of dissolution.
- *Required notice*: ▸ Actual notice (i.e., oral or mailed notice) is required if a third party has previously dealt with the partnership. ▸ Notice by publication in a newspaper is sufficient notice for third parties that have not previously dealt with the partnership.
- *Notice not required*: ▸ Notice does not have to be given to partners. ▸ Notice to third parties is not required if (1) a partnership is dissolved by operation of law or by judicial decree or (2) a dissolution occurs because a dormant or secret partner withdraws.

VII. DISTRIBUTION OF ASSETS

- After dissolution, partnership assets are distributed in the following order: (1) payment of debts owed to third party creditors; (2) payment to partners for loans or advances, or reimbursement for money spent on behalf of the partnership; (3) return of capital contributions to partners; and (4) equal division of remaining assets, if any, among the partners unless otherwise agreed.
- In the event of a loss, partners share equally in the loss unless otherwise agreed.

REVIEW OF CHAPTER

REVIEW OF TERMS

Select the term that best matches a statement below. Each term is the best match for only one statement.

TERMS

a. Actual notice
b. Dissolution
c. Notice by publication

d. Terminated
e. Winding up

STATEMENTS

Answer

_____ 1. Notice of dissolution that may be given to members of the general public who have not previously dealt with a partnership.

_____ 2. Completing outstanding partnership business and distributing assets in manner required by law.

_____ 3. Change in purpose of a partnership from conducting a business to concluding the business.

_____ 4. Notice of dissolution required to be given to parties who have previously dealt with a partnership.

_____ 5. No longer in existence; status of a partnership following winding up of partnership affairs.

REVIEW OF CONCEPTS

Directions: Indicate **T** for true and **F** for false in the answer column.

_____ 1. A dissolution of a partnership immediately ends the partnership's existence.

_____ 2. A majority of partners have the right at any time to dissolve a partnership that has a definite term.

_____ 3. If a partnership does not have a definite term, partners can withdraw at any time without liability.

_____ 4. Stu was a partner in S&S Partnership, and he properly withdrew from the partnership. By withdrawing, Stu forfeited his right to be paid his contributions and share of undistributed profits.

_____ 5. A partner has the power to withdraw from a partnership at any time even if the withdrawal breaches the partnership agreement.

_____ 6. Upon a sale of a partnership interest, the buyer becomes a partner in the partnership and the buyer is entitled to participate in the management of the partnership.

_____ 7. If a partner wrongfully withdraws, the other partners may be able to continue the business.

_____ 8. Jinx and Jeb are partners. On occasion Jinx and Jeb disagree on various business decisions. In this case, Jinx can properly request a court to issue a decree dissolving the partnership.

_____ 9. Bankruptcy of a partnership causes a dissolution, but bankruptcy of only one partner does not.

_____ 10. A and B were partners. A died. A's personal representative has the right to act as a partner in A's place.

_____ 11. A partnership can complete existing contracts following a dissolution.

_____ 12. A third party can never hold a partnership liable on a contract that is made after dissolution.

_____ 13. Duties that partners owe to each other continue until a partnership winds up and terminates.

_____ 14. Notice of dissolution does not need to be given to anyone if a court orders the dissolution.

_____ 15. Partners are entitled to a return of contributions before partnership creditors are paid.

REVIEW OF CONCEPT APPLICATIONS

Answer

Directions: Indicate your choice in the answer column.

_____ 1. Bruce, Mark, and Erwin are partners in B-MER Partnership. The agreement states that the partnership will continue until January 1, 2001. The partnership agreement allows any two partners to expel another partner at any time. Which event would *NOT* cause a dissolution?

a. On May 1, 1998, Bruce sold his partnership interest to Harold.

b. On May 1, 1998, Mark and Bruce expelled Erwin from the partnership.

c. On May 1, 1998, all of the partners agreed to dissolve the partnership.

_____ 2. Lee and Mindy are partners in L&M Partnership. The partnership agreement states that the partnership will continue until June 1, 2004. In which situation can Lee request a court to enter a decree dissolving the partnership prior to June 1, 2004?
   a. Mindy has pneumonia and cannot work for one month.
   b. Lee and Mindy repeatedly disagree on all important business decisions. As a result, the partnership cannot carry out its business.
   c. The partnership business is not as profitable as it was in the past.

_____ 3. Glenn, Jane, and Shelli are partners in a partnership whose sole business is making Styrofoam containers. Which event may cause a dissolution of the partnership by operation of the law?
   a. Glenn files for bankruptcy and receives a discharge in bankruptcy.
   b. Jane dies.
   c. The federal government passes a law making it illegal to make Styrofoam containers.
   d. All of the above.

_____ 4. Jerry and Jill were partners in a partnership that bought and sold plumbing supplies. The partnership was dissolved due to Jerry's proper withdrawal. After dissolution, Jill contracted on behalf of the partnership to buy a shipment of supplies from Manufacturer who had previously dealt with the partnership. Manufacturer did not know of the dissolution. Jill intended to sell the supplies to new customers that she hoped to solicit on behalf of the partnership. In this case:
   a. Jill was entitled to make the contract on behalf of the partnership.
   b. Jill was not entitled to make the contract on behalf of the partnership.
   c. The partnership is liable on the contract.
   d. b and c.

CASE PROBLEM

Clay and Cora are partners in C&C Partnership. Clay and Cora equally share the profits and losses of the partnership. By mutual agreement, the partnership has been dissolved. The partnership has $70,000 cash. The partnership owes Cora $10,000 for a loan she previously made to the partnership, and it owes $20,000 to Rosco, an outside creditor. Clay contributed $10,000 to the partnership, and Cora contributed $15,000. Under these facts, in what order are the partnership assets distributed?

_____

_____

_____

BUSINESS LAW PARTNER EXERCISE

Directions: Using the Online feature of the Business Law Partner CD-ROM, identify at least four states that have enacted the Revised Uniform Partnership Act.

_____

_____

_____

CHAPTER 33 QUIZ

Section A

DIRECTIONS: Following each question below, indicate your answer by placing a "Y" for "Yes" or an "N" for "No" in the Answers column.

	Answers	For Scoring
1. If the partnership agreement fixes the date the partnership will cease, are the partners prohibited from terminating it at any other time?...	_____	1. _____
2. If a partner wrongfully withdraws, can the other partners continue the business?	_____	2. _____
3. Must a withdrawing partner pay for damages caused to the partnership by withdrawing prior to the date stated in the articles of partnership?................................	_____	3. _____
4. In case a partner makes a voluntary sale of an interest in the firm, does the buyer become a partner by the purchase?...	_____	4. _____
5. Is the partnership dissolved if one partner's interest is involuntarily sold to pay the partner's debts?..	_____	5. _____
6. Must an incapacity normally be permanent in order to warrant a court decree of dissolution of a partnership?...	_____	6. _____
7. May the partners dissolve a partnership by mutual agreement at any time?...................	_____	7. _____
8. Is it sufficient to give notice of dissolution to existing customers and creditors by publication?...	_____	8. _____
9. May the representative of a deceased partner act as a partner while protecting the interests of heirs?...	_____	9. _____
10. Does dissolution relieve the partners of their duties to each other?...............................	_____	10. _____

Score _____

Section B

DIRECTIONS: In the Answers space in Column II, select the appropriate letter from Column I that indicates the nature of the dissolution which is caused in each situation.

Column I	Column II	Answers	For Scoring
Dissolution by:	1. Definite date fixed in original agreement	_____	1. _____
a. Acts of parties	2. Illegality of the business	_____	2. _____
b. Court decree	3. Futility of the business..	_____	3. _____
c. Operation of law	4. Withdrawal of a partner..	_____	4. _____
	5. Bankruptcy of a partner	_____	5. _____
	6. Achieving the purpose of the partnership......................	_____	6. _____
	7. One partner persistently violates the partnership agreement...	_____	7. _____
	8. Expulsion of a member..	_____	8. _____
	9. Insanity of a member	_____	9. _____
	10. Death of a partner	_____	10. _____

Score _____

Section C

DIRECTIONS: Complete each of the following statements by writing the missing word or words in the Answers column.

	Answers	For Scoring
1. The change in the relation of the partners caused by any partner ceasing to be associated in carrying on the business is called	_____	1. _____
2. The process of taking care of outstanding obligations and distributing remaining assets of a partnership is ??? the partnership.................................	_____	2. _____
3. If, at the time a partnership is formed, the partners fix a time when the relation will cease, the partnership will dissolve by	_____	3. _____
4. When the act of the parties causes dissolution of a partnership, third parties that have done business with the firm must be given	_____	4. _____
5. When a partner makes a voluntary sale of an interest or loses the interest through an involuntary sale to satisfy personal creditors, the partnership is dissolved by..	_____	5. _____
6. When a partner is permanently unable to perform duties agreed upon in the partnership agreement because of illness or injury, the other members may request a court to issue a decree of dissolution because of the partner's ???.	_____	6. _____
7. If a member of the partnership behaves in a way that is harmful to the continuation of the business, a dissolution may be sought on the grounds of	_____	7. _____
8. When it is clear that the objective of a partnership cannot be achieved, the court may, upon proper request, order a dissolution because of	_____	8. _____

Score _____

Section D

DIRECTIONS: Following each statement below, indicate your answer by placing a " T " for " True " or an " F " for " False " in the Answers column.

	Answers	For Scoring
1. A partner who rightfully withdraws from a partnership is liable for any loss sustained by the other partners because of the withdrawal..	_____	1. _____
2. In a partnership for a definite term, a partner has the power, but not the right, to withdraw at any time.	_____	2. _____
3. Expulsion of a partner terminates the business unless the partnership agreement provides otherwise.	_____	3. _____
4. One partner may compel the others to assume continued losses after the success of the business becomes highly unlikely...	_____	4. _____
5. A court order is necessary when a partnership is dissolved by operation of law.	_____	5. _____
6. A trustee in bankruptcy has the right to assume control of a debtor partner's share of the partnership business..	_____	6. _____
7. After dissolution, no new contracts (except minor contracts necessary to complete existing contracts) can be made by the partnership.	_____	7. _____
8. If notice of dissolution is not given, every member of the old firm may be held liable for acts of the former partners taken within the scope of the business.	_____	8. _____
9. Temporary incapacity of a partner justifies dissolution of the partnership.....................	_____	9. _____
10. Notice to creditors is always required when a firm is dissolved by operation of law.	_____	10. _____
11. After dissolution and the payment of creditors, each partner is entitled to the return of capital contributed, and then advances are paid.	_____	11. _____
12. Unless there is an agreement to the contrary, losses at termination are shared equally by the partners.	_____	12. _____

Score _____

CHAPTER 34
NATURE OF A CORPORATION

CHAPTER OUTLINE

I.   CLASSIFICATION BY PURPOSE

A. PUBLIC CORPORATIONS

General rules.   ‣ A public corporation is created by a government body to accomplish a government purpose. Public corporations may assess taxes, impose fines, and condemn property. ‣ A quasi-public corporation is similar to a public corporation, but it typically has fewer powers.
Examples.   ‣ Public corporation: a city. ‣ Quasi-public corporation: a school board.

B. PRIVATE CORPORATIONS

Individuals form private corporations for private, nongovernmental purposes. Two important types of private corporations are:

- *Not-for-profit corporations*: ‣ Defined: corporations formed for charitable, educational, religious, or social purposes. ‣ Stock is not issued, and membership is by agreement.

- *Profit corporations*: A profit corporation is a corporation formed by private persons to engage in a business for profit. Types of profit corporations include:

  ‣ *Stock corporation*: corporation in which ownership is represented by shares of stock.
  ‣ *Close (closely held) corporation*: one person or a few people own all shares of stock.
  ‣ *S corporation*: corporation that has elected special tax treatment by which income is not taxed to the corporation, but is taxed as personal income to shareholders. S corporation avoids double taxation that results when corporate profits are taxed to the corporation and are taxed again when distributed to shareholders as dividends.

II.   CLASSIFICATION BY STATE OF INCORPORATION

- *Domestic corporation*: corporation doing business in the state in which it was incorporated.
- *Foreign corporation*: corporation doing business in a state other than the state of incorporation.
- *Alien corporation*: corporation incorporated in a foreign country.

III.   FORMATION OF A CORPORATION

‣ Promoters are persons who initiate formation of a corporation. A corporation may be formed in any state the promoters choose, and it may do business as a foreign corporation in other states. ‣ Minor defects in forming a corporation do not affect its validity. Major defects may cause a state to revoke the corporation's charter, and may cause promoters to be held personally liable as partners.

IV.   LIABILITY ON PROMOTER'S CONTRACTS AND EXPENSES

General rule.   If a promoter makes a contract on behalf of a corporation prior to its incorporation (formation), then the parties' liability for the contract is as follows: (1) *liability of corporation*: corporation is not liable unless the corporation expressly or by implication adopts the contract after incorporation; (2) *liability of promoter*: promoter is personally liable on the contract unless the contract expressly states, or otherwise indicates, that the promoter does not have personal liability.
Study hint.   It is customary (but not required) for a corporation to reimburse a promoter for expenses incurred by the promoter in forming the corporation.

V. ISSUANCE OF STOCK (SUBSCRIPTION TO STOCK)

General rules. ▸ Subscriber: party who offers to buy stock in a proposed corporation. ▸ Stock subscription: an *offer* to buy stock. ▸ Enforceability of subscriptions: In most states, a subscriber can revoke an offer to purchase stock at any time before the corporation has accepted it.

Study hints. ▸ A subscription to buy stock in a corporation that has not been formed cannot be accepted by the corporation until after it is incorporated. ▸ As soon as a corporation accepts a subscription, the subscriber has rights of a shareholder even though a certificate has not been issued.

VI. ARTICLES OF INCORPORATION

▸ Articles of incorporation is a document that states information required by law, and it is filed with a state officer in order to form a corporation. ▸ Once articles have been filed and approved by the state, a certificate of incorporation (charter) is issued and the corporation is formed. ▸ Articles state basic information regarding the corporation, including its name, the names of incorporators (persons who sign and file articles), and the amount and types of stock the corporation may issue.

VII. POWERS OF A CORPORATION

A. EXPRESS POWERS

A corporation may exercise the powers granted by statutes and by the articles of incorporation.

B. INCIDENTAL POWERS (AND OBLIGATIONS)

In general, corporations have the following incidental powers (and obligations):

- *Corporate name*: A name is required. Any name is generally permitted provided: (1) a name cannot be the same as another corporation or business within the state; and (2) many states require a name to contain the words "Corporation" or "Incorporated" (or an abbreviation).

- *Continuous existence*: A corporation continues for the time for which its charter is issued, which may be forever (perpetual succession). Death of a shareholder does not dissolve a corporation.

- *Property rights*: A corporation can generally own, buy, and sell property.

- *Bylaws and regulations*: The board of directors adopts bylaws (rules governing the internal affairs of a corporation). Bylaws cannot conflict with statutes or public policy.

- *Legal actions*: A corporation can sue and be sued in its own name.

- *Corporate seal*: A corporation may adopt a seal. A seal is necessary only if (1) the instrument that is signed would require a seal if signed by an individual or (2) a law otherwise requires a seal.

C. IMPLIED POWERS

A corporation generally has the implied power to do all acts reasonably necessary to carry out the purpose of the corporation. Thus, a corporation may have the power to (1) borrow money, (2) issue, indorse, and accept negotiable instruments, and (3) mortgage property.

VIII. *ULTRA VIRES* CONTRACTS

▸ An *ultra vires* contract is a contract that exceeds the corporation's powers as granted by the corporation's articles or applicable law. ▸ An *ultra vires* contract is binding between the corporation and the other contracting party. ▸ A shareholder may bring an action to prevent a corporation from making an *ultra vires* contract, or to recover damages from directors who authorized the contract. ▸ In some cases, a state may request a court to revoke a corporation's charter if it repeatedly makes *ultra vires* contracts.

REVIEW OF CHAPTER

REVIEW OF TERMS

Select the term that best matches a statement below. Each term is the best match for only one statement.

TERMS

a. Articles of incorporation
b. Bylaws
c. Close (closely held) corporation
d. Incorporator

e. Not-for-profit corporation
f. Profit corporation
g. Promoter

h. Public corporation
i. Stock corporation
j. Subscriber

STATEMENTS

Answer

_____ 1. Person who takes the initial steps to form a corporation.
_____ 2. Private corporation that is formed to carry on a business for profit.
_____ 3. Corporate document that states required information regarding a corporation and that is filed with an appropriate state officer in order to form a corporation.
_____ 4. Corporation that is owned by one person or a few people.
_____ 5. Private corporation, ownership of which is represented by shares of stock.
_____ 6. Corporate document stating rules that govern the internal affairs of a corporation.
_____ 7. Private corporation formed for charitable, educational, religious, or social purposes.
_____ 8. Person who offers to purchase stock of a proposed corporation.
_____ 9. Person who signs and files articles of incorporation.
_____ 10. Corporation formed by a governmental body to carry out a government function.

REVIEW OF CONCEPTS

Directions: Indicate **T** for true and **F** for false in the answer column.

_____ 1. Public corporations may have the power to impose taxes and condemn (take) private property.
_____ 2. A corporation is automatically treated as an S corporation unless the corporation elects otherwise.
_____ 3. The profits and losses of an S corporation are taxed to the shareholders and not to the corporation.
_____ 4. A corporation can transact business only in the state in which it is incorporated (formed).
_____ 5. A state may revoke a corporation's charter if there are major defects in forming the corporation.
_____ 6. Lon was a promoter who helped form Kemp Inc. Lon spent $1,000 in connection with formation of Kemp Inc. In this case, Kemp Inc. is prohibited from reimbursing Lon for his expenditures.
_____ 7. Fonda signed a subscription to buy 500 shares of F&F Inc., a corporation not yet formed. In most states this subscription was a binding contract when Fonda signed and she cannot revoke it.
_____ 8. A subscriber has the rights of a shareholder as soon as a subscription is accepted by the corporation, even if a stock certificate has not been issued yet.
_____ 9. A corporation has only the powers expressly given to it by statute or its articles of incorporation. A corporation does not have any incidental or implied powers.
_____ 10. An *ultra vires* contract is one that exceeds the lawful powers of a corporation.

REVIEW OF CONCEPT APPLICATIONS

Answer

Directions: Indicate your choice in the answer column.

_____ 1. Phyllis and Rod are the only shareholders of P&R Inc., which was incorporated in Iowa. P&R Inc. sells corn (for profit) to wholesalers and to the public in Arizona. P&R Inc. is a:
   a. Domestic corporation with regard to its business in Arizona.
   b. Quasi-public corporation.
   c. Public corporation.
   d. Close corporation.

_____ 2. Sylvia planned to form a corporation to own and operate a food store. Prior to incorporation, Sylvia leased a store, signing the contract in her individual name and on behalf of the corporation to be formed. The corporation has now been incorporated. In most states:
   a. The corporation is liable on the contract even if it does not adopt the contract.
   b. The corporation is liable on the contract only if it expressly or by implication adopts the contract.
   c. Sylvia does not have any personal liability on the contract.

_____ 3. Polly wishes to incorporate Polly's Pets Inc. In this case, select the correct answer.
   a. Polly must file articles of incorporation with a state officer to form the corporation.
   b. Polly must file bylaws with a state officer to form the corporation.
   c. Polly must perfectly comply with all requirements to form the corporation. If there are any minor defects in formation, the corporation's charter will be canceled by the state.

_____ 4. Freedom Corp. buys and sells stocks. Freedom's articles prohibit the corporation from buying stock of any company that does business in a country allows racial discrimination. The board of directors of the corporation authorized a purchase of stock that violated this restriction, and the sale has been completed. Under these facts:
   a. The contract is binding on Freedom Corp.
   b. The contract is not binding on Freedom Corp. The corporation can rescind the contract.
   c. Freedom Corp. shareholders can sue the directors for authorizing this _ultra vires_ contract.
   d. a and c.

CASE PROBLEM

Ted and Alice intend to form a corporation. The purpose of the corporation will generally be to acquire, develop, and sell land. Ted and Alice are trying to determine what powers the corporation may have, and what requirements may apply to the corporation. In this case: (1) What express powers will the corporation have? (2) Will the corporation have the power to buy and sell real estate; to mortgage real estate? (3) Must the corporate name indicate that it is a corporation? (4) Can the corporation be formed to have perpetual succession? (5) Must the corporation have a corporate seal?

_____

_____

_____

BUSINESS LAW PARTNER EXERCISE

Directions:

1. Access your Business Law Partner CD-ROM and find the document "Articles of Incorporation."
2. Help Hill complete the above-referenced document using the information provided in the following case study. Furnish any additional information necessary.

Case Study: _Planning is the Best Policy_

Hill, Todd, and Fran are forming a corporation called HT&F, Inc. The corporation will be authorized to sell 100,000 shares of no-par-value common stock. Hill, Todd, and Fran will sign the Articles of Incorporation and they will comprise the initial board of directors. There will be no preemptive rights or restrictions on sales of stock by shareholders. HT&F, Inc. will indemnify the directors against all losses, except those arising from reckless or intentional wrongdoing.

_____

_____

_____

CHAPTER 34 QUIZ

Section A

DIRECTIONS: Complete each of the following statements by writing the missing word or words in the Answers column.

		Answers	For Scoring
1-3.	The three types of powers a corporation has are	_____	**1.** _____
	....	_____	**2.** _____
	....	_____	**3.** _____
4.	A corporation formed to carry out a governmental function, such as a city or a state university, is a(n) <u>???</u> corporation..	_____	**4.** _____
5.	A public body with powers similar to those of a corporation is a(n)...........	_____	**5.** _____
6.	Corporations formed by individuals to perform a nongovernmental undertaking are called <u>???</u> corporations.	_____	**6.** _____
7.	A corporation formed by private individuals to perform a charitable, educational, or social service is a(n) <u>???</u> corporation.	_____	**7.** _____
8.	A(n) <u>???</u> corporation is organized to run a business and earn money.	_____	**8.** _____
9.	Corporations organized for profit with the membership represented by shares of stock are called <u>???</u> corporations...	_____	**9.** _____
10.	A business corporation that has only a few shareholders is called a(n) <u>???</u> corporation.	_____	**10.** _____
11.	To achieve tax savings, a corporation with a small number of shareholders may choose to be a(n) <u>???</u> corporation.................................	_____	**11.** _____
12.	In the state in which a corporation receives its charter, it is called a(n) <u>???</u> corporation.	_____	**12.** _____
13.	In states other than the one in which a corporation received its charter, it is called a(n) <u>???</u> corporation...	_____	**13.** _____
14.	If a corporation is formed in another country, it may be referred to as a(n) <u>???</u> corporation.	_____	**14.** _____
15-16.	The person who initially forms a corporation is called a(n).......................	_____	**15.** _____
	OR a(n)...	_____	**16.** _____
17.	A prospective stockholder who signs an agreement to buy stock in a new corporation that is to be formed is a(n)	_____	**17.** _____
18.	A written contract between the corporation and the state setting forth facts required by law and stating that the corporation has complied with those requirements is the	_____	**18.** _____
19.	Corporate rules that govern the internal operations of a corporation are known as..	_____	**19.** _____
20.	A contract that is beyond the powers of the corporation or is otherwise unauthorized is called a(n)	_____	**20.** _____

Score _____

Section B

DIRECTIONS: Following each statement below, indicate your answer by placing a "T" for "True" or an "F" for "False" in the Answers column.

	Answers	For Scoring
1. A corporation may be used to run any size business.		1. _____
2. Public corporations' powers may be much greater than those of private corporations...		2. _____
3. Nonstock corporations are organized for profit.		3. _____
4. The stockholders of close corporations are typically not active in the management of the corporations' business.		4. _____
5. If there are major defects in the formation of a corporation, the people organizing it will be held liable as partners or joint venturers.		5. _____
6. A corporation is automatically liable for contracts made by the promoters who organized the corporation.		6. _____
7. A corporation is required to pay the expenses that were incurred in its organization.....		7. _____
8. Once a valid subscription agreement is signed, the subscriber has rights in the corporation even if the stock certificates have not been issued.		8. _____
9. The articles of incorporation include the amount and types of stock the corporation has authorization to use.		9. _____
10. A corporation must have a corporate name.		10. _____
11. The death of a major stockholder dissolves a corporation.		11. _____
12. A corporation is required to use a seal in all transactions.		12. _____
13. A corporation generally has the implied power to issue commercial paper.		13. _____
14. As between the parties to an ultra vires contract, the contract is binding.		14. _____
15. The attorney general of a state may obtain a court order revoking the articles of incorporation of a corporation that enters into any ultra vires contract.		15. _____

Score _____

Section C

DIRECTIONS: Indicate whether or not the statements below are correct by marking a "Y" for yes or a "N" for no.

	Answers	For Scoring
1. A shareholder is not liable for business debts beyond the amount of his or her investment.		1. _____
2. Corporations must be organized for the purpose of making a profit.		2. _____
3. Minority shareholders have a legal right to be employed by the corporation		3. _____
4. Each shareholder has an equal voice in managing the corporation.		4. _____
5. A corporation is formed as a result of a contract with the state		5. _____

Score _____

CHAPTER 35
OWNERSHIP OF A CORPORATION

CHAPTER OUTLINE

I. OWNERSHIP

General rules. ▸ Ownership in a stock corporation is represented by shares of stock. ▸ A shareholder may acquire stock by: (1) subscription; (2) gift; or (3) purchase from a shareholder. ▸ A corporation may be validly formed even if some authorized stock has not been issued or sold.

Example. ABC Inc. is authorized to sell 100,000 shares of stock. ABC issued and sold 50,000 shares. If Jerry owns 25,000 shares of ABC stock, then Jerry owns 50 percent of the corporation.

Study hints. ▸ Authorized stock: stock that a corporation may sell. ▸ Outstanding stock: stock that a corporation has issued and that is owned by shareholders. ▸ Capital stock: declared money value for corporation's outstanding stock.

II. STOCK CERTIFICATE

Ownership of stock in a corporation is usually represented by a stock certificate.

III. CLASSES OF STOCK

The classes of stock a corporation may issue is determined by statute and the articles of incorporation. Two important classes of stock are common stock and preferred stock.

A. COMMON STOCK

General rules. ▸ Common stock is the usual type of stock issued by a corporation. ▸ Common stockholders ordinarily vote for the board of directors. ▸ Common stockholders are entitled to dividends when declared by the board, and a share of assets on dissolution of the corporation.

Limitation. Stockholders do not have a right to directly manage a corporation's business.

B. PREFERRED STOCK

- *Preferred as to assets*: Preferred shareholders ordinarily receive their share of the corporation's assets upon dissolution before common shareholders receive theirs.

- *Preferred as to dividends*:

  ▸ *Cumulative preferred stock*: ▸ Dividends for cumulative preferred stock accumulate each year that dividends are not paid. All unpaid dividends must be paid before dividends are paid to common stockholders. ▸ Example: In 2000, Alpha Corp. does not pay dividends. In 2001, Alpha declares a dividend. Alpha must pay holders of its cumulative preferred stock dividends for 2000 and 2001 before it pays dividends to common stockholders. ▸ Preferred stock is presumed to be cumulative unless the stock certificate specifically states otherwise. ▸ Limit: Unpaid dividends do not accumulate in a year that a corporation has a loss unless preferred stock is expressly stated to be cumulative.

  ▸ *Noncumulative preferred stock*: Noncumulative preferred stock is entitled to dividends for only the current year; unpaid dividends for past years do not accumulate (even if the directors do not declare a dividend when there are sufficient funds to pay a dividend).

  ▸ *Participating preferred stock*: ▸ Participating preferred stock shares with common stock in additional dividends that are declared after preferred and common stockholders have each received an equal dividend. ▸ Preferred stock is participating only if this is stated in the articles and on the stock certificate. The extent of participation must be stated in the articles.

  ▸ *Nonparticipating preferred stock*: ▸ Nonparticipating preferred stock is entitled to receive only the dividend stated on the certificate; it is not entitled to share in additional dividends that may be declared. ▸ Preferred stock is presumed to be nonparticipating.

IV.   KINDS OF STOCKS

- *Par-value stock*: ▸ Defined: stock that has an assigned face value. ▸ A corporation must *initially* sell par-value stock for at least the par value. A shareholder can resell par-value stock for any price the shareholder chooses. ▸ Example: Ajax Corp. sells $10 par-value common stock to Terri. Ajax must sell Terri the stock for at least $10 per share. Terri can resell the stock for any price she can get. ▸ Liability: If a buyer pays a corporation less than the par value, the buyer is liable to subsequent corporate creditors for the difference between the price paid and the par value.

- *No-par-value stock*: ▸ Defined: stock that does not have an assigned face value. ▸ No-par-value stock can be sold by a corporation for any price determined by the board of directors.

- *Treasury stock*: ▸ Defined: stock that has been issued and repurchased by a corporation. ▸ A corporation can sell treasury stock for any price determined by the board, regardless of par value. While owned by the corporation, treasury stock is not entitled to dividends and it cannot be voted.

- *Watered stock*: ▸ Defined: stock paid for with property that has an inflated value. ▸ If a corporation is insolvent, a shareholder is liable to corporate creditors for the difference between the actual value of property given for stock and the par value of the stock. ▸ Example: Helen purchased $10,000 of par-value stock from Esprit Inc. Helen paid with a truck that was worth only $4,000. If Esprit Inc. becomes insolvent, its creditors can recover $6,000 from Helen.

V.   TRANSFER OF STOCK

General rules.   ▸ In general, a shareholder transfers stock by indorsing the stock certificate and delivering it to the buyer. The buyer should have the corporation issue a new certificate in his or her name, and register the stock on the corporation's books in the buyer's name. ▸ Rights of unregistered owner: (1) Under the Uniform Stock Transfer Act, an unregistered owner is entitled to distributions that represent a return of capital (amount originally paid for stock). (2) Under common law rules, an unregistered owner is not entitled to dividends that represent profits.

Study hint.   Unregistered owners of stock are not entitled to vote.

VI.   STOCK OPTIONS

General rule.   A stock option is a contract between a corporation and a person that grants the person a right to purchase a stated number of shares for a stated price, within a certain period of time.

Example.   Simmons Inc. granted Charlie an option to buy 100 shares of Simmons' stock at $5 per share until June 1, 2005. Charlie may, but is not obligated to, purchase the shares in accordance with the terms of the option.

Study hint.   Stock options are often used as a form of compensation for officers and employees.

VII.   DIVIDENDS

- *Form of dividends*: ▸ In general, dividends are profits distributed to shareholders. ▸ Dividends may be paid in cash, property, stock of the corporation, or stock of another company.

- *Right to dividends*: ▸ The board of directors has complete discretion to determine (in good faith) whether to declare a dividend on common or preferred stock. ▸ Once a cash dividend is declared, it cannot be rescinded. ▸ Stock dividends can be rescinded before the shares are delivered.

- *Funds available for dividends*: ▸ With one exception, cash dividends can be declared only to the extent the corporation has (1) retained earnings (undistributed profits) or (2) donated or paid-in surplus (amount paid for stock in excess of the stock's par value). ▸ Stock dividends paid in the stock of the corporation can be paid to the extent the corporation has retained earnings or surplus.

VIII. LAWS REGULATING STOCK SALES

A. BLUE-SKY LAWS

▸ Every state has "blue-sky laws" that regulate intrastate (not interstate) sales of securities. ▸ Common provisions: (1) criminal penalties; (2) licensing of dealers; (3) registration of stocks.

B. SECURITIES ACT, 1933 (REGULATION OF INITIAL SALE OF SECURITIES)

- *Scope of law*: The Securities Act of 1933 applies to any offering to sell a new issue of securities to the public in interstate commerce.

- *Exempt transactions*: Requirements of the Securities Act of 1933 do not apply to: (1) intrastate sales of securities; (2) most sales of securities for less than $5 million; or (3) resales of securities after their initial issuance by a corporation.

- *General requirements*: A company selling its securities must: (1) file a registration statement with the SEC; and (2) provide a prospectus to each buyer. ▸ A prospectus must state certain detailed information regarding the issuing company and the securities being sold.

- *Liability for violations*: ▸ If a registration statement or prospectus contains false statements or fails to state important facts, then: (1) the SEC will not permit the securities to be sold; (2) if the securities have already been sold, a buyer may rescind the contract and sue the company, or any officer or director who signed the registration statement, for damages; and (3) officers of the company offering the securities may be subject to criminal penalties.

C. SECURITIES EXCHANGE ACT, 1934 (REGULATION OF RESALE OF SECURITIES)

- *Scope of law*: This Act primarily regulates the resale of securities in interstate commerce.

- *Registration*: ▸ Brokers, dealers, and exchanges dealing in securities in interstate commerce or on an exchange must register with the SEC. ▸ Regulated companies must file periodic statements with the SEC, disclosing financial and other corporate information.

- *Antifraud provisions*: ▸ It is illegal for a party, including any broker, dealer, or exchange, to use the mail, interstate commerce, or an exchange to make any untrue statement of material fact or to otherwise defraud a person in connection with the purchase or sale of any security. ▸ These provisions apply to both sellers and buyers of securities.

- *Disclosure by insiders*: This Act requires that insiders (officers, directors, and owners of more than 10 percent of any class of security in a company): (1) file statements making certain disclosures; and (2) pay to the corporation any profits made by buying and selling the company's securities within a six-month period. ▸ The corporation (or a shareholder suing on behalf of the corporation) may sue insiders to recover these profits.

D. SECURITIES PROTECTION ACT OF 1970

This Act requires brokers, dealers, and members of securities exchanges to belong to the Securities Investors Protection Corporation (SIPC), and to contribute to a fund administered by the SIPC. The fund is used to pay certain customer claims that are made against SIPC members.

REVIEW OF CHAPTER

REVIEW OF TERMS

Select the term that best matches a statement below. Each term is the best match for only one statement.

TERMS

a. Blue-sky laws
b. Common stock
c. Cumulative preferred stock
d. Dividends
e. Insider

f. Noncumulative preferred stock
g. Nonparticipating preferred stock
h. No-par-value stock
i. Participating preferred stock
j. Par-value stock

k. Preferred stock
l. Prospectus
m. Stock option
n. Treasury stock
o. Watered stock

STATEMENTS

Answer

_____ 1.   Preferred stock for which unpaid, past dividends accumulate.

_____ 2.   Profits of a corporation that are distributed to shareholders.

_____ 3.   Class of stock that generally has voting rights, but no preferences to dividends.

_____ 4.   Stock that does not have an assigned face value.

_____ 5.   Document required by the Securities Act of 1933 to be given to purchasers of securities.

_____ 6.   Class of stock that typically is nonvoting, but generally has a preference to dividends or to assets upon dissolution of a corporation.

_____ 7.   Stock that has an assigned face value.

_____ 8.   Preferred stock that shares with common stock in additional dividends that are declared.

_____ 9.   Agreement between a corporation and an individual that grants the individual the right to purchase a certain number of shares at a stated price.

_____ 10.   State laws that regulate the intrastate sale of securities.

_____ 11.   Officer, director, or owner of 10 percent or more of a class of securities of a company.

_____ 12.   Preferred stock that has a right to receive a stated dividend, but does not have a right to share with common stock in additional dividends that may be declared.

_____ 13.   Stock that is paid for with property that has an inflated value.

_____ 14.   Preferred stock for which unpaid, past dividends do not accumulate.

_____ 15.   Corporation's stock that has been issued and repurchased by the corporation.

REVIEW OF CONCEPTS

Directions: Indicate **T** for true and **F** for false in the answer column.

_____ 1.   Ownership in a corporation is represented by bonds and promissory notes.

_____ 2.   A corporation can pay cash dividends whenever it chooses to do so. A corporation is not required to have certain types of funds available in order to pay cash dividends.

_____ 3.   Dividends can be paid only with cash or with the corporation's own stock. Dividends cannot be paid with property or stock of another corporation.

_____ 4.   Preferred stockholders generally have a preference to dividends, but do not have a right to vote for the board of directors.

_____ 5. If preferred stock has a preference as to corporate assets upon dissolution, this means that the preferred stockholders have a right to receive all assets that remain after creditors are paid.

_____ 6. Preferred stock is presumed to be nonparticipating unless it is expressly stated to be participating.

_____ 7. Karl owned 6 percent, participating preferred stock in Cap Co. In 2000, Karl was paid a 6 percent dividend and common stockholders were paid an equal dividend. Later in 2000, the board declared an additional dividend. Karl was entitled to share in this additional dividend.

_____ 8. The par value for stock is typically printed on the face of the stock certificate.

_____ 9. In general, it is illegal for a corporation to issue shares of stock without a par value.

_____ 10. A buyer of stock does not have the right to vote the stock until the buyer's ownership has been registered with the corporation.

_____ 11. State blue-sky laws generally regulate both the intrastate and interstate sale of securities.

_____ 12. Every sale of securities that is made in interstate commerce, regardless of the amount of securities issued, must satisfy all requirements of the Securities Act of 1933.

_____ 13. In some cases, a corporate officer who violates the Securities Act of 1933 may be subject to both civil liability for damages and criminal prosecution.

_____ 14. The Securities Exchange Act generally regulates the initial sale of securities by a company.

_____ 15. The SIPC administers a fund that pays certain customer claims against stockbrokers and dealers who are members of the SIPC.

REVIEW OF CONCEPT APPLICATIONS

Answer

Directions: Indicate your choice in the answer column.

_____ 1. Milco Corp. has retained earnings of $1 million. On June 1, the board of directors declared a $500,000 dividend. The dividend has not been paid. After hearing several objections to this dividend, the board of directors is now reviewing the legality and desirability of the dividend. Under these facts, the board of directors should determine that:
   a. The dividend is illegal. Only shareholders can declare dividends.
   b. The dividend is illegal. The board of directors was legally required to declare a dividend for the full amount of the corporation's retained earnings.
   c. The dividend is legal, and the board of directors cannot rescind the dividend.
   d. The dividend is legal, but the board of directors can rescind the dividend.

_____ 2. XYZ Inc. has common stock and cumulative preferred stock. In 2001, the board of directors of XYZ did not declare a dividend even though it made a profit and had retained earnings sufficient to pay a dividend. In 2002, the directors intend to declare a dividend. Under these facts:
   a. Preferred stock must be paid a dividend for 2001 before common stock is paid a dividend.
   b. Preferred stock must be paid a dividend for 2002 before common stock is paid a dividend.
   c. Common stock must be paid a dividend before preferred stock is paid any dividends.
   d. a and b.

_____ 3. Necco Inc. has one class of stock, $10 par-value common stock. Necco sold 2,000 shares of stock to Alice. Later, Alice sold 1,000 shares to Jeff. Alice sold the other 1,000 shares back to Necco, and Necco resold these shares to Larry. Under these facts, which answer is correct?
   a. Necco was legally obligated to sell the 2,000 shares to Alice for at least $20,000.
   b. Alice was legally obligated to sell the 1,000 shares to Jeff for at least $10,000.
   c. Necco was legally obligated to sell the 1,000 shares to Larry for at least $10,000.
   d. All of the above are correct.

_____ 4. Benito is a shareholder in Benco Inc. Benito purchased 5,000 shares of $10 par-value common stock from the corporation. Benito paid for the stock with real estate that was clearly worth only $20,000. Later, the corporation became insolvent and it failed to repay a $100,000 loan to Creditor. Under these facts, Benito may be personally liable to Creditor for:

      a. $0.

      b. $30,000.

      c. $50,000.

      d. $100,000.

_____ 5. R&V Corp. is planning to issue and sell 1 million shares of common stock. The stock will be sold for a total price of $50 million. The stock will be offered to the public in every state. Under these facts, what must R&V do to comply with the Securities Act of 1933?

      a. R&V is not required to comply with this Act. R&V must only comply with state blue-sky laws.

      b. R&V is only required to file a registration statement with the SEC.

      c. R&V is only required to provide a prospectus to purchasers of the stock.

      d. R&V must file a registration statement with the SEC and provide a prospectus to purchasers of the stock.

CASE PROBLEM

Nassau Inc. owns several gold mines. Nassau is a regulated, publicly-held company that is subject to all requirements of the Securities Exchange Act of 1934. Bonnie owns 25 percent of the common stock of Nassau, and Dick is a director of Nassau. Discuss whether any of the actions below this Act or related SEC rules.

1. Nassau refuses to disclose any information to the SEC regarding its organization or finances.
2. In 2001, Bonnie bought and sold Nassau stock within a six-month period, earning a $10,000 profit.
3. In 2002, Nassau engineers made a secret discovery of a massive new gold deposit. After this discovery, Dick bought shares of Nassau stock from Buyer. Dick misrepresented to Buyer that Nassau had not discovered any new gold deposits. Buyer did not know that this was untrue.

_____

_____

_____

BUSINESS LAW PARTNER EXERCISE

Directions: Using the Online feature of the Business Law Partner CD-ROM, locate the federal law entitled the National Securities Markets Improvement Act ("NSMIA"). Then answer the questions below.

Case Study: *Blue-Sky Laws Cut Down to Size*

Precious Metals, Inc. (PMI) is a publicly-held corporation and its stock is traded on NASDAQ, a national stock exchange. The PMI board of directors has authorized the public offering of 1 million shares of the corporation's common stock for an aggregate price of $100 million. The PMI board has asked you the following questions:

1. Is this stock offering subject to the registration and prospectus requirements of the Securities Act of 1933?
2. Does the NSMIA exempt this stock offering from having to comply with state blue-sky laws?

_____

_____

_____

CHAPTER 35 QUIZ

Section A

DIRECTIONS: Complete each of the following statements by writing the missing word or words in the Answers column.

	Answers	For Scoring
1. Capital stock is divided into units called..	_____	1. _____
2. The owners of a corporation are known as	_____	2. _____
3. A corporation may not pay a stock dividend in its own stock if there is no ...	_____	3. _____
4. The amount of ownership, or the number of shares owned, is evidenced by a(n)...	_____	4. _____
5. Stock that entitles its owner to vote is ??? stock.	_____	5. _____
6. Stock that gives shareholders a preference to the corporation's assets in case of dissolution is called ??? stock.	_____	6. _____
7. Stock on which dividends must be paid for all years before dividends are paid to the holders of common stock is called ??? stock.	_____	7. _____
8. Stock that has the right to receive only current dividends before dividends are paid to common stockholders is	_____	8. _____
9. Preferred stock, the holders of which may share in profits that exceed a fixed rate, is called ??? preferred stock.	_____	9. _____
10. Preferred stock on which the maximum dividend is a stated percentage is	_____	10. _____
11. Stock that has an assigned face value is ??? stock.	_____	11. _____
12. Stock to which no face value has been assigned is ??? stock.........	_____	12. _____
13. If a corporation purchases stock that it has sold, the stock is referred to as ??? stock.	_____	13. _____
14. When stock is issued as fully paid up but the price is paid with property of inflated values, it is said to be ??? stock.	_____	14. _____
15. A contract entered into by the board of directors giving an individual a right, for a stated period, to purchase a certain number of shares of stock in the corporation at a stated price is called a(n)	_____	15. _____
16. Whether or not to declare dividends is left to the discretion of the................	_____	16. _____
17. State laws that regulate the sale of securities and prevent fraud in the sale of worthless stocks and bonds are called ??? laws............................	_____	17. _____
18. A document that gives specified information about a corporation is a(n)	_____	18. _____
19. An officer, director, or owner of more than 10 percent of a corporation's stock is a(n)...	_____	19. _____
20. A corporation set up to pay claims of customers of stockbrokers in severe financial difficulty is the..	_____	20. _____

Score _____

Section B

DIRECTIONS: Following each statement below, indicate your answer by placing a "T" for "True" or an "F" for "False" in the Answers column.

	Answers	For Scoring
1. The capital stock of a corporation is the declared money value of its outstanding stock.		1. _____
2. The amount of capital stock authorized in the charter cannot be altered without the consent of the state and the stockholders.		2. _____
3. Shares of stock may only be obtained by purchasing them from the corporation.		3. _____
4. Stock dividends may be in the corporation's own stock or another corporation's stock.		4. _____
5. Unlike a declared cash dividend, a declared stock dividend may later be rescinded by the directors.		5. _____
6. Minority stockholders cannot get a court to require a corporation to declare a dividend out of surplus.		6. _____
7. A stock certificate merely represents the fractional interest in a corporation that is owned by a shareholder.		7. _____
8. There are only two classes of stock.		8. _____
9. Common stockholders elect directors, who in turn hire managers.		9. _____
10. A stockholder has a right to be employed by the corporation to help run it.		10. _____
11. The most frequent stock preference relates both to dividends and assets.		11. _____
12. Preferred stockholders usually give up the right to receive a share of corporate assets and the right to stock options.		12. _____
13. The stock certificate establishes the rights of preferred shareholders.		13. _____
14. Unless specifically stated to be cumulative, preferred stock does not cumulate in the years when the corporation operates at a loss.		14. _____
15. Par-value stock must be issued for property at least equal in value to its par value.		15. _____
16. Common stock may be either par-value or no-par-value.		16. _____
17. Dividends are paid on treasury stock.		17. _____
18. The purchasers of par-value stock sold by the corporation at a discount are liable to subsequent creditors for the amount of the discount.		18. _____
19. Most state statutes prohibit the watering of stock by corporations.		19. _____
20. Individuals to whom stock is transferred are entitled to the rights and privileges of a stockholder from the time the previous owner signs and delivers the certificate.		20. _____
21. If stock options are made available to all employees of a corporation, the option price is often less than the fair market value for such stock.		21. _____
22. An issuance of securities in excess of $5 million must be registered with the Securities Investor Protection Corporation.		22. _____
23. An investor who purchases newly issued stock in a corporation that has issued an incorrect registration statement may sue anyone who signed the statement.		23. _____
24. An insider is free to purchase and sell stock in the corporation without restriction or penalty.		24. _____
25. All registered brokers and dealers must contribute to a fund to pay claims of customers.		25. _____

Score _____

CHAPTER 36
MANAGEMENT AND DISSOLUTION OF A CORPORATION
CHAPTER OUTLINE

I.   INTRODUCTION

The business of a corporation is managed by a board of directors. Shareholders exercise indirect control through their power to elect the board. Day-to-day management is carried out by officers.

II.   STOCKHOLDERS' MEETINGS

‣ In general, shareholder action is effective only if taken at a valid meeting. ‣ Regular meetings are held at the time and place stated in the articles or bylaws; notice of the meeting is not required. ‣ Special meetings may be called by directors or, in some cases, by other parties. Shareholders must be given notice of the meeting, and the notice must state the proposed business of the meeting.

A. QUORUM

A valid shareholder meeting requires the presence of a quorum (number of shares required to be represented at a meeting in order for shareholders to legally act). Statutes or articles generally require that holders of a majority of the outstanding stock must be represented to have a quorum.

B. VOTING

- *Who may vote*: ‣ Persons who are registered in the corporate records as the owners of common stock are entitled to vote. ‣ A buyer of stock cannot vote until his or her ownership is registered in the corporate records. ‣ A subscriber cannot vote until the stock is paid for.

- *Matters entitled to vote upon*: ‣ Election of board of directors. ‣ Extraordinary matters that require shareholder approval (e.g., changing the corporation's capital; mergers or consolidations; sale of all corporate assets; dissolution; changing the number of directors).

- *Normal voting*: ‣ Common stockholders normally get one vote per share on each matter voted upon. ‣ Unless otherwise required by statute or the articles of incorporation, an affirmative vote of a majority of shares present at a meeting can authorize a matter. ‣ Under this type of voting, an owner of 51 percent or more of the voting stock can elect the entire board of directors.

- *Cumulative voting*: ‣ In order to allow minority shareholders some voice on the board of directors, cumulative voting for the directors may be authorized or required. ‣ Cumulative voting: a shareholder has a number of votes equal to the number of shares owned multiplied by the number of directors being elected. A shareholder can cast all votes for one candidate, or the shareholder can allocate the votes among several candidates.

- *Voting trusts*: ‣ A voting trust is an agreement by two or more shareholders to transfer stock to a trustee who votes the stock. ‣ State laws may limit the permitted term for voting trusts.

- *Absentee voting (voting by proxy)*: ‣ A proxy is a written authorization permitting another person to vote one's stock. ‣ A shareholder can generally give a proxy to anyone. ‣ In some states proxies are valid for only a limited time. ‣ A proxy can be revoked at any time.

C. PROXY WARS

A proxy war is an attempt by parties to obtain a right to vote a majority of the outstanding stock.

III. RIGHTS OF STOCKHOLDERS

In addition to the rights to vote and receive dividends, shareholders have the following rights:

- **Transfer of shares**: Shareholders can ordinarily sell and transfer shares to whomever they wish.

- **Preemptive rights**: ‣ If a corporation increases its stock (which requires shareholder approval), existing shareholders have a right to buy a proportionate share of this new stock when it is offered for sale. ‣ Example: Liz owns 20 percent of the common stock of XYZ Co. XYZ authorizes the sale of 10,000 new shares of common stock. Liz has a right to buy 2,000 shares of this stock.

- **Inspection of books**: ‣ A shareholder may inspect corporate books if it is done for a proper purpose. ‣ The right to inspect is not absolute; inspection for improper purposes is not permitted.

- **Distributions on dissolution**: ‣ After a corporation is dissolved, shareholders are entitled to receive a pro rata share of corporate assets that remain after payment of creditors. ‣ Common stockholders' rights to distributions may be subject to preferences of preferred shareholders.

IV. DIRECTORS

- **Qualifications**: In most states, a board of directors is required to have at least three directors. Otherwise, the number and qualifications of directors is determined by the articles or bylaws.

- **Powers**: ‣ The board of directors has the power to manage the corporation, and to do anything reasonably necessary to carry out the purpose of the corporation. Among other things, the board may (1) elect officers, (2) appoint agents, and (3) appoint two or more directors to act for the board. ‣ The board of directors cannot do anything prohibited by statute or the articles, nor can it authorize an extraordinary matter that requires shareholder approval.

- **Duties**: ‣ Directors must (1) establish corporate policy, (2) appoint officers to carry out policies, and (3) supervise officers. ‣ Directors may delegate routine duties, but they cannot delegate responsibility for major matters. Directors must vote in person (i.e., they cannot vote by proxy).

- **Liabilities**: ‣ A director is personally liable to a corporation for damages resulting from (1) the director's negligence or bad faith, or (2) authorization of an illegal or *ultra vires* act. ‣ Negligence test: Did the director exercise the care that a reasonably prudent person would have exercised in that situation? ‣ Bad faith test: Did the director act for personal reasons that conflicted with the interests of the corporation? ‣ Directors are not liable for losses if they act reasonably, with diligence, and in good faith. ‣ Directors who attend a meeting are deemed to have voted in favor of all matters unless they do an act in opposition (e.g., cast a negative vote).

V. OFFICERS

‣ A corporation typically has a president, at least one vice-president, a secretary, and a treasurer. ‣ The officers of a corporation are selected and removed by the board of directors. Officers are frequently authorized by the board to carry out its policies. Because officers are agents of the corporation, their authority is largely determined by agency law.

VI. CORPORATE COMBINATIONS

‣ Consolidation: two corporations combine; the combining corporations terminate, and a new corporation is created. ‣ Merger: two corporations combine; one corporation terminates, and the other corporation continues to exist. ‣ Tender offer: offer to buy stock in a target company at a stated price. Tender offers are an approach that is used to take over another company.

VII. DISSOLUTION

‣ A corporation may voluntarily dissolve by paying its debts, distributing its assets, and then surrendering its charter. ‣ A state may request a dissolution for several reasons, including violation of state law, fraud in obtaining the charter, and (in some states) failure to pay certain taxes.

REVIEW OF CHAPTER

REVIEW OF TERMS

Select the term that best matches a statement below. Each term is the best match for only one statement.

TERMS

a. Consolidation
b. Cumulative voting
c. Merger

d. Preemptive right
e. Proxy
f. Proxy war

g. Quorum
h. Tender offer
i. Voting trust

STATEMENTS

Answer

_____ 1. Shareholder's right to buy a proportionate share of newly authorized stock that is offered for sale by a corporation.

_____ 2. Agreement by which shareholders transfer stock to a trustee who votes the stock on behalf of the shareholders.

_____ 3. Corporate combination whereby two corporations combine, terminating the separate existence of the combining corporations, and creating a new corporation.

_____ 4. Attempt by competing parties to obtain the right to vote a majority of the stock of a corporation.

_____ 5. Minimum shares required to be represented at a shareholder meeting in order to have a valid meeting.

_____ 6. Shareholder's written authorization of another person to vote the shareholder's stock.

_____ 7. Offer made to shareholders of a corporation to purchase their shares for a stated price.

_____ 8. Type of voting for a board of directors that may enable minority shareholders to elect a director.

_____ 9. Corporate combination whereby two corporations combine and only one corporation continues to exist.

REVIEW OF CONCEPTS

Directions: Indicate **T** for true and **F** for false in the answer column.

_____ 1. ABC Inc. has 100,000 shares of outstanding common stock. Most modern statutes or articles would require 50,001 or more shares to be present to have a quorum, and to hold a valid meeting.

_____ 2. To have a valid special meeting of shareholders, the shareholders must be given notice of the meeting, and the notice must state the proposed business of the meeting.

_____ 3. A shareholder cannot authorize another person to vote his or her shares of stock.

_____ 4. Cumulative voting enables a minority shareholder to elect a majority of the board of directors.

_____ 5. The board of directors of a corporation is generally elected by the common stockholders.

_____ 6. State laws typically require a board of directors to have at least five directors.

_____ 7. The board of directors can delegate total control of a corporation to a corporate officer.

_____ 8. A director is personally liable to a corporation whenever it suffers a loss due to any action by the director.

_____ 9. The board of directors selects the officers of a corporation.

_____ 10. Officers are agents of a corporation, and their authority is largely governed by agency law.

_____ 11. A state does not have the power to seek the dissolution of a corporation.

REVIEW OF CONCEPT APPLICATIONS

Answer

Directions: Indicate your choice in the answer column.

_____ 1. Hee Haw Inc. owns and operates a fun house. Which transaction can be authorized by the Hee Haw Inc. board of directors without obtaining shareholder approval?
   a. Consolidation of Hee Haw Inc. with Fun Inc., a separate corporation.
   b. Dissolution of Hee Haw Inc.
   c. Remodeling of the fun house.
   d. The board cannot authorize any of the foregoing transactions without shareholder approval.

_____ 2. Nanco Inc. has three shareholders, Amy, Brason, and Count. Each shareholder owns 10,000 shares of common stock. The articles grant preemptive rights. Under these facts:
   a. Amy cannot sell her stock to a third party without first offering it to Brason and Count.
   b. If Nanco Inc. is authorized to sell 15,000 new shares of common stock, then Amy, Brason, and Count each have the right to buy 5,000 shares of this stock when it is offered for sale.
   c. Count cannot inspect the corporate records in order to determine the value of his stock or for any other purpose. Shareholders have no right to inspect corporate records.

_____ 3. Sue was a director of Money Corp., a commercial lender. Sue voted in favor of three actions that each caused a loss to the corporation. In which situation is Sue liable to the corporation?
   a. Sue voted in favor of a loan to Lynx Co. Lynx Co. was investigated and found to be solvent, and the loan was secured by collateral. Lynx Co. failed to pay due to a recession.
   b. Sue voted in favor of a transaction that involved the illegal laundering of money belonging to organized crime figures. This transaction was a crime.
   c. Sue voted in favor of delegating normal advertising decisions to the company's president.
   d. Sue is liable in all of the situations above.

_____ 4. The shareholders of Acme Corp. and Belco Corp. have voted in favor of combining their corporations. Pursuant to this combination, Acme Corp. and Belco Corp. will be terminated, and a new corporation, Cactus Inc., will be created. This combination is a:
   a. Consolidation.
   b. Merger.
   c. Tender offer.

CASE PROBLEM

Earl and Antonio are the sole shareholders of Antlers Inc. Earl owns 60,000 shares of common stock, and Antonio owns 40,000 shares of common stock. The articles require cumulative voting for board of director elections. At its annual meeting, the shareholders are to: (1) elect a board composed of three directors; and (2) approve or disapprove an extraordinary bonus plan for the board of directors. Earl and Antonio each have three candidates that they would like to elect to the board. Both shareholders plan to attend the meeting. Under these facts: (1) How many directors can Earl and Antonio elect? (2) If Earl votes in favor of the bonus plan and Antonio votes against it, will the plan be approved?

BUSINESS LAW PARTNER EXERCISE

Directions:

1. Access your Business Law Partner CD-ROM and find the document entitled "Corporate Proxy."
2. Help Felipe complete the above-referenced document using the information provided in the following case study. Provide any additional information that is necessary to complete the document, making certain that any other terms reasonably protect Felipe's interests.

Case Study: *Every Vote Counts*

Felipe owns 500,000 shares of the common stock of Acme Corporation. The annual meeting of the shareholders is being held at 10:00 a.m. on June 1, 2000. The meeting is taking place at 110 Miami Street, Fourport, State of *X*. Felipe cannot attend the meeting, but he wants his brother, Carlos, to attend and vote his shares. Carlos has agreed to attend the shareholders meeting. Felipe wants Carlos to be able to use his discretion in deciding how to vote the shares. Felipe has asked you to help him prepare an appropriate proxy.

CHAPTER 36 QUIZ

Section A

DIRECTIONS: Complete each of the following statements by writing the missing word or words in the Answers column.

	Answers	For Scoring
1. In order to be valid, a stockholders' meeting requires the presence of a(n)....	_____	1. _____
2. Some states provide in elections of the board of directions, a stockholder's vote may equal the number of shares owned multiplied by the number of directors to be elected. This is called ??? voting.	_____	2. _____
3. One who is authorized to vote for another at a stockholders' meeting is a(n)	_____	3. _____
4. A stockholder's right to buy the same percentage of a new stock offering as is currently owned is called a(n)	_____	4. _____
5. A combination of two corporations whereby one corporation survives and the other ceases to exist is a(n)	_____	5. _____

Score _____

Section B

DIRECTIONS: In the space at the right, place the letter of the group of words that most correctly completes the statement.

	Answers	For Scoring
1. Stockholders may exercise control over their investment by a. discharging the directors b. electing a new board of directors c. taking over the management themselves	_____	1. _____
2. A stockholders' meeting a. requires a quorum in order to be valid b. may be called by a stockholder c. never requires any notice to stockholders	_____	2. _____
3. Those stockholders who may vote at stockholders' meetings include a. all subscribers b. anyone who has purchased stock c. owners of voting stock as shown on the corporate record books	_____	3. _____
4. A new investor who purchases common stock has a right to vote a. if the charter is silent on voting rights b. as soon as stock has been subscribed c. as soon as the certificate is recorded on the corporate books	_____	4. _____
5. A stockholder may subscribe for new stock to be issued by the corporation in order to a. give more power in management b. allow participation in dividends c. protect proportionate interest in accumulated surplus	_____	5. _____
6. Directors may be held personally liable for a. unpaid state and local taxes b. losses on loans of corporate funds to officers or directors c. unsecured debts	_____	6. _____

7. A stockholder's execution of a proxy
a. authorizes another to vote for the stockholder
b. is irrevocable
c. prevents the stockholder from attending the stockholders' meeting.............................. _____   **7.** _____

8. A corporation's dissolution is complete
a. when it distributes any remaining assets to the stockholders
b. when it surrenders its articles of incorporation
c. when it pays all its debts .... _____   **8.** _____

9. The officers a corporation must have are
a. specified in the bylaws and state statutes
b. specified by the chairman of the board of directors
c. president, vice-president, secretary, and treasurer .... _____   **9.** _____

10. When a corporate takeover is attempted
a. the acquiring corporation must first notify the board of directors of the
     target corporation before making a tender offer to its shareholders
b. a formal tender offer must be made
c. the price of the stock of the target company normally rises.. _____   **10.** _____

Score _____

Section C

DIRECTIONS: Following each statement below, indicate your answer by placing a "T" for "True" or an "F" for "False" in the Answers column.

	Answers	For Scoring
1. Corporations can conduct business transactions only through actual persons acting as agents.	_____	**1.** _____
2. Directors generally act as agents for a corporation	_____	**2.** _____
3. The board of directors appoints the agents and subagents of the corporation.	_____	**3.** _____
4. A corporation must have one stockholders' meeting every year.	_____	**4.** _____
5. Regular stockholders' meetings are held at the place and time specified on the stock.	_____	**5.** _____
6. The majority of the outstanding stock must be represented in order to constitute a quorum at the stockholders' meetings.	_____	**6.** _____
7. The only matter upon which stockholders may vote is the annual election of directors.	_____	**7.** _____
8. A corporation may have both voting and nonvoting common stock.	_____	**8.** _____
9. Normally, each stockholder has one vote for each share of common stock owned.	_____	**9.** _____
10. Cumulative voting sometimes enables minority stockholders to gain representation on the board of directors.	_____	**10.** _____
11. A voting trust is primarily a device to give minority stockholders a voice on the board of directors.	_____	**11.** _____
12. State laws encourage the use of voting trusts.	_____	**12.** _____
13. It is unlawful for the management of a corporation to solicit proxies for candidates selected by the board of directors.	_____	**13.** _____
14. Proxy wars are a common occurrence.	_____	**14.** _____
15. Each stockholder has the right to sell and transfer stock.	_____	**15.** _____
16. In the absence of a statute to the contrary, a stockholder has the right to inspect the corporation books.	_____	**16.** _____
17. Directors may vote by proxy.	_____	**17.** _____
18. Directors are insurers of the success of the business.	_____	**18.** _____
19. Dissolution of a corporation may be voluntary or involuntary.	_____	**19.** _____
20. Upon dissolution of a corporation, if there are not enough assets to pay the creditors, the stockholders are personally liable for any unpaid corporate obligations	_____	**20.** _____

Score _____

CHAPTER 37
PRINCIPLES OF INSURANCE

CHAPTER OUTLINE

I.   INTRODUCTION

General rule.   Insurance is a contract whereby a party transfers a risk of financial loss to an insurance company, the risk bearer. An individual pays a certain sum of money to the insurance company in return for the company's agreement to assume a specified risk and to pay an agreed-upon amount if a loss occurs.

Study hints.   ▸ The insurance contract specifies the risks that are insured against. The name of the policy does not determine the policy coverage. ▸ The insured must not increase risks.

II.   TERMS USED IN INSURANCE

- *Insurer (underwriter)*: company agreeing to pay a person for a specified loss.
- *Insured (policyholder)*: person who is protected against a specified loss by an insurance policy.
- *Beneficiary*: person who receives proceeds of life insurance.
- *Policy*: written contract of insurance.
- *Face*: maximum amount that an insurer agrees to pay for a specified loss.
- *Premium*: consideration paid by an insured to an insurer for a policy.
- *Risk (peril)*: danger or type of loss that is covered by a policy (e.g., property damage to a car).
- *Hazards*: types of risks or perils, e.g., fires; floods; earthquakes.
- *Rider*: addition that modifies, extends, or limits an insurance contract.

III. TYPES OF INSURANCE COMPANIES

- *Stock companies*: ▸ A stock insurance company is a corporation owned by shareholders who elect directors to manage the business. ▸ Shareholders receive profits (dividends), and shareholders do not have personal liability for losses. ▸ A corporation must set aside in a reserve account part of the capital paid for stock and part of the premiums received.

- *Mutual companies*: ▸ A mutual insurance company is a corporation owned by members who are also the policyholders of the company. ▸ A member shares in profits of the company. A member has personal liability for losses of the company if: (1) the company is an assessment mutual insurance company; and (2) the policy specifically requires a member to share losses.

IV. WHO MAY BE INSURED

General rules.   ▸ A policyholder must: (1) have an insurable interest in the insured person or property (i.e., the party will sustain a financial or other recognized loss if a risk or peril occurs); and (2) be competent to contract. ▸ In general, a minor can disaffirm an insurance contract. ▸ For life insurance, the insurable interest must exist at the time the policy is taken out. ▸ For property insurance, the insurable interest must exist both when the policy is issued and at the time of loss.

Limitations.   ▸ Some states forbid disaffirmance of insurance contracts by minors. ▸ Some states allow minors to recover only the unearned premium (premium for period following disaffirmance).

Study hints.   ▸ In general, a party has an insurable interest to the extent the party will suffer a financial loss if the insured risk occurs. ▸ If a policyholder does not have an insurable interest, the insurer is not obligated to pay for a loss.

V.   SOME LEGAL ASPECTS OF THE INSURANCE CONTRACT

Contract law applies to insurance policies. The following contract concepts are quite important.

A. CONCEALMENT

General rules.   ▸ Concealment is an insured's willful failure to disclose relevant, material information to an insurer. ▸ An insurer may void a policy due to an insured's concealment.

Example.   Tim applied for life insurance. The insurer requested all relevant information from Tim. Tim intentionally failed to disclose that he recently had two heart attacks.

Limitations.   ▸ An insurer typically cannot raise the defense of concealment in connection with property insurance if an insurance agent had an opportunity to inspect the insured property. ▸ Ocean marine insurance policies generally provide that an insurer may void a contract whenever pertinent information is withheld, and no intent to defraud is required.

B. REPRESENTATION

General rules.   ▸ A false representation is an oral or written misstatement of a material fact that is made by an insured prior to execution of an insurance contract. ▸ An insurer may void a policy due to a false representation, whether it was made intentionally or not.

Example.   Olivia purchased fire insurance for a manufacturing plant. Prior to signing the insurance contract, Olivia told the insurer that the plant would only make plastic pellets. The plant actually assembles munitions for weapons. The insurance company can avoid the policy.

Limitation.   Misrepresentations of insignificant facts do not affect the validity of a policy.

Study hint.   Most life insurance contracts provide that if an insured misstates his or her age, the policy is not voided. Instead, the amount paid on the death of an insured is only the amount that would have been paid if the insured's correct age had been stated.

C. WARRANTY

General rules.   ▸ A warranty is an insured's statement or promise relating to a risk that is made in the insurance contract or in a document incorporated into the contract. ▸ An insurer may void the contract if a warranty is not completely true, or if it is not perfectly performed.

Example.   Prep School signed a public liability insurance contract which warranted that students were 11 to 18 years old. If some students are 6 years old, the contract can be voided.

Study hints.   ▸ Warranties differ from representations in three ways: (1) warranty: made in the contract; representation: stated outside of the contract. (2) warranty: insurer can void contract for a breach of warranty, even if not material; representation: insurer can void contract only if misrepresentation is material. (3) warranty: must be absolutely correct; representation: only needs to be substantially correct. ▸ Courts construe warranties as representations when possible.

D. SUBROGATION

General rule.   An insurer who pays an insured's claim "steps into the shoes" of the insured and acquires the insured's legal rights and claims against the party who caused a loss or harm.

Example.   Marty vandalized Eric's car, and Eric's insurance company paid to have the car repaired. The insurance acquires Eric's rights against Marty, and it can sue Marty for damages.

E. ESTOPPEL

General rule.   The doctrine of estoppel prevents a person from misleading a second person and then taking unfair advantage of the second person's mistaken belief.

Example.   Insurance company told Eve that her homeowner's policy was paid up and in effect. Eve reasonably relied on this statement. If a loss occurs, the company is estopped from denying coverage if it turns out that Eve's premium check had actually been lost in the mail.

REVIEW OF CHAPTER

REVIEW OF TERMS

Select the term that best matches a statement below. Each term is the best match for only one statement.

TERMS

a. False representation   c. Peril   e. Property insurance
b. Life insurance   d. Policyholder   f. Underwriter

STATEMENTS

Answer

_____ 1. Insured under a contract of insurance.
_____ 2. Hazards that may be insured against.
_____ 3. Insurance that insures against the death of the insured.
_____ 4. Insurance company that insures against specified hazards.
_____ 5. Insurance that insures against specified casualties to personal or real property.
_____ 6. Willful failure to disclose relevant, material information to an insurer.

REVIEW OF CONCEPTS

Directions: Indicate **T** for true and **F** for false in the answer column.

_____ 1. The coverage actually provided by an insurance policy may be somewhat different than that indicated by the name of the policy.
_____ 2. A premium is the amount paid to an insured for a covered loss.
_____ 3. Policyholders of a stock insurance company do not have to bear losses suffered by the company.
_____ 4. Members in an assessment mutual insurance company may be required to pay a pro rata share of the losses of the company if this is stated in their respective policies.
_____ 5. Members of a mutual insurance company are also the persons who are insured by the company.
_____ 6. Hank applied for a life insurance policy on the life of Wilma. However, Hank will not suffer a loss if Wilma dies. In this case, Hank does not have an insurable interest.
_____ 7. Chris purchased a fire insurance policy on a building. Chris failed to disclose that he stored flammable fluids in the building. However, prior to issuance of the policy, an agent of the insurer inspected the building. In this case, the insurer cannot void the policy.
_____ 8. An insurer can void a policy due to concealment if an insured fails to tell an insurer any fact relating to the policy, whether the concealed fact is material or not.
_____ 9. An insurer cannot void an insurance contract due to an insured's unintentional misrepresentation.
_____ 10. In most states, an insurance contract may be avoided if a warranty is not absolutely true.
_____ 11. An insurer is not subrogated to the rights of an insured.

REVIEW OF CONCEPT APPLICATIONS

Answer

Directions: Indicate your choice in the answer column.

_____ 1. Mae purchased a life insurance policy from Insurer. When Mae applied for the insurance, Insurer requested that she furnish her complete medical history. Mae knowingly failed to disclose that she had a tonsillectomy (removal of tonsils) when she was a child, and that she now has lung cancer. Insurer would have insured Mae despite the tonsillectomy, but it would not have insured her had it known of the cancer. In this case:
  a. Insurer can void the policy due to Mae's concealment of the tonsillectomy.
  b. Insurer can void the policy due to Mae's concealment of the lung cancer.
  c. Insurer cannot void the policy due to Mae's concealment.
  d. a and b.

_____ 2. Gray purchased a standard life insurance policy on her own life, and she named Melvin as beneficiary. Gray misrepresented to the insurance company that she was 65 years old; Gray was actually 70 years old. The face of the policy was $25,000. Had Gray told the truth, the premium she paid would have purchased a policy with a $20,000 face. If Gray dies, how much will Melvin probably recover?
   a. $0.
   b. $20,000.
   c. $25,000.

_____ 3. Victor purchased property insurance on a storage facility that was composed of 10 warehouses. The policy insures Victor against burglaries at the facility. In the insurance contract, Victor warranted that he would install a burglar alarm system in all of the warehouses. Victor installed a burglary alarm system in only nine warehouses. In most states:
   a. The insurer cannot cancel the policy since Victor substantially performed the warranty.
   b. The insurer cannot cancel the policy if the failure to install the burglar alarm system in one warehouse is not a material breach of the warranty.
   c. The insurer can cancel the contract due to Victor's breach of warranty.

_____ 4. Char's insurer intentionally mislead her into believing that her antique Ford was insured for its full restoration value, when in fact it was only insured for "blue book" value, a much lesser amount. Which concept prevents the insurer from paying the lesser amount in case of a loss?
   a. Estoppel.
   b. Concealment.
   c. Subrogation.

CASE PROBLEM

Marcus bought a car on his sixteenth birthday. Marcus immediately purchased a one-year insurance policy on the car. Marcus paid the $1,500 premium. Six months later, Marcus decided to disaffirm the insurance contract. Under these facts: (1) Did Marcus have an insurable interest in the car? (2) In most states, can Marcus disaffirm the contract? (3) If Marcus disaffirms, how much is he entitled to be repaid?

_____

_____

_____

_____

BUSINESS LAW PARTNER EXERCISE

Directions: Access your Business Law Partner CD-ROM and find the document entitled "Personal Fact Sheet." Complete this document using the information provided in the case below. Supply any other necessary information.

Case Study: *Hi, My Name is Amber*

Amber is single, thirty-three years of age, and recently graduated from college. She has a four-year-old child, Penelope, from a prior marriage. She owns a car and has $20,000 in the bank. She has also recently started her own florist shop. She does not have a will, but she has made a living will.

CHAPTER 37 QUIZ

Section A

DIRECTIONS: In the Answers space in Column II, place the letter of the corresponding word or words from Column I.

Column I	Column II		Answers	For Scoring
(a)	assessment mutual	**1.**	A contract whereby a party transfers risk of financial loss to a risk bearer for a fee is .... _____	**1.** _____
(b)	beneficiary	**2.**	A clause added to an insurance contract that modifies, extends, or limits the base contract is called a(n) .... _____	**2.** _____
(c)	concealment	**3.**	The person protected against loss by insurance is the..... _____	**3.** _____
(d)	estoppel	**4.**	In life insurance the person who is to receive the benefits or proceeds from insurance is known as the ..... _____	**4.** _____
(e)	face	**5.**	A written contract of insurance is called the .... _____	**5.** _____
(f)	hazards	**6.**	Maximum amount the insurer will pay for a loss is known as the .... _____	**6.** _____
(g)	insurable interest	**7.**	The consideration paid by an insured for protection is the .... _____	**7.** _____
(h)	insurable risk	**8.**	The danger of a loss of, or injury to, property, life, or anything insured is called a(n)... _____	**8.** _____
(i)	insurance	**9.**	A factor that contributes to the uncertainty is called a(n) _____	**9.** _____
(j)	insured	**10.**	Insurance companies for which the original investments were made by stockholders and whose business is conducted by boards of directors are called.................... _____	**10.** _____
(k)	insurer	**11.**	Insurance companies in which the policyholders are the members and owners are .... _____	**11.** _____
(l)	mutual companies	**12.**	An insurance company in which each insured must pay a share of the company's losses equal to a ratio of the face of the insured's policies compared to the face of all policies issued by the company is a(n) .... _____	**12.** _____
(m)	policy			
(n)	premium			
(o)	representation			
(p)	rider	**13.**	When two people have a relationship such that one has a reason-able expectation of benefit being derived from the continued existence of the other, the first person has a(n) .... _____	**13.** _____
(q)	risk			
(r)	stock companies			
(s)	subrogation	**14.**	A willful failure by the insured to disclose information pertinent to the risk is known as .... _____	**14.** _____
(t)	waiver	**15.**	A statement of a material fact made by the insured prior to the making of an insurance contract is a(n) .... _____	**15.** _____
(u)	warranty	**16.**	A statement or promise of the insured that relates to the risk and appears in the contract is a(n) .... _____	**16.** _____
		17.	The right of the insurer to " step into the shoes" of the insured is.. _____	**17.** _____
		18.	Doctrine that prohibits a party from denying the existence of a represented fact that another person has detrimentally relied upon is called.................................. _____	**18.** _____

Score _____

Section B

DIRECTIONS: Following each question below, indicate your answer by placing a "T" for "True" or an "F" for "False" in the Answers column.

	Answers	**For Scoring**
1. Insurance exists to provide a fund of money when a loss covered by a policy is sustained.	_____	1._____
2. The name by which the policy is identified controls as to the coverage of the policy....	_____	2._____
3. Insurance companies must place a major part of their original capital in a reserve account..	_____	3._____
4. The law covering insurable interest is different for life and for property insurance.......	_____	4._____
5. Dependency upon the insured is necessary to be a life insurance beneficiary...............	_____	5._____
6. One partner usually has an insurable interest in the life of another partner.	_____	6._____
7. The seller has an insurable interest in goods sold on the installment plan when title is retained as security.	_____	7._____
8. A change in title to the insured property will not affect the insurable interest...............	_____	8._____
9. The laws that apply to contracts in general do not apply to insurance contracts.	_____	9._____
10. The willful failure to disclose a material fact renders an insurance contract voidable....	_____	10._____
11. The rule of concealment applies equally to all types of insurance contracts.	_____	11._____
12. Representations are incorporated by reference in the actual contract of insurance.........	_____	12._____

Score _____

Section C

DIRECTIONS: Following each question below, indicate your answer by placing a "Y" for "Yes" or an "N" for "No" in the Answers column.

	Answers	**For Scoring**
1. Does the insurance contract specify the risk being transferred?	_____	1._____
2. Is negligence by the insured a normal hazard of insurance?..	_____	2._____
3. Does a policyholder in a stock company share its losses?	_____	3._____
4. Must the beneficiary have an insurable interest in the insured's life?.............................	_____	4._____
5. To have a concealment, must the concealed facts be material?	_____	5._____
6. Does a willful concealment render the contract void?	_____	6._____
7. If the age of the insured is misstated, will the life insurance policy usually be voided?.	_____	7._____
8. Does a breached warranty void the policy in all states?..	_____	8._____
9. Is subrogation particularly applicable to some types of automobile insurance?.............	_____	9._____
10. Does the rule of concealment apply with equal force to all kinds of insurance?	_____	10._____

Score _____

CHAPTER 38
TYPES OF INSURANCE

CHAPTER OUTLINE

I. **LIFE INSURANCE**

Life insurance is a contract whereby an insurance company agrees to pay a stated sum of money to a beneficiary upon the death of the insured party.

A. TYPES OF LIFE INSURANCE CONTRACTS

1. Term insurance

Term life insures a person's life for the number of years stated in the policy. Term policies are pure life insurance; they have no savings aspect. Variations are discussed below.

- *Renewable term insurance*: ▸ Defined: term insurance that allows an insured to renew a policy without a physical exam. ▸ Premiums for renewal terms are higher.

- *Nonrenewable term insurance*: Defined: term insurance that does not allow an insured to renew the policy unless the insurer consents to the renewal.

- *Level term insurance*: ▸ Described: face amount remains the same throughout the policy term. ▸ Example: Fred buys a $10,000 face value policy for a five-year term. The insurer will pay $10,000 to a beneficiary if Fred dies during the five-year term.

- *Decreasing term insurance*: ▸ Described: amount paid to a beneficiary decreases during the policy term according to a schedule of benefits or formula. ▸ Amounts are paid to a beneficiary periodically (e.g., monthly) or in a lump sum. ▸ Example: Wade bought a ten-year, decreasing term policy. According to the policy, the beneficiary is to receive $400 per month for the remainder of the term. If Wade died after 24 months, a beneficiary would collect $400 per month for the remaining 96 months of the term.

2. Endowment insurance

▸ Defined: decreasing term insurance plus a savings account. ▸ Benefits: (1) If an insured dies before expiration of the policy term, the beneficiary receives the policy's face value. (2) If the insured is alive when the policy expires, the insured receives the face value.

3. Whole life Insurance

Whole life insurance is essentially endowment insurance. The face is paid to a beneficiary on the insured's death, or it is payable to the insured (if living) at age 100.

4. Combinations (and other types of policies

- *Combinations*: ▸ Term, endowment, and whole life policies can be combined to form many types of policies. ▸ Examples: universal life insurance; Family Income Policy.
- *Riders*: Common riders: (1) disability income riders (provide disability benefits); and (2) double indemnity (twice the ordinary amount is paid in the event of accidental death).

B. LIMITATION ON RISKS IN LIFE INSURANCE CONTRACTS

Most policies do not cover death by suicide or death resulting from war.

C. PAYMENT OF PREMIUMS

▸ Premiums must be paid when due. Failure to do so may result in automatic lapse (termination) of a policy, or it may allow an insurer to terminate a policy. ▸ If an insured pays a certain number of premiums and then fails to pay additional premiums, state law or a policy may require an insurer to extend the policy, although the policy may have a reduced face value.

D. GRACE PERIOD

In general, an insurer must grant a 30- or 31-day grace period after the due date for a life insurance premium. If the insured pays a premium within this period, the policy will not lapse.

E. INCONTESTABILITY

In general, a life insurance policy cannot be contested by an insurer after a certain period has elapsed (usually one or two years) since the policy was issued. After this time, a claim typically cannot be contested for any reason except nonpayment of premiums.

F. CHANGE OF BENEFICIARY

General rule. An insured can ordinarily change a beneficiary at any time and can name successive beneficiaries.

Limitation. If a court order (e.g., a divorce decree) names a beneficiary, the beneficiary cannot be changed.

G. ASSIGNMENT OF THE POLICY

▪ *Assignment of policy*: An insured is free to assign rights under a policy without affecting the validity of the contract. An assignment may be made to a creditor as security for a loan.

▪ *Assignment of rights by a beneficiary*: A beneficiary can assign rights to proceeds under a policy. The assignee's rights may be terminated, however, if the insured changes beneficiaries.

H. ANNUITY INSURANCE

▸ Defined: Contract that pays monthly income from a specified age until death. ▸ Purpose: Provides guaranteed income for the entire life of the person acquiring the policy. ▸ Joint and Survivor's Annuity: annuity pays income until the second of two insureds dies. For example, Sam purchased a Joint and Survivor's Annuity that pays $700 per month until Sam and his wife die. If Sam died in 1999, Sam's wife receives $700 per month until her death.

II. PROPERTY INSURANCE

General rules. ▸ Property insurance is a contract whereby an insurer, for compensation, agrees to pay an insured for damage or loss to specified property resulting from a covered hazard. ▸ An insured is paid the lesser of: (1) the actual loss; or (2) the face amount of the policy.

Example. Lee insured his condo for $40,000. The actual value of the condo is $35,000. If the condo is destroyed by a covered hazard, the insurance company is required to pay only $35,000.

A. LOSSES RELATED TO FIRE

General rules. ▸ Fire insurance pays for damage to insured property only if a hostile fire (a fire outside its normal place) causes the damage. ▸ Fire insurance does not compensate for: (1) damage caused by a friendly fire (a fire in its normal place); (2) heat damage not caused by a fire; or (3) economic losses caused by a fire (e.g., lost profits; cost of higher rent).

Examples. ▸ Hostile fire: fire policy covers damage if sparks escape from a fireplace and ignite a carpet. ▸ Friendly fire: fire policy does not cover smoke damage caused by a fire in a fireplace. ▸ Heat: fire policy does not cover losses caused by heat from a defective furnace. ▸ Economic damage: fire policy does not cover profits that are lost if a fire forces a store to close.

Study hint. Insurance is available to cover losses excluded by fire insurance. Such insurance includes: (1) business interruption insurance (covers lost profits); (2) leasehold interest insurance (covers the cost of increased rent if an insured must evacuate leased premises); and (3) extended coverage (covers with riders losses from named hazards, such as wind, water, or riots).

B. THE PROPERTY INSURANCE POLICY

- *Open policy*: The maximum amount payable is stated by the policy. Subject to this limit, an insured must prove, and only recovers, the actual loss that the insured suffered.

- *Valued policy*: The policy states a fixed value for each item of property. In the event of a loss, the insured recovers up to the stated value for each item of lost property.

- *Specific policy*: Insurance covers only one specified item (e.g., a house; boat; fur coat).

- *Blanket policy*: Insurance covers: (1) many similar items at different locations (inventory at several stores); or (2) different property that is at a single location (building and inventory).

- *Floating policy*: ▸ Insurance covers specified property no matter where it is. ▸ This policy is appropriate for property moved from place to place (trucks), and property taken on a trip.

- *Homeowners' policy*: Covers house and its contents from almost every peril. Also provides liability insurance in case someone is injured on the insured premises.

- *Reporting Form for Merchandise Inventory*: ▸ This type of policy covers a merchant's inventory. The amount of insurance (and premiums) adjusts according to how much inventory an insured reports from time to time. ▸ Example: Star Fashions has a Reporting Form for Merchandise Inventory policy. If Star reports $20,000 inventory on May 1, Star will be covered for $20,000 and will pay premiums for this amount. If Star reports $15,000 inventory the next month, coverage and premiums will be reduced accordingly.

C. DESCRIPTION OF THE PROPERTY

- *Description of property*: ▸ In order to recover for a loss, an insured must describe the insured property with reasonable accuracy. ▸ Property must be sufficiently described to enable the insurer to (1) value the property, and (2) determine the risk.

- *Location of property*: ▸ An insured must state where insured property is located, and reasonably describe such premises (e.g., brick house). ▸ Unless a floating policy is obtained, most property insurance covers insured items only: (1) while located at a named location; (2) during transit to another location; and (3) for several days after being moved to another location. ▸ Example: John moved from a home in the city to a home in the suburbs. John's policy covers his household effects for only several days after the move.

D. COINSURANCE

General rule. Policies may require property to be insured for a minimum percent of its value (usually 80 percent). If a lesser amount is carried, payment for a partial loss is reduced.

Example. Ina's policy on her $20,000 boat required that it be insured for at least 80 percent of its value, i.e., $16,000. Ina insured the boat for $12,000. If the boat suffers $10,000 damage, the insurer will pay only $7,500 (75 percent of the loss) because Ina carried only 75 percent of the minimum required insurance ($12,000 face, divided by the $16,000 required).

E. REPAIRS AND REPLACEMENTS

An insurer can pay for a loss, or repair or replace damaged property. If property is repaired, materials of like kind and quality must be used, and repairs must be done in a reasonable time.

III. AUTOMOBILE INSURANCE

A. PHYSICAL DAMAGE INSURANCE (DAMAGE TO INSURED'S AUTOMOBILE)

- *Fire insurance*: ▸ Fire insurance covers damage to a car that results from a fire. ▸ Comprehensive automobile insurance normally includes fire insurance.

- *Theft insurance*: Theft insurance covers: (1) theft of an auto or any part permanently attached to the auto; and (2) damage that may be caused by a theft or attempted theft. Theft insurance does not cover: (1) theft of articles in a car (e.g., clothes) or equipment not firmly attached to the car (e.g., radar detector); or (2) loss of use of a car.

- *Collision insurance*: ▸ Collision insurance covers damage to an insured's car that is caused by: (1) the car striking another object; (2) another car or an object striking the car; or (3) a fire caused by a collision. ▸ To reduce premiums, most policies have a deductible clause that requires an insurer to pay for a loss only to the extent it exceeds a specified amount. ▸ Collision insurance only covers accidental collisions, and it does not cover damage resulting from natural causes, such as hail. ▸ Collision insurance on a car usually is void if a trailer is attached to the car and the trailer is not covered by the same type of insurance.

- *Comprehensive coverage*: Comprehensive coverage insures against a variety of named risks, such as hail, rain, wind, floods, vandalism, battery acid, and glass breakage.

B. PUBLIC LIABILITY INSURANCE (INJURIES OR DAMAGE TO THIRD PARTIES)

- *Bodily injury insurance*: ▸ Covers injuries to anyone other than the insured. ▸ An insurer is liable for injuries up to the policy limits. Policy limits are usually stated as three numbers, such as 25/50/10. In the order stated, these numbers refer to the maximum amount that the insurer must pay for: (1) injuries to one person in one accident; (2) injuries to all persons in one accident; (3) damage to the property of others. ▸ Auto insurance may not cover a loss if: (1) the car is driven by a person who is under the legal age to drive; (2) a car is used to carry persons for pay; (3) a car is used for a purpose not stated in a policy; or (4) a car is operated outside the U.S. and Canada. ▸ A defense clause requires an insurer to bear the cost of defending an insured, but permits the insurer to accept or reject settlement offers.

- *Property damage insurance*: ▸ Subject to policy limits, property damage insurance covers damage to property of others resulting from an insured's use, ownership, or maintenance of a vehicle. ▸ Not covered: damage to property owned, leased, loaned, or transported by the insured (physical damage insurance may cover this damage).

C. MEDICAL PAYMENTS AND UNINSURED MOTORIST INSURANCE

▸ Medical payment insurance covers injury to an insured and to those in an insured's car.
▸ Uninsured motorist covers an injured insured if the other driver is at fault but is uninsured.

D. NOTICE TO THE INSURER

An insured must cooperate with an insurer by giving prompt notice of an accident, providing all relevant information regarding the accident, and assisting in preparing a defense.

E. RECOVERY EVEN WHEN AT FAULT (RIGHT TO RECOVER DAMAGES)

At common law, a plaintiff could not recover if in any way at fault. Some states now have no-fault insurance; others use the last clear chance rule or comparative negligence.

F. REQUIRED INSURANCE

Under assigned risk rules, states can make an insurer provide insurance to a driver who is legally required to carry liability insurance but who cannot buy it elsewhere.

REVIEW OF CHAPTER

REVIEW OF TERMS

Select the term that best matches a statement below. Each term is the best match for only one statement.

TERMS

a. Annuity insurance
b. Assigned risk rule
c. Bodily injury insurance
d. Business interruption policy
e. Coinsurance
f. Collision insurance
g. Comprehensive coverage

h. Deductible clause
i. Double indemnity
j. Endowment insurance
k. Extended coverage
l. Floating policy
m. Open policy
n. Physical damage

o. Property damage
p. Public liability
q. Rider
r. Specific policy
s. Term insurance
t. Valued policy
u. Whole life insurance

STATEMENTS

Answer

_____ 1.   Insurance (in the nature of endowment insurance) that is paid to an insured, if living, at age 100.

_____ 2.   Insurance that pays a guaranteed monthly amount to the insured from a specified age until death.

_____ 3.   Broad class of automobile insurance that covers damage to property of third parties.

_____ 4.   Agreement that is attached to an insurance policy, thereby modifying or changing the policy.

_____ 5.   Insurance that states a specific value for each item of insured property.

_____ 6.   Insurance that insures the life of a person for the time specified in the policy.

_____ 7.   Life insurance benefits are paid for twice the ordinary policy amount if death is accidental.

_____ 8.   Insurance requiring payment of the face amount to a beneficiary if an insured dies during a policy term and, if the insured is alive at the end of the term, the face amount is paid to the insured.

_____ 9.   Insurance that covers property that is moved from place to place.

_____ 10. Insurance that states a maximum amount of coverage and requires an insured to prove his or her actual loss in order to recover.

_____ 11. Principle that reduces the amount that can be recovered for a loss if an insured failed to carry the required amount of insurance.

_____ 12. Insurance that covers only a single, specified item of property.

_____ 13. Insurance that covers a loss of profits due to a fire.

_____ 14. Insurance added to a fire policy by riders covering losses to property that may result from a number of named hazards.

_____ 15. Broad class of automobile insurance that insures against liability to third parties for personal injuries or property damage.

_____ 16. Public liability insurance that covers damage to property of third parties.

_____ 17. Law that allows a state to make an insurance company provide insurance for certain drivers.

_____ 18. Term that obligates an insurer to pay for a loss only to the extent it exceeds a specified amount.

_____ 19. Physical damage insurance covering damage to an insured's car that results from hitting an object.

_____ 20. Physical damage insurance that covers damage to an insured's car from a number of hazards.

_____ 21. Public liability insurance that covers injuries to third parties.

REVIEW OF CONCEPTS

Answer

Directions: Indicate **T** for true and **F** for false in the answer column.

_____ 1. The amount paid under decreasing term insurance is not affected by when the insured dies.

_____ 2. If an insured dies during the term of an endowment or whole life insurance policy, the beneficiary is entitled to be paid the face amount of the policy.

_____ 3. An insured living at age 100 is entitled to be paid the face amount of a whole life policy.

_____ 4. Life insurance contracts cannot be modified by riders.

_____ 5. Life insurance companies are not required to grant a grace period for payment of premiums.

_____ 6. In 1995, Gil purchased life insurance containing a typical two-year incontestability clause. In 2001, Gil died of a heart attack and Beneficiary filed a claim. When Gil acquired the policy, he failed to disclose an existing heart condition. In this case, the insurer cannot contest the claim.

_____ 7. A beneficiary can assign rights to benefits under an insurance contract.

_____ 8. Annuity insurance typically pays a lump sum upon the death of the insured.

_____ 9. Carol insured her $500 ring for $1,000. If the ring is lost in a fire, Carol can recover $1,000.

_____ 10. Smoke damage from a friendly fire is not covered under most fire insurance policies.

_____ 11. Vi's Candies suffered a fire, and Vi's was forced to rent a new store for a higher rent. In this case, a standard fire insurance policy would cover the cost of the higher rent.

_____ 12. Fire insurance does not typically cover heat or smoke damage unless it results from an actual fire.

_____ 13. Kit had a floating policy on her mink coat. Kit took the coat on a trip to New York, and the coat was lost in a fire in her hotel room. In this case, the policy covers the loss of the coat.

_____ 14. Insured negligently started a fire that damaged his home. In this case, the insurer that issued a fire policy on the home is not liable for the loss since the fire was caused by Insured's negligence.

_____ 15. An insurer must actually replace damaged property; an insurer cannot simply pay for the loss.

_____ 16. Carl was having his car transported to Utah by train. During shipment the train caught fire and the fire destroyed Carl's car. In this case, Carl's fire insurance will cover the loss to the car.

_____ 17. Pat owns a sports car. The car is equipped with a CD player that is installed in the dash. If the CD player is stolen, Pat's theft insurance will not cover the loss.

_____ 18. Jake was pulling a large house trailer with his truck when the trailer came loose, causing the truck to collide with another car. Jake had collision insurance on the truck, but not on the trailer. In this case, the collision insurance will not cover the damage to the truck or to the trailer.

_____ 19. Lance's car is struck by lightning. Lance's collision insurance will cover this loss.

_____ 20. Amelia has bodily injury insurance. Amelia was involved in an auto accident with Rod, and Rod was at fault. In this case, Amelia's insurer must pay for Rod's injuries.

_____ 21. Under a defense clause an insurer has the option to defend or not to defend the insured.

_____ 22. Carrie was in an auto accident with Ellen. Ellen was at fault, but she has no insurance. If Carrie has an uninsured motorist policy, Carrie's insurer must cover certain losses suffered by Carrie.

_____ 23. Property damage insurance covers damage to the contents of the insured's vehicle.

_____ 24. In case of an accident, an insured is only required to give minimal cooperation to the insurer.

_____ 25. In a state with a comparative negligence statute, a driver who contributes even slightly to an accident cannot recover from a driver who bears most of the fault.

_____ 26. Under the "assigned risk" rule, an insurance company determines or assigns a risk factor to the various hazards it may cover under its policies.

REVIEW OF CONCEPT APPLICATIONS

Directions: Indicate your choice in the answer column.

_____ 1. Oliver is 40 years old. Oliver wants to buy a life insurance policy that will provide him with a lump sum payment if he is living at age 60. What kind of insurance should he buy?
   a.   Term insurance.
   b.   Endowment insurance.
   c.   Annuity insurance.

_____ 2. Marvin purchased a life insurance policy on his own life and he named Jolene as the beneficiary. Jolene assigned her rights to Last Bank as collateral for a loan. Marvin wants to change the policy to name his brother George as beneficiary. Under these facts:
   a.   Marvin cannot name George as beneficiary without Jolene's consent.
   b.   Marvin cannot name George as beneficiary because George has no insurable interest.
   c.   Jolene could not assign her rights as a beneficiary to Last Bank.
   d.   Jolene could assign her rights as beneficiary to Last Bank. However, these rights will be terminated if Marvin changes the policy and names George as the beneficiary.

_____ 3. Which loss would be covered by a standard form of fire insurance policy?
   a.   Smoke damage that was caused by a clogged fireplace.
   b.   Scorching of wallpaper that was caused by a defective electric heater.
   c.   Heat damage to corn that was stored in a grain silo.
   d.   Damage to a carpet caused by a fire that started when a cigar was accidentally dropped.

_____ 4. Mario owns a fire insurance policy on his home. The policy has a coinsurance clause requiring Mario to insure the home for at least 80 percent of its value. The value of the home is $50,000. Mario insured the home for only $20,000. If the house is damaged by fire and suffers $10,000 damage, how much will the insurance company pay Mario?
   a. $0.
   b. $5,000.
   c. $10,000.

_____ 5. Greg owned a standard form of theft insurance on his car. One day, Greg's car was broken into and vandalized. Which loss or damage is covered by the theft insurance?
   a.   Theft of a portable CD player that Greg had hidden under the front seat.
   b.   Theft of a leather jacket that was in the trunk of the car.
   c.   Damage to the driver's window that was shattered when the thieves broke into the car.
   d.   All of the above.

_____ 6. Lisa's car collided with a truck. Lisa's collision insurance has a $10,000 policy limit, and it contains a $500 deductible. Lisa's car suffered $5,000 damage. Under these facts, how much must Lisa's insurer pay?
   a. $0.
   b. $500.
   c. $4,500.
   d. $5,000.

_____ 7. Tom's public liability insurance coverage is 25/50/10. Tom was responsible for an accident that injured two people and destroyed another person's car. One party suffered $40,000 damages due to personal injuries, and the other person suffered $30,000 damages due to personal injuries. The accident caused $15,000 damage to the other car. How much must Tom's insurer pay?
   a.   The insurer must pay a total of $50,000 for the personal injuries to the other parties.
   b.   The insurer must pay a total of $70,000 for the personal injuries to the other parties.
   c.   The insurer must pay $15,000 for the damage to the other car.
   d.   The insurer must pay a total of $85,000 for this accident.

_____ 8.   Alvin is involved in an automobile accident with Kristen. Both parties are at fault. It is determined at trial that Alvin was 75 percent at fault, and Kristen was 25 percent at fault. Kristen suffered $100,000 damages. The accident occurred in a state that has adopted comparative negligence. Under these facts, for how much is Alvin liable?
   a. $0.
   b. $25,000.
   c. $75,000.
   d. $100,000.

_____ 9.   Sarah owned two standard, term life insurance policies. Sarah failed to timely pay the premiums on either policy. Sarah is 90 days delinquent in paying the premiums on policy No. 1; she is 10 days delinquent on policy No. 2. Under these facts:
   a.   Policy No. 1 has not lapsed. Sarah is entitled to a 90-day grace period in which to pay the premium.
   b.   Policy No. 2 has not lapsed. Sarah is entitled to a 30-day grace period in which to pay the premium.
   c.   Both policies have lapsed. Sarah is not entitled to a grace period in which to pay premiums.
   d.   Neither policy has lapsed. Sarah is entitled to a 120-day grace period in which to pay the premiums.

CASE PROBLEM

Bruce is considering acquiring automobile insurance. Bruce wants to know (1) If he buys insurance, should he agree to a reasonable deductible? (2) What types of insurance does he need to cover the following losses: (a) damage to his car that may result from an accident; (b) hail damage to his car; (c) liability for physical injuries to third parties; (d) medical expenses he may incur due to an accident? Please answer Bruce's questions.

_____

_____

_____

BUSINESS LAW PARTNER EXERCISE

Directions: Using the Online feature of the Business Law Partner CD-ROM, complete the assignments below.

Case Study: *Janice (from Chapter 37) Returns With More Insurance Needs*

Remember Janice from Chapter 37? If not, refer back to that chapter and review the Personal Fact Sheet that you helped complete.

In Amber's college law class, she studied insurance, among other things. Now, she is trying to decide what type of personal and/or business insurance she needs to adequately protect herself, her child, and her business. Towards this end, she has asked you to do the following:

1.   Locate and identify one or more Internet web sites that provide practical information regarding what insurance is most appropriate for an individual or business.
2.   Identify two types of personal and two types of business-related insurance that Amber should acquire.

_____

_____

_____

CHAPTER 38 QUIZ

Section A

DIRECTIONS: Following each statement below, indicate your answer by placing a "T" for "True" or an "F" for "False" in the Answers column.

	Answers	For Scoring
1. An insured has the legal right to renew term life insurance.	_____	1. _____
2. Sickness is an acceptable reason for nonpayment of insurance premiums.	_____	2. _____
3. Most life insurance policies are incontestable after a specified time.	_____	3. _____
4. An annuity protects against outliving one's savings.	_____	4. _____
5. The actual value of the property is the maximum that can be collected in case of a total loss.	_____	5. _____
6. Fire insurance on a building and contents covers loss of profits while the building is being restored.	_____	6. _____
7. The location of the insured property is unimportant.	_____	7. _____
8. Most insurance policies give the insurer the option of paying the amount of loss, or repairing or replacing the property.	_____	8. _____
9. "Automobile insurance" refers to insurance that the insured obtains to cover a car, injuries the insured and family members sustain, and liability insurance......................	_____	9. _____
10. A car must be in motion in order to have a collision.	_____	10. _____

Score _____

Section B

DIRECTIONS: Indicate your decision in each of the following cases in the space at the right.

	Answers	For Scoring
1. Bell took out a life insurance policy on her life. The premiums were due every six months. Bell got a fellowship to study abroad for the summer. She did not receive a notice that the premium was due until she returned. The premium was one week overdue. Can Bell do anything to prevent the policy from lapsing?	_____	1. _____
2-4. Abbott requested a fire insurance policy and was issued an open policy for $75,000 on her home. When it was destroyed by fire, the insurer employed appraisers who placed a value of $55,000 on the building. Abbott thought she should receive the $75,000 on which she had paid premiums. What must Abbott do to recover $75,000?	_____	2. _____
For a valued policy, what would Abbott have to do to collect $75,000?........	_____	3. _____
Had Abbott suffered a partial loss of $22,000, how much would she collect?	_____	4. _____
5-7. Roger had taken out a $30,000 coinsurance policy containing an 80 percent clause on his stock of goods at $50,000. What percentage of a partial loss will the insurance company pay?...	_____	5. _____
If the entire stock is destroyed, he would collect	_____	6. _____
If he suffers a partial loss of $5,000, he will collect	_____	7. _____
8. Potter had a "fender bender" with Mashburn's car and paid for the minor repairs to both vehicles. Since the damage was so minor, Potter did not report it to his insurance company, because he did not want his premium rate to increase. Two years later, Mashburn sued him alleging personal injuries, so Potter reported the accident to his auto insurer. Did Potter properly notify the insurer?	_____	8. _____

Score _____

Section C

DIRECTIONS: Complete each of the following statements by writing the missing word or words in the Answers column.

	Answers	For Scoring
1. A contract by which the insurer agrees to pay a specified sum to a beneficiary upon death of the insured is	_____	1. _____
2. Twice the ordinary amount of the policy paid when death is caused by accident is	_____	2. _____
3. In health and accident, hospitalization, and group medical insurance, the beneficiary is always the	_____	3. _____
4. A fire out of its normal place is called a(n) ??? fire.	_____	4. _____
5. Riders to a fire policy which add coverage from loss by wind-storm, explosion, falling aircraft, and water damage create	_____	5. _____
6. The principle by which the insured recovers on a loss in the same ratio as the insurance bears to the amount of insurance which the company requires is called	_____	6. _____
7. Insurance which covers the risks of injury or damage to the car itself is	_____	7. _____
8. Automobile insurance that covers all damage done to the car by being upset or by colliding with an object is called ??? insurance.	_____	8. _____
9. The division of automobile insurance that covers liability for damage to property and the life of other persons is ??? insurance.	_____	9. _____
10. Insurance which protects the insured when injury results from the negligence of another driver who does not have liability insurance is called ??? coverage.	_____	10. _____

Score _____

Section D

DIRECTIONS: Following each question below indicate your answer by placing a "T" under "True" or an "F" under "False" in the Answers column.

	Answers	For Scoring
1. May term insurance be either level or decreasing term?	_____	1. _____
2. Are all life insurance policies either term or whole life insurance policies?	_____	2. _____
3. Can the insured pay an additional premium for a policy which does not require the payment of premiums while the insured is disabled?	_____	3. _____
4. If a life insurance policy is incontestable, does it mean the insurance company cannot contest the validity of a claim on any grounds?	_____	4. _____
5. If the insured obtains a loan from the insurer, is the policy assigned to the insurer?	_____	5. _____
6. Does a fire insurance policy on household effects cover them at any location?	_____	6. _____
7. Do fire insurance policies permit either party to cancel the insurance without giving notice?	_____	7. _____
8. Does automobile theft insurance cover personal items left in the car?	_____	8. _____
9. If collision but not fire insurance is carried on a car, will the policy always cover both the fire loss and the collision loss occurring in the same wreck?	_____	9. _____
10. If the insured is not liable for damages, is the insurance company relieved of all duties and liability under bodily injury coverage?	_____	10. _____
11. May the insurer accept or reject any settlement offered out of court?	_____	11. _____
12. Does slight negligence on the part of one involved in an automobile accident always bar recovery?	_____	12. _____

Score _____

CHAPTER 39
SECURITY DEVICES

CHAPTER OUTLINE

I. INTRODUCTION

Three important security devices that are used to assure that a party will perform an obligation are: (1) a guarantee contract; (2) a surety contract; and (3) a secured credit sale.

II. GUARANTY AND SURETYSHIP

A contract of guaranty or suretyship is an agreement whereby one party promises to be responsible for the debt, default, or obligation of another party.

A. PARTIES

General rule.   Parties to a guaranty or suretyship are: (1) guarantor or surety: party undertaking responsibility for another's obligation; (2) creditor: party to whom a guarantee or promise of suretyship is made; and (3) principal debtor (principal): party primarily liable for an obligation.
Examples.   ‣ Suretyship: Nanco Inc. (principal) borrowed $10,000 from Bank (creditor). Nanco's president (surety) agreed to be a surety for the loan. ‣ Guaranty: Lad (principal) bought a car for $2,000 on credit from Seller (creditor). Brother (guarantor) guaranteed Lad's debt.

B. DISTINCTIONS (NATURE OF LIABILITY)

- *Suretyship*: ‣ A surety agrees to be *primarily liable* to a creditor for a principal's debts. In essence, the liability of a surety and principal are the same. ‣ Example: Principal borrowed $20,000 from Creditor, and Craig agreed to be surety. Payment is due May 1. On May 1, Creditor can demand payment from Principal or Craig. ‣ In general, the rules regarding suretyships apply equally to a paid surety (surety paid compensation) and an accommodation surety (gratuitous surety, e.g., parent co-signing a contract with a child).

- *Guaranty*: ‣ A guarantor agrees to be *secondarily liable* for a principal's debt. This means that a guarantor promises to pay only if a principal fails to pay. A creditor must first attempt to collect from the principal before proceeding against a guarantor. ‣ Example: Principal bought a plane from Seller on credit, and Todd guaranteed the debt. When payment is due, Seller must first try to collect from Principal before Seller can demand payment from Todd.

C. IMPORTANCE OF MAKING A DISTINCTION

- *Form (of contract)*: ‣ A contract of guaranty or suretyship must generally satisfy the basic requirements for a contract. ‣ Writing requirement: Most suretyship contracts can be oral or written. Contracts of guaranty must be written.

- *Notice of default*: ‣ Suretyship: A creditor can hold a surety liable without notifying the surety that a principal defaulted. ‣ Guaranty: A creditor must notify a guarantor that a principal defaulted before enforcing a guarantee. Damages resulting from a failure to give notice may reduce the guarantor's obligation.

- *Remedy*: ‣ Suretyship: A suretyship is unconditional. A surety has full liability with the principal.
‣ Guaranty: A guaranty is conditional. A guarantor is liable to pay only if (1) the principal defaults and (2) reasonable attempts by a creditor to collect are unsuccessful.

D. RIGHTS OF THE SURETY AND THE GUARANTOR

- *Indemnity*: ▸ A surety or guarantor who pays a debt is entitled to reimbursement by the principal. ▸ Example: Carlos defaulted on a debt and Surety paid the debt. Surety is entitled to be repaid by Carlos.

- *Subrogation*: ▸ A surety (guarantor) who pays a creditor acquires (1) the creditor's claim against the principal and (2) any security interests of the creditor. In this situation, the surety can collect the debt from the principal, and the surety can enforce the creditor's lien. ▸ The foregoing rights arise only after the entire debt has been paid by one or more of the parties.

- *Contribution*: ▸ Cosureties are two or more sureties who are liable for a debt. ▸ A cosurety (coguarantor) who pays a debt may seek contribution from the other sureties (guarantors) if they fail to pay their share of a debt. ▸ Example: Al and John were cosureties. When the principal defaulted, Al paid the debt. Al can recover half of the payment from John.

- *Exoneration*: A surety (guarantor) may be released from liability if a debt was not paid because the creditor failed to compel payment by the principal when payment was due.

E. DISCHARGE OF A SURETY OR A GUARANTOR

A surety (guarantor) may be discharged by: (1) performance; (2) agreement of the parties; or (3) bankruptcy of the surety (guarantor). Discharge may also result from:

- *Extension of time*: A surety (guarantor) is discharged if a creditor extends the time for payment (in exchange for consideration) without the consent of the surety.

- *Alteration of the terms of the contract*: A surety (guarantor) is discharged if a principal's contract or debt is materially altered. Lowering an interest rate does not cause a discharge.

- *Loss or return of collateral by the creditor*: ▸ A surety (guarantor) is discharged if collateral securing the debt is impaired due to: (1) the negligence of a creditor; or (2) a creditor's voluntary return of collateral to a principal. ▸ A creditor's failure to perfect or otherwise protect a security interest may cause a discharge.

III. SECURED CREDIT SALES

Article 9 of the UCC governs secured credit sales. This type of transaction allows a seller or creditor (secured party) to create a security interest in a buyer's or debtor's goods or fixtures (collateral). A secured party is permitted to repossess and sell collateral if a debtor fails to perform an obligation.

A. CREATION OF A SECURITY INTEREST AND BASIC RIGHTS

- *Security agreement*: A security interest is enforceable if: (1) the debtor signs a written security agreement that describes the collateral and names the parties; (2) the secured party gives value (e.g., sells goods on credit or loans money to debtor); and (3) the debtor owns or has a right to possess the collateral (e.g., debtor leases the collateral).

- *Rights of the seller*: ▸ A seller (secured party) may assign a debtor's debt and related security interest to a third party. ▸ Under FTC rules, if the debt arose out of a sale of consumer goods, the original contract must contain a notice that the third party takes the debt subject to any defense the consumer may have against the seller.

- *Rights of the buyer*: ▸ A debtor generally has the right to transfer collateral to others even if it is subject to a security interest. ▸ The transferee usually takes the property subject to the security interest. ▸ A debtor can make a secured party verify the amount of the debt.

B. PERFECTION OF SECURITY INTEREST

- *Nature of perfection*: ‣ A perfected security interest in collateral gives a seller a superior right to collateral over (1) most creditors who later obtain a security interest in the collateral, and (2) most subsequent purchasers of the collateral. ‣ How a security interest is perfected depends on what type of collateral the goods are at the time the security interest is perfected.

- *Key definitions*: ‣ *Inventory*: goods intended primarily for sale or lease. ‣ *Equipment*: goods intended primarily to be used in a business, profession, or farming concern. ‣ *Fixtures*: personal property permanently attached to real estate. ‣ *Consumer goods*: goods intended primarily for personal, household, or family use. ‣ *Financing statement*: writing, signed by a debtor and secured party, stating the parties' addresses and describing collateral.

- *Inventory and equipment*: ‣ A security interest in inventory or equipment is usually perfected by filing a financing statement with an appropriate government office. ‣ Buyers of inventory in the ordinary course take goods free from a prior perfected security interest. ‣ Example: Secured Party had a perfected security interest in Debtor's inventory of stoves. Buyer purchased a stove. Buyer takes the stove free from the security interest.

- *Fixtures*: Filing a financing statement in the government office where a mortgage for the real estate in question would be recorded perfects a security interest in fixtures.

- *Consumer goods*: ‣ In most cases, a security interest in consumer goods is automatically perfected; filing of a financing statement is not necessary. However, a secured party may elect to file a financing statement to perfect the security interest. ‣ An *automatically perfected security interest* in consumer goods is inferior to the rights of a subsequent buyer of the goods if the buyer purchased the goods (1) without knowledge of the security interest, (2) for value, and (3) for his or her personal, family, or household use.

- *Collateral with certificate of title*: If title to collateral is represented by a certificate of title, (e.g., automobile; truck) and state law requires liens to be stated on the certificate, then stating the security interest on the certificate of title perfects the security interest, and filing a financing statement is not required.

- *Duration of filing*: Filing a financing statement perfects a security interest for five years. Continuation statements may be filed to perfect for additional five-year periods.

C. EFFECT OF DEFAULT

- *Repossession*: ‣ On a debtor's default, a secured party can repossess collateral; a court order is not required. But, a secured party cannot use self-help to repossess collateral if doing so would cause a breach of the peace. In this case, a party must first get a court order to repossess. ‣ A seller may retain collateral as payment of a debt unless a debtor objects.

- *Resale*: ‣ After repossession, collateral may be sold at a private or public sale. A sale must be commercially reasonable. ‣ A secured party must give a debtor prior notice of sale unless goods are perishable. ‣ If a debtor paid 60 percent or more of the price for consumer goods, goods must be sold within 90 days after repossession unless the debtor agrees otherwise.

- *Redemption*: ‣ A debtor may recover (redeem) collateral from a secured party at any time before the secured party has sold, or entered into a contract to sell, the collateral. ‣ To redeem, a debtor must pay the entire debt, plus any expenses incurred by the secured party.

- *Accounting (proceeds)*: Proceeds from a sale of collateral are applied in the following order: (1) expenses incurred in repossessing collateral; (2) payment of the obligation owed to the secured party; (3) payment of debts owed to other parties with a security interest in the collateral. ‣ A debtor remains liable for any deficiency (amount of debt unpaid by proceeds from the sale). ‣ A seller must return any surplus to a debtor.

REVIEW OF CHAPTER

REVIEW OF TERMS

Select the term that best matches a statement below. Each term is the best match for only one statement.

TERMS

a. Consumer goods
b. Contribution
c. Equipment
d. Exoneration
e. Financing statement

f. Fixtures
g. Guaranty
h. Indemnity
i. Inventory
j. Perfected security interest

k. Principal (debtor)
l. Secured credit sale
m. Security agreement
n. Subrogation
o. Suretyship

STATEMENTS

Answer

_____ 1. Right of a surety or guarantor to be reimbursed by the principal.

_____ 2. Writing that is filed with an appropriate public office to perfect a security interest in certain types of collateral.

_____ 3. Right of a guarantor or surety to be released from a debt because a creditor wrongfully failed to demand payment from a principal debtor when the debt was due.

_____ 4. Goods intended primarily for sale or lease by a debtor.

_____ 5. Goods intended primarily for personal, family, or household use.

_____ 6. Agreement by a third party to be secondarily liable for the debt of another.

_____ 7. Transaction whereby a seller may retake goods sold to a debtor on credit if the debtor fails to pay.

_____ 8. Security interest that gives a secured party priority to collateral over most other parties who subsequently acquire an interest in the collateral.

_____ 9. Goods intended primarily to be used in a business, profession, or farming concern.

_____ 10. Right of a cosurety to seek reimbursement from other sureties for their proportionate share of a debt paid by the cosurety.

_____ 11. Agreement by a party to be primarily liable for another person's debt.

_____ 12. Goods that are permanently attached to real estate.

_____ 13. Agreement signed by a debtor that grants a security interest in collateral to a secured party.

_____ 14. Right of a surety or guarantor to enforce a creditor's claim against a principal.

_____ 15. Party who has the original, primary liability to pay a debt.

REVIEW OF CONCEPTS

Directions: Indicate **T** for true and **F** for false in the answer column.

_____ 1. In general, suretyship contracts do not need to be in writing.

_____ 2. When a debt becomes due, a creditor can collect immediately from the principal or a surety.

_____ 3. A creditor can collect from a guarantor only if the principal is unable or unwilling to pay.

_____ 4. Sureties cannot be held liable unless they are first given notice that the principal has defaulted.

_____ 5. First Bank is a guarantor for the unpaid price of goods sold to Principal. Later, First Bank paid this sum to the seller. In this case, First Bank has a right of indemnification against Principal.

_____ 6. A guarantor's liability for an obligation may be terminated if the obligation is materially modified without the guarantor's consent.

_____ 7. A bonding company is an example of an unpaid surety.

_____ 8. Oral security agreements are generally valid and enforceable.

_____ 9. In general, a perfected security interest gives a secured party a superior right to collateral over most subsequent creditors and purchasers of the collateral.

_____ 10. Diane granted Lender a security interest in her car. Title to the car is represented by a certificate of title. State law requires a lien to be stated on the certificate. In this case, Lender does not need to file a financing statement to perfect its interest if the lien is stated on the certificate.

_____ 11. How a security interest is perfected is determined by the type of collateral involved.

_____ 12. If a financing statement is filed in the wrong office, it does not perfect a security interest.

_____ 13. Filing a financing statement perfects a security interest for ten years.

_____ 14. A security interest in equipment can be perfected only by a secured creditor's possession of the equipment.

_____ 15. A secured party must resell collateral. A secured party can never keep collateral in satisfaction of a debt.

REVIEW OF CONCEPT APPLICATIONS

Answer

Directions: Indicate your choice in the answer column.

_____ 1. Carlsbad Co. purchased some equipment on credit from Seller. Michael guaranteed Seller that it would be able to collect payment from Carlsbad. The debt is now due and payable. Under these facts:
   a. Michael has secondary liability to pay the purchase price.
   b. Michael has primary liability to pay the purchase price.
   c. Seller can demand payment from Michael without first attempting to collect from Carlsbad.
   d. If Carlsbad defaults, Seller does not have to give Michael notice of the default prior to demanding payment from Michael.

_____ 2. First Federal Bank lent Decca Corp. $100,000. David and Janet agreed to be cosureties for this loan. Decca defaulted on the loan. Under these facts:
   a. First Federal must sue Decca Corp. before it can demand payment from David and Janet.
   b. If Janet repays the entire loan, she is entitled to $50,000 contribution from David.
   c. If Janet repays the entire loan, she does not have a right to indemnification by Decca Corp.
   d. If Janet and David repay the entire loan, they do not have a right of subrogation that would entitle them to enforce First Federal's claim against Decca Corp.

_____ 3. Roberto granted Secured Party a security interest in several items of property belonging to Roberto. In which case did Roberto grant a security interest in a fixture?
   a. Roberto granted a security interest in a refrigerator that he intended to use in a restaurant.
   b. Roberto granted a security interest in a stereo that he intended to sell in his stereo store.
   c. Roberto granted a security interest in a table saw that he intended to use at home.
   d. Roberto granted a security interest in a large generator and boiler system that he permanently installed in an office building.

_____ 4. Spokes sold Dee exercise equipment on credit. Dee intended to use the equipment for her personal workouts. Dee granted Spokes a security interest in the equipment to secure payment of the unpaid price. Spokes did not file a financing statement. Under these facts:
   a. The security interest is invalid. It is unlawful to obtain a security interest in consumer goods.
   b. The security interest in the equipment is not perfected.
   c. If Dee sells the equipment to Helen for her personal use, and Helen pays value and takes the equipment without knowledge of the security interest, then Helen's right to the equipment is superior to Spokes' security interest.
   d. b and c.

_____ 5. On May 1, First Bank perfected a security interest in Debtor's inventory of boats. On June 1, Bob bought a boat from Debtor in the ordinary course of business. On July 1, Second Bank perfected a security interest in Debtor's inventory of boats. Under these facts:

    a.   Bob's interest in the boat that he purchased is superior to First Bank's security interest.

    b.   First Bank's security interest is superior to Bob's interest in the boat that he purchased.

    c.   First Bank's security interest in Debtor's inventory of boats is superior to Second Bank's security interest.

    d.   a and c.

CASE PROBLEM

Acme Co. has a perfected security interest in Debtor's inventory to secure repayment of a $50,000 loan. Debtor has defaulted on three $1,000 monthly loan payments, and Acme has accelerated the entire loan. Under these facts:

(1) Can Acme repossess the inventory without obtaining a court order?

(2) Can Acme commit a breach of the peace if necessary to repossess the inventory?

(3) If Acme repossesses the inventory, briefly describe the procedure for selling the collateral.

(4) Can Debtor redeem the collateral?

(5) How are proceeds from the sale to be applied?

_____

_____

_____

BUSINESS LAW PARTNER EXERCISE

Directions:

1.   Time to go shopping, but beware of unknown secured parties! Using the Online feature of the Business Law Partner CD-ROM, find and identify two products that are for sale; one new and one used.

2.   If you purchased these items, would a party with a perfected security interest in each of these items have priority to these items and, therefore, have the right to retake them from you?

_____

_____

_____

Section A

DIRECTIONS: Complete each of the following statements by writing the missing word or words in the Answers column.

	Answers	For Scoring
1-2. An agreement whereby one party promises to be responsible for the debt, default, or obligation of another is known as ???	_____	1. _____
or ???	_____	2. _____
3. The party to whom a guaranty is given is the	_____	3. _____
4. A contract of suretyship which guarantees the faithful performance of a person entrusted with another's money is a(n)	_____	4. _____
5. The guarantor or surety who pays the obligation of the principal is entitled to reimbursement, which is known as the right of	_____	5. _____
6. The right of the guarantor to all property held by the creditor to secure payment of the debt is called	_____	6. _____
7. The right of the surety to insist the debt be paid and to bring suit against the principal to bring that about is the right of	_____	7. _____
8. Transactions in which sellers retain the right to repossess the items sold if the buyer's breach the sales contracts are called	_____	8. _____
9. When the seller's rights to the collateral are superior to the rights of third persons, the seller has a(n)	_____	9. _____
10. Articles purchased with the intention of reselling them are called	_____	10. _____
11. Goods used or purchased for use in a business are	_____	11. _____
12. A writing signed by the debtor and the secured party giving their addresses and a description of the collateral is a(n)	_____	12. _____

Score _____

Section B

DIRECTIONS: Following each statement below, indicate your answer by placing a "T" for "True" or an "F" for "False" in the Answers column.

	Answers	For Scoring
1. The obligation of a guarantor is primary.	_____	1. _____
2. The law of suretyship applies with equal force to both paid sureties and accommodation sureties.	_____	2. _____
3. It is necessary to notify the surety if the debt is defaulted.	_____	3. _____
4. The right of subrogation does not arise until the creditor has been paid in full.	_____	4. _____
5. Guarantors who have paid more than their proportionate share of a debt may not recover the excess from the other guarantors.	_____	5. _____
6. If the creditor extends the time of the debt without consent of the surety and for consideration, the surety is discharged.	_____	6. _____
7. A security interest cannot attach or become enforceable until the buyer and seller agree it shall attach.	_____	7. _____
8. After default, the seller must sell the collateral at a public sale.	_____	8. _____

Score _____

Section C

DIRECTIONS: Following each question below, indicate your answer by placing a "Y" for "Yes" or an "N" for "No" in the Answers column.

	Answers	For Scoring
1. Does a bonding company's obligation arise from its contract with the employee?		1. _____
2. Is a surety's obligation identical to the obligation of the one for whom responsibility is assumed?		2. _____
3. Does a guarantor's obligation arise simultaneously with the principal's obligation?		3. _____
4. Must all the essential elements of a contract be present in both contracts of guaranty and contracts of suretyship?		4. _____
5. Is it unnecessary to notify sureties if the debt is defaulted?		5. _____
6. Is the guarantor liable only if the other party cannot pay?		6. _____
7. If the creditor reduces the interest rate charged is the surety discharged?		7. _____
8. Does loss of the collateral security by the creditor discharge a surety or guarantor?		8. _____
9. May a creditor have an enforceable security interest before the buyer signs a security agreement?		9. _____
10. In the case of a consumer sale, is the assignee of the seller free of any claims or defenses that the buyer could assert against the seller?		10. _____
11. Can the transfer of collateral be subject to the security interest?		11. _____
12. Can a buyer require a seller to approve or correct a statement indicating the amount of unpaid indebtedness owed?		12. _____
13. Is filing unnecessary when the law requires a security interest to be noted on a title?		13. _____
14. After repossession, can the seller sell the collateral without notice to the debtor?		14. _____
15. Does the buyer have a right to redeem the property after repossession?		15. _____

Score _____

Section D

DIRECTIONS: Indicate your decision in each of the following cases in the Answers space.

	Answers	For Scoring
1. Higley, a composer, purchased by secured credit sale a small, lightweight cassette recorder with earphones to use while composing. Later Higley decided to compose without the recorder and just used the recorder to listen to language tapes while jogging. When sued by other creditors, the question arose as to whether the seller of the recorder had a perfected security interest. No filing had been made. Was the security interest perfected?		1. _____
2-4. Burns agreed to pay Grahm for repairs on Hale's car if Hale did not pay. Grahm was to retain the car until paid. On Hale's plea of great need, Grahm surrendered the car to him and then demanded payment from Burns. Burns denied liability. Would Burns' promise have to be written to be enforceable?		2. _____
Was this a contract of guaranty or suretyship?		3. _____
Even if Burns' promise had been enforceable, did Grahm's surrender of the security discharge Burns?		4. _____
5. Cowlings purchased furniture by means of a secured credit sale. He was laid off at work and missed a payment. The seller repossessed the furniture and before the seller sold it, Cowlings was called back to work. What right does Cowlings have?		5. _____

Score _____

CHAPTER 40
BANKRUPTCY

CHAPTER OUTLINE

I. INTRODUCTION

Bankruptcy gives debtors a new start, and it gives creditors an equal chance to collect their claims.

II. WHO CAN FILE A PETITION FOR BANKRUPTCY

General rule. Virtually any party residing or doing business in the U.S. can file for bankruptcy.
Limitation. Banks, insurance firms, savings and loans, and some cities cannot file for bankruptcy.
Study hint. The Bankruptcy Code provides several types of bankruptcy. Parties who can file for various types of bankruptcy include: ‣ Chapter 7: any person. ‣ Chapter 9: certain municipalities. ‣ Chapter 11: businesses (and other persons). ‣ Chapter 13: individuals with regular income.

III. KINDS OF DEBTORS

- *Voluntary debtors*: ‣ With the exception of the entities noted above, anyone can file a voluntary petition for bankruptcy. ‣ A husband and wife can file a joint petition for bankruptcy.

- *Involuntary debtors*: ‣ Creditors can sometimes force a debtor into bankruptcy by filing an involuntary petition. ‣ If a debtor has 12 or more creditors, at least three creditors with unsecured claims totaling $5,000 or more must sign an involuntary petition. If there are fewer than 12 creditors, any creditor with an unsecured claim of $5,000 or more may sign. ‣ A court will enter an order of relief (assume jurisdiction) if: (1) a debtor is not paying debts as they become due; or (2) within 120 days prior to filing, a custodian was appointed for a debtor's property.

- *Automatic stay*: A filing of a voluntary or involuntary petition gives rise to an automatic stay that prohibits creditors from beginning, or continuing, any legal action to collect debts from a debtor.

IV. PROCEDURE IN A LIQUIDATION CASE (CHAPTER 7 BANKRUPTCY)

‣ Creditors are notified that a petition has been filed, and a meeting of creditors is called. ‣ Creditors elect a trustee. The trustee assumes ownership of the debtor's property, collects debts owed to the debtor, preserves assets, and ultimately distributes the assets in accordance with the law.

V. EXEMPT PROPERTY

General rules. ‣ Federal bankruptcy law and state law may exempt certain property from being taken to satisfy claims of creditors. ‣ A debtor is allowed to keep exempt property even though the debtor has filed for bankruptcy. In general, a debtor can choose to keep either the property that is exempted by federal law, or the property that is exempted by state law.
Example. Exempt property commonly includes: a limited interest in a residence and vehicle; household goods; a *reasonable amount* of tools of a trade; clothing; personal effects, such as a Bible.
Limitation. States can limit exempt property to that property which is exempted by state law.

VI. INCLUDED PROPERTY

A debtor's bankruptcy estate includes: (1) debtor's nonexempt property owned at time of filing of a petition; (2) property acquired by a debtor by inheritance, divorce, or as a beneficiary of life insurance within 180 days after filing of a petition; and (3) property transferred by a debtor to a creditor within 90 days prior to filing, if done with an intent to prefer that creditor over other creditors.

VII. DUTIES OF THE DEBTOR

- *Duties*: ▸ Cooperate with trustee. ▸ File list of creditors. ▸ File schedule of assets and liabilities.
- *Penalties for not cooperating*: ▸ No discharge from debts. ▸ In some cases, criminal prosecution.

VIII. PROOF OF CLAIMS

Chapter 7: A creditor must file a proof of claim within 90 days after the first meeting of creditors.

IX. RECLAMATIONS

- *Reclamations*: If a debtor has possession of another person's property, the owner of the property should file a reclamation claim. This claim will entitle the owner to recover his or her property.
- *Checks*: ▸ Uncertified checks: A party holding an uncertified check of a debtor is merely a creditor who must file a proof of claim; the party is not entitled to have the check cashed. ▸ Certified check: If a party has a certified check, the party is entitled to payment by the bank.

X. TYPES OF CLAIMS

- *Fully secured claim*: Claims fully secured by assets are paid in full from proceeds from the assets.
- *Partially secured claims*: Claims that are partially secured by assets receive the proceeds from a sale of the assets. The unpaid portion of claims become unsecured claims.
- *Unsecured claims*: Claims that are not secured by any assets are paid with assets that remain after secured creditors receive payment under the foregoing rules.

XI. PRIORITY OF CLAIMS (UNSECURED CLAIMS)

▸ Assets that remain after secured creditors have enforced their security interests are paid to unsecured creditors in the following order: (1) bankruptcy administration expenses; (2) debts incurred by a debtor after the filing of an involuntary petition, but before an order of relief is granted; (3) maximum of $2,000 per employee, for wages earned within 90 days prior to the debtor's filing for bankruptcy; (4) certain fringe benefits owed employees; (5) certain claims by individuals who have deposited money with a debtor for undelivered consumer goods; (6) certain tax claims.

▸ After the foregoing claims are paid, unpaid claims share pro rata in the remaining assets, if any.

XII. DISCHARGE OF INDEBTEDNESS

A debtor who performs his or her duties receives a discharge. A discharge voids most unpaid debts.

XIII. DEBTS NOT DISCHARGED

A debtor is not discharged from liability for: (1) alimony and child support; (2) unpaid taxes incurred within three years; (3) debts owed due to embezzlement, fraud, or intentional wrongs; (4) wages owed to employees for work done within three months of bankruptcy; and (5) educational loans.

XIV. NONLIQUIDATION PLANS

- *Business reorganization*: ▸ Under Chapter 11, a voluntary or involuntary petition may be filed for businesses (and certain individuals). ▸ The debtor generally continues to run the business, and the debtor typically proposes a rehabilitation plan. ▸ A plan indicates to what extent creditors will be paid. A court may confirm a plan if it is fair, equitable, feasible, and proposed in good faith.
- *Chapter 13 plans*: ▸ A person can typically file for a Chapter 13 bankruptcy if he or she has regular income (wages or commissions), unsecured debts less than $100,000, and secured debts less than $350,000. ▸ Under Chapter 13, a debtor may file a plan that provides for full or partial payment of debts over an extended time. However, the plan cannot pay unsecured creditors less than they would receive under Chapter 7. ▸ After a plan is carried out, the debtor is discharged from most unpaid debts that are dischargeable in a Chapter 7 bankruptcy.

REVIEW OF CHAPTER

REVIEW OF TERMS

Select the term that best matches a statement below. Each term is the best match for only one statement.

TERMS

a. Chapter 7 bankruptcy
b. Chapter 11 bankruptcy
c. Chapter 13 bankruptcy

d. Discharge of indebtedness
e. Exempt property
f. Involuntary petition

g. Proof of claim
h. Reclamation claim
i. Voluntary petition

STATEMENTS

Answer

____ 1. Bankruptcy petition filed by creditors against a debtor.
____ 2. Liquidation proceeding. Bankruptcy proceeding in which a trustee sells a debtor's nonexempt property for the benefit of creditors.
____ 3. Claim by an owner that requests return of property that is in the possession of a debtor.
____ 4. Bankruptcy petition filed by a debtor.
____ 5. Assets that a debtor may keep even though the debtor has filed for bankruptcy.
____ 6. Bankruptcy proceeding in which a business reorganizes its affairs, proposes a plan to pay creditors, and continues in business.
____ 7. Claim by a creditor that requests payment of a debt owed by a debtor.
____ 8. Court decree that voids (bars) a debtor's unpaid debts upon conclusion of bankruptcy proceedings.
____ 9. Bankruptcy proceeding in which a person with regular income can propose a plan for paying off his or her debts over an extended period of time.

REVIEW OF CONCEPTS

Directions: Indicate **T** for true and **F** for false in the answer column.

____ 1. Bankruptcy law is intended solely to protect debtors and to give debtors a new start on life.
____ 2. Banks and insurance companies cannot file a voluntary petition for Chapter 7 bankruptcy.
____ 3. After a petition for bankruptcy has been filed, creditors are generally prohibited from filing or continuing any lawsuits against a debtor.
____ 4. Federal bankruptcy law allows states to specify what property is exempt in a bankruptcy action.
____ 5. Exempt property that a debtor can keep typically includes a limited interest in a house, a reasonable amount of tools of a trade, and clothing.
____ 6. Thirty days prior to filing for bankruptcy, Debtor paid an old debt owed to XYZ Co. Debtor paid XYZ with the intent to prefer XYZ over other creditors. (XYZ would receive nothing in bankruptcy.) In this case, the trustee cannot recover Debtor's payment to XYZ.
____ 7. If a debtor fails to cooperate with the bankruptcy trustee, the debtor may be denied a discharge.
____ 8. A creditor is not required to file a proof of claim in a Chapter 7 bankruptcy.
____ 9. Under Chapter 11, a debtor's business is liquidated, and assets are distributed to creditors.
____ 10. Anyone with regular income (regardless of amount of debts) can file for a Chapter 13 bankruptcy.
____ 11. A Chapter 13 plan may provide for less than full payment of certain creditors.

REVIEW OF CONCEPT APPLICATIONS

Answer

Directions: Indicate your choice in the answer column.

____ 1. Lance is a construction worker who earns a regular wage. Lance has $20,000 of unsecured debts, and he is no longer paying his debts as they become due. Lance has 10 creditors, including ABC Finance to whom Lance owes $7,000. Under these facts:
    a. Lance cannot file a voluntary petition for Chapter 7 bankruptcy.
    b. Lance cannot file a voluntary petition for Chapter 13 bankruptcy.
    c. ABC Finance can file an involuntary petition for Chapter 7 bankruptcy against Lance.
    d. b and c.

_____ 2.	Melpha has just filed for Chapter 7 bankruptcy. One of Melpha's creditors is Arco Finance. Melpha is delinquent on a loan owed to Arco. Under these facts:
   a.	Arco cannot sue Melpha in state court to collect the loan.
   b.	Melpha will retain possession of her assets, and she will administer her bankruptcy estate.
   c.	Melpha will not be entitled to keep any property. All of Melpha's property will be taken to satisfy the claims of her creditors.
   d.	Melpha does not have to cooperate with the bankruptcy court.

_____ 3.	Barbara recently filed for Chapter 7 bankruptcy. Which property is included in Barbara's bankruptcy estate?
   a.	$500 that was in Barbara's bank account at the time she filed for bankruptcy.
   b.	A stereo that Barbara purchased 90 days after she filed for bankruptcy.
   c.	$5,000 that Barbara inherited 60 days after she filed for bankruptcy.
   d.	a and c.

_____ 4.	Ramon filed for Chapter 7 bankruptcy, and he received a discharge. Certain debts were not paid in Ramon's bankruptcy. Which of the following unpaid debts is discharged?
   a.	Child support owed for Ramon's minor children.
   b.	$1,500 owed to MasterCard.
   c.	Federal income taxes owed for the preceding two years.
   d.	$5,000 judgment resulting from Ramon's embezzlement of money from a former employer.

CASE PROBLEM

Fuller Co. filed for Chapter 7 bankruptcy. Fuller's bankruptcy estate included a building, equipment, and $16,000. The bankruptcy trustee sold the building for $100,000, and sold the equipment for $10,000. Fuller has the following creditors: (1) First Bank is owed $100,000. This debt is secured by the building. (2) Budget Co. is owed $30,000. This debt is secured by the equipment. (3) Stephanie is owed $1,000 for wages she earned 30 days prior to Fuller's filing for bankruptcy. (4) Case Co. is owed $10,000 for supplies. This debt is unsecured. Please discuss the rights of Fuller's creditors to be paid.

_____

_____

_____

BUSINESS LAW PARTNER EXERCISE

Directions: Using the Online feature of the Business Law Partner CD-ROM, answer the questions in the case below.

Case Study: *Are There More Generous Pastures Elsewhere?*

Linda is experiencing significant financial difficulties and she recognizes that bankruptcy may not be out of the question. She has learned, however, that the extent to which a person's primary residence may be exempt property in a Chapter 7 bankruptcy often depends on state law. She has asked you to answer the following questions:

1.	Does federal bankruptcy law allow states to grant different exemptions than are allowed under federal law?
2.	Identify three states that have more generous residence or personal property exemptions than are offered under the U.S. Bankruptcy Code. Identify the amount of the state exemptions.

_____

_____

_____

CHAPTER 40 QUIZ

Section A

DIRECTIONS: Following each question below, indicate your answer by placing a "T" for "True" or an "F" for "False" in the Answers column.

	Answers	For Scoring
1. Is one of the purposes of bankruptcy to give an insolvent person a new start?	_____	1. _____
2. Is a bankruptcy proceeding less wasteful of the debtor's assets than individual suits by creditors?	_____	2. _____
3. May any person having a place of business in the United States be a debtor under the Bankruptcy Code?	_____	3. _____
4. If there are twelve or more creditors, must five seek an involuntary bankruptcy?	_____	4. _____
5. When an involuntary petition is filed, will a court order relief if the debtor is not paying debts as they become due?	_____	5. _____
6. Is the liquidation procedure the same if the bankruptcy is voluntary or involuntary?	_____	6. _____
7. Does filing a petition in bankruptcy court stay the filing of proceedings to recover a claim against the debtor that arose before the bankruptcy petition was filed?	_____	7. _____
8. Do many federal exemptions set a limit on the value of items which may be excluded?	_____	8. _____
9. May some property acquired by the debtor after the beginning of bankruptcy proceedings be included in the debtor's estate?	_____	9. _____
10. Are there circumstances under which property transferred with the intention of giving preference to a creditor may be restored to the debtor's estate?	_____	10. _____
11. Can a business work out a Chapter 13 plan?	_____	11. _____
12. Can a Chapter 13 plan pay unsecured creditors less than they would receive under a Chapter 7 liquidation?	_____	12. _____
13. Can a creditor of a Chapter 7 debtor normally collect from the trustee if proof of a claim is not filed within 90 days after the date of the first meeting of creditors?	_____	13. _____
14. Is a reclamation a preference which would defraud creditors?	_____	14. _____
15. Do partially secured creditors have liens on assets sufficient to fully pay the debts?	_____	15. _____
16. Are debts incurred after the filing of an involuntary petition and before an order of relief or appointment of a trustee priority claims?	_____	16. _____
17. Are claims for alimony and child support discharged by bankruptcy?	_____	17. _____
18. Are debts due on a judgment for intentional injury discharged by bankruptcy?	_____	18. _____
19. May a debtor who has hidden a few assets be denied a discharge by the court?	_____	19. _____
20. After the discharge of indebtedness, can creditors sue the debtor for collection of debts not fully paid by the proceedings?	_____	20. _____

Score _____

Section B

DIRECTIONS: Following each statement below, indicate your answer by placing a " T" for " True" or an " F" for " False" in the Answers column.

	Answers	For Scoring
1. Bankruptcy is a judicial declaration of a debtor's willingness to pay debts....................	_____	1. _____
2. Bankruptcy proceedings allow creditors to be paid in proportion to their claims; therefore, a more equitable settlement is achieved.	_____	2. _____
3. An insurance company cannot be a debtor under the Bankruptcy Code, but may be the subject of rehabilitation proceedings.	_____	3. _____
4. Chapter 7 applies to any person who may be a debtor under the Bankruptcy Code.......	_____	4. _____
5. A husband and wife must file a joint petition in bankruptcy.	_____	5. _____
6. An involuntary petition may be filed against a farmer..	_____	6. _____
7. The trustee is chosen by the bankruptcy judge.	_____	7. _____
8. The trustee in bankruptcy sets a deadline for filing proof of claims.............................	_____	8. _____
9. All life insurance must be used to pay the debtor's debts.	_____	9. _____
10. Each state exempts certain property from seizure for the payment of debts..................	_____	10. _____
11. A debtor must file a schedule of all assets and liabilities with the trustee.	_____	11. _____
12. A debtor may be liable for criminal prosecution for failure to obey orders of, and cooperate with, the trustee.	_____	12. _____
13. If a debtor involved in bankruptcy proceedings has possession of bailed goods, the true owner cannot recover the property.	_____	13. _____
14. A person in possession of a check drawn by the debtor may be able to get it paid.	_____	14. _____
15. Tax claims have first priority on the assets of the debtor...	_____	15. _____
16. Debts incurred by means of fraud are discharged by bankruptcy proceedings...............	_____	16. _____
17. Under Chapter 11, a business is liquidated.	_____	17. _____
18. If no acceptable plan of reorganization can be worked out, the business is released from court supervision..	_____	18. _____
19. A Chapter 13 plan attempts to achieve for an individual debtor the same advantages that the business reorganization act gives to a business..	_____	19. _____
20. A minority of creditors can prevent a Chapter 13 plan for a debtor.	_____	20. _____

Score _____

CHAPTER 41
NATURE OF REAL PROPERTY

CHAPTER OUTLINE

I.   DISTINGUISHING REAL PROPERTY

General rules. ▸ Real property includes land, soil, minerals, water on the land, and all things permanently attached to the land, such as fences and buildings. ▸ Real property also includes: (1) trees, orchards, and *perennial* crops while attached to the land; (2) the riverbed (but not the water) of non-navigable rivers; and (3) fixtures (personal property that is so securely attached to land or buildings that it becomes part of it).

Examples. ▸ House. ▸ Orange grove. ▸ Evergreen forest. ▸ Coal deposits. ▸ Attached furnace.

Limitation. Real property does not include crops planted annually and cultivated (e.g., corn).

Study hints. ▸ A landowner cannot dam or impound river water if doing so denies its use to others. ▸ A tenant cannot remove fixtures without a lessor's permission. ▸ Tests to determine if property is a fixture: (1) Can property be removed without damaging real property? (If not, it is real property.) (2) Intent of the party attaching the property. (3) Purpose for which property is attached. (4) Who installed the property? (If a landlord installed the property, it is presumed to be real property. If a tenant installed the property, it is presumed to be personal property.)

II.   MULTIPLE OWNERSHIP

When more than one person owns the same land, each owner has the right to use and possess that land. The most common ways real property can be owned by more than one person are:

A. TENANCY IN COMMON

General rules: ▸ Defined: Form of multiple ownership in which upon one co-owner's death, his or her share passes to the person named in his or her will. (If there is no will, the share passes to the deceased's heirs.) ▸ Co-owners each own an undivided fractional share of the entire property rather than a specific portion of the land. ▸ Co-owners may give away or sell their fractional shares while they are living. A new owner becomes a tenant in common with the remaining owner(s). ▸ The law makes a presumption that property held by multiple owners is held by them as tenants in common.

Example: James and Juan equally own a ten-acre tract as tenants in common. James cannot sell five of the acres as his share of the tract. Juan can sell his one-half interest in the ten acres to Marguerite, who then owns the property as a tenant in common with James.

Study hint: Tenants in common may own unequal interests in the property.

B. JOINT TENANCY

General rules: ▸ Defined: Form of multiple ownership in which at the death of one co-owner, the remaining co-owners automatically own the entire property (i.e., co-owners have a right of survivorship). ▸ Each co-owner owns an undivided fractional share of the entire property rather than a specific portion of the land. ▸ To create a joint tenancy, language must clearly indicate that intent. ▸ If one joint tenant gives away or sells his or her interest, the new owner becomes a tenant in common rather than a joint tenant. ▸ Any joint tenant may sue for partition or division of the property. Partition destroys the joint tenancy.

Study hint: A joint tenant cannot transfer his or her interest by will.

C. TENANCY BY THE ENTIRETY

General rules: ▸ Defined: Co-ownership of property by husband and wife with the right of survivorship. ▸ Creditors of only one co-owner cannot claim the property. ▸ The husband or wife alone cannot convey the property.

Limitation: This form of multiple ownership is only recognized in about half of the states.

Study hint: If tenants by the entirety divorce, they become tenants in common with regard to the property.

D. COMMUNITY PROPERTY

General rule: Defined: Property acquired by a husband and wife during their marriage is owned in separate and equal shares no matter how it is titled.

Limitations: ▸ Only eight states recognize community property. ▸ Property owned by one spouse before the marriage is normally that spouse's separate property.

III.   ESTATES IN PROPERTY

An estate in property defines the nature and extent of a person's interest in the property. A person may hold one of the following estates in personal or real property:

- *Fee simple estate*: ▸ A party with an estate in fee simple owns all rights to a property, and the party can sell, lease, or dispose of the property, or pass the property by will. ▸ Real property is owned from the center of the earth to the heavens (although planes have a right to fly overhead).

- *Life estate*: ▸ A person with a life estate owns property for a lifetime. On the death of that person, property passes to whomever the original owner (grantor) directed. Title may pass back to the grantor (a reversion), or to a third party (a remainder). ▸ Example of a reversion: Susan conveyed a life estate in a cottage to Audrey. When Audrey dies, the cottage reverts back to Susan. ▸ Example of a remainder: By will, Grandpa left a life estate in a ranch to Joe, and a remainder to Claire. Joe owns the ranch until he dies; then the ranch passes to Claire.

IV.   OTHER INTERESTS IN REAL PROPERTY

- *Easement*: ▸ Defined: interest in property that gives a holder a right to use (not exclusively possess) property. ▸ Easements are acquired by deed or adverse possession. ▸ Example: right-of-way across land.

- *License*: ▸ Defined: interest in property that gives a holder a right to perform an act on property. A license can be terminated at any time by the grantor. ▸ Example: Owner grants Stan a license to hunt rabbits on his land. Owner can revoke the license at any time.

V.   ACQUIRING REAL PROPERTY

Title to real property may be acquired in many of the same ways as personal property. For example, property can be acquired by purchase, will (transfer upon owner's death following probate) or descent (transfer upon death of owner without a will), and gift. Title to real property may also be acquired by:

- *Accretion*: Real property is enlarged by a build-up of soil or silt, or by a river changing course.

- *Adverse possession*: ▸ A person occupying land for a certain period of time may obtain title by adverse possession. ▸ Requirements: occupation must be: (1) continuous; (2) open; (3) hostile; (4) visible; (5) actual; and (6) exclusive. ▸ The required occupation varies by state statute from seven to twenty-one years. ▸ Example: Hal does not have title to a cabin, but he lived in the cabin for 25 years, telling everyone he was the owner. Hal may own the cabin by adverse possession.

REVIEW OF CHAPTER

REVIEW OF TERMS

Select the term that best matches a statement below. Each term is the best match for only one statement.

TERMS

a. Accretion
b. Adverse possession
c. Color of title
d. Community property
e. Easement
f. Estate in fee simple

g. Fixture
h. Joint tenancy
i. License
j. Life estate
k. Partition
l. Personal property

m. Real property
n. Remainder
o. Reversion
p. Right of survivorship
q. Tenancy in common
r. Tenancy by the entirety

STATEMENTS

Answer

_____ 1. Ownership of all rights to property.

_____ 2. Interest in property that gives one the nonexclusive right to use (not possess) the property.

_____ 3. Property that is movable. This property includes all property that is not real property.

_____ 4. Title to land is acquired by continuous, open, hostile, visible, and exclusive occupation of property for the statutorily required period of time.

_____ 5. Ownership of property for a lifetime.

_____ 6. Interest in property that gives one the right to perform an act on another person's property.

_____ 7. Property is increased by a build-up of soil or silt deposits.

_____ 8. Land, soil, minerals, fences, and permanently attached buildings.

_____ 9. Personal property so securely attached to real property that it becomes part of it.

_____ 10. Multiple ownership in which at co-owner's death, his or her share passes by will or to heirs.

_____ 11. Multiple ownership in which at co-owner's death, his or her share passes to remaining owners.

_____ 12. Automatic ownership of property by survivors.

_____ 13. Lawsuit to divide property held in joint tenancy.

_____ 14. Co-ownership by husband and wife with right of survivorship.

_____ 15. Property acquired during marriage and owned equally by both spouses.

_____ 16. Grantor's interest in life estate that returns to grantor upon death of grantee.

_____ 17. Grantor's interest in life estate that goes to someone other than grantor upon grantee's death.

_____ 18. Person's apparent title.

REVIEW OF CONCEPTS

Directions: Indicate **T** for true and **F** for false in the answer column.

_____ 1. Tony planted a wheat crop on land he was renting. In this case, the crop is real property.

_____ 2. Peter sold some land to Yin. Yin is entitled to a house and forest that are on the land.

_____ 3. Tim owns land that is bounded by a non-navigable stream. In this case, Tim is entitled to divert the stream and impound all of the water to create a private reservoir for his exclusive use.

_____ 4. If a landlord installs equipment in leased premises, the equipment is presumed to be a fixture.

_____ 5. Phil can prohibit planes from flying over his property if he owns the land in fee simple.

_____ 6. If an earthquake causes a river to shift its course, the owner of property bounded by the river may gain additional land by accretion.

_____ 7. Lenny built a fence at his home. The fence was misplaced, and the fenced-in property included a strip of land belonging to a neighbor. For 23 years, Lenny used and maintained this strip, always acting as its owner. In this case, Lenny may own this strip of land by adverse possession.

REVIEW OF CONCEPT APPLICATIONS

Directions: Indicate your choice in the answer column.

_____ 1. Shanti leased a building. Shanti installed a stove and a boiler in the building. Upon expiration of the lease, Shanti intends to remove the stove, but not the boiler. The stove can be easily removed without harming anything. Removal of the boiler, however, will seriously damage both the building and the boiler. Are the stove and boiler fixtures?
   a. The stove and the boiler are both fixtures.
   b. The stove is not a fixture, but the boiler is a fixture.
   c. The stove is a fixture, but the boiler is not a fixture.

_____ 2. Martin owned the entire title to the Lazy B Ranch. Martin executed a deed transferring title to the ranch to Roger for the duration of Roger's life and, upon Roger's death, title was to pass to Beth. Under these facts, what type of estate or interest did the parties have?
   a. Prior to passing title, Martin had an estate in fee simple.
   b. Prior to passing title, Martin had a life estate.
   c. Roger did not have any estate because title passed to Beth on Roger's death.
   d. Beth had a reversionary interest.

_____ 3. Sherman owns a large farm. Sherman granted Sam the right to build a road across his farm and to indefinitely use the road so that Sam could reach his own property. Sherman also granted Benjamin the (revocable) right to camp on the farm. What kinds of interests did Sherman grant?
   a. Sherman granted easements to both Sam and Benjamin.
   b. Sherman granted licenses to both Sam and Benjamin.
   c. Sherman granted Sam a license, and Benjamin an easement.
   d. Sherman granted Sam an easement, and Benjamin a license.

CASE PROBLEM

Winslow owned all rights to a farm and a lot in the city. He conveyed the farm "to Abe and Max as joint tenants with the right of survivorship." Abe died and had a clause in his will conveying his interest in the farm to Chris. Winslow deeded his city lot to his mother for her lifetime, and then the lot was to go back to Winslow. What types of interests did each of the parties have? Briefly explain.

_____

_____

_____

BUSINESS LAW PARTNER EXERCISE

Directions:

1. Access your Business Law Partner CD-ROM and find the document entitled "License Agreement." Also read the accompanying material under "Legal Help."
2. Can a person obtain a license to use either real property or personal property?
3. For what type of license is the License Agreement intended?

_____

_____

_____

CHAPTER 41 QUIZ

Section A

DIRECTIONS: Following each question below, indicate your answer by placing a "Y" for "Yes" or an "N" for "No" in the Answers column.

	Answers	For Scoring
1. Are trees always classified as real property?	_____	1. _____
2. Can the owner of property through which a nonnavigable river flows impound or divert the water in any way desired?	_____	2. _____
3. If personal property is so securely attached that it cannot be removed without damaging the real property, does it cease to be personal property?	_____	3. _____
4. Must the owners of land held as a tenancy in common own the land equally?	_____	4. _____
5. May a tenant in common convey the interest while alive?	_____	5. _____
6. When property is conveyed to more than one person, does the law presume they hold it as tenants in common?	_____	6. _____
7. May a joint tenant determine who owns the property at death?	_____	7. _____
8. If the interest of one joint tenant is sold, does the buyer become a joint tenant?	_____	8. _____
9. May a joint tenant dispose of the interest in the tenancy by will?	_____	9. _____
10. May a wife's creditors claim property held as a tenancy by the entirety?	_____	10. _____
11. Does a divorce change a tenancy by the entirety to a tenancy in common?	_____	11. _____
12. Do all states recognize the community property form of ownership?	_____	12. _____
13. Does property owned by one spouse prior to the marriage normally become community property?	_____	13. _____
14. Does a fee simple owner of property have the right to possess the property forever?	_____	14. _____
15. Does the owner of land have an absolute right to the air above the land?	_____	15. _____
16. Can one own only the surface of land?	_____	16. _____
17. Does the owner of a life estate direct to whom title passes on the death of such owner?	_____	17. _____
18. May the person granting a license normally terminate it at will?	_____	18. _____
19. Is the period required to establish title by adverse possession the same in every state?	_____	19. _____
20. Is it adequate for adverse possession that the occupancy of the land is continuous, open, and hostile?	_____	20. _____

Score _____

DIRECTIONS: Complete each of the following statements by writing the missing word or words in the Answers column.

	Answers	For Scoring

1. Land and all permanent attachments to the land such as fences are ??? property. .... _____ 1. ____

2. Perennial crops are classed as ??? property.. _____ 2. ____

3. Personal property securely attached to land is known as a(n)........................ _____ 3. ____

4-5. When more than one person owns land, each person has the right to ??? and ??? it. .... _____ 4. ____

   .... _____ 5. ____

6. Multiple ownership in which at the death of one owner, that owner's interest passes as directed in the deceased's will or to heirs is called............. _____ 6. ____

7. Multiple ownership whereby the share of a deceased owner passes to the surviving owners is called .... _____ 7. ____

8. Automatic ownership of property by the surviving owners is called the........ _____ 8. ____

9. A suit to divide property held in joint tenancy is a suit for .... _____ 9. ____

10. Co-ownership of property by a husband and wife such that the survivor becomes the sole owner of the property is called... _____ 10. ____

11. A type of ownership reserved for married couples whereby both spouses own a separate and equal share of the property no matter how titled is called .... _____ 11. ____

12. The nature and extent of interest a person has in property is a(n).................. _____ 12. ____

13. The largest, most complete right which one may possess in property is a(n) . _____ 13. ____

14. If, at the time of death of the owner of a life estate, the title goes back to the grantor, the interest of the grantor is called a(n).. _____ 14. ____

15. If, at the time of death of a life estate, the title goes to someone other than the grantor, the interest in the estate is called a(n)... _____ 15. ____

16. An interest in land for non-exclusive or intermittent use is a(n)..................... _____ 16. ____

17. A right to do certain acts on land, but not a right to stay in possession is a(n) _____ 17. ____

18. When additional real estate is acquired by the addition to land as a result of the gradual deposit by water of solids, the owner acquires land by .... _____ 18. ____

19. Acquiring title to real property by occupying land owned by another for a period fixed by statute is called .... _____ 19. ____

20. A person's apparent title is called .... _____ 20. ____

Score _____

CHAPTER 42
TRANSFER OF REAL PROPERTY

CHAPTER OUTLINE

I. INTRODUCTION

▸ Real property may be transferred by sale, gift, or lease. ▸ A transfer of title to real property that is made by sale or gift must be evidenced by a deed.

II. DEEDS

A deed is a writing signed by a grantor (seller) that transfers title to real property from the grantor to a grantee (buyer). A deed must be in the form required by statute. Types of deeds include:

- *Quitclaim deed*: ▸ A quitclaim deed transfers whatever interest the grantor has to property. However, a grantor under a quitclaim deed does *not* warrant that the grantor owns good title or that there are no liens. ▸ Example: Wayne conveyed land to Maria by quitclaim deed. Wayne owned a one-half interest in the land. Maria now owns Wayne's interest in the property. Wayne did not breach any warranties even though Maria did not receive title to the entire property.

- *General warranty deed*: ▸ A general warranty deed transfers the grantor's title to property, and the grantor warrants that: (1) title is good; (2) all previous owners had good title; and (3) the property is not subject to any liens or claims of others. ▸ Example: Art conveyed title to land to Bob by general warranty deed. Carl owns a one-third interest in the land, and ABC Bank has a lien on the land. Art has breached two warranties, and Art is liable to Bob for damages.

- *Special warranty deed*: ▸ A special warranty deed transfers a grantor's title to property, and the grantor warrants only that the grantor has the authority to transfer the property. Under a special warranty deed, a grantor does not warrant that the grantor has good title, or that the title is free from defects. ▸ This type of deed is used by sheriffs, trustees, and personal representatives who transfer property belonging to others.

Most courts now impose an implied warranty of fitness or habitability on homebuilders.

III. PROVISIONS IN A DEED

- *Parties*: A deed must identify both the grantor and the grantee. If the grantor is married, the grantor's spouse should also be identified.

- *Consideration*: ▸ In general, a deed must state that consideration has been given, but the actual amount need not be stated. ▸ Example: "One Dollar and other valuable consideration" is proper.

- *Covenants*: ▸ Covenants are promises stated in a deed. ▸ Types of covenants: (1) an affirmative covenant is a promise by a grantee to do an act (e.g., maintain a fence); and (2) a negative covenant is a promise by a grantee not to do an act (e.g., promise not to keep horses). ▸ Covenants frequently arise when an owner subdivides land into lots, and covenants are then placed in the deeds to the lots. ▸ Most covenants "run with the land," i.e., they are binding on all future owners of the land. ▸ Example: Steven purchased a house in a subdivision. The deed to Steven's house contains a covenant that prohibits building a fence on the property. In this case, neither Steven nor any future owner of the house can build a fence on the property.

- *Description*: ▸ A deed must accurately describe the property. Any description is sufficient if the property can be identified. ▸ Common types of description: (1) lots and blocks (city property); and (2) section, range, and township, or metes and bounds (rural property). ▸ Deeds frequently use the description that was used in a prior deed. ▸ Deeds may sometimes describe property by reference to surveys or natural boundaries.

- ▪ *Signature*: ▸ A grantor must sign a deed, although the grantor can sign by making a mark. ▸ Most states require deeds to be attested by witnesses. ▸ If a grantor is married, the grantor's spouse should sign for the purpose of conveying any rights the spouse may have to the property.

- ▪ *Acknowledgment*: ▸ An acknowledgment is a declaration by a notary public or other authorized official that the grantor acknowledged that he or she signed a document of his or her free will. ▸ In virtually all states, a deed cannot be recorded unless it is acknowledged.

IV.   DELIVERY

General rules.   ▸ Title to property vests in a grantee as soon as (1) the grantor executes a deed and (2) the deed is delivered to the grantee or to the grantee's agent. ▸ Delivery requires that a grantor give up possession and control over the deed.

Examples.   ▸ Title passes: Evelyn executed a deed, and Evelyn gave the deed to Grantee. ▸ Title does not pass: Isaac executed a deed, but Isaac kept the deed.

Limitations.   ▸ A deed is not effective (does not transfer title) until it is delivered. ▸ A deed is not delivered if (1) the grantor keeps possession of the deed, (2) the deed is placed in a safety deposit box that is controlled by the grantor, or (3) the deed is in the possession of an agent of the grantor.

V.   RECORDING

General rules.   ▸ It is not necessary to record a deed in order to pass title. ▸ However, recording a deed gives notice of the grantee's ownership, and it protects the grantee from having his or her title impaired by: (1) a subsequent sale of the property by the grantor; or (2) a lien the grantor may subsequently create against the property.

Example.   Lucas signed a deed to his farm, conveying title to Cohen. Lucas delivered the deed to Cohen, but Cohen failed to record the deed. Later, Lucas borrowed money from Bank and he granted Bank a mortgage on the farm. Bank recorded the mortgage. In this situation, Cohen has title to the farm, but Cohen holds title subject to Bank's mortgage. If Cohen had recorded the deed before the mortgage was recorded, Cohen would hold the land free from the mortgage.

VI.   ABSTRACT OF TITLE

General rule.   An abstract of title provides a complete history of transactions relating to the real property in question. An abstract also shows whether there are any outstanding mortgages, liens, unpaid tax assessments, or judgments against the property.

Example.   Ray contracted to buy a house from Ben. Ray ordered an abstract of title prior to paying. The abstract showed that the house was subject to a lien for repair work that Ben had failed to pay. This knowledge allows Ray to take appropriate steps to protect his rights.

VII.   TITLE INSURANCE

General rules.   ▸ Title insurance insures a party against defects in the title to real estate. ▸ An insured pays one premium, and the policy protects the insured for as long as the insured owns the property.

Limitations.   ▸ Title insurance may expressly exclude coverage for certain defects. ▸ Title insurance only protects the named insured; it does not protect a future owner or any other party.

Study hint.   Title insurance helps to protect against defects that cannot be detected by an abstract of title (e.g., forged signatures on prior deeds; adverse possession claims; fraud or duress).

REVIEW OF CHAPTER

REVIEW OF TERMS

Select the term that best matches a statement below. Each term is the best match for only one statement.

TERMS

a. Abstract of title
b. Acknowledgment
c. Covenant
d. Deed
e. Delivery
f. General warranty deed
g. Quitclaim deed
h. Special warranty deed
i. Title insurance

STATEMENTS

Answer

_____ 1. Promise stated in a deed.

_____ 2. Writing signed by a grantor that transfers title to real property to a grantee.

_____ 3. Warranty deed that transfers a grantor's title and guarantees good title to property.

_____ 4. Declaration by a grantor before a notary public that the grantor is signing of his or her free will.

_____ 5. Deed that transfers the title, if any, held by the grantor, but does not make any guarantees.

_____ 6. Insurance that protects an insured against defects in title.

_____ 7. Document that shows whether there are any liens or other claims recorded against real property.

_____ 8. Warranty deed that transfers a grantor's title, but only guarantees that the grantor has the right or authority to transfer the property in question.

_____ 9. Giving up possession and control of a deed.

REVIEW OF CONCEPTS

Directions: Indicate **T** for true and **F** for false in the answer column.

_____ 1. Royce executed a general warranty deed to Richard. The deed effectively transferred Royce's title, but the property is subject to a lien. In this case, Royce has not breached any warranties.

_____ 2. A special warranty deed makes more guarantees than are made by a general warranty deed.

_____ 3. Administrator executed a special warranty deed to Buyer transferring an estate's title to real property. Administrator has breached a warranty to Buyer if the title is not good.

_____ 4. A deed does not pass title unless the deed identifies the grantor and the grantor signs the deed.

_____ 5. A grantor may describe property in several ways so long as it sufficiently identifies the property.

_____ 6. Karen, a married woman, owns some land. Karen intends to convey the land to Grantee. In this case, Grantee should request that Karen's husband also sign the deed.

_____ 7. Seller sold land to Buyer. The deed states that Buyer and all subsequent owners promise to maintain a retaining wall on the property. This promise is an affirmative covenant.

_____ 8. A deed does not have to be acknowledged in order to be recorded.

_____ 9. Title to property does not pass until a signed deed is delivered by the grantor to the grantee.

_____ 10. Grantor gave a signed deed to Fran, but she failed to record it. Grantor then executed another deed to Bill, and Bill recorded his deed. In this case, Bill has a superior title to the property.

_____ 11. Buyer received a general warranty deed to property, but title is defective because a prior deed was forged. In this case, title insurance would not protect Buyer from a loss due to the forgery.

REVIEW OF CONCEPT APPLICATIONS

Answer

Directions: Indicate your choice in the answer column.

_____ 1. Porter executed a quitclaim deed, and he delivered the deed to Bonnie. The deed passed Porter's title to Bonnie. As it turns out, Porter owned only half of the property, and the property was subject to a lien. Under these facts:

    a. Porter breached a warranty that he owned good title to the property.

    b. Porter breached a warranty that the property was free of liens.

    c. Porter did not breach any warranties.

    d. a and b.

____ 2.   Sydney signed a deed, and the deed was acknowledged. The deed accurately described certain property by section, range, and township. The deed stated: "I, Sydney Austin, do hereby transfer to Grantee the above-described property in consideration for One Dollar and other valuable consideration." The deed did not identify the grantee. Is the deed valid?
   a.   Yes. The deed was signed, acknowledged, and it described the property.
   b.   No, because the deed described the property by section, range, and township.
   c.   No, because the deed stated the consideration as One Dollar and other valuable consideration.
   d.   No, because the deed did not identify the grantee.

____ 3.   Acme Development subdivided land into residential lots. Acme sold one lot to Charles. The deed from Acme to Charles contained a covenant prohibiting construction of a two-story home on the lot. The covenant runs with the land. Charles sold the lot to Jane. Under these facts:
   a.   The covenant was binding on Charles, and it is binding on all future owners, including Jane.
   b.   The covenant was binding on Charles, but it is not binding on future owners, such as Jane.
   c.   The covenant is void. Negative covenants are illegal.

____ 4.   Margaret wanted to give Lex a small seaside cottage for his birthday. Margaret executed a proper deed to convey title to Lex, and the deed was acknowledged. Under these facts:
   a.   Title passed to Lex as soon as the deed was signed and acknowledged.
   b.   Title will pass as soon as Margaret delivers the deed to her attorney, for delivery to Lex.
   c.   Title will pass as soon as Margaret delivers the deed to Lex.
   d.   Title will not pass until Margaret delivers the deed to Lex, and Lex records the deed.

CASE PROBLEM

Chris plans to buy a 100-year-old house from Gloria. The house is subject to a recorded mortgage, and it is also subject to a recorded judgment against Gloria. In addition, a neighbor claims to own a portion of the property in question by adverse possession. In this case: (1) Should Chris obtain an abstract of title? What will the abstract show? What will the abstract not show? (2) Should Chris obtain title insurance?

_____

_____

_____

BUSINESS LAW PARTNER EXERCISE

Directions:

1.   Using the Online feature of the Business Law Partner CD-ROM, find an advertisement for a company that is offering title insurance. Identify the web site where this advertisement is located.
2.   Describe what benefits and costs are associated with the proferred title insurance

_____

_____

_____

CHAPTER 42 QUIZ

Section A

DIRECTIONS: Complete each of the following statements by writing the missing word or words in the Answers column.

	Answers	For Scoring
1. As a party to a deed the seller of real estate is called the	_____	1. _____
2. A deed by which the seller gives up any claim in real estate but makes no warranty is a(n) <u>???</u> deed.	_____	2. _____
3. A deed in which the seller warrants title and that the buyer shall have peaceful possession, freedom from encumbrances, and defense against all claims	_____	3. _____
4. A deed in which the seller warrants only a right to sell the property is a(n) <u>???</u> deed.	_____	4. _____
5. The amount paid to the seller for property is the	_____	5. _____
6. A promise contained in a deed is a(n)	_____	6. _____
7. A declaration by an authorized officer that the grantor has stated the execution of the instrument was a free act is a(n)	_____	7. _____
8. The giving up of possession and control over the deed is called	_____	8. _____
9. A complete history of a piece of real estate is a(n)	_____	9. _____
10. Protection from defects in title such as forgery of signatures, claims of adverse possession, and fraud can be obtained through	_____	10. _____

Score _____

Section B

DIRECTIONS: Following each question below, indicate your answer by placing a "Y" for "Yes" or an "N" for "No" in the Answers column.

	Answers	For Scoring
1. Title to real property is conveyed as a gift. Must the transfer be made by a deed?	_____	1. _____
2. Can the parties use any form they wish for a deed?	_____	2. _____
3. Does a quitclaim deed convey a grantor's interest as effectively as a warranty deed? ...	_____	3. _____
4. When a new house is sold, are all warranties on the sale contained in the deed?	_____	4. _____
5. If the person conveying property is single, should this fact be indicated in the deed? ...	_____	5. _____
6. Is it necessary that the consideration stated in a deed be the actual amount?	_____	6. _____
7. Are affirmative and negative covenants only binding on the parties to the deed?	_____	7. _____
8. If the description in a deed is indefinite, does the grantor retain title?	_____	8. _____
9. Should a spouse join a married seller in the execution of a deed?	_____	9. _____
10. Is it unlawful for an agent to execute a deed if the grantor is incapable of signing?	_____	10. _____
11. Is a deed valid before it is recorded?	_____	11. _____
12. Does recording protect grantees against a second sale of the property and liens?	_____	12. _____
13. Do recording officials stamp a deed with the date and time it is left for recording?	_____	13. _____
14. Can all defects in title be detected by an abstract?	_____	14. _____
15. Does a title insurance policy benefit a subsequent purchaser?	_____	15. _____

Score _____

Section C

Ralph Alexander and Paula Alexander, husband and wife, are selling the N.W. 1/4 of the N.E. 1/4 of Section 42, Township 33 N., Range 15 W., consisting of 65 acres more or less, in the township of Delta, County of Warren, and State of Iowa. The purchaser is Theresa Reynolds, a single woman, and the price is fifty thousand dollars to be paid in full at the time and place of delivery and acceptance of the deed. Both parties reside in the village of Delta.

Prepare the warranty deed for the signatures of the Alexanders. Use the current date. Sign the names of the parties who should execute the instrument. Use an X to signify the signatures of two witnesses. Affix your own signature to the acknowledgment as notary public.

For Scoring

Know All Men By These presents

That _____

in consideration of _____

to _____ paid by _____

the receipt of which is hereby acknowledged, do   hereby Grant, Bargain, Sell, and Convey to

the said _____ , _____ h _____ heirs and assigns forever the

following described real property: _____

_____

_____

and all t he Estate, Title, and Interest of the said grantor _____ in and to the said premises; Together with all the privileges and appurtenances to the same belonging; and all the rents,
issues, and profits thereof; To have and to hold the same to the only proper use of the said grantee
_____, _____ h _____ heirs and assigns forever.

And the said _____

do _____ hereby Covenant that _____ the true and lawful owner _____ of the said premises, and ha___ full power to convey the same; and that the title so conveyed is Clear, Free, and Unencumbered; And further, That _____ Will Defend the same against all claim or claims, of all persons whomsoever.

In Witness Whereof, The grantor _____ ha___ hereunto set _____ hand and

seal this _____ day of_____ in the year of our Lord one thousand
nine hundred _____ .

Signed and acknowledged in presence of

_____   _____

_____   _____

_____   _____

STATE OF _____ , COUNTY OF _____ , ss.
On this _____ day of_____ in the year of our Lord
onethousand nine hundred _____ before me, the subscriber, a _____ in and for said
county, personally came _____ the grantor in the
foregoing Deed, and acknowledged the signing thereof to be _____ voluntary act and
deed.

IN TESTIMONY WHEREOF, I have hereunto subscribed my name and
affixed my seal
on the day and year last aforesaid

_____
Notary Public

1. _____
2. _____
3. _____
4. _____
5. _____
6. _____
7. _____
8. _____
9. _____
10. _____
11. _____
12. _____
13. _____
14. _____
15. _____
16. _____
17. _____
18. _____

_____

Score _____

CHAPTER 43
REAL ESTATE MORTGAGES

CHAPTER OUTLINE

I.   INTRODUCTION

General rule.   A mortgage is a lien on real estate that is granted by a mortgagor (owner) to a mortgagee to secure payment of a debt. The mortgagor retains possession of the property. However, if the mortgagor fails to pay, the mortgagee can have the property sold at a foreclosure sale.

Study hint.   A person can mortgage land without mortgaging buildings on the land, or vice versa.

II.   THE MORTGAGE CONTRACT

General rules. ‣ Mortgages must be in writing, and they must be acknowledged by a mortgagor. ‣ A mortgage attaches to (1) property described in the contract, and (2) any future additions or improvements to the property, such as fixtures that are subsequently attached. ‣ A mortgage secures repayment of (1) the debt stated in the contract and (2) future debt, if this is stated in the contract.

Example.   Lance granted a mortgage on land to secure the unpaid purchase price for the land. Later, Lance built a house on the land. The mortgage attaches to the land and house.

III.   RECORDING

General rule.   An owner may grant more than one mortgage on property. In this event, the mortgage that is recorded first generally has priority.

Example.   Al grants mortgages to two lenders. The lender to record first generally has priority.

Limitation.   In some states, a recorded mortgage may be inferior to a prior, unrecorded mortgage if the party recording the mortgage was aware of the unrecorded mortgage.

IV.   DUTIES OF THE MORTGAGOR

- *Interest and principal*: ‣ A mortgagor must pay all interest and principal when due; failure to do so is a default entitling a mortgagee to foreclose. ‣ Most mortgages have an acceleration clause that allows a mortgagee to declare the entire debt due if any payment is late. ‣ A mortgagor cannot avoid interest by paying a loan early unless this right is reserved in the contract.

- *Taxes, assessments, and insurance premiums*: ‣ A mortgagor must pay taxes and assessments. A mortgage may state that a failure to pay taxes or assessments is a default. ‣ If a mortgagee pays these items, the mortgagee is entitled to be reimbursed by the mortgagor. ‣ The law does not require a mortgagor to insure property, but the mortgage contract may require insurance.

- *Security of the mortgagee*: ‣ A mortgagor is forbidden from doing anything that materially impairs the value of ("wastes") the property (e.g., destroy a building). ‣ A mortgagee's remedy for this type of misconduct may include: (1) foreclosure; (2) an injunction; or (3) a receivership.

V.   RIGHTS OF THE MORTGAGOR

- *Possession of the property*: ‣ A mortgagor generally retains possession of property. But if a mortgagor defaults, a mortgagee may take possession to collect rents and profits. ‣ Some states do not allow a mortgagee to take possession. Instead, a receiver is appointed to collect rents.

- *Rents and profits*: Unless otherwise agreed, a mortgagor has the right to all rents and profits that are derived from the mortgaged property.

- *Cancellation of lien*: Upon final payment, a mortgagor is entitled to have the mortgage canceled. A mortgage is canceled by having this fact noted on the public records in the recorder's office.

- **Redemption**: ► After default, a mortgagor may have a right of redemption that entitles the mortgagor to discharge the mortgage and recover the property. Redemption requires payment of the entire mortgage debt and costs of foreclosure within the time specified by law. ► In general, only persons with an interest in the property (mortgagor; heirs; second mortgagees) may redeem.

- **Sale of mortgage property (by mortgagor)**: In general, a mortgagor may sell mortgaged property. If this is done, then the liabilities of the purchaser and the mortgagor are as follows:
    - ► **Liability of purchaser**: ► If a purchaser "assumes" a mortgage loan, the purchaser is primarily liable for the loan. ► If a purchaser buys property "subject to the mortgage," the purchaser may lose the property in a foreclosure, but does not have any liability to pay the loan.
    - ► **Liability of mortgagor**: ► In general, a mortgagor remains liable for a mortgage loan even if a purchaser assumes the loan or the purchaser buys the property subject to the mortgage. ► Exception: A mortgagor is released from a debt (by novation) if: (1) the mortgagee in writing releases the mortgagor; or (2) the mortgagee modifies the mortgage (e.g., extends time for payment) without first obtaining the mortgagor's consent.

VI. FORECLOSURE

- **Foreclosure**: Foreclosure is a legal proceeding to sell mortgaged property to pay a debt. A mortgagee can foreclose if a mortgagor fails to pay any sum when due, or breaches the contract.

- **Procedure**: A mortgagee files a judicial action to foreclose. Sale of mortgaged property is made by a court officer, pursuant to a court order. The mortgagor must be given proper notice of sale.

- **Proceeds**: Proceeds are distributed in the order set by state law. Costs of sale and taxes are paid before mortgages and mechanic's liens (liens for materials or labor that benefit the property).

- **Deficiency**: A mortgagor is liable for any deficiency (debt that is unpaid after foreclosure sale).

VII. ASSIGNMENT OF THE MORTGAGE

► A mortgagee may assign rights under a mortgage. ► The assignee receives no greater rights than the mortgagee held. However, if the mortgagor signs an estoppel certificate stating that there are no claims against the mortgagee, then the mortgagor is barred from asserting past claims against the assignee. ► If a mortgage is assigned more than once, the assignment recorded first has priority.

VIII. DEED OF TRUST

► In some states, a deed of trust is used instead of a mortgage. ► A deed of trust creates a lien on property, and it creates the same basic rights as a mortgage. However, a deed of trust transfers title to a third party (a trustee) to hold in trust for the benefit of the creditor. The trustee can sell the property without using judicial foreclosure proceedings that are required for mortgages.

IX. MORTGAGE INSURANCE

Private companies and public agencies may guarantee payment of mortgage loans in consideration for a fee that is paid by the mortgagor. Two important types of government-insured loans are:

- **Federal Housing Administration (FHA) loans**: ► Anyone may obtain this loan if they meet certain financial criteria. ► The maximum loan is based on the average home sale price in the area. ► Benefits of this type of loan are a smaller down payment and lower interest rates.

- **Veteran's Administration (VA) loans**: ► Certain military veterans may apply for these loans that require no down payment and provide low interest rates. ► Maximum loan amount is $144,000.

REVIEW OF CHAPTER

REVIEW OF TERMS

Select the term that best matches a statement below. Each term is the best match for only one statement.

TERMS

a. Acceleration clause   e. Mortgage   h. Receiver
b. Deed of trust   f. Mortgagee   i. Redemption
c. Foreclosure   g. Mortgagor   j. Trustee
d. Mechanic's lien

STATEMENTS

Answer

_____ 1. Party who may be appointed (by a court) to collect rents and profits for a mortgagee.
_____ 2. Lien granted to persons who provide materials or labor for improving or repairing property.
_____ 3. Agreement (similar to a mortgage) that transfers title to a trustee to hold for a creditor's benefit.
_____ 4. Party to whom a mortgage is granted.
_____ 5. Term in a mortgage contract that allows a mortgagee to declare an entire debt due and payable.
_____ 6. Procedure that allows a mortgagor to discharge a mortgage and recover property after foreclosure by paying the entire debt and costs of sale.
_____ 7. Legal proceedings pursuant to which mortgaged property is sold to pay a debt.
_____ 8. Party to whom title to property is transferred under a deed of trust.
_____ 9. Contract between a mortgagor and mortgagee that creates a lien on real estate to secure payment of a debt.
_____ 10. Party who grants a mortgage.

REVIEW OF CONCEPTS

Directions: Indicate **T** for true and **F** for false in the answer column.

_____ 1. Mortgages may be oral or written.
_____ 2. Greg recorded a mortgage on Ira's home. Unknown to Greg, Mandy already held an unrecorded mortgage on the home. In this case, Greg's mortgage has priority over Mandy's mortgage.
_____ 3. A mortgagor is required, by law, to insure mortgaged property.
_____ 4. Rene granted Mortgagee a mortgage on some farmland. Rene harvested and sold a bean crop that was grown on the property. In this case, the proceeds from this sale belong to Mortgagee.
_____ 5. Sam bought a mortgaged ranch from John, and Sam assumed the mortgage loan. In this case, Sam and John are both personally liable to pay the loan.
_____ 6. Fay defaulted on a $10,000 mortgage. The mortgaged property was sold for $5,000. Expenses of sale were $500. In this case, Fay is liable for a $5,500 deficiency.
_____ 7. Kyle granted a mortgage to Lender. Lender assigned the mortgage to Assignee. In this case, Assignee takes the mortgage subject to any defense that Kyle could have raised against Lender.
_____ 8. A trustee must file judicial foreclosure proceedings in order to sell property under a deed of trust.
_____ 9. FHA loans are available to only certain retired military personnel.
_____ 10. VA loans may not require a down payment.

REVIEW OF CONCEPT APPLICATIONS

Answer

Directions: Indicate your choice in the answer column.

_____ 1. Marvin granted Lender a mortgage on certain undeveloped land to secure a $10,000 loan and any future sums that Marvin might borrow from Lender. Six months later, Lender lent Marvin an additional $5,000. One year later, Marvin built an office building on the land. Under these facts:
     a. The mortgage attaches to the land, but the mortgage does not attach to the building.
     b. The mortgage attaches to the land and building.
     c. The mortgage secures payment of only the $10,000 loan. It cannot secure payment of future debts.

____ 2.   Char granted Bank a mortgage on her home as security for the loan. The mortgage contains an acceleration clause, and it states that a failure to pay taxes is a default. Char failed to pay the taxes on her home, and she did not pay the last month's loan payment. Under these facts:
   a.   Char breached a duty to pay all sums when due. Bank can declare the entire loan due.
   b.   Char breached a duty to pay taxes. Bank can pay the taxes, and recover this sum from Char.
   c.   Char's failure to pay the taxes and the loan entitle Bank to foreclose on the home.
   d.   All of the above.

____ 3.   F&G Co. granted Arriva Bank a mortgage on a warehouse to secure an outstanding $100,000 loan. F&G is delinquent on two $750 mortgage payments, and Arriva has accelerated the loan. Arriva has commenced foreclosure proceedings. Under these facts:
   a.   F&G cannot redeem the property. A mortgagor cannot redeem after the mortgagor defaults.
   b.   F&G may be able to redeem the property. To redeem, F&G must pay Arriva $1,500.
   c.   F&G may be able to redeem the property. To redeem, F&G must pay Arriva the unpaid balance of the $100,000 debt, plus the foreclosure expenses that Arriva has incurred.

____ 4.   Jason granted Fidelity a mortgage on his house, and the mortgage was recorded. Supplier then recorded a mechanic's lien against the house for materials used to build the house. Affiliated then recorded a mortgage against the house. When Jason defaulted on its mortgage, Fidelity foreclosed. In most states, in what order are the proceeds from the foreclosure sale distributed?
   a.   First: Fidelity   Second: Affiliated   Third: Supplier
   b.   First: Fidelity   Second: Supplier   Third: Affiliated
   c.   First: Supplier   Second: Fidelity   Third: Affiliated

CASE PROBLEM

Helen obtained a loan from Bank to help finance her daughter's education. Helen granted Bank a mortgage on her home as security for the loan, and the mortgage was recorded. Helen subsequently sold the home to Buyer who purchased the home "subject to the mortgage."

Under these facts: (1) Is Helen still liable for the loan? (2) Is Buyer personally obligated to pay the loan? (3) If the loan is not repaid, can Bank foreclose on the home even though it has been sold to Buyer?

_____

_____

_____

BUSINESS LAW PARTNER EXERCISE

Directions: Using the Online feature of the Business Law Partner CD-ROM, find and identify three different types of mortgages that are offered over the Internet by various mortgage companies. Compare the terms of these mortgages, and contrast the major pros and cons for each type of mortgage.

_____

_____

_____

CHAPTER 43 QUIZ

Section A

DIRECTIONS: Following each question below, indicate your answer by placing a "Y" for "Yes" or an "N" for "No" in the Answers column.

	Answers	For Scoring
1. Does the mortgage contract, as a rule, have the same form as a deed?............................	_____	1. _____
2. Does the mortgage generally attach to additions to the mortgaged property?	_____	2. _____
3. Does a mortgagor's payment of the mortgage debt destroy the mortgagee's lien on mortgaged property?...	_____	3. _____
4. Can there be more than one mortgage on the same piece of real estate?	_____	4. _____
5. Is the mortgage recorded for the benefit of subsequent purchasers?	_____	5. _____
6. Does failure by the mortgagor to pay periodic payment of interest give the mortgagee the right to foreclose?	_____	6. _____
7. Must the mortgagee make all the payments expected of the owner of the land?............	_____	7. _____
8. If the mortgagor does not pay taxes, can the mortgagee pay them and compel reimbursement from the mortgagor?	_____	8. _____
9. Do both the mortgagor and the mortgagee have an insurable interest in the property to the extent of their interest or maximum loss?..	_____	9. _____
10. Might the mortgagor be guilty of a criminal offense by willfully impairing the security of mortgaged property?...	_____	10. _____
11. Can the right of redemption be exercised at any time after foreclosure and sale of the property?..	_____	11. _____
12. Does a mechanic's lien normally have priority over recorded mortgages no matter when the lien attaches?	_____	12. _____
13. Are foreclosure proceedings uniform throughout the United States?	_____	13. _____
14. Does the mortgagee's extension of the time of payment for the purchaser of mortgaged property without the mortgagor's consent void the mortgage?	_____	14. _____
15. Can the mortgagee assign rights under the mortgage agreement?	_____	15. _____
16. Can the assignee of rights in a mortgage obtain greater rights than the assignor?.........	_____	16. _____
17. Should the assignee of a mortgage have the assignment recorded?...............................	_____	17. _____
18. Does a deed of trust, like a mortgage, involve two parties?..	_____	18. _____
19. Are the proceedings in the foreclosure of a trust deed similar to the foreclosure of an ordinary mortgage?...	_____	19. _____
20. Is the only mortgage insurance available from the federal government?.......................	_____	20. _____

Score _____

Section B

DIRECTIONS: Following each statement below, indicate your answer by placing a "T" for "True" or an "F" for "False" in the Answers column.

	Answers	For Scoring
1. A mortgage is a lien given upon real estate to secure a debt.	_____	1. _____
2. Land may not be mortgaged separately from its improvements.	_____	2. _____
3. A mortgage must be in writing.	_____	3. _____
4. The purpose of providing notice can be accomplished even if recording of a mortgage is not proper.	_____	4. _____
5. An acceleration clause allows the mortgagor to pay off the mortgage debt so as to save interest.	_____	5. _____
6. The law requires the mortgagor to keep the property insured.	_____	6. _____
7. In some states, if the mortgagor cuts timber or tears down buildings on the mortgaged property, the mortgagee has the right to foreclose.	_____	7. _____
8. The mortgagee usually has the right of possession of the mortgaged property.	_____	8. _____
9. The mortgagee is entitled to rents and profits from mortgaged property.	_____	9. _____
10. Anyone may exercise the right of redemption.	_____	10. _____
11. The costs of foreclosure and taxes always take precedence over a first mortgage.	_____	11. _____
12. In case the proceeds of the sale of mortgaged property are greater than the amount of the debt and expenses of foreclosure, the surplus belongs to the mortgagee.	_____	12. _____
13. The purchaser of mortgaged property who assumes the mortgage agrees to become primarily liable for the debt.	_____	13. _____
14. Some states limit the amount of a deficiency judgment.	_____	14. _____
15. If the buyer of mortgaged property takes it "subject to the mortgage" and default occurs, the property may be lost, but no more.	_____	15. _____
16. The original mortgagor is automatically released when mortgaged property is sold.	_____	16. _____
17. When a mortgagee assigns the mortgage to more than one party, the one who records an assignment first has preference.	_____	17. _____
18. A deed of trust involves two parties just as a mortgage does.	_____	18. _____
19. A trustee under a deed of trust need not go to court in order to foreclose.	_____	19. _____
20. The interest rate for FHA mortgages is slightly higher than for conventional ones.	_____	20. _____

Score _____

CHAPTER 44
LANDLORD AND TENANT

CHAPTER OUTLINE

I. THE LEASE

General rules. ▸ A lease is a contract whereby a landlord (lessor) allows a tenant (lessee) to use land or buildings in exchange for compensation (rent). ▸ Leases may be oral or written; express or implied; formal or informal.

Limitation. Leases for a term longer than one year must be in writing.

II. TYPES OF TENANCIES

- *Tenancy for years*: ▸ Described: tenancy for a definite time, no matter how long; expiration date stated in lease. ▸ Example: Pam leased a home until May 1, 1999. ▸ Termination: Lease ends automatically on the date stated in lease; no notice is needed to terminate.

- *Tenancy from year to year*: ▸ Described: tenancy for indefinite period; rent is fixed as an annual amount. ▸ Example: Tenant leased office for an indefinite time; lease states that Tenant shall pay $4,800 annual rent. ▸ Termination: Notice required by state law must be given to terminate lease.

- *Tenancy at will*: ▸ Described: tenancy for an indefinite duration. ▸ Example: Joe leased a room at Bill's Boardinghouse for an indefinite time. ▸ Termination: Either party may terminate the lease at any time, and the death of the landlord or tenant automatically terminates the lease.

- *Tenancy at sufferance*: ▸ Described: without the landlord's permission, tenant holds over after a lease expires. ▸ Tenancy continues until landlord decides whether (1) to treat the tenant as a trespasser and sue for eviction and damages, or (2) to recognize the tenant as a continuing tenant.

III. RIGHTS OF THE TENANT

- *Right to possession*: ▸ A tenant has the right to (1) exclusive, timely possession of leased premises and (2) quiet enjoyment of the premises. ▸ A landlord is liable to a tenant for damages if either of these rights are violated. ▸ If a landlord has control over a nuisance (e.g., disruptive tenants; health hazards) and fails to eliminate the nuisance, a tenant can (1) terminate the lease and sue for damages, or (2) obtain an injunction. ▸ A landlord is not liable if a nuisance existed when a lease was made and the tenant knew of the nuisance, or landlord has no control over a nuisance.

- *Right to use the premises*: ▸ Unless otherwise agreed, a tenant can use leased premises in any manner that is consistent with the nature of the premises. ▸ Premises cannot be converted to an inconsistent use.

- *Right to assign or sublease*: ▸ Assignment: tenant transfers entire lease to third party who agrees to perform lease. ▸ Sublease: tenant transfers rights to part of the premises, or rights for only a portion of the term. ▸ Assignments and subleases are permitted unless a lease states otherwise.

IV. DUTIES OF THE TENANT

- *To pay rent*: ▸ If rent is not paid on time, a landlord can (1) terminate a lease and evict a tenant, or (2) permit the lease to continue and sue for rent. ▸ The common law right to retain a tenant's personal property for unpaid rent has been restricted or eliminated by modern statutes.

- ▪ *To protect and preserve the premises*: ▸ Traditional rule: A tenant has a duty to repair any damage, excluding damage caused by ordinary wear and tear or by natural elements (e.g., sun). ▸ Under modern statutes, a tenant must repair damage caused by the tenant's negligence. Otherwise, modern statutes take three approaches: (1) landlord is obligated to repair premises; (2) landlord is obligated to assure that premises are habitable (reasonably livable); or (3) tenants may make needed repairs that a landlord refuses to do, and deduct the expense from the rent.

V.   RIGHTS OF THE LANDLORD

- ▪ *To regain possession*: ▸ If necessary, a landlord may bring an ejectment action to regain possession of leased premises after a lease terminates. ▸ Unless otherwise agreed, a landlord may retain all permanent improvements and fixtures which have become part of the real estate.

- ▪ *To enter upon the property to preserve it*: A landlord has the right to enter leased premises if necessary to preserve the premises. Otherwise, a landlord does not have a right to enter without the tenant's consent (in the lease or otherwise).

- ▪ *To assign rights*: A landlord can assign his or her rights under a lease without terminating the lease, but the assignment does not terminate the landlord's liability under the lease.

VI.   DUTIES OF THE LANDLORD

- ▪ *To pay taxes and assessments*: ▸ Landlord pays taxes and assessments unless the lease provides otherwise. ▸ If a lease requires a tenant to pays taxes, this does not include special assessments.

- ▪ *To protect the tenant from concealed defects*: ▸ A landlord is liable for a tenant's injuries caused by a concealed defect that the landlord knew about, or should have known about, at time of leasing. ▸ A landlord may not be liable if a defect was apparent or reasonably discoverable.

- ▪ *To mitigate damages upon abandonment by tenant*: If a tenant abandons leased property before the end of the term, the landlord has a duty to try to find a new tenant.

VII.   TERMINATION OF THE LEASE

- ▪ *Destruction of leased room*: If a tenant is merely leasing a room or an apartment, destruction of the leased premises terminates the lease.

- ▪ *Destruction of building*: If a tenant is leasing a building, several rules may apply: (1) common law: destruction of leased building does not terminate a lease; the tenant must continue to pay rent; or (2) some modern statutes and leases: destruction of a building may terminate the lease if landlord refuses to rebuild.

- ▪ *Voluntary termination*: If a tenant surrenders leased premises prior to expiration of the lease term and the landlord consents to the surrender, the lease terminates. If the landlord does not consent, the tenant's abandonment of the premises is a breach of contract for which the tenant is liable.

- ▪ *Notice*: Statutes determine whether a party may terminate a lease by giving notice.

- ▪ *Eviction*: A forcible entry and detainer action is a summary (brief) judicial action to evict (expel) a tenant who refuses to leave. After written notice and a court hearing, a landlord may recover possession in a short time.

VIII.   IMPROVEMENTS

When a lease expires, a tenant can remove his or her personal property and trade fixtures, such as display cases, but a tenant cannot remove fixtures, such as wall-to-wall carpeting.

IX.   DISCRIMINATION

Landlords cannot discriminate based on race, color, religion, sex, national origin, whether a tenant has children, and in some states, age, handicap, or marital status.

CHAPTER 44

REVIEW OF CHAPTER

REVIEW OF TERMS

Select the term that best matches a statement below. Each term is the best match for only one statement.

TERMS

a. Action of ejectment

b. Assignment

c. Eviction

d. Forcible entry and detainer

e. Lease

f. Sublease

g. Tenancy at sufferance

h. Tenancy at will

i. Tenancy for years

j. Tenancy from year to year

STATEMENTS

Answer

_____ 1. Tenancy that arises if, without the landlord's consent, a tenant holds over after a lease expires.

_____ 2. Transfer by a tenant of his or her entire interest in a lease to a third party.

_____ 3. Contract by which an owner of real property allows another party to possess and use the property in consideration for the payment of rent.

_____ 4. Tenancy for an indefinite duration that can be terminated by either party at any time.

_____ 5. Summary judicial action that allows a landlord to evict a tenant within a relatively short time.

_____ 6. Tenancy that is for a definite term.

_____ 7. Transfer by a tenant of rights to a portion of leased premises.

_____ 8. Tenancy that is for an indefinite duration, with rent fixed as an annual amount.

_____ 9. Judicial action to regain possession of leased premises from a holdover tenant.

_____ 10. Expulsion of a tenant from leased premises.

REVIEW OF CONCEPTS

Directions: Indicate **T** for true and **F** for false in the answer column.

_____ 1. Mary wants to lease her house to John for two years. This lease must be in writing to be valid.

_____ 2. Anne leased a home as a tenant at will. If Anne dies, the lease is automatically terminated.

_____ 3. Tenant leased an office from Landlord. Subsequently, gangs started to frequent the neighborhood, driving away Tenant's clients. Landlord has no control over the gangs. In this case, the gangs constitute a nuisance that entitles Tenant to terminate the lease.

_____ 4. Unless otherwise stated in a lease, a tenant can assign a lease without the landlord's consent.

_____ 5. In most states, landlords still enjoy the unrestricted common law right to retain a tenant's personal property if the tenant fails to pay his or her rent.

_____ 6. A landlord does not have the right to enter leased premises without a tenant's consent, even if the landlord is entering to make emergency repairs to the premises.

_____ 7. Unless otherwise agreed, a landlord has the duty to pay taxes and assessments on leased premises.

_____ 8. If a landlord assigns a lease, the assignment terminates the tenant's rights under the lease.

_____ 9. Larry leased a building to Tom. Tom was injured when a stairway collapsed. Larry knew the stairway was defective, but he did not tell Tom about the danger. Tom did not know that the stairway was defective, and the danger was not apparent. In this case, Larry is liable to Tom.

_____ 10. Forcible entry and detainer is an action by a tenant to gain possession of leased premises.

REVIEW OF CONCEPT APPLICATIONS

Answer

Directions: Indicate your choice in the answer column.

_____ 1. Janice leased a beach house for the summer. The lease term is stated to run from May 31 to September 1. Janice's leasehold interest in the beach house is a:
   a. Tenancy for years.
   b. Tenancy from year to year.
   c. Tenancy at will.
   d. Tenancy at sufferance.

_____ 2. Jesse leased an apartment in the Cascade Arms. The lease is silent regarding the right of the landlord to enter the premises, permitted use of the apartment, and subleases. Under these facts:
   a. Jesse has the right to prohibit the landlord from entering the apartment to show it to prospective renters.
   b. Jesse has the right to open a dance studio in the apartment.
   c. Jesse has the right to sublease the apartment to a friend.
   d. a and c.

_____ 3. Marvin leased a home. The lease is silent regarding repairs. During the term of the lease, the following items require repair: various doors require repainting due to normal use; the furnace requires repair because it was damaged when it short-circuited; two windows need to be replaced because they were broken during a party given by Marvin.
   a. Under traditional rules, Marvin has a duty to repaint the doors.
   b. Under traditional rules, Marvin has a duty to replace the windows, and repair the furnace.
   c. Under modern statutes in some states, Marvin can repair the furnace if the landlord refuses to do so, and he can deduct the repair charges from his rent.
   d. b and c.

____ 4. Lee leased a store to Oppy. Oppy installed a permanent air conditioning system in the store, together with some removable shelving. The lease has expired, but Oppy refuses to vacate the premises. Under these facts:
    a. Lee has the right to file an action of ejectment in order to regain possession of the store.
    b. Lee has the right to keep the air conditioning system and the shelving.
    c. Lee does not have the right to keep the air conditioning system or the shelving.

CASE PROBLEM

Targo Inc. leased a manufacturing plant from Landlord for five years. After two years, a fire destroyed the plant. The landlord refuses to rebuild the plant. The lease is silent regarding the parties' rights if the plant is destroyed. (1) Under traditional common law rules: (a) Is the lease terminated? (b) What duties does Targo have? (2) Would the lease be terminated under some modern statutes? (3) What should Targo have done to better protect its rights?

_____

_____

_____

BUSINESS LAW PARTNER EXERCISE

Directions:

1. Access your Business Law Partner Exercise and find the document entitled "Complaint to Landlord." Complete this document using the information provided in the case below.
2. What rights does Kim have in this case?

Case Study: *Rats - In My Apartment!*

Kim leased an apartment for one year from Beachwood Corp. Kim signed a standard form of lease agreement. The agreement is silent regarding the lessor's duties to provide habitable living quarters. After moving in, Kim discovered that rats lived inside her kitchen wall and roamed throughout her apartment. Kim has verbally complained to the manager, but nothing has been done to solve the problem.

_____

_____

_____

CHAPTER 44 QUIZ

Section A

DIRECTIONS: Following each question below, indicate your answer by placing a " Y" for " Yes" or an " N" for " No" in the Answers column.

	Answers	For Scoring
1. Is the relation of landlord and tenant created by a contract?	_____	1._____
2. Can a lease be either oral or written?	_____	2._____
3. In a tenancy from year to year does a lease last until proper notice of termination is given?	_____	3._____
4. Is the tenant who remains on the premises after the expiration of the lease without permission of the landlord automatically a trespasser?	_____	4._____
5. Do tenants have the same right to exclusive possession of the property during the term of the lease as if they owned the property?	_____	5._____
6. If a nuisance existed and the tenant was aware of it at the time the property was leased, has the tenant waived the right to complain about it?	_____	6._____
7. Does the tenant have a right to use the leased premises in any way desired?	_____	7._____
8. May a tenant of farmland cut wood from the premises for personal use?	_____	8._____
9. Does the tenant surrender control over the leased property under a joint occupancy?	_____	9._____
10. If rent is paid to a former agent after the death of the principal, and the agent does not remit it to the proper party, is the tenant's duty to pay rent fulfilled?	_____	10._____
11. If the tenant fails to pay rent on time, may the landlord terminate the lease and order the tenant to vacate?	_____	11._____
12. Must tenants repair damage caused by their negligence?	_____	12._____
13. Has the landlord the right to show the leased property to prospective purchasers or tenants if this right has not been reserved in the lease?	_____	13._____
14. Can the tenant avoid duties if the landlord assigns the rights under the lease?	_____	14._____
15. Is it the tenant's duty to pay the taxes on the leased premises?	_____	15._____
16. Does the tenant bear the risk of injury caused by defects which are apparent?	_____	16._____
17. If a tenant abandons leased premises before the end of the term, does the landlord have a duty to mitigate the tenant's damages by attempting to secure a new tenant?	_____	17._____
18. Does death of either party ordinarily affect a lease that terminates after a fixed time?	_____	18._____
19. Do the statutes usually prescribe the time and manner of giving notice of intention to terminate a lease that runs from month to month?	_____	19._____
20. Do all states have summary eviction laws?	_____	20._____

Score _____

Section B

DIRECTIONS: Following each statement below, indicate your answer by placing a " T" for " True" or an " F" for " False" in the Answers column.

	Answers	For Scoring
1. A tenant is the same as a lodger.	_____	1._____
2. The law does not limit the length of time a lease may last.	_____	2._____
3. A lease should be in writing and include a clear identification of the property.	_____	3._____

4. The termination date is not fixed by the lease in a tenancy for years. .... _____   4. _____
5. It is possible to have a tenancy from year to year with the rent paid quarterly or monthly. _____   5. _____
6. Tenancy at will terminates if the landlord sells the property. .... _____   6. _____
7. The existence of a nuisance is rarely the cause of dispute between the landlord and
   tenant. .... _____   7. _____
8. The tenant is liable for any damage to the leased property. .... _____   8. _____
9. Assigning or subleasing the property is not usually restricted by the lease. .... _____   9. _____
10. The tenant's major responsibility is to pay the rent. .... _____   10. _____
11. The landlord may enter upon the premises occupied by the tenant at any time............. _____   11. _____
12. The assignment of the landlord's rights does not release the assignor from the contract
    without consent of the tenant... _____   12. _____
13. The tenant bears the risk of injury caused by defects in the leased property that can be
    observed by inspection at the time the property is rented.................................... _____   13. _____
14. An abandonment of the premises without the consent of the landlord is a surrender
    which merely terminates the lease. .... _____   14. _____
15. If improvements made by the tenant are trade fixtures and can be removed without
    substantial injury to the leased property, the tenant may remove them at the
    termination of the lease.. _____   15. _____

Score _____

Section C

DIRECTIONS: Complete each of the following statements by writing the missing word or words in the Answers column.

Answers   For Scoring

1-2. The owner of the property who leases it is the ??? .... _____   1. _____
      or ???. .... _____   2. _____
3-4. The person who is given possession of the property is the ??? .... _____   3. _____
      or ???. .... _____   4. _____
5. The amount of compensation the owner of property is to receive for the use
   of the property is the.. _____   5. _____
6. A tenancy for a definite period of time is a(n) .... _____   6. _____
7. An indefinite tenancy in which the rent is set at a monthly amount and
   payable monthly is.. _____   7. _____
8. When the tenant has possession of the property for an uncertain period,
   there is a(n) .... _____   8. _____
9. When a tenant holds over tenancy without permission after the expira-
   tion of the lease, there is a tenancy... _____   9. _____
10. During the term of a lease, the individuals renting the property have the
    right to exclusive ??? of the property. .... _____   10. _____
11. A transfer of the entire premises by the tenant to someone who then pays
    rent directly to the landlord is a(n) .... _____   11. _____
12. When someone other than the tenant takes over the premises for less than
    the term of the lease or only part of the premises and pays rent to the
    tenant, this is a(n) .... _____   12. _____
13. The action brought by the landlord to have the sheriff forcibly remove the
    tenant and any property is an action of... _____   13. _____
14. The expulsion of the tenant from the property is called a(n) .... _____   14. _____
15. A summary action by the landlord to regain possession from a tenant
    refusing to surrender possession of the premises after expiration of the
    lease is called a(n)... _____   15. _____

Score _____

Your tenant, E. J. Sarge, who is occupying a residence you own at 9063 Forest Drive, Alexandria, Campbell County, Kentucky, is three months in arrears with rent payments.

Fill in the blanks of the following "Notice to Quit" as of the current date, over your own signature as landlord, and require the tenant to quit by one week from the date.

NOTICE TO QUIT

To _____

You are hereby notified that you are required to quit, surrender, and deliver possession of the premises hereinafter described, which you now hold as a tenant.

Said premises are located at: _____

_____

City of _____ County of _____ State of _____

_____

You must comply with this notice by_____

_____

Dated this _____ day of _____ 19 ____

1. _____

2. _____

3. _____

4. _____

5. _____

_____

Score _____

CHAPTER 45
WILLS, INHERITANCES, AND TRUSTS

CHAPTER OUTLINE

I.   INTRODUCTION

General rules.   ▸ A will is a written instrument that disposes of the property (estate) of a person on his or her death. ▸ A person executing a will is a testator (man) or testatrix (woman). ▸ A party must have capacity to make a will at the time the will is executed. Capacity means one: (1) knows the natural objects of one's bounty (family and friends); (2) understands the nature and extent of one's property; (3) understands that a will is being made; and (4) is able to dispose of one's property.

Example.   Testator, age 75, executed a will in the form required by law. Testator was eccentric, but he knew who his family and friends were, what property he owned, and that he was making a will. Testator left everything to a charity for the homeless. The will is valid.

Limitation.   For the most part, minors or insane persons cannot make a valid will.

II.   LIMITATIONS ON DISPOSITION OF PROPERTY

General rule.   In general, a person is free to dispose of his or her property in whatever manner the person chooses. A person can disinherit anyone he or she chooses, including children.

Limitations.   The right to freely dispose of one's property is subject to the following restrictions:

- *Spouse's right to take against the will*: ▸ Unless a surviving spouse is guilty of misconduct (e.g., desertion), the spouse may ignore a deceased spouse's will, and take whatever property he or she would have received had there been no will. ▸ Example: Testator's will made no provision for Testator's wife, Mildred. Under state law, Mildred would receive one-half of the estate if there were no will. Mildred can take against the will, and she will receive one-half of the estate.

- *Rule against perpetuities*: Persons receiving property from an estate must receive their interests within 21 years after the death of persons who were alive at the time the testator died.

Study hints.   ▸ The amount that a surviving spouse receives if there is no will depends on the number of surviving children ▸ A person does not have to mention persons who are disinherited (except for children), and nothing needs to be given to such persons.

III.   TERMS COMMON TO WILLS

- *Beneficiary*: person receiving any type of property under a will.
- *Devisee*: person receiving real property under a will.
- *Legatee*: person receiving personal property under a will.
- *Devise*: gift of real property under a will.
- *Legacy (bequest)*: gift of personal property under a will.
- *Executor (executrix)*: person named in a will to administer the estate.
- *Intestate*: dying without a will.
- *Administrator (administratrix)*: person appointed by a court to settle an intestate's estate.

IV.   DISTINGUISHING CHARACTERISTICS OF A WILL

▸ Courts construe wills less strictly than other documents. ▸ Wills devising real property must comply with the law where the property is located. Wills that bequeath personal property must comply with the law where the decedent was domiciled (lived). ▸ A testator may revoke a will.

V. FORMALITIES

General rules. ▸ To be valid, a will must be: (1) written; (2) signed by the testator or testatrix; and (3) in most states, be witnessed by two or three witnesses. ▸ Many states also require publication, i.e., a testator states to witnesses that it is the testator's will that is being signed.

Example.   Testatrix typed a will and signed it. The will was not witnessed by two persons as legally required. The will is invalid, and it will not dispose of Testatrix's estate.

Study hints.   ▸ A will is valid if it satisfies the legal requirements where it was executed. ▸ Witnesses must verify their signatures and the signature of the testator at the time of probate. If witnesses cannot be found, other persons must identify the testator's signature.

VI. SPECIAL TYPES OF WILLS

- ***Holographic will***: ▸ Defined: will written entirely in the testator's handwriting. ▸ State laws regarding holographic wills vary. Many states recognize holographic wills, but some do not. ▸ In some states, a holographic will does not require witnesses. ▸ Example: Testator drafted his will. He typed half of the will, and he wrote the remainder in longhand. This is *not* a holographic will because it is not entirely handwritten.

- ***Nuncupative will***: ▸ Defined: oral will made by testator during a last illness. ▸ This will can only transfer personal property. ▸ Witnesses must generally reduce the will to writing shortly after it is made. ▸ Example: A few hours before dying, Testator orally bequeathed his ring to his son.

- ***Soldiers and sailors***: Military personnel can typically dispose of personal property by oral wills, or by written wills with few formalities. These wills remain in effect unless they are revoked.

VII. THE WORDING OF A WILL

General rules. ▸ No special words are required to make a will so long as the will clearly expresses the intention of the testator. ▸ Property is disposed of strictly in accordance with the terms of a will.

Example.   Testator's will bequeathed 100 shares of stock to Wanda, and $5,000 to Bob. Testator thought the stock was worth $5,000, and he wanted Wanda and Bob to get property of equal value. A court will enforce Testator's will even if the stock is worth only $1,000.

VIII. REVOCATION

A will can be revoked or changed at any time prior to death by:

- ***Codicil***: ▸ A codicil is a separate writing that modifies a will. ▸ A codicil must be executed with the same formality as a will. ▸ A codicil does not terminate a will; it only changes specific terms.

- ***Destruction or alteration***: ▸ A will is revoked if a testator destroys the will with an intent to revoke. ▸ Example: With an intent to revoke, Testatrix throws her will in a fire. ▸ Alteration of part of a will may or may not revoke it. ▸ Scratching out a clause does not revoke a will.

- ***Marriage and divorce***: ▸ Marriage: A marriage that occurs after a will is made revokes the will, in whole or in part (depending on the state), unless the will was made in contemplation of marriage. Example: Nina executed a will that left everything to her parents. Later, Nina met Ken, and they were married. Under state law, Ken inherits everything if Nina dies without a will. In this situation, the marriage may revoke Nina's will. ▸ Divorce: A divorce revokes a will to the extent that a spouse receives property under a property settlement agreement.

- ***Execution of a later will***: ▸ In general, a will automatically revokes an earlier will if the will is inconsistent with the earlier will. If a will is inconsistent with only a few provisions of an earlier will, then the new will may revoke only those provisions. ▸ Example: Testator executed a will in 1997, leaving everything to Wilbur. In 2001, Testator executed a new will, leaving everything to Marilyn. In this situation, the new will automatically revokes the earlier will.

- ***After-born child***: The birth or adoption of a child after a will is made revokes a will, in whole or in part, if the will (or a codicil) does not provide for that child.

IX.   ABATEMENT AND ADEMPTION

- *Abatement*: ▸ If a testator makes specific bequests of money to beneficiaries, but there is insufficient money in the estate to pay the bequests in full, then the bequests abate (are reduced) proportionately. ▸ Example: Testatrix bequeathed $10,000 to Collen and $5,000 to Wendy. If the estate has only $7,500, then Collen will receive $5,000, and Wendy will receive $2,500.

- *Ademption*: ▸ If a testator bequeaths a specific item of property, but the estate does not own that property at time of death, the bequest is adeemed (canceled). ▸ Example: Testator bequeathed his racehorse to Bart. Prior to Testator's death, the horse died. Bart will receive nothing.

X.   PROBATE OF A WILL

General rules.   ▸ Probate is a judicial proceeding to determine the validity of a will. ▸ In general, a will must be probated. ▸ A will usually names an executor who preserves and administers the estate and distributes the assets. ▸ An executor is liable for losses resulting from his or her negligence, bad faith, or breach of trust. ▸ An executor must furnish a bond unless the will provides otherwise.

Limitation.   In a contest of a will (validity of will is challenged), a court may void a will if the court determines that it was executed due to fraud, duress, mental incapacity, or undue influence. If a will is invalid, then property is distributed under the laws of descent. (See Section XII.)

XI.   WHEN ADMINISTRATION IS UNNECESSARY

Administration is not required if a decedent did not own any property, or if all property was owned jointly with another person with a right of survivorship.

XII.   TITLE BY DESCENT

▸ If a person dies intestate, laws of descent distribute the decedent's property. Typical order of distribution:
(1) surviving children (grandchildren) and surviving spouse take all, and share in manner fixed by law;
(2) surviving parents take all if no spouse or child survives; (3) surviving brothers or sisters take all if no spouse, child, or parent survives; (4) grandparents and their descendants take the estate if no one else survives.
▸ If there are no "next of kin," the state takes the property.

XIII.   PER CAPITA AND PER STIRPES DISTRIBUTION

- *Per capita*: ▸ If a person dies intestate, property is distributed to his or her children per capita, meaning equally. ▸ Example: Amanda died intestate. Amanda had two sons, Jim and Todd. Jim and Todd will share equally in Amanda's estate.

- *Per stirpes*: ▸ If a party dies intestate and the party had children, both living and deceased, the estate is divided into a number of parts equal to the number of (1) living children and (2) deceased children who have living children. The share belonging to a deceased child is divided equally among that person's children. ▸ Example: Tony died intestate. Tony had two children, Guy and Ian. At the time of Tony's death, Guy was dead, but he had two living sons. Ian receives one-half of Tony's estate, and Guy's sons each receive one-quarter of the estate.

XIV.   ADMINISTRATORS

▸ A court may appoint an administrator to preserve and distribute an estate if a decedent did not name an executor. ▸ An administrator has basically the same rights and duties as an executor, except an administrator must post a bond. ▸ In some states the order of priority for being an administrator is: (1) surviving spouse; (2) children; (3) grandchildren; (4) parents; (5) brothers and sisters.

REVIEW OF CHAPTER

REVIEW OF TERMS

Select the term that best matches a statement below. Each term is the best match for only one statement.

TERMS

a. Abatement
b. Ademption
c. Administrator
d. Codicil
e. Devise

f. Estate
g. Executor
h. Holographic will
i. Intestate
j. Legacy (bequest)

k. Nuncupative will
l. Probate
m. Publication
n. Testator (testatrix)

STATEMENTS

Answer

_____ 1. Will written entirely in the handwriting of a testator.

_____ 2. Writing that modifies a will.

_____ 3. Person appointed by a court to preserve and distribute a decedent's estate.

_____ 4. Gift of real property under a will.

_____ 5. Real and personal property belonging to a person at time of death.

_____ 6. Statement by a testator to witnesses that the testator is signing his or her will.

_____ 7. Person named in a will to administer an estate.

_____ 8. Oral will made during a person's last illness.

_____ 9. Dying without a will.

_____ 10. Judicial proceeding to determine the validity of a will.

_____ 11. Proportionate reduction of monetary bequests if an estate has insufficient funds to pay in full.

_____ 12. Person making a will.

_____ 13. Failure of a bequest of a specific item of property because an estate no longer owns the property.

_____ 14. Gift of personal property under a will.

REVIEW OF CONCEPTS

Directions: Indicate **T** for true and **F** for false in the answer column.

_____ 1. For the most part, minors do not have the capacity to make a will.

_____ 2. A person cannot make a will unless the person can understand what property he or she owns.

_____ 3. If a spouse dies, the surviving spouse generally can choose to forego what is bequeathed by the deceased spouse's will, and take what the spouse would have received had there been no will.

_____ 4. A testator cannot revoke a will once it has been executed and witnessed.

_____ 5. A testator can disinherit a child only if the child is left at least a token (small) bequest.

_____ 6. The difference between an executor and an administrator is that an executor is named in a will to administer an estate, whereas an administrator is appointed by a court to perform this function.

_____ 7. Reggie owns land in one state, but he lives in another state. In general, Reggie's will can validly devise the land only if the will complies with the law of the state where the land is located.

_____ 8. With a few exceptions, a will must be written to be valid.

_____ 9. States no longer require wills to be witnessed.

____ 10. Many states require publication, i.e., that a testator declare that a will is his or her will.

____ 11. Felicia executed a will in 1998. In 2002, Felicia executed a new will. The new will changes most of the provisions of the earlier will, but it does not specifically mention the earlier will. In this case, execution of the new will revokes the will that Felicia made in 1998.

____ 12. If a testator bequeaths a specific article of personal property which is no longer in the estate at the time of the testator's death, the legatee will take a proportionate share of the cash in the estate.

____ 13. Probate of a will is typically an optional procedure; a will is not required to be probated.

____ 14. Danny executed a will in 1994. The will made numerous devises and bequests. In 1996, Danny executed a codicil that changed one bequest. In this case, the codicil revokes the entire will.

____ 15. Property of a person who dies with an invalid will is distributed according to the laws of descent.

____ 16. In most states, a spouse has priority for being named administrator of a deceased spouse's estate.

REVIEW OF CONCEPT APPLICATIONS

Answer

Directions: Indicate your choice in the answer column.

____ 1. Ollie suffered from Alzheimer's disease. Ollie recalled that he owned a large ranch, but he could not recognize or remember his family. Ollie executed a properly witnessed, published will. The will left everything to Ollie's friends in a nursing home. Ollie did not leave anything to Chip, his son, whom Ollie had forgotten about. Under these facts:
   a. The will is invalid because Ollie did not have the capacity to make a will.
   b. The will is invalid because a testator cannot disinherit a child.
   c. The will is valid. A testator can disinherit a child, and a will is valid if it is properly executed, witnessed, and published.
   d. a and b.

____ 2. Select the correct answer.
   a. Testator typed a will, and he signed it. In most states, this will is valid.
   b. Testator wrote out a will in longhand, and he signed and dated it. The will was witnessed by three persons. In some states, this will is a valid holographic will.
   c. Testator was dying of incurable cancer. Two days before his death, Testator orally devised his ranch to his brother. This oral will is a valid nuncupative will.
   d. b and c.

____ 3. While single, Ralph executed a will, leaving his estate to his parents. Several years later, Ralph met Lisa, and they were married. Two years later, Lisa gave birth to Ralph's son. During that same year, Ralph mistakenly tore his will in half, thinking that it was waste paper. Under the laws of at least some states, which event may have revoked Ralph's will (in whole or in part)?
   a. Ralph's marriage to Lisa.
   b. The birth of Ralph's son.
   c. Ralph's tearing of the will.
   d. a and b.

____ 4. In her will, Josette bequeathed her Studebaker automobile to Andrew. The auto was worth $20,000.
Josette also bequeathed $50,000 each to John and Marsha. Prior to her death, Josette sold the Studebaker.
After payment of creditors, there was only $30,000 cash remaining for distribution to beneficiaries. Under
these facts:
   a.   Andrew, John, and Marsha will each receive $10,000.
   b.   Andrew will receive $20,000, and Andrew and Marsha will each receive $5,000.
   c.   Andrew will receive nothing. John and Marsha will each receive $15,000.
   d.   Andrew, John, and Marsha will receive nothing. A will is invalid if there are insufficient assets to
        fulfill all bequests.

____ 5. Lawrence died without a will. He is survived by his wife, two children, mother and father, and two
brothers. How will Lawrence's estate be distributed in most states?
   a.   Lawrence's wife will receive the entire estate. The children have no rights.
   b.   Lawrence's wife and children will share the estate in the proportion established by statute.
   c.   Lawrence's surviving kin who are named above will each receive one-seventh of the estate.
   d.   The state will take the entire estate since Lawrence died intestate.

CASE PROBLEM

Sarah (a widow) died intestate. Sarah had four children: Adam, Baker, Claire, and Dedre. At the time of Sarah's
death, Adam and Baker were living, but Claire and Dedre were deceased. Claire was survived by two children, Edith
and Flo, who were alive when Sarah died. Dedre was not survived by any children or other descendants. Who is
entitled to receive Sarah's estate? What portion of the estate will each of these persons receive? Explain.

_____

_____

_____

BUSINESS LAW PARTNER EXERCISE

Directions:

1. Using the Online feature of the Business Law Partner CD-ROM, locate and identify a uniform state act that deals
    with the allocation of trust funds between principal and interest.
2. Under this act, when does the right of the income beneficiary begin and end?

_____

_____

_____

CHAPTER 45 QUIZ

Section A

DIRECTIONS: Following each question below, indicate your answer by placing a "Y" for "Yes" or an "N" for "No" in the Answers column.

	Answers	**For Scoring**
1. Must the testator meet as high a standard of capacity to make a will as to make a contract?	_____	1. _____
2. Does a person of sound mind, other than a minor, ordinarily have the competence to make a will?	_____	2. _____
3. Can a testator deprive a spouse of the share the spouse would have received had the testator died intestate?	_____	3. _____
4. With the exception of children, may a testator disinherit persons without even mentioning the disinherited persons in the will?	_____	4. _____
5. Do all states prescribe formalities for wills?	_____	5. _____
6. Must a will devising real property be executed in conformity with the laws of the state in which the testator was domiciled?	_____	6. _____
7. Must the witnesses and testator usually sign in the presence of each other?	_____	7. _____
8. When a will is proved, are witnesses usually called upon to testify that they signed the will as indicated by their signatures?	_____	8. _____
9. Is a will executed in another jurisdiction valid if it was correctly executed in that other jurisdiction?	_____	9. _____
10. Are any words that convey the intention of the testator sufficient in a will?	_____	10. _____
11. Can a will be revoked at any time during the life of the testator?	_____	11. _____
12. Must a codicil be signed and witnessed in the same manner as the original will?	_____	12. _____
13. If the testator deliberately destroys a will does this action constitute revocation?	_____	13. _____
14. Does marriage always act as a complete revocation of a will?	_____	14. _____
15. Does divorce have an effect on a will when there has been no property settlement?	_____	15. _____
16. If a will makes no provision for an afterborn child, and no codicil is added to provide for such a child, is the will at least partially revoked?	_____	16. _____
17. If a will contest results in nullification of a will, is the property of the testator distributed according to the law of descent?	_____	17. _____
18. If an intestate has no relatives, will the property pass to charity?	_____	18. _____
19. Can an administrator be excused from furnishing a bond for faithful performance?	_____	19. _____
20. Is the prime duty of an administrator the same as that of an executor?	_____	20. _____

Score _____

Section B

DIRECTIONS: Complete each of the following statements by writing the missing word or words in the Answers column.

	Answers	For Scoring

1. An instrument prepared in the form prescribed by law, which provides for the disposition of a person's property to take effect after death is a(n).......... _____ 1. _____

2. The property left by a person who has died is called a(n)............................ _____ 2. _____

3. The person who makes a will is called a(n) .... _____ 3. _____

4. A spouse's right to take the share of the deceased's estate provided by statute if the will leaves a smaller share is called the................................... _____ 4. _____

5. The one receiving a gift of real property is a(n).. _____ 5. _____

6-7. A gift of personal property by will is a(n) **???** .... _____ 6. _____

or **???**... _____ 7. _____

8. The person named in a will as the one to administer the estate is a(n) .... _____ 8. _____

9. One who dies without having made a will is said to die .... _____ 9. _____

10. A person appointed by a court to settle the affairs of an intestate is a(n)....... _____ 10. _____

11. **???** occurs when the testator informs the witnesses that the instrument being signed is a will. .... _____ 11. _____

12. Wills written entirely in longhand by the testator are **???** wills. .... _____ 12. _____

13. An oral will is a(n) **???** will... _____ 13. _____

14. A separate writing which modifies a will is a(n)... _____ 14. _____

15. If the testator bequeaths cash gifts of specific sums, but there are not sufficient funds to pay the full amounts specified, the cash gifts will........... _____ 15. _____

16. When property that is bequeathed is not in existence at the time of the testator's death, the gift is... _____ 16. _____

17. The court procedure that determines the validity of a will is called .... _____ 17. _____

18. When a person dies intestate, the property is distributed in accordance with the state law of... _____ 18. _____

19. The distribution of property per head, or equally, is called .... _____ 19. _____

20. Property distributed among heirs according to their relationship to the deceased is said to be distributed.. _____ 20. _____

Score _____